A Poetics of Resistance

A Poetics of Resistance

The Revolutionary Public Relations of the Zapatista Insurgency

Being a true tale of
a possible better world
in its first untamed imaginings

Jeff Conant

In memory of Howard Zinn,
who taught so many of us that history
is made down below.

AK PRESS
EDINBURGH • OAKLAND • BALTIMORE

A Poetics of Resistance:
The Revolutionary Public Relations of the Zapatista Insurgency
by Jeff Conant

ISBN 978 1 849350 00 6
Library of Congress Number: 2009907356

Cover Design: Brian Awehali
Interior: Charles Weigl

Printed in Canada on 100% recycled, acid-free paper by union labor

AK Press
674-A 23rd Street
Oakland, CA 94612
www.akpress.org
akpress@akpress.org
510.208.1700

AK Press U.K.
PO Box 12766
Edinburgh EH8 9YE
www.akuk.com
ak@akedin.demon.co.uk
0131.555.5165

The main battle in imperialism is over land, of course; but when it came to who owned the land, who had the right to settle and work on it, who kept it going, who won it back, and who now plans the future—these issues were reflected, contested, even for a time decided in narrative.

—Edward Said, ***Culture and Imperialism***

Discourse is not simply that which translates struggles or systems of domination, but that for which and by means of which struggle occurs.

—Michel Foucault, ***The Order of Discourse***

At times we wish that our word were the incandescent lava of a volcano wiping out everything in its path, devouring the last vestiges of retrograde ideas, to found a humanitarian society at the feet of true equality.

—Francisco Severo Maldonado and Rafael de Zayas Enríquez

Words without action are empty; action without words is blind; words and action outside of the spirit of community are death.

— Pueblo Nasa, Colombia

Contents

Introduction: A World Made of Stories

The poet Muriel Rukeyser said, "The world is not made of atoms, but of stories." Emerging at the very tail end of the twentieth century in remote jungle enclaves deep in the storied outlands of Mesoamerica, the Zapatista rebellion has had the force of an atom smasher, reinventing what makes the world. Poetics, the making of meaning through language, is central to the Zapatista project. My purpose in *A Poetics of Resistance* is to examine the narrative of the Zapatistas, to look at what it means, to unravel its poetics, and to discover, in part, by what means it makes its meaning.

As if it's not clear enough when thousands of women, men and children cover their faces, raise their machetes in the air, and shout "*Ya basta!*"

The Zapatistas' famous "*Ya basta!*"—enough already!—is one of many ways into their narrative, a prelude to a set of stories they tell, stories of historical resistance and contemporary re-existence. Stories of resistance, of course, help to strengthen resistance, rooting it more deeply in belief and in practice, and thus sustain it. It was Ivan Illich, that great nomadic thinker, who pointed out, "Through argument you can only come to conclusions. Only stories make sense." And what revolution has not been built on stories and sustained by poetry? And, without revolution, what is poetry but dry sustenance in a prosaic world?

Amid the vibrant and oftentimes desperate cacophony that is contemporary Mexico, a plenitude of social movements raise their voices ceaselessly, demanding work, land, justice, dignity. But something—many things, in fact—has made the Zapatista movement distinct, and has "attracted the world's attention" to a set of demands that "the world" would generally prefer to ignore. By meeting at the crossroads of European tradition and Mesoamerican native history, and by inhabiting the language and the mythistory of both, the language of *Zapatismo* serves as a gateway for outsiders into indigenous methods of resistance, revealing to the outside world "what the Indians want." Of course, "what the Indians want" is based on profound, historical cultural values and often has little to do with categories of modern power like the nation-state, access to the free market, or "social services." The eleven demands that the Zapatistas articulated in The First Declaration of the Lacandon Jungle—"work, land, housing, food, health, education, independence, freedom, democracy, justice, and peace"—are not easily delivered in a government aid package; they are also not easily understood, as words such as "democracy," "peace," and "education" carry dramatically differing meanings in varying cultures and contexts. As Flavio Santi, an indigenous Quichua/Shuar activist from Ecuador, says in regard to his village's struggle to maintain access to forest resources, "We don't want a piece of land like a piece of bread. We want territory. It is not the same thing."

This distinction between conventional "western" thinking and "what the Indians want"—the recognition that "it is not the same thing"—makes clear the need for translation, *poesis,* literature; that is, the need for stories that help to reframe the narratives we're familiar with, words and phrases that help to reorient the language. (As if the cry "*tierra y libertad!*"—land and liberty—doesn't ultimately say it all.) The stories of *Zapatismo*, then, offer up a reflection on our postcolonial, capitalism-in-crisis moment—a mirror that we may find familiar, whether or not we immediately understand it. If the road is made by walking, as the Zapatistas are fond of saying, then the communiqués and the web of propaganda that they've created offer a roadmap of sorts. We have only to learn to read it. And then to walk, and to keep walking.

Zapatismo is immediately recognizable through its symbols. In various political cultures of Europe and the Americas beginning in the late 1990s, seeing a ski mask brought to mind, as if by magic, the struggle of indigenous people for land and liberty. Just as seeing the current struggle in Chiapas as part of a larger history allows us to understand it better, looking at the collected fables and manifestos of Subcomandante Marcos and the Zapatista Army of National Liberation (EZLN, in its Spanish initials), along with the masks, the guns, and the entire armature of resistance not as a random stream or packet of propaganda, but as a distinctly and intentionally constructed *mythos,* gives a better grasp of what the symbols mean and how they work.

In telling the history of the movement in 2003, Subcomandante Marcos articulated three strategies: "The strategy we call fire, which refers to military actions, preparations, battles, military movements. And the one called the word, which refers to meetings, dialogues, communiqués, wherever there's the word or silence, the absence of the word. The third strategy would be the backbone of everything else—the organizational process that the Zapatista communities evolve over time."[1]

Supporters of *Zapatismo*—participants in organizational processes inspired by or in support of the movement—have often faced the critique that they—we—are engaged in a facile romanticizing of both indigenous cultures and armed struggle; an overreliance on superficial imagery (what we might term "the Che Guevara T-shirt phenomenon"), and a dangerous oversimplification of an incredibly complex socio-historical situation. Indeed, these are real concerns, and are no less valid for the fact that they are used by the Mexican government, the U.S. State Department, and the *New York Times* to discredit the deeply ethical commitment and profoundly imaginative vision of social movement activists. By dedicating attention to the terms of the debate and to the *poesis* that has given *Zapatismo* its transnational resonance, one hopes that we can get beyond such surface readings to the meanings carried within the mythology of resistance.

The Zapatistas have taken territory, occupied it, and struggled to expand its boundaries, both geographically and psychologically. They have achieved this taking of territory in part through action—military action on the ground, community development initiatives, legal struggles, acts of solidarity—and, in part, through the winning (and, it must be said, occasional losing) of hearts and minds. The poetics of resistance as I define it is the sum of the values and the visions that resound in the voice of *Zapatismo*—the symbols and sense used to win the battle for public opinion.

In her wonderful book, *Hope in the Dark*, Rebecca Solnit sums up a piece of what has attracted so many to the Zapatista cause:

> They were not just demanding change, but embodying it; and in this, they were and already are victorious. "*Todo para todos, nada para nosotros*," is one of their maxims—"Everything for everyone, nothing for ourselves," and though, ten years later, they have more survived than won their quarrel with the Mexican government, they have set loose glorious possibilities for activists everywhere. They understood the interplay between physical actions, those carried out with guns, and symbolic actions, those carried out with words, with images, with art, with communications, and they won through the latter means what they never could have won through their small capacity for violence. Some of their guns were only gun-shaped chunks of wood, as though the Zapatistas were actors in a pageant, not soldiers in a war. This brilliantly enacted pageant caught the hearts and imaginations of Mexican civil society and activists around the world.

Still, not everyone got it, and, as they say, the struggle continues. An article in the *New York Times* Sunday Travel Section on November 16, 2008, entitled "Frugal Mexico," attributes part of the allure of Chiapas (as a cheap tourist destination) to the Zapatistas, "whose failed revolution," says author Matt Gross, "has given Chiapas a frisson of danger." Given the years of counter-revolutionary press the *New York Times* has given to the uprising, it is not surprising that the paper of record should further the myth of an emasculated revolution, peopled by shadowy rebels of unclear motivation "tolerated by the government but limited in their movement." From the perspective of short-term gains, without the benefit of history, any social rebellion might appear disarticulated from its causes, its core demands, and its meanings—might seem to have "failed"—especially when it exists under permanent threat of attack. In 1963 when Medgar Evers was assassinated and churches throughout the American South were bombed with impunity, one might have spoken of "the failed civil rights movement." The "frisson of danger" that our frugal traveler senses in Chiapas is nothing less than the slow burning of resistance that is always just beneath the surface here (as it is in most postcolonial societies), which every now and again, under the right conditions and with the right fuel, bursts into flames of open rebellion. This *frisson*, I dare say, is the engine of history churning beneath the veil of everyday life.

What the Zapatistas give us is historical perspective—a story of the true men and women, as they have it, from before the beginnings of time, well before the conquest and colonization, to now, a moment in history when resistance to that conquest can be glimpsed at certain times and in particular places, fully out in the open. It should also be said that historical perspective, for the Zapatistas, does not end in the present, but opens prophetically toward the future, because history, of course, includes the future. As my friend Trinidad Perez Cruz, a Zapatista insurgent and peasant farmer from the village of Roberto Barrios, slain by paramilitaries in 1998, said to me, "We are not fighting for ourselves. We are fighting for our grandchildren. Our grandchildren want justice."

In seeking justice, the Zapatistas have been, if anything, shockingly inclusive for an armed, revolutionary movement: if you dream of a better world for yourself and your community and everyone else, there is a place for you within the movement. This, of course, is the genius of their strategy: creating a world in which many worlds fit. They prefigure the diversity of ends they are struggling toward, now, by the diversity of means and media they employ to get there: jokes, fables, masks, dolls, songs, radio broadcasts, videos, posters, popular theater, poems, and murals, etc; they accompany all of these, without doubt, with marches, caravans, road blockades, voter boycotts, civil disturbances, land occupations, *encuentros*, as well as the construction of schools, clinics, *bodegas*, collectives, autonomous governing councils, etc. Each and all of these serve to reinforce the values and visions that drive the movement.

It has been remarked a dozen dozen times that the strength of the Zapatista struggle, and its broad appeal, is that it does not seek to take state power, but to "open a space for democracy," to transform social relations. What this effort at transformation implies is that power does not reside merely in the authority of the state or in the hand of the market, visible or invisible; popular power, people's power, and ultimately, the power of mass movements to shape history, resides in culture and in the fonts of culture's creation and proliferation—work, play, love, child-rearing, art-making, stewardship of the land, the cultivation of community. This is to say that one of the lessons to be gleaned from the Zapatistas—

both from their fire and from their word—is that power resides in the production and reproduction of human dignity, and—for a lack of my own words to name it—in the revolution of everyday life.

So: this book. *Zapatismo* is one of the most storied resistance struggles of the past two decades, and admittedly there are few tales herein that have not been told. Jan de Vos, one of the great historians of Chiapas, comments in passing that "the avalanche of interpretive and informative literature [about the Zapatistas], rather than stimulating the appetite, more likely provokes indigestion."[2] There are certainly many books by and about the Zapatistas, and many scholars who have staked their territorial claims to Chiapas and all it represents. But I believe this particular territory—what I term the poetics—requires a more thorough look, one that goes beyond the bounds of a simple reciting of history or an academic illustration of "social movement theory." My hope is that the material here will not merely elucidate the communications strategies of the Zapatistas, of which a good deal has been written, but will offer a broader context—that of the Americas, and of the last several centuries of history, and of development and decolonization—by approaching the material from diverse contexts.

With that said, it must be admitted that the "public relations" of the book's subtitle is something of a joke: as a whole, the purpose here is to examine profound questions of historical representation, strategies for cultural survival, and the mythological and material underpinnings of the Zapatista movement. At the same time, "public relations," I think, is a sensible term to cover the complex and varied ways in which the Zapatistas have managed to convey their truths to the public (a.k.a., global civil society) in order to build awareness of, and support for, their cause.

The book arrives in six chapters that follow a rough plan, though the reader should be warned that I have not attempted to offer a simple structure or framework, preferring the twisting path to the toll road. Rather than follow the standard academic format of introducing theories and dismissing them in favor of a new theory, i.e, *mine*, I intersperse my own analyses and close readings of *Zapatismo* with theories and approaches from a variety of thinkers in a variety of disciplines, to offer what I hope is a unique and engaged perspective.

Chapter 1, "We Are Named, Now We Will Not Die," introduces the terms of discussion and offers insight into what I have dared to call "the Zapatista brand." Chapter 2, "Living Myth, Reviving History," examines the mythistorical underpinnings of Marcos's communiqués and the Zapatistas' approach to communications, and walks through some of the basic iconography of the movement, looking at how this iconography calls upon the collective historical memory of resistance. Chapter 3, "Of Masks, Mirrors and Metamorphosis," unravels the Zapatistas' less-verbal messaging—the ski masks, the dolls, and the guns—with a few side-trips into their use of humor and their inhabiting of what one anthropologist has called "the space of terror and of death." Chapter 4, "So That the True Tongue is Not Lost," uses a study of Tojolabal sociolinguistics and historical records of the early conquest to show how the Zapatistas' use of language reflects their profound sense of dignity, and how their appropriation of media technology is a continuation of indigenous methods of resistance that have been in play for centuries. Chapter 5, "Tilting at Windmills," looks at the character and the characters of Subcomandante Marcos, the merchandizing of *Zapatismo*, and what it means for "a ragged band of Indians" to emerge at the forefront of postmodernity. Chapter 6 attempts to sew things up by examining the proactive aspects of the struggle—the construction of autonomy, democracy, gender equity, and plurinationality—showing how the Zapatistas have made the journey from collective resistance to collective re-existence, and how they have opened the door onto an entirely *other* modernity.

That, then, is the general road map of the book—but there are several subplots that force us, from time to time, to drift off the road in order to stay on the path. The book contains numerous communiqués and close readings of them, essentially using the writings of Marcos as the armature on which to hang the material; through the communiqués and other forms of communication, we return to key concepts more than once, repetition being a key strategy for getting the messages across.

My hope is that the book will be of interest to those who have studied and accompanied the Zapatista struggle as well as those for whom the subject is altogether unfamiliar. To this end, I have tried to allow the chronology of the Zapatista struggle to guide the narrative, so the key events of Zapatista history emerge more or less in order, beginning with the uprising of January 1, 1994, and ending with *la festival de la digna rabia* in January 2009. Of course, the history of the present moment includes both the distant past and the near future, so we make some visits there as well.

Because of the many facets of the topic, it seems to me important to clarify as well what this book is *not*. Many people close to the movement talk about two *Zapatismos*—that which reaches in, takes root, and grows in the autonomous villages of Chiapas—and that which reaches out, interpreting for the world beyond those villages what goes on there and how, and why, and to what end. This book is about the latter; the topic, broadly, speaking, is the manner in which *Zapatismo* represents itself to the eyes and ears, the hearts and minds, of those outside the movement. Thus, it engages only superficially with questions of the movement's internal structure (barely touching, for example, the oft-noted conflict between the military hierarchy of the Zapatista National Liberation Army and the horizontal structure of the base communities it serves), the development of autonomy, the coherence (or lack of it) between speech and action, or other questions more relevant to the movement-building aspects of *Zapatismo*. How deeply Zapatista values—liberty, justice, democracy, diversity, dignity—are *lived* as daily cultural practice and praxis, and how truly Zapatista communities and the EZLN leadership adhere to the vision do not, precisely, constitute the subject at hand, though they are, of course, relevant, and profoundly important for the Zapatista movement and the many movements that it inspires.

I lived in Zapatista communities for a period, but the material here is based more on a study of the literature than personal fieldwork. It is also not an attempt to either glorify Subcomandante Marcos or criticize and lay bare the contradictions that he embodies. That discussion is best left to the experts.

Finally, it should go without saying that the ideas here are the fruit of much collective thinking; I take credit only for putting them down in this form, and for any errors of fact or of omission.

A Note on the Text

Zapatista communiqués have poured forth in an endless stream since 1994, and they keep coming. There is no intention here to catalogue or otherwise delimit or define the range of writing that has come out of the Lacandon jungle in recent years, simply an attempt to collectively read a small but representative cross-section of it.

The best collections of the communiqués currently available in English are *Our Word Is Our Weapon* (New York: Seven Stories, 2001), *The Speed of Dreams* (San Francisco: City Lights, 2007), and *Conversations with Durito: Stories of Zapatistas and Neoliberalism* (Brooklyn, NY: Autonomedia, 2005), each of which also contains useful introductory material that, without doubt, illuminates the points I am trying to bring across here. Without these antecedents, this book would have been much diminished. Communiqués old and new are also widely available on the Internet.

Despite the enormous value of these books and online resources, I have translated many of the communiqués here myself, though many, too, have been translated by others, both named and unnamed. This is not out of any disregard for the work of other translators, but simply because, in some cases, my own translation was done before other English versions were available; in other cases, I rendered my own versions in English for the pleasure of it, or, on rare occasions, because I felt that the existing translations might be improved upon by bringing out a particular tone or stylistic approach.

See the bibliography for the wide range of editions of the communiqués, both in English and in the original Spanish. The text contains several communiqués and many fragments of communiqués, picked up from various sources, noted when possible. This treatment attempts to give credit where it is due while also respecting one of the signal aspects of the communiqués: the fact that they are not copyrighted, but live in the public domain, and thus have been widely and variously translated and reproduced. Where other cited texts were originally in Spanish, I have undertaken the translations myself, and, as in the rest of the material, am wholly responsible for any errors, inaccuracies, or misrepresentations.

Several key words have been left in Spanish when their meaning cannot be translated directly and clearly, as is the case for example with the word "*campesino*," or where one can reasonably assume that the meaning is evident to non-Spanish speakers.

Some names of native peoples have a variety of spellings; I have kept to one standard spelling except in quoted sources, such that two of the *pueblos indios* of Chiapas are herein called both Tzeltal and Tseltal, and Tzotzil and Tsotsil.

The endnotes contain most of the sources I have used, as well as occasional interventions into the text that did not fit or were inappropriate elsewhere. When endnotes refer to sources not cited in the bibliography, it is because they were found as quotes in non-source materials. The bibliography lists both books and texts that informed *A Poetics of Resistance* directly, and others that have influenced my thinking on the subject more generally or have served as touchstones.

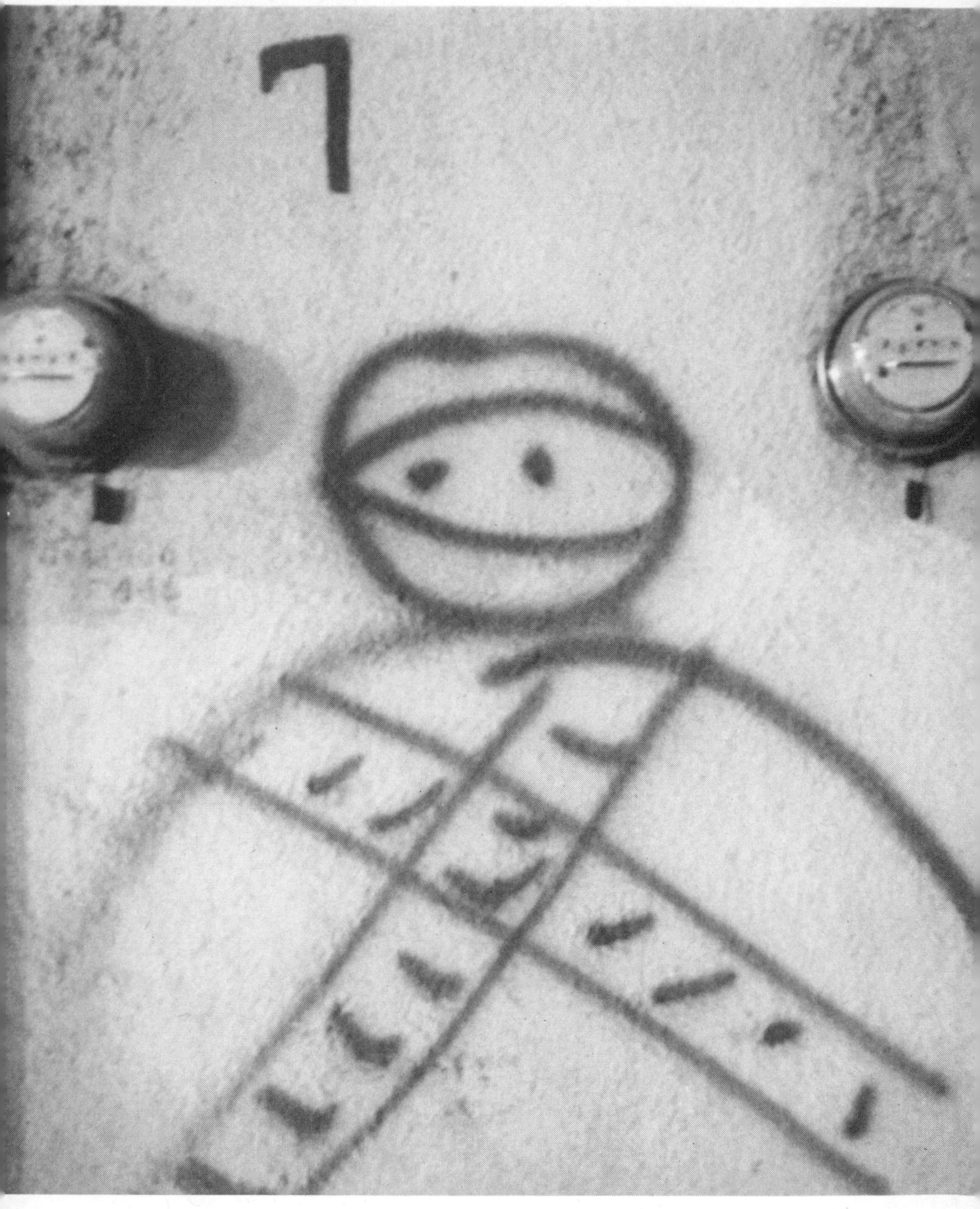
7

I
We Are Named, Now We Will Not Die

Un pueblo con memoria es un pueblo rebelde.
—Subcomandante Insurgente Marcos

Against Oblivion

In late 1994, toward the end of the first year of "the first postmodern revolutionary struggle,"[1] a ceremony took place somewhere in the Lacandon jungle. It was the eleventh anniversary of the Zapatista Army of National Liberation (EZLN) and Subcomandante Insurgente Marcos, the *mestizo* spokesman for the indigenous Zapatista movement, was being given seven staffs of military command representing the seven ethnicities united behind the Zapatista ski mask. The exact place, somewhere in the Lacandon jungle, was where Marcos and a few *compañeros* had made shelter from the driving rain eleven years before—the EZLN's first clandestine guerilla encampment.

On a stage replete with fruits of the harvest—corn, bananas, squash, and sugarcane—Comandante Tacho handed Marcos the order to renew his commitment to the Zapatistas' struggle. The ceremony revolved around seven symbolic objects. One by one, Tacho named the objects and spoke these words:

The Seven Messages[2]

• The National Flag: With this fabric go the words of all poor Mexicans and their struggle since ancient times. You must struggle for them, never for yourself, never for us. Everything for everyone, nothing for ourselves. We are Mexicans who want to be free. This is the flag of our history. Remember always that our struggle is for liberty.

• The Flag of the EZLN: In this five-pointed star lives the human figure: the head, the two hands and the two feet, and the red heart that unites the five parts and makes them one. We are human beings and this means that we have dignity. Remember always that our struggle is for humanity.
• The Gun: In this weapon lives our warrior heart. It is our dignity that obliges us to take up arms so that nobody will have to take up arms again. We are soldiers who want to stop being soldiers. This is the weapon of peace. Remember always that our struggle is for peace.
• The Bullet: In this bullet lives our tender fury. It is our longing for justice that sends this bullet on its path, that it may speak what our words do not say. We are voices of fire in need of a rest. This is the bullet of justice. Remember always that our struggle is for justice.
• Blood: In this blood lives our indigenous blood. It is our pride that we inherited from the ancestors, that which brings blood is that which makes us brothers. We are blood, which nourishes the soil and cries out the thirst of all our brothers and sisters. This is the blood of the true men and women. Remember always that our struggle is for truth.
• Corn: In this corn lives the flesh of our people. We are the men and women of corn, the sons and daughters of the first gods, the makers of the world. We are the corn that nourishes our history, that which tells us that we must command by obeying. It is the corn which, in its suffering, relieves the suffering of our brothers and sisters. Remember always that our struggle is for democracy.
• Earth: In this earth is the home of our great dead. We are the forever dead, those who must die so that we may live. We are the death that has life. This is the death that gives life to all of our brothers. Remember always that our struggle is for life.
• Seven powers: tzotzil, tzeltal, tojolobal, chol, mame, zoque and mestizo,[3] that seven to the power of seven the struggle will grow. Seven words and seven roads: life, truth, humanity, peace, democracy, liberty, and justice. Seven words that give force to the staff of command of the leader of the true men and women.

> Receive, then, the staff of command of the seven forces. Carry it with honor, and never allow it to give rise to words that are not spoken by the true men and women. Now you are not you, now and forever you are us.

This is the poetic outfitting in which the Zapatistas, a guerilla army and a civil political force, dress their struggle. The language is rich with symbols in which the word and the deed are made one: *the seven words live in the staff of command; the bullet speaks what our words do not say; we are voices of fire in need of a rest.* The Zapatistas' sophisticated propaganda, their poetics, hinge on an almost alchemical process of transformation, as if freeing the symbols—the corn, the flag, the weapon, the handful of earth, etc.—will free the objects themselves. As Marcos noted early in 1994, and has continued to demonstrate since with a stunning barrage of verbiage—sometimes profound and incisive, sometimes banal and overblown, often comic and self-effacing—a revolution is not fought merely with arms, but with words. As Comandante David has said, "We *are* the Word."

In Mexico, a national culture given to a vivid symbolic vocabulary—from the iconic rogue figure of Emiliano Zapata, whose heritage is claimed equally by the EZLN and by the chief executive (Carlos Salinas de Gortari, the ex-president forced to flee the country when his private crimes became publicly known, was a fan), to the eagle devouring the serpent that appears on the flag and on every Mexican coin, the territory of symbols, the aesthetic sphere, the signifying instance from which history is constructed, is a battle zone, a zone that each side struggles to occupy in any given moment. Even in the clandestine ritual of the Seven Messages that took place "somewhere in the Lacandon jungle" before perhaps a few hundred indigenous warriors, away from both the press and the public, the flags, the guns, the blood, and the earth are invoked as symbols to animate the army.

In the fifteen-year history of *Zapatismo*, as in any history, the lexicon of symbols shifts with each twist and counter-twist of the historical plot, but certain persistent features remain. At political rallies and in the graffiti scrawled across the nation's walls, you hear the cry, "*Zapata vive, la lucha sigue!*": "Zapata lives, the struggle continues!" The resounding echo of Zapata's name suggests that as long as the symbol of this martyred horse-trader and hero is held aloft there is hope—hope for land reform, hope for an indigenous agrarian identity, hope for dignity among Mexico's embattled and disenfranchised. As long as the spirit of Zapata lives, the echoing cry tells us, there will be resistance to Power with a capital "P." As long as the political territory signified by Zapata, the indigenous leader of the first Mexican revolution, remains open, this territory will be the arena of struggle upon which the indigenous of Mexico and all of the Americas fight to recapture their land, resist oppression and misery, and build autonomy. *Zapata vive vive, la lucha sigue sigue!* From the frigid highland villages above San Cristóbal de las Casas to the *zocalo* of Makesicko City[4] to the brown and toxic waters of the Rio Bravo and beyond, hope lives in these words and in the voices that echo them.

Every society and every state controls public discourse to one degree or another—whether through political repression or corporate buy-off, through state censorship or through proliferation of official "truths" masqueraded as history—and in every state there appears a dissenting voice—or, better, a multitude of dissenting voices—that echo against the hollow untruths of state and corporate propaganda. A quick survey of the literary track records of the twentieth century's great repressive regimes reminds us how the voice of dissent inspires fear in the powers-that-be: the Soviet regime that silenced or exiled the poets Mayakovsky, Mandelstam, Voznesensky, and so many more; the repression of intellectuals in China that began during the Cultural Revolution and continues to the present day; Hitler's frontal attack on "degenerate art"; the Latin American dictatorships of Pinochet, Somoza, Batista, Banzer, Duarte, and the rest that tore the tongues from the mouths of their poets and very literally burned them alive; the House Un-American Activities Committee that attempted to silence artists such as Charlie Chaplin, Pete Seeger, Lillian Hellman, Paul Robeson, and so many others. As a political figure, the artist is immediately suspicious, whether populist, like a Langston Hughes or a Victor Jara, vanguardist, like a Mayakovsky or a Khlebnikov, or some hybrid, like a Roqué Dalton, a Federico García Lorca, a John Lennon, or a Subcomandante Marcos. And rightly so: the first front in any war of liberation is the front of language. If the territory of symbols is not liberated and given new life—in songs, poems, street theater, on banners and flags, in murals, on the very face and façade of culture, everywhere—no movement to revitalize society can thrive. Upon entering San Cristóbal de las Casas on New Year's Eve, 1994, the EZLN did what any literate guerillas would do: they occupied the heights and captured the radio station. Hope lives and dies in the language, and, as Marcos has repeated ad infinitum, the Zapatistas are not professionals of violence, but professionals of hope.

In a communiqué of March 19, 1995, Subcomandante Marcos speaks of this voice and its power to redeem hope:

> Brothers and Sisters,
>
> With old pain and new death our heart speaks to you so that your heart will listen. It was our pain that was, it was hurting. Keeping quiet, our voice was silenced. Our voice was of peace, but not the peace of yesterday, which was death. Our voice was of peace, the peace of tomorrow.

And he repeats the mantra:

> We are named.
> Now we will not die.
> We have a name. Now we will not die. We will dance.
> Now we will not die. We are named.
> Health, brothers and sisters! Let death die! Long live the EZLN!

He makes the point that naming and speaking, the power to name oneself, and the power to articulate one's self, one's community, one's history, is the territory of struggle. When memory has been erased by terror and forced migration, crop failures and beatings, hunger and the destruction of cultural symbols, sacred places, whole pantheons of gods, when the conquest or the inquisition or the dictatorship or the global economy silences a people, the first casualty (beyond the bodies broken and the lives taken) is history. The Zapatistas and their primary spokesman and voice, Subcomandante Marcos, recognize that the struggle is to retake history, to reoccupy it: the revolution is the moment when the true past meets the true future and history is made anew.

Even as the news media have blacked-out the details—especially in the United States where, in the glut of entertainment, news and history have little to do with one another—the popular media has done much to inflate the Zapatista image. The Zapatistas have so carefully managed their image through the conscious creation of a mythology and the painstaking documentation of their own history that, though they may be misunderstood, and while they, along with all the poor of Mexico, continue to suffer repression and marginalization, they cannot be ignored. There is a voice behind that ski-masked image that always somehow manages to get through: as one of their many slogans declares—in this case declaring the presence not just of an insurgent voice but of an *indigenous* insurgent voice—"*Nunca más un Mexico sin nosotros.*" Never again a Mexico without us.

The romp through the communiqués and other forms of Zapatista public relations that follows is not so much a look at the way these voices have been represented and misrepresented by the media—from the sometimes fawning but always fascinating reportage of left-leaning Mexican daily *La Jornada* to the mythic misinformation campaign carried out by the two-headed Mexican media monopoly of Televisa and TV Azteca,[5] to the crafty, finely honed minimalism of the *New York Times*—as it is a look at how the voice behind that ski-masked image has somehow always managed to get through, and how that voice, amplified by autonomous organizations everywhere, helped foment the rise of the global movement against (take your pick) neoliberalism, corporate globalization, state terror, colonialism, neocolonialism, empire, misery, miserablism, or whatever we may, today, choose to call it.

For their part, the Zapatistas call it "oblivion," as in "the war against oblivion."

What I call the Zapatistas' poetics of resistance is the collective speaking voice they have brought to bear as their primary armament in this, the war against oblivion.

Insurgent Narrative, Narrative Insurgence

> For a country to have a great writer … is like having another government. That's why no regime has ever loved great writers, only minor ones.
>
> —Aleksandr Solzhenitsyn

Historically, EZLN communiqués are issued either by the Clandestine Revolutionary Indigenous Committee–General Command (CCRI-CG) (the body that guides EZLN strategic decisions) or come directly from the hand of Marcos, who speaks, he often repeats, as the voice of the EZLN. Back in 1994, the first epistles, legend has it, were banged out on a battered Olivetti portable typewriter. Always late, they still somehow managed to arrive at the offices of Mexican media outlets and in the in-boxes of insurgent computer geeks from San Cristóbal to San Francisco, from Chilangolandia to Manhatitlan, always bearing as an approximate return address, "*las montañas del Sureste Mexicano.*" Later, with the international awareness of his needs as a postmodern Cyrano de Bergerac, Marcos received a laptop and printer, bringing state-of-the-art to the state-of-the-jungle. The messages were carried out of the jungle on foot and traveled through the Catholic diocese of San Cristóbal or the slim pages of a local weekly, *El Tiempo,* before they reached the national dailies and the Internet lists where they would proliferate. Later, when Marcos left Chiapas for periods of time with the Otra Campaña, communiqués tended to come no longer from "*las montañas del Sureste Mexicano,*" but from every corner of the Republic.

As in the ceremony of the seven staffs, the word is a weapon; as in that ceremony, the word is accompanied, often, by the symbolic gesture—the ski masks donned by the rebel warriors and the wooden guns they carried in their first uprising, the dolls they weave and sell in their noisy, crowded markets and the precise numbers of peasant warriors who walk every inch of Mexico to be heard. These gestures, the acts that constitute the history of *Zapatismo*, embody the living spirit of the communiqués. The communiqués themselves—mock travel brochures, childrens' tales, autobiographical anecdotes, myths of origin, ballads and songs, manifestos, personal missives, literary imitations, and military discourses—have poured out of the jungle of southeastern Mexico since that cold January of 1994 when the ski mask first appeared as a symbol of resistance throughout the New World and the New World Order. The voice has been so strong that when it falls silent for a time—as it did in the first days of the uprising, and in the summer of 1998, and in late 2000 during the presidential campaign which, after seventy-odd years of "the perfect dictatorship,"[6] saw the changing of the palace guard, and again after the March for Indigenous Dignity in 2001 resulted in a mass public fraud that threatened to discredit the Zapatistas at the height of their popularity—the silence itself rings thick with meaning. From the ancient codices of the Maya to versions of Shakespeare, Cervantes, Coleridge, Borges, Pessoa, Eluard, Leon Felipé, Galeano, and Umberto Eco, from Aesop and *Alice in Wonderland* to Bugs Bunny and Speedy Gonzalez, from popular songs to statistics from the *Wall Street Journal* and the *BBC World News*, in dialects that mock old-world Spanish and *caló*, or new-world Spanglish street slang, the communiqués have managed to ricochet their echo off of every voice in the canon of modern literature and pop culture. Beyond the communiqués are the *other* communiqués—the murals, the videos, the *corridos* written and sung both within and outside of Zapatista rebel territory, the appearance of Marcos's voice in pop music recordings far and wide, most famously perhaps on Manu Chao's galvanizing 1998 record *Clandestino*.

Along with an often adept military strategy based on popular support, this range and depth of voice has kept the Zapatista struggle moving in and out of the media spotlight in a political climate that easily does away with less articulate players. It has also brought to the world's attention a particularly Mexican brand of surrealism, where we are forced to wonder which is the real reality—the subterranean reality of talking beetles and Indian women running through the jungle with ski masks and submachine guns, or the above-board reality of the stock market and the global banking system, where virtual trading in non-commodities trades wealth for hunger as quickly as the sun sets over the bulls and bears of Wall Street and rises over the tigers of Asia. As the Zapatista National Liberation Movement has brought about the first mass insurgency in Latin America since the end of the Cold War (known to the Zapatistas as the "Third World War"), sparking a global rebellion against corporate globalization (known to the Zapatistas as "World War Four"), the communiqués of Subcomandante Marcos and the voice of popular *Zapatismo* are the texts that write the postmodern rebellion into history and give currency to what André Breton, seventy years ago in the pages of *International Surrealism*, called "art in the service of the revolution."

Subcomandante Marcos, or "*el Sup*" as he is known informally, is not by any means the sole author of the Zapatista communiqués; but his voice is so strongly identified as the voice of *Zapatismo* that any study of the communications strategies of the movement as a whole of necessity must focus largely on the writings produced by his hand. Marcos, a political strategist and *guerrillero*, is not first and foremost an author or a "literary figure" in the way that, say, a Solzhenitsyn is, or a Jorge Luis Borges, or an Alice Walker; he is also not primarily a poet in the way that, say, Bretón is, or Ginsberg; to the extent that his oeuvre exists largely in service to the political aims he serves—as opposed to his political aims being best expressed in his poetry—he is not a Roqué Dalton, a García Lorca, or an Ernesto Cardenal. While he is a "political writer," one would hardly say that writing is his vocation; he is first and foremost a "political actor," whose writings represent a movement more than an individual. Absent his role as military propagandist for the EZLN, Marcos as *auteur* barely exists.

The writings of Subcomandante Marcos, filled as they are with native voices, hybrid styles, and demanding, sometimes mystifying content, have not been embraced by any literary establishment, in Mexico or elsewhere, and it will undoubtedly be long after his death (or perhaps not so long, given the hungry proclivities of the culture industry) that his work gains significant recognition *as literature.* But there can be little doubt that Marcos's writing deserves literary treatment and literary analysis. In recent years, with the publication of his pulp-noir *Muertos Incomodos*, written collaboratively with Paco Ignacio Taibo II, and the mysterious erotic book, *Las Noches de Fuego y Desvelo,*[7] Marcos has strayed from communiqués that represent the Mayan rebels of Chiapas into a territory that is more conventionally "literary," in that it is his own voice speaking rather than that of the "voiceless" speaking through him.

With the biographical material that we have available, there is no question that Marcos's thinking evolved from a love of literature *as* literature toward literary engagement as a means to effect social revolution. Telling Gabriel García Marquez about his history of reading and the love for books he inherited from his family, Marcos cites *Don Quixote* as one of the first of the great books he was exposed to, at age twelve, in "a beautiful cloth edition. Next came Shakespeare. But the Latin American boom came first, then Cervantes, then García Lorca, and then came a phase of poetry. So in a way you [looking at Marquez], are an accessory to all this."[8]

One goal of story telling is to name things, while at the same time getting beyond names, to mythic essences—to complicate, diversify, problematize, mystify. While many of the unstoried communiqués, the ones that serve as manifestos, declarations, invitations—in short, the more utilitarian communiqués—contain a more or less static lexicon of signifiers ("democracy," "justice," "liberty"), the storied ones, where we are greeted by the tough little beetle Don Durito and the wise elder Old Antonio, where the immediately political content is delivered in a sugar-coated literary package, dive into the manifold meanings of these words, showing us, in ways that are appealingly shifting, ungrounding, dodgy even, what justice is, whither liberty, what democracy looks like.

The poet Diane DiPrima has said, "the only war is the war against the imagination"—a powerful slogan for those whose work, like hers, unites a revolutionary praxis with a poetics of liberation. But it falls short, because in fact, the war against the imagination takes shape, everywhere, as a war against the physical body as well: hunger, disease, brutality, and violence. It might be better said that the assault on imagination is the first front of violence in the war against everything. It follows, then, that the counter offensive should take the form of poetry—necessarily accompanied, of course, by physical resistance in all of its diverse renderings.

The British art critic, novelist, poet, and fellow traveler John Berger tells how, in the eighteenth century, Peter the Great of Russia, in imitation of the French Academy of Louis XIV, decreed an Academy to control all artistic activity in Russia. Berger acutely reminds us that the tsar's autocratic approach to creating a national art is emblematic of the frequently imperial function of the arts:

> Academies were and are formed as instruments of the State. Their function is to direct art according to a State policy: not arbitrarily by *Diktat*, but by codifying a system of artistic rules which ensure the continuation of a traditional, homogenous art reflecting the State ideology. This ideology may be conservative or progressive. But it is intrinsic to all academic systems that theory is isolated from practice. Everything begins and ends with the rules.[9]

In contrast, revolution, and revolutionary art, is always about aligning theory and practice: the praxis of everyday liberation and the timeless ideal of Human Liberty. Thus we find in Marcos's communiqués, and the entire panoply of visual images and text issuing from the remote mountains of southeastern Mexico—the fire and the word—a literature that escapes the bounds of literature, combining discursive passages with poetic narrative and fictional journeys, invented characters with autobiographical material. Unique to them, as well, is a sense of irony, of humor, of self-mockery. From the comic chuckle "*Yepa, yepa!*"[10] to the anthemic *grito*, "filled with fire to demand and cry out our longings, our struggle,"[11] from the early and ongoing polemical discourses where "through Marcos's voice speaks the voice of the EZLN," to the more recent erotic ruminations which, one supposes, represent only Marcos himself, everything is permitted, nothing excluded.

In this sense, as we shall see, *Zapatismo* represents postmodernism in aesthetics as well as in praxis, as it embodies "extreme complexity, contradiction, ambiguity, diversity, interconnectedness or interreferentiality"[12]—that is to say, in Zapatista phraseology, "a world in which many worlds fit." If the communiqués are literature, they are a hybrid form: neither poetry nor testimony, neither fiction nor nonfiction, neither essay nor journalism, they are an apparently unceasing cascade of "*relatos*," meaning stories, "*cuentos*," meaning fables, "*cronicas*," meaning reportage, and "*communicados*," meaning, in the military language of the guerilla, communiqués, but in a more literal sense simply meaning "communications." So, what is being communicated? And if communication is a two-way street, what response is invited? The stories of *Zapatismo* were, and are, often published in the newspapers, the most ephemeral of media, and yet they are, somehow, intended to shape history, to make news, to be news.

As the American modernist poet William Carlos Williams wrote:

> It is difficult
> to get the news from poems,
> yet men die miserably every day
> for lack
> of what is found there.[13]

We Are Here, We Resist

When the Zapatistas assert on banners and aloud, chanting in time during marches in Mexico City and San Cristóbal de las Casas, "We are here! We resist!" their very presence is an act of resistance. Their presence as living people after a five-hundred-year war of attrition means they have resisted and are resisting still. We are here because we resist, they are telling us; our being here means resistance; if we didn't resist, we wouldn't be here. "*Aqui estamos! Resistimos!*"

For the indigenous Zapatistas, resistance is a strategy for cultural survival. In biology, resistance is the ability of a living thing to adapt and protect itself from eradication. We hear about plants that are resistant to blight or to pesticides. Plants, like people, like cultures and subcultures, develop resistances of various sorts to protect themselves from disease. They evolve mechanisms for protecting their own kind from outside invaders. The vast majority of indigenous peoples in Mexico and the entire "New World" were destroyed by disease early in the conquest because they had no resistance to the viruses and bacteria introduced by the conquerors and missionaries from Europe.

People develop resistance in much the same sense that animals, plants, and even viruses and bacteria develop resistance. An example from the history of medicine illustrates: In the seventeenth century, the age of Discovery, the Aguaruna Jivaro Indians taught Spanish doctors about the healing properties of cinchona bark in order to save the Countess of Cinchon, wife of the Viceroy of present-day Peru—and namesake of the tree—from the disease malaria, or "bad air." Since that time cinchona and its derivatives have been used worldwide in treating malaria; the microorganism that carries malaria was not *resistant* to the chemistry of *cinchona*, and so it was kept largely under control, for a time. Large-scale malaria control allowed for the undertaking of large-scale projects such as, among other things, the construction of the Panama Canal through dense, mosquito-infested lowland swamps and the ability of the American military to wage effective warfare across the South Pacific theater in World War II.

But by the turn of the twenty-first century, the parasite has developed resistance to quinine—the compound synthesized from cinchona—and, for this and other reasons, the disease is again reaching pandemic proportions. Humans develop ways of resisting invasive pathogens and eventually the pathogens themselves develop resistance. Technology fails and nature develops strategies to regenerate. This is one way that resistance works—a cycle of pushing and pulling, of opposing forces struggling for survival, struggling to engage creatively with their environment, to adapt. Resistance is always aware of the variety of external threats it faces, and adapts to the struggle as it happens.

In politics, resistance is the act of standing up against injustice or against an invading or colonizing force. The French resistance waged a campaign against Nazism and the Vichy government from inside occupied France during World War II. This kind of resistance struggles to prevent the invader from taking more territory, both geographical and cultural. Part of the struggle, in the case of French resistance, was to keep the press and literature alive, to maintain a voice against the bombardment of Nazi propaganda. Resistance demands flexibility, strategic adaptation to the means of the invader, a changing of tactics to fit the moment. In plant populations and in human populations, resistance has a common meaning—to doggedly hold on to one's customs and one's habitat in the face of an enemy intent on overtaking that habitat and those customs. In both cases, resistance remains dormant until a threat appears. But when the threat appears, watch out. As graffiti on the streets of Oaxaca declared during the 2006 uprising that erupted to oust a corrupt governor, "*The more you repress, the more we resist.*"

Native peoples of the New World, even as they fell to disease and cultural onslaught, have fiercely resisted the colonial invader since 1492. In the case of the Zapatistas and their struggle against the loss of indigenous territory and indigenous culture, this resistance takes many forms, changing tactics with the times. The type of resistance varies according to the nature of the threat—armed resistance, passive resistance, vocal resistance, silent resistance. The very ability of the rural indigenous farmer—the *campesino*—to cultivate rocky hillsides while military helicopters circle above and troops stand just across the river awaiting orders to invade—a common scenario in Chiapas—is one type of hardened, passive resistance. In this sense, resistance has become the very soil in which native cultures grow.

Santos de La Cruz Carrillo, a Wixarika (Huichol) lawyer from the state of Durango, and a delegate to Mexico's National Indigenous Congress, says:

> What does resistance mean? Resistance means to defend what belongs to us as indigenous people: territory, resources, culture. If, among our peoples, we didn't have resistance, we would no longer exist as peoples. Thanks to our resistance, we have maintained our cultures.[14]

For the Zapatista communities, resistance means rejecting handouts from the "*mal gobierno,*" the bad government, and from any other national or international agency whose intention is not to build local self-sufficiency but to undermine it through paternalism, clientism, charity, or other forms of low-intensity warfare. This rejection is the "no" in the Zapatista slogan, "one no and many yeses." Of course, for a people living at the margins of the capitalist economy, on poor soils and with only the most basic resources, this kind of resistance is accompanied by hunger, thirst, illness, and want. For the Zapatista communities, the decision to resist is a daily one, made next to a cold stove in an empty kitchen on yet another day without beans, let alone meat, or vegetables, or sugar.

The Second Declaration of the Lacandon Jungle, issued six months into the uprising, on June 10, 1994, defines resistance and its cost:

> We will accept nothing from the supreme government, although they may increase our suffering and our pain, although death continues to accompany us at our table, in our bed, and in our lands, although we watch others selling themselves to the hand that oppresses them; although everything hurts; although pain wrings

> tears from the very stones. We will accept nothing. We will resist. We will accept nothing from the government. We will resist until he who commands, commands by obeying.[15]

There is an aspect of resistance that roots itself in language and in the symbols of culture, in the hidden meanings of ritual or custom, myths, and daily acts, in the stories and songs and in the dreams of a people. More than simply keeping literature or oral tradition alive, and not limited to something as programmatic as "propaganda," we might think of this as poetic resistance, as the resistance of memory against forgetting. When the Spanish conquistadors forced the people of highland Chiapas and Guatemala to wear distinct patterns to mark their home villages, allowing insurrectionaries to be quickly recognized and reckoned with, the native women fought back, everywhere, by weaving stunningly beautiful *huipiles.*[16] In the words of journalist and poet John Ross, they "turned apartheid into art."[17]

Again, *poesis*—creation, or creating—is the first front in the war against oblivion. Ofelia Rivas, Tohono O'odham from the Sonora/Arizona border, who insists on speaking her native language when she addresses a crowd, says, "my language is my resistance."[18] Poetic resistance—the resistance of language against the oblivion of silence—has been a part of indigenous survival for the last five centuries—the fiery blooming of flowers from the hardened soil.

A poetics of resistance develops around stories and histories, fables and fabrics and old wives' tales, songs and symbols, all of the poetic outfitting that keeps a culture alive, that gives it memory and hope; it is the armature of belief, the means by which history is spelled out day by day becoming culture, becoming memory, becoming codes of action handed down by gods, heroes and saints. The poetics that crops up under dangerous circumstances is easy to find in any anti-imperial struggle: the songs of the Spanish Civil War, the murals of the Sandinistas, the street-theater of Yippics and Diggers during the sixties in the United States. We can find poetic resistance in hip-hop and *tropicalismo* and punk rock, in the hard bop and free jazz of the black arts movement, in the graffiti of French Situationists and students of 1968 ("Beneath the paving stones, the beach!") and the posters and pranks of Dadaists in 1918, in the union songs of the American labor movement of the early twentieth century, in the quilts of abolitionists. Like any flowering of culture, and like the manifold expressions of life itself, once you begin to look for it, it's everywhere. On the wall of the pub where I sometimes write are the words, painted in calligraphy, of the Irish freedom fighter James Connolly, intoning, "No revolutionary movement is complete without its poetic expression"; he is echoed by Roqué Dalton and Ernesto Cardenal, Pablo Neruda and Cesar Vallejo, Daisy Zamora and Aimé Cesaire, Paul Eluard and June Jordan and Allen Ginsberg and Amiri Baraka. Even the American Revolution, with its myths of Betsy Ross the flag maker, Paul Revere's ride ("one if by land, two if by sea"), the Boston Tea Party, and young George Washington chopping down the cherry tree and confessing, "I cannot tell a lie," has a poetics born of anti-imperial struggle, a mythic language or lexicon of stories that has rooted itself in the consciousness of the United States. "The Star-Spangled Banner," its singular lyric, is still sung fervently at baseball games, and the Pledge of Allegiance, hymn to American nationalism, has been recited in public schools since the 1950s, two centuries after the end of British colonial rule, in a perverse show of resistance to the "communist menace" of the Cold War years. Similarly, several Mexican revolutions have given birth to bodies of myth, narratives of hope and stories of national pride and unity, symbols of strength, songs and endless stories that roll together over the course of years to become history. Along with bread—that is, survival—history is the object of revolution. History is made by telling stories as you go.

Rick Rowley of Big Noise Tactical, a radical film collective born out of *Zapatismo*, that has documented—from down below and to the left—the global resistance to globalization and the ongoing wars for territory that wrack our historical moment, notes that it takes more than collective imagination, or the will to truth, to transform the world:

> The truth is not something that is just in the facts and in the information, the truth is something that has to be fought for, it's something that has to be defended ... so when the Zapatistas say "named are we now we will not die," they're saying we've conquered a place in reality, we exist now because our movement has made a name for us that circulates, that our name echoes in the

rocks, our name resonates inside of movements all over the world, and so we've conquered those realities and we exist. It's not a war of information, it's a war of dreams and images that ... animate information, make that information true, or make it a lie.[19]

Branding Popular Resistance

"No space has been left unbranded."

—Naomi Klein[20]

Digging into the poetics of *Zapatismo*, analyzing the communiqués for their symbolic and literary content, seems a valid and valuable exercise, but it begs a question: if a story is told in the jungle and no one is there to hear it, is it still a story?

Introducing Gloria Muñoz Ramirez's book *The Fire and the Word: A History of the Zapatista Movement*, Subcomandante Marcos has written the story of the Zapatistas' early days: "According to our calendar, the history of the EZLN prior to the beginning of the war had seven stages."[21] Marcos goes on to tell of the events in the jungle during the early years, 1983 to 1993, from the first camp established in the Lacandon to the night of the uprising. The telling serves to build the myth of *Zapatismo*—but who has the ears to hear it? That is to say, while the Zapatista communiqués have been widely published in many languages, perhaps rivaling in our time the viral spread of older insurgent literature like *The Communist Manifesto* and *The Declaration of the Rights of Man*, and have been serialized in major Mexican periodicals, the numbers of actual readers, one can guess, is minimal. It would be disingenuous to suggest that the *relatos* of Old Antonio or of Don Durito serve to bring new sympathizers to the Zapatista cause, or to win them territory, either physical or psychological: by the time a reader has approached these stories, has taken the time to read and digest them, most likely she is already sympathetic to the cause. Still, the narrative itself has a certain intention and a certain promise. So how does the poetics of resistance, then, have its effect?

Aside from countless converging historical factors, what has drawn people in such numbers to a movement beginning in the most obscure corner of Mexico has been a web of stories and grand historical gestures: a ski-masked face and a rebel cry; a man on horseback, serenely smoking a pipe, with bullet belts marking a wide X across his chest; crowds of miniscule women in flower-embroidered dresses shoving and screaming at a ragged platoon of worried soldiers. Beginning in the mid-1990s, these images, seen worldwide, have evoked a global uprising against state and corporate capitalism, corrupt bureaucracy, and power wielded by the few against the interests of the many. *Zapatismo*, aside from creating a new kind of social movement that seeks to build local alternatives to power rather than to take the power of the state, has created an image and a mythic space that is unique among liberation movements, and that has allowed it to survive in the popular imagination, and therefore on the ground, for a decade and a half now.

By taking early and strategic advantage of the Internet and the news media, the Zapatistas have kept their story in the headlines, at least in their own country, and sometimes elsewhere. By using folktales, myths, jokes, and other ways of engaging an audience, they have filled what might be described as a psycho-emotional need for stories of resistance in the international left, and among those with a leftward tendency. By framing themselves as sympathetic characters—Subcomandante Marcos the charismatic and self-effacing wit, Comandanta Ramona the diminutive but persistent female presence who overcame illiteracy to speak before millions, and the rest of the Zapatistas, the unbending will of popular resistance—they have created a living history that wins them press, solidarity, and the attention of international human rights organizations, and that, generally, prevents the Mexican government from attacking them outright.

Dubious as it may at first appear, I'd suggest that the web of propaganda of which the communiqués are one piece—and perhaps the principal piece, the Rosetta Stone that allows us to decipher the meanings of the masks, the dolls, the *encuentros*, the public spectacles—goes beyond the means of literature, and certainly beyond the traditional limits of political pamphleteering, to function as *branding*.

To refer to the Zapatistas' representation of a deeply marginalized multitude as branding might appear cynical or ill-considered, but it is fair to say that just as the Nike swoosh calls to mind not only athletic equipment but also athletics itself (and, for many, a supreme dog-eat-dog competitiveness, the fundamental ideology of predatory capitalism), and just as Starbucks represents not only gourmet coffee but yuppie comfort and conformity, the ski mask and other symbols of *Zapatismo* serve to deliver a dense package of information wrapped in a single visual icon—and to create name recognition for it. It is precisely this careful image management, along with a clear and consistent message, that prevented the Zapatistas from suffering the same fate as the multitudes slaughtered in neighboring Guatemala in the 1980s, and that has led them, instead, to inspire and represent global popular resistance.

As branding serves to expand the market of a product and broaden its market share by targeting a particular consumer profile, and as a national mythology serves to project qualities of authority, rightness and permanence—using such familiar advertising slogans as "The sun never sets on the British Empire," "*Como Mexico No Hay Dos,*" "America the Beautiful," "Land of the Free and Home of the Brave," etcetera—the poetics of *Zapatismo* act as a portal to understanding the projected values, ideals, ideologies, and goals of the Zapatista movement.

Naomi Klein, in her era-defining opus *No Logo*, discusses the power of branded images, pointing out that "logos, by the force of ubiquity, have become the closest thing we have to an international language, recognized and understood in more places than English," and describes them as a kind of magical shibboleth within "this global web of logos and products … couched in the euphoric marketing rhetoric of the global village, an incredible place where tribespeople in remotest rain forests tap away on laptop computers."[22]

Indeed, just as Nike's swoosh acts as a psychic trigger, urging the mind to recreate a set of relationships, feelings, urges, desires, there is a "magical" element to the way the ski-mask affects one's perception of an indigenous woman, her face covered in order to be seen. The "magic" lies, in part, in what the mask implies through the Zapatistas' manipulation of historical symbols, names, dates, and images. Just as "successful corporations must primarily produce brands, as opposed to products,"[23] successful movements must engage in name recognition, guerilla marketing, and product placement, constantly opening "fresh new spaces to disseminate the brand's idea of itself."[24] This is the cynic's view, indeed, but it is fair to say that, just as the folk art of José Guadalupe Posada (you know the images even if you don't recognize the artist's name) in some sense *brands* a Mexican popular mythology at the turn of the last century—insurgent, satirical, redolent of class antagonism and the reclamation of native cultural symbols—the ski-masked face and the comical image of Don Durito de la Lacandona have branded Mexico's grassroots rebellion at the vertiginous turn of our own century.

In the world of business, the objective of branding is, of course, to increase sales, or, put another way, to draw increased capital exchange. Since the Zapatistas are not a profit-seeking venture, the objective of their brand is not to increase revenue, but rather to encourage other forms of exchange: solidarity, reciprocity, material aid, human rights accompaniment, and so on. That is to say, the Zapatista brand attracts *social and political capital.* How else is it possible to explain that while impoverished people, rebel people, people demanding a voice exist everywhere, Zapatista rebel territory has attracted aid and accompaniment from so many since 1994? Human Rights Watch and the Red Cross, congressional delegations, cultural celebrities from Danielle Mitterrand and Oliver Stone to Rage Against the Machine, Manu Chao and the Indigo Girls, celebrated intellectuals, documentary film makers, boatloads of journalists and social scientists, educators, health workers, medical professionals, agronomists, organic farmers, collectivists, fair trade entrepreneurs, poets, community organizers, religious delegations, video artists, and scores of so-called "revolutionary tourists," not to mention the steady stream of political visionaries, anarchists, and seekers and adventurers of all description. Where else on the planet do the likes of John Berger, Jose Saramago, and Susan Sontag chat with Catalan solidarity activists and peasant farmers in thatch-roofed huts?

Such is the power of branding. "*We are branded, we cannot die.*" Swoosh!

But, aside from its superficial goal of attracting capital, whether in the form of shekels or of solidarity, there is a key difference between corporate branding and the sort engaged in by the Zapatistas. In his subversive classic, *The Society of the Spectacle*, Guy Debord examines the role of the mass-mediated spectacle in the reproduction of capitalist ideology, arguing that social life has become mediated by images; beyond mediated, he argues, social life has lost any quality of unmediated experience—it is reduced, in late capitalism, to the endless reproduction of images. The function of the spectacle, in Debord's thought, is to alienate each from each, to shape reality—social space, interpersonal relations, the subjective realms of desire, need, and community—according to the images provided by the machinery of capitalist production: "The spectacle within society corresponds to a concrete manufacture of alienation."[25] The opening section of the book, "Separation Perfected," begins with the proclamation, "In societies where modern conditions of production prevail, all of life presents itself as an immense accumulation of spectacles. Everything that was directly lived has moved away into a representation."[26]

In a certain sense, the Zapatistas are masters at creating spectacle. Yet, where Debord sees in spectacle the function of separation, or alienation, the Zapatista web of propaganda creates and manipulates spectacle to re-establish connection—to reject the alienation of individuals from both history and society, and to reunite each to each and all to all. To further mine Debord's lexicon, the Zapatista brand and the spectacle it projects function as *détournement*, gathering the symbols and sense of capital, and turning them about to both empty them of their force, and create a liberatory space to be filled by collective acts of insurgent imagination.

It might be noted that in much of Mexico, deep Mexico, on the eve of the North American Free Trade Agreement's implementation in 1994, "modern conditions of production" did not and still do not, to a large extent, prevail. The figures are widely available: Chiapas supplies 20 percent of Mexico's oil and 40 percent of its natural gas, yet 60 percent of the population cooks with firewood; roughly the same percentage lacks clean drinking water, and the same percentage again is chronically malnourished.[27] A particularly telling figure, illustrative of the economic means of most Chiapanecos, is that, of the 118 municipalities in the state of Chiapas, only 25 percent have banks. In the municipality of Ocosingo, with an area of 10,000 square kilometers, there were, at the time of the uprising, two banks.[28]

However, to say that modern conditions of production are absent from Chiapas is a vast oversimplification; in fact, modern production exists, but, as throughout the global south, the wealth produced is shipped inexorably northward. While Mexico's oil, gas, beef, coffee, timber and other products leave the state, Chiapas suffers the lowest literacy rate in Mexico (30 percent statewide and almost 50 percent in the zone of conflict); in eastern Chiapas, over 80 percent of homes have mud floors.[29]

Perhaps this odd but oddly prevalent condition—the coexistence of the digging stick and the laptop, the presence of the *campesino* in *huaraches* and his burro on the interstate toll road—is what has allowed the unique spectacle of *Zapatismo* to bloom. The collision of modernity with peasant culture, perhaps, presents conditions where the commodified and commodifying spectacle of Debord lives alongside the "directly lived" experience of land-based peoples engaged in age-old seasonal rhythms of production. Perhaps it is this "leak" in the spectacle—a still uncommodified and unalienated corner of the world, off in the periphery of Southeast Mexico—that gives the Zapatista spectacle both its allure and its power of *détournement*.

Autonomy vs. Insurgency: A Word on Contradictions

When we talk about "the Zapatistas," it is important to note, we are not referring to a single, unitary organization or structure; "Zapatistas" generally refers to both the EZLN—the military command whose function is to serve and protect the civilian population and bring the government to the negotiating table—and to the "*bases de apoyo*"—the rural communities that support the EZLN, governed by autonomous municipal authorities, and more recently by the Juntas de Buen Gobierno (Good Government Councils).

The EZLN, organized as a hierarchical structure with Subcomandante Marcos as the supreme military commander and the Clandestine Revolutionary Indigenous Committee-General Command (CCRI-CG, known informally as the Comandancia*)*, acting as a leadership council, takes the decisions that guide military strategy in what we might call the project of insurgency. Marcos, often mistakenly characterized as the "leader" of the Zapatistas in general, is designated "subcomandante" because, being non-indigenous, he cannot form a part of the executive committee or collective leadership council.

In his own words:

> I have the honor of having as my superiors the best women and men of the Tzotzil, Chol, Tojolobal, Mam, and Zoque ethnicities. I have lived with them for more than ten years and I am proud to obey them and serve them in my arms and my life. They have taught me more than they now teach the country and the whole world. They are my commanders and I will follow them along whatever path they choose.[30]

Linked closely with the insurgency in ever-evolving ways are the Zapatista communities themselves—the villages, settlements, and peri-urban neighborhoods that form the base of the Zapatista movement. Their struggle, beyond the work of simply meeting daily needs, is to build and maintain self-sufficiency in governance, education, health care, rural production, and basic services such as the provision of water, sanitation, and energy.

Autonomous municipal authorities, generally acting according to traditional collective methods of governance, guide decision making in the communities. The Comandancia guides decision making among the insurgents; it acts on its own authority, though sometimes with direct input from the communities (as in the decision to go to war on January 1, 1994), and sometimes not.

Inevitably, there are tensions between these parallel structures—that of the EZLN and that of the autonomous communities—and sometimes there are outright contradictions. In a series of discussions I carried out in Chiapas in October 2008, numerous people shared the perspective that, when we speak of *Zapatismo*, we are speaking of two different things—the theory, or ideal, of *Zapatismo*, and the ways in which it is carried out in practice. Generally speaking, the theory is grounded in the structures of democratic governance that emerge from the autonomous communities, while the practice hinges largely on tactical decisions made by Marcos and the Comandancia.

Paco Vazquez of ProMedios, an independent organization started in the late 1990s to provide media training to the embattled communities of Chiapas, says:

> The construction of autonomy in infrastructure, agriculture, education, health services, political decision-making, brings with it the need for an autonomous voice, and Marcos has introduced many speeches and communiqués, "through my voice speaks the voice of the EZLN." However, the voice of the EZLN, the Zapatista military, is not the voice of the indigenous communities that the EZLN exists to defend and protect. It's easy to forget that we're talking about two different entities. Related, but different.[31]

Jorge Santiago Santiago, founding director of the non-governmental organization DESMI (Desarollo Economico y Social de los Méxicanos Indígenas, or Economic and Social Development of Indigenous Mexicans), present in Chiapas since 1970, has a different perspective:

> It's not like there's a struggle [between Marcos and the Comandancia and the *bases de apoyo*] about who represents more authentically; they have different roles. There could be, for example, a *convocatoria* (a large public meeting) organized by the communities that has nothing to do with the EZLN, and vice-versa. In the Other Campaign, Marcos is the representative, the speaking voice. But for the communities, each community represents itself; the Good Government Council represents itself. I think the EZLN

> has a type of organizational strength that allows them to represent themselves with great articulation at different levels—with the NGOs, the military, the government, within their own organization. There isn't a conflict, because they're very agile—each group and person has its own role; they know that one has to address different problems in different ways, at different levels. Like in medicine—you give children's medicine to children, adult's medicine to adults, you do prevention when necessary, and it's not as if there are conflicts between the different approaches.[32]

Underlying much of the movement's action, then, is a tension between the largely democratic and autonomist project of the communities, based on building and exercising popular power, and the military project of defending rights and territory, whose leadership clearly rests with the Comandancia and with Subcomandante Marcos. This tension without a doubt results in frequent contradictions, disappointments, and frustrations of the hopes of those who invest all of their revolutionary ideals in Marcos, on the one hand, or in the project of autonomy on the other. Some who have watched the movement evolve consider this tension irreconcilable, fearing that within it lies the movement's ultimate failure. But, as the timeless wisdom of the *campesino* might say: *ni modo, asi es.* Too bad, that's how it goes. I would argue that, all theory and all revolutionary ideals aside, the ways in which this tension plays out in practice is precisely *Zapatismo*.

The communiqués and other acts of "public relations," it should be noted, tend to be responses to the political moment—an uprising, an invasion, an election, a presidential decree, a media blitz, etc. In some cases, depending on what is at stake at the moment, the communiqués promote the autonomist project—they are the words of a collective whose focus is on a long-term political process of building autonomy. In other cases, they represent the insurgency—they are the words of a single man (Marcos) or a core of clandestine leaders (the Comandancia), whose focus is to drive a time-bound political agenda with force and immediacy to further the insurgent strategy. Taken as a whole, they create the narrative, the story, of *Zapatismo*.

II
Living Myth, Reviving History

> It hasn't taken long for the excitement inspired by the manic renditions of globalization to wear thin, revealing the cracks and fissures beneath its high-gloss façade. More and more ... we in the West have been catching glimpses of another kind of global village, where the economic divide is widening and cultural choices are narrowing.
>
> —Naomi Klein[1]

> On the side of oblivion are the multiple forces of the market. On the side of memory is the solitary reason of History.
>
> — Subcomandante Marcos[2]

The Story of January 1, 1994

If the story has been told and retold so often that it has become legend, it is because the first bursting forth of the Zapatista insurgency was crafted with pure cinematic genius, every aspect shot through with the material of legend. As the clock strikes midnight in Mexico City, President Salinas de Gortari is toasting the North American Free Trade Agreement (NAFTA) and Mexico's much-ballyhooed entrance into the First World. In remote Chiapas, an invisible army has gathered in the mist of highland villages, uniformed in dark colors, faces masked, some armed with bolt-action rifles, some with sticks, some armed only with their rage and shielded only with their dignity. Like a confluence of waters roiling into a flash flood, thousands of Mayan rebels, some trained for a decade, some for a month, others for a lifetime, descend onto the colonial bastions of San Cristóbal, Ocosingo, Altamirano, and Las Margaritas, spilling into the streets under cover of night. Few shots ring out, mingled with the fireworks of the Mexican New Year. Government offices are taken, files are ransacked, land titles destroyed, computers smashed. The walls are covered with graffiti and wheat-pasted with proclamations of war. From the balcony of the government palace in San Cristóbal, first in Tzotzil, and then in Spanish, a ski-masked rebel pronounces:

The First Declaration of the Lacandon Jungle[3]

To the people of Mexico

Mexican brothers and sisters,

We are the product of 500 years of struggle: first against slavery, then in the insurgent-led War of Independence against Spain; later in the fight to avoid being absorbed by North American expansion; next to proclaim our constitution and expel the French from our soil; and finally, after the dictatorship of Porfirio Diaz refused to fairly apply the reform laws, in the rebellion where the people created their own leaders. In that rebellion Villa and Zapata emerged, poor men like us.

We are denied the most elementary education so they can use us as cannon fodder and plunder the wealth of our country, uncaring that we are dying of hunger and curable diseases. Nor do they care that we have nothing, absolutely nothing, no decent roof over our heads, no land, no work, no health care, no food, no education. We do not have the right to freely and democratically elect our political representatives, nor are we independent from foreigners, nor do we have peace and justice for ourselves and our children.

But today, we say ENOUGH. We are the inheritors of the true builders of our nation. The dispossessed, we are millions and we call on our brothers and sisters to join this struggle as the only path that will allow us not to die of hunger due to the insatiable ambition of a seventy-year-old dictatorship led by a clique of traitors that represent the most conservative groups ready to sell out our country. They are the same ones that opposed Hidalgo and Morelos, the same ones that betrayed Vicente Guerrero, the same ones that sold half our country to the foreign invader, the same

> ones that imported a European prince to rule our country, the same ones that formed the "scientific" Porfirista dictatorship, the same ones that opposed the Petroleum Expropriation, the same ones that massacred the railroad workers in 1958 and the students in 1968, the same ones that today take everything from us, absolutely everything.
>
> As our last hope, after having exhausted every option to exercise the legal rights in the Carta Magna, we return to her, our Constitution, to apply Article 39, which says, "National sovereignty resides essentially and originally in the people. All public power issues from the people and is instituted for the people's benefit. The people have, at all times, the inalienable right to alter or modify their form of government." Thus, in keeping with our Constitution, we issue the present declaration of war against the Mexican federal army, that basic pillar of the dictatorship under which we live, monopolized by the party in power, headed by the federal executive office, which is today unlawfully held by the illegitimate head-of-state, Carlos Salinas de Gortari.
>
> According to this Declaration of War, we ask that other powers of the nation advocate to restore the legitimacy and the stability of the nation by overthrowing the dictator.

The declaration goes on to enumerate the specific demands of the EZLN and then closes with the assertion that their course is a just one:

> To the People of Mexico: We, men and women, upright and free, are conscious that the war we have declared is our last resort, but is also just. The dictatorship has been waging an undeclared genocidal war against our people for many years. Therefore we ask for your participation, your decision to support this plan of the people of Mexico who struggle for work, land, housing, food, health care, education, independence, freedom, democracy, justice and peace. We declare that we will not stop fighting until the basic demands of our people have been met by forming a government of our country that is free and democratic.

The press is gathered, and the words fly out across the ether. Within a day the Declaration is rendered into other languages, flashing on computer screens from Bogotá to Bilbao, Strasbourg to San Francisco. Retreating from the town centers, the rebels attack Rancho Nuevo military base, freeing weapons and ammunition; they kidnap the hated land baron General Abasalón Castellanos; according to legend, they liberate the typewriter that Marcos would use henceforth to launch his incendiary communiqués. They open prisons and release the prisoners. In San Cristóbal, anxious tourists crow to the guerillas about their disrupted travel plans—an anonymous masked rebel famously replies, "I'm sorry for the inconvenience, but this is a revolution."[4]

For twelve days, the highlands are at war: firefights and skirmishes in the hills, the government strafing and bombing from the air. The civilian population, too, is under siege. At least 200 are killed. Government troops can't tell Mayan rebels from ordinary Maya. Ranches and *haciendas* are occupied, their former owners fleeing. The Zapatistas take back lands that once belonged to them, or might have, or should have. In the space of weeks, their territory is established, the lowland jungle *cañadas* closed off, bridges are downed and roadblocks built, and signs go up throughout the jungle: *Welcome to Zapatista rebel territory*.

Desperate to undermine the legitimacy of the uprising, the Salinas government released a statement: "some professional mercenaries and a group of foreigners, alien to the efforts of Mexican society, struck a painful blow in the zone of Chiapas and in the heart of all Mexicans."[5]

But the uprising had already stirred the Mexican psyche. With a single striking blow, the Zapatistas launched an offensive whose inertia set the establishment off kilter, winning crucial support from many sectors of the population. As Mexican anthropologist Gilberto López y Rivas points out, "It was the revelation of an identity that was always present in the formation of the Mexican nation, coming from an otherness that had been consistently undervalued. The social indicators that situated the indigenous peoples as the most impoverished sectors of the Mexican population were suddenly profoundly relevant, and were rendered starkly visible."[6] Suddenly, like never before, a spotlight shone on the indigenous problem, the poverty problem, the human rights problem, the democracy problem. In the course of a single night, the corrupt and violent nature of the Mexican nation was exposed like a patient in a surgical theater.

After twelve days of fighting, civil society demanded that the government call off its assault. President Salinas, eager to minimize the problem, complied. By the end of February, peace talks had been organized in the Cathedral of San Cristóbal, convened by Bishop Samuel Ruiz, known to the native people of Chiapas as Tatik, or Father. The scene of the peace talks itself was profoundly theatrical: twenty members of the EZLN's Clandestine Revolutionary Indigenous Committee, their faces masked, and Marcos wearing the bandoliers of the *guerillero* across his chest, albeit empty of shells, spread out at a long conference table in the nave of the haunting stone Cathedral. Their bearing was not that of fugitives or bandits, but of women and men who held their truth before them like a talisman. Clearly they welcomed this opportunity to speak. The *comandantes* ably and defiantly demonstrated that this was their rebellion, speaking truth to the government's lie that the uprising was the work of foreign agitators. After each of the *comandantes* had spoken, the littlest *comandanta*, Ramona, handed Marcos a folded Mexican flag which he dramatically unfurled before speaking. By the end of the first session the government representative, Manuel Camacho, had no choice but to recognize that, whatever their intentions, "the EZLN is an organization of Chiapanecos, Mexicans, in their majority indigenous."[7]

They had won a major PR victory, setting the stage for a dramatic turn in Mexican national politics, and arguably setting in motion global events as well. An unnamed Colombian *guerillero* quoted at the time expressed awe, tempered by frustration, at the overnight success of the EZLN:

> They fought for twelve days and occupied a handful of municipalities.... We have been fighting for thirty years, we are controlling large parts of the national territory ... and even so, nobody is interested in our actions, while theirs have created a furor around the world."[8]

To put it simply, in January 1994, a legend was born.

Living Myth

Fundamental to our narrative, then, is the creation of legends, the notion of history in the making, and of myth as the fundament of history. Author and scholar Ronald Wright offers a helpful definition:

> Myth is an arrangement of the past, whether real or imagined, in patterns that reinforce a culture's deepest values and aspirations.... Myths are so fraught with meaning that we live and die by them. They are the maps by which cultures navigate through time.[9]

For the Zapatistas, revolution means reclaiming the map of the past in order to build roads into a just future from an ignoble present. But what form does this past take, when it has been claimed by so many, when it has been mythologized and demythologized, claimed and re-claimed so many times that its content cannot possibly remain "authentic" or "transparent"? Historian Victoria Bricker, while documenting the Mayan regions of Chiapas, Guatemala, and the Yucatán, acknowledges that, in a largely oral culture like the Mesoamerican indigenous culture, history is atemporal and blends with myth and legend in a way that differ fundamentally from the established Western view of history as an objective sequence of events that *actually happened.*

Or is it really so different, when every side, dominator or dominated, writes history in its favor, sanctifies its heroes and glorifies or negates its defeats? Bricker argues that the indigenous of southern Mexico do not differentiate myth, legend and history: "Myths constitute theories of history, and the creators of myths are historians in the same sense as [Arnold] Toynbee and [Oswald] Spengler." She continues, "in sum ... the intent to discover schemes in the sequence of events is not history but the *science* of history"; "if we accept that myths constitute theories of history, then it is evident that we must analyze them as such."[10] The Zapatistas, with their ski masks and their storied narrative resistance, show us that myth and history are woven of the same material.

Another scholar of things Mayan, Dennis Tedlock, in the introduction to his translation of the Popul Vuh, council book of the Quiché Maya, elaborates:

> We tend to think of myth and history as being in conflict with one another, but the authors of the inscriptions at Palenque and the alphabetic text of the Popul Vuh treated the mythic and historical parts of their narratives as belonging to a single, balanced whole....
>
> In fact we already have a word that [describes this whole]: mythistory, taken into English from Greek by way of Latin. For the ancient Greeks, who set about driving a wedge between the divine and the human, this term became a negative one, designating narratives that should have been properly historical but contained mythic impurities. For Mayans, the presence of a divine dimension in narratives of human affairs is not an imperfection but a necessity, and it is balanced by a necessary human dimension in narratives of divine affairs.[11]

Gods and humans mingle with one another, creating myth and history together in dreams, legends, fables, and books. How can they not? Further on we will look at "the presence of a divine dimension" in the communiqués, the way in which Marcos introduces the voices of gods long presumed dead to speak to contemporary conditions from their mythistorical vantage point.

For us in the post-industrial "first" world, these gods automatically assume a mythic role, because they exist outside of our lived or perceived experience. But, as part of the living history of the Mayan people, the reintroduction of these gods into national ethical-political discourse gives their presence the qualities of history. The gods' existence (for us) is mythical, but their presence as signs in a historically bound narrative brings them into history. They bring back the sense of mythistory that is so loudly and rudely absent from the nightly news.

In *Myth and the Origin of Religion*, Vine Deloria surveys an impressive array of Western social scientists, including Émile Durkheim, Franz Boas, R. G. Collingwood, Carl Jung, Joseph Campbell, Alan Watts, and Mircea Eliade, and demonstrates that, for virtually all of them, "the definition of myth, or at least religious myth, excludes the possibility of extracting from myth any historical reality. It finds myth to possess verbal existence only, confining it to the realms of ancient intellectualism or psychological phenomena that occur 'in here' rather than 'out there' in the world of physical existence."[12]

Deloria asserts, by contrast, that myth is likely always constructed from lived historical reality: "The point that seems to escape all of these men is that the ancient sources and accounts that we have in hand today may simply be the way people wrote about the events that affected their lives."[13] Deloria, a native American scholar deeply immersed in the question of how Western science and indigenous science differ, points out throughout his writings that for indigenous peoples, there is no qualitative difference between the objective—what occurs "out there"—and the subjective—what occurs "in here.' That which *actually happened*, in other words, is not limited to measurable, quantifiable, material events. Thus, there is no reason to differentiate between Bricker's sense of "myths as *theories* of history," and Tedlock's assertion that mythic and historical narratives belong to a single, balanced whole. Perhaps, Deloria suggests, myths are history, but history that explicitly includes visions, dreams, interpretations, and other apparently subjective ways of reading the world.

Tzvetan Todorov, in *The Conquest of America*, gives another perspective on the question of the (re)production of historical narratives. Speaking of the difficulty of comprehending the early history of the conquest due to the absence (read: destruction) of earlier indigenous texts and the subjugation of conquest-era texts to the laws—at once linguistic, structural, and religious—of New Spain, Todorov suggests:

> Our only recourse is not to read these texts as transparent statements, but to try at the same time to take into account the action and circumstances of their utterance.... The questions raised here refer less to a knowledge of the truth than to a knowledge of verisimilitude. That is, an event may not have occurred, despite the allegations of one of the chroniclers. But the fact that the latter could have stated such an event, that he could have counted on its acceptance by the contemporary public, is at least as revealing as the simple occurrence of an event which proceeds, after all, from chance. In a way, the reception of the statements is more revealing for the history of ideologies than their production; and when an author is mistaken, or lying, his text is no less significant than

> when he is speaking the truth; the important thing is that the text be "receivable" by contemporaries, or that it has been regarded as such by its producer. From this point of view, the notion of "false" is irrelevant here.[14]

Put more simply, history is not events that happened, but stories about events that might have happened or not. Once these stories enter the public record, they must be reckoned with. Once the gods of Mayan antiquity appear in the national daily newspapers, they have entered national history. The very fact that the stories have been passed along means there is something in them that speaks to *someone*. Like the old Earth goddess Tonantzin, whose shrine exists, still, beneath and within the heart of the Basilica of Guadelupe in Tepayac near Mexico City, the old and the new blend and mix. Catholicism and the old indigenous religions mix in the market stalls in Tepayac, blending Western history and indigenous myth, Western myth and indigenous history.

A similar syncretism, a similar blending, appears in the poetics of Marcos and the EZLN. When the observations, declarations, testimonies and manifestos of the indigenous communities in resistance come in the form of "story" or "myth," there is an entrance of myth into history, another voice speaking. The propaganda of the Mexican government, which counts on state and corporate-sponsored news media to repeat its versions of events, also counts on a species of mythology to give weight to its authority and legitimacy. Both sides of the propaganda war (we limit our discussion to two sides for the time being) propagate stories, and both employ carefully constructed iconography to support and maintain their discourse. Arguably the discourse of Marcos serves to reveal historical "truths," while that of the state serves to conceal them, as Marcos accuses throughout his writings.

Discourse is the means of struggle; in some cases this means visual imagery, in some cases, narrative, in some cases graffiti or music or other forms of spontaneous expression that serve in one way or another as propaganda. It is notable that the word "*propaganda*" in Spanish does not carry the negative charge of "untruth" that it does in American English. Propaganda is the production of information, simply speaking. Whether it is "true" or "false" depends on its reception by an audience. In this propaganda war, both sides invent their histories as they go, creating new myths or retelling past ones. The narrative shifts as they gain or lose moral ground and popular approval or disapproval. The cycle of repression and resistance generates myths and stories like mechanical friction generates heat.

Marcos's fictions often come in the form of actual fables—stories told around a campfire in the night—while the "official version" masks itself as historical fact. One of the hallmarks of totalitarian history is that it vigorously presents itself as the one truth, the one story, while the history of the "subaltern"—the person without access to state power and official media channels—is more like a collection of stories reflecting a diversity of voices. In the end, history usually belongs to the side with the most guns. But Marcos understands well the importance of creating an alternative discourse, of allowing a diversity of voices to speak. He refers to this discourse reflexively and repeatedly as "the wind from below." It is this wind from below, this diversity of voices and visions, that is the real history, because it is the history of everyone at once—messy, divergent, inharmonious, colorful, violent, and vibrantly human.

Once we accept the fact that the making of history, both in terms of enacting historical events and in terms of the recording, classifying, and subsequent restructuring of these events, is not the privileged activity of the dominant culture and its scholars, and has in it nothing of truth per se, we can look at the activities of Marcos as a historical mover, mythmaker, and rewriter of histories in a fresh context, in the context of one writer or speaker creating histories to defeat and derail and debunk others' histories.

The history of the Mexican state of Chiapas, indeed, the history of the entire "New World" is a history of resource conflicts that has not seen pause since Hernán Cortés first set foot in the Valley of Mexico. Centuries of rebellions and regional wars form a crucial nexus in indigenous self-conception at the opening of the twenty-first century, especially with respect to the current uprising. That is, the EZLN uprising must be seen in the context of indigenous uprisings in the region over the course of centuries. Similarly the struggle must be seen in its global context and not as an ahistorical phenomenon surging out of some regional conflict that will disappear quietly again once the political climate shifts a bit.

The Mexican government offers this latter perspective as it systematically denies indigenous histories and disregards indigenous cultures and rights. The official version—which the successive governments of Carlos Salinas de Gortari, Ernesto Zedillo, Vicente Fox, and Felipe Calderón have relied on as part of their campaign to suppress the Zapatista voice and to create legal arguments against the presence of foreigners in the conflict zone—determined the uprising to be a small, illegitimate power struggle with no historical base. The indigenous have no history except as it is assigned to them by the powers that be; the imperial power consistently tries to pull the rug of history out from under the feet of the social majorities. But in this case, a new rug—a tapestry of resistance—is woven as quickly as the old one is pulled away.

Ward Churchill, in his essay "Literature and the Colonization of American Indians," outlines the strategy at work here:

> Direct attack is obsolete. In the post-holocaust era there is no viable ability to justify Sand Creek, the Washita and Wounded Knee. Rather, these are to be purged through a reconstitution of history as a series of tragic aberrations beginning and ending nowhere in time. The literal meaning of such events must at all costs be voided by sentiment and false nostalgia rather than treated as parts of an ongoing process. The literal is rendered tenuously figurative, and then dismissed altogether.[15]

The holocaust referred to is the genocide of native peoples of the Americas. As Churchill makes clear, one of the central strategies in this genocide, a strategy that has allowed it to continue even into the present era of enlightened concern for human rights and liberal democracy, is the substitution of indigenous history by official history. Massacres of native peoples like the events at Sand Creek and Wounded Knee in the nineteenth century are called "battles" in military history, invasions are called "discoveries," and imperial genocide is called "manifest destiny" and "the march of progress." Similar massacres, like the one at Acteal in the highlands of Chiapas on December 22, 1997, are called interethnic, interfamily strife, and are separated from their history—though this precise mountain pass has witnessed dozens of uprisings like the

Zapatista uprising and countless similarly harsh reprisals throughout the centuries—as if they "just happened." Yet everybody involved, from the men with guns to the men that govern, knows that the massacre at Acteal did not "just happen."

As will become clear when we look at a selection of the communiqués themselves, the work of Marcos, to a large extent, is to put the struggle in its global and historical context, to counter the government's propaganda, and to reveal the historical and human forces that have motivated the current phase of indigenous uprising. The notion that myth and history are interpenetrating concepts, that mythic events as well as real ones compose the current moment, will prove useful in looking at Marcos's deconstruction and reconstruction of history in service to the indigenous revolution. We will return to these concepts further on.

If we think of history as stories with differing amounts of truth and fiction, myths that derive from and go on to support particular understandings of events, there is another side of myth, then, that we must acknowledge before we go any further. In an essay called "American Indians and American History," Neal Salisbury writes of a certain kind of mythology:

> When Europeans began their invasion of America they sought to understand, legitimize and elevate their actions through a mythology in which they juxtaposed themselves as "civilized" Christians to the "savage," heathen natives. In so doing they maximized the differences between themselves and the Indians in moral, biological and cultural terms. It is not surprising that these myths informed historical as well as first-hand imaginative representations of Indian-white relations for several centuries; what is surprising is their staying power among contemporary scholars supposedly emancipated from the religious and racial superstitions of the past. For while the convention of distinguishing Indians and whites as two different species of humanity is largely outmoded, a vestige of it survives in the assumption that Indians have not participated in "history," except in their encounters with the whites who actually "made" that history.[16]

This kind of myth undergirds any history; understandings of the nature of "us" and "them" are based in cultural values, which find their expression through cultural mythologies, or, as they've been called, "imagined communities." As Edward Said notes, "culture comes to be associated, often aggressively, with the nation or the state; this differentiates 'us' from 'them,' almost always with some degree of xenophobia. Culture in this sense is a source of identity, and a rather combative one at that."[17] In the case of the Spanish missionaries who landed in the New World, there was a clash between the myths of biblical Catholicism—Adam and Eve and the Serpent, Christ on the cross, Jonah inside the whale, the presence of a single divine Being behind all of these events, and the guidance of events in an ever-forward motion toward redemption and salvation—and the myths of the indigenous religions with their multiple deities—Quetzalcoatl, Ixchel, Itzamná, and the rest—carved in stone, supported by bloodlettings and sacrifices, and their vision of time as an endless spiral in which humans continually reenact the events of the world's origin and, through their actions, perpetuate the cycles of time, of death and rebirth, fertility and mortality, feasting and fasting. These are some of the myths that began to clash and to fuse when the Spaniards, and soon afterward the British, French, Dutch, and Portuguese—came upon the New World. And of course the vision of America as a "New World" is part of a fundamentally mythic viewpoint that allowed the European visitors to conceive of these inhabited lands as without history and without culture. These myths have proven intractable and incredibly destructive.

Thinking about myth, we can include both statist and capitalist propaganda and the entire mechanism of what is called "neoliberalism." Neoliberalism, which we'll look at later from the perspective of an animated beetle on the floor of the Mesoamerican cloud forest, is girded by an array of beliefs or mythic conceptions like "progress," "advanced technology," "global information systems," "free markets," "national security," and so on. These concepts have become so engrained in the contemporary Western mind-set that they are assumed to be "natural," or at least inevitable, and to prompt actions that are, more often than not, directly threatening to both nature and culture, in the same way that the myth of an uninhabited, "virgin" territory was deadly to the ancient, historical inhabitants of that territory. Reinforced by daily rituals of buying and selling goods and services, from properties and natural resources to weapons of mass destruction, these beliefs take on the quality of myth.

As we delve into this story, we will move between the fairly recent myths of neoliberalism and the more ancient indigenous myths of the natural intelligence of all living things, the origins of humankind from mud, clay, gold, and finally corn, and the eternal returns and cycles of history. There is an entire system of beliefs—rather, many systems of belief—based on mythic events that, according to the fact-bound science of history, may never have occurred, but which nevertheless have the most profound effect on the changes occurring before us. The ability to move between these poles, between ancient myths and modern myths, is crucial to an understanding of the present conflict. Indigenous history is fundamentally different from occidental history; the difference between these two histories is largely the ground of struggle. [18] The fables, jokes, anecdotes, epistles, diatribes and manifestos written by Subcomandante Marcos tell the story—one of the stories, some of the stories—of the place between these two histories, the moving ground occupied by those whose history is in motion between other histories, where the two histories collide like weather patterns and create a front, building toward what Marcos calls a gust of wind from below.

Tourism at the End of the World
An Invitation to Bear Witness

> A new wind is rising, a wind made from the air of yesterday and an air that smells unquestionably of tomorrow.
>
> —Subcomandante Marcos, "The Long Journey from Despair to Hope"[19]

The story begins, cordially, with an invitation.

That is, the story begins brusquely, with a gunshot, a series of gunshots followed by all-out war on New Year's Day, 1994. But the invitation, whispered in the remote canyons where subterranean forces gathered, came before, in a piece written by Marcos in 1992, "The Southeast in Two Winds: A Storm and a Prophecy." First published in *La Jornada* on January 27, 1994, Marcos wrote "The Southeast in Two Winds" in

August 1992 as a teaching aid for courses on history and political analysis among EZLN troops during a period when they were deciding whether or not to take up arms. This story, one of many tales inside the larger history, is at once an invitation—first to the EZLN recruits, *indigenas* of the *cañadas* of Chiapas, and secondly to us, the listener, herein known as "civil society"—and an invocation, a welcoming of the winds that stir the restless history into turbulence. As an invocation, the piece revolves around the metaphor of a storm provoked by two winds, one a wind from above provoked by the cruel government that exploits and oppresses, and the other, appearing out of the Mexican Southeast, a wind that is a powerful ally of the Mayan people in their millenarian quest for greater autonomy from the concrete and steel world of Western capitalism into the more familiar world of the forest and jungle, the harvest, the cycles of living and dying, the processes that have allowed them to survive as a people for so long. As an invitation, "The Southeast in Two Winds" takes the form of a travel brochure, an ironic journey through the poverty and misery that is present-day Chiapas. One of Marcos's first public jokes, the communiqué-as-travel-brochure exemplifies the power of his ambivalent and playful wit; it might be read both as a parody of the literature of imperialism—with comedic echoes of Joseph Conrad's *Heart of Darkness*, mocking the exoticism of the world-expanding imperial gesture—and of the contemporary tourism industry: "Come to Jamaica! Where you are free to exploit both land and people to your infinite pleasure." At the same time, the piece introduces a number of metaphors that are central to the Zapatistas' lexicon.

It is in "The Southeast in Two Winds" that we first see Marcos's fascination with Cervantes' *Don Quixote de la Mancha*, the first comic novel of the modern age. Published in Spain in 1605, *Don Quixote* is contemporaneous with the colonization of Mexico, and the dozens of documents, maps, testimonies, and books that recount the history of the colonization and, for the first time in roman script, document the lives and cultures of indigenous America. Spanish chroniclers at the time include Andrés de Olmos, Motolinia, Bernardino de Sahagún, Diego Duran, and Diego de Landa. Original inhabitants of Mexico also wrote many chronicles at the time. Among the books written by indigenous contemporaries of Cervantes, there are the *Anales de Cuautitlán* (1570), the *Cronica mexicana*

(1599), the *Historia de la conquista de Tenochtitlán* (1554), the *Cronica Mexicayotl* (1607), and, most famously, the Popul Vuh.[20] Not long after the invention of the printing press, the Age of Discovery—or the Age of Conquest, depending on which side you found yourself on—saw what we might call the first global information revolution.

Each of the five chapters of "The Southeast in Two Winds" begins with an epigraph in the style of *Don Quixote* and other seventeenth-century picaresque novels, where each chapter is introduced with a brief summary of the action ahead. The technique became common to European literature of the time, not really going out of fashion until the advent of modernism in the twentieth century. Retreading the history of literature in the postmodern age, Marcos echoes Cervantes, leading us into "The Southeast" with characteristic irony:

> Narrating how the supreme Government has been moved by the misery of the indigenous people of Chiapas and how it has endowed the state with hotels, jails, military headquarters and a military airport. And narrating as well how the beast feeds upon the blood of these people, and other unhappy and wretched occurrences.[21]

Marcos presents the "supreme Government" as a "beast," a kind of leviathan feeding on the poor and the downtrodden—exactly the sorts that Don Quixote de La Mancha, knight errant and righter of wrongs, seeks to defend in his noble adventures, and exactly the people who make up the ranks of the EZLN, and who, as of January 1, 1994, are engaged in a battle to the death with this "beast." By establishing an archaic language mimicking Cervantes and the travel narratives of the Age of Discovery,[22] Marcos sets up a mechanism of irony that mocks the contemporary Mexican state's insistence that Mexico is "modern," "advanced," and so on, forcing the reader to recognize that, despite all appearances to the contrary, the passage of five centuries has done very little to change the relations between the indigenous people of the Americas and the colonial authorities that dominate and exploit them.

After the epigraph, the piece turns from picaresque novel to a sardonic travel brochure:

> Suppose that you heed the old slogan of the Department of Tourism, "Get to know Mexico first." Suppose that you decide to get to know the Southeast of Mexico, and suppose that in the Southeast you decide to travel to the state of Chiapas. [23]

Here Marcos describes the faulty condition of the highways, the lack of infrastructure, and statistics showing how much the state produces in agriculture, industry, and natural resources as contrasted with the poverty of its people. He begins with a look at the geography, the rivers that generate hydroelectric power, the Pacific ports with their fishing industry and commerce, the forests, the minerals, and the croplands:

> Chiapas loses blood through many veins: through oil and gas ducts, electric lines, railways, through bank accounts, trucks, vans, boats and planes, through clandestine paths, gaps and forest trails. This land continues to pay tribute to the imperialists: petroleum, electricity, cattle, money, coffee, banana, honey, corn, cacao, tobacco, sugar, soy, melon, sorghum, mamey, mango, tamarind, avocado, and Chiapaneco blood flows as a result of the thousand teeth sunk into the throat of the Mexican Southeast.[24]

It is a list not unlike lists we might find in the logs of adventurers like Christopher Columbus and Sir Walter Raleigh, Renaissance narratives detailing the wealth of the newly discovered world and all of its sensual and material riches and exotic oddities. Only in this narrative, 500 years later, the terrain has been despoiled. The exotic oddities are not examples of God's infinite blessing and the wonders of the natural world, but, more explicitly, a "tribute to the imperialists." Marcos details the extensive oil holdings beneath the soil here:

> In Chiapan earth there are eighty-six fangs of Pemex[25] clenched into the municipalities of Estacion Juarez, Reforma, Ostuacan, Pichucalco and Ocosingo. Every day they suck 92,000 barrels of petroleum and 516.7 thousand million cubic feet of gas. They take away the gas and petroleum and leave, in exchange, the stamp

> of capitalism: ecological destruction, agrarian ruin, hyperinflation, alcoholism, prostitution, and poverty. The beast doesn't stop there and extends its tentacles over the Lacandon Jungle: eight oil deposits are under exploration. Openings are made in the forest by machetes, machetes wielded by the same *campesinos* who have no land of their own because of the insatiable beast. The trees fall, felled by explosions of dynamite in areas where only the *campesinos* are prohibited from felling trees for planting.[26]

Marcos reviews statistics on the export of hardwood and corn, sugar and hydroelectric power, avocados and bananas, coffee and chocolate, and leads up to the question that an economist might ask in justifying the free market economy and massive exports: "What does the beast leave in exchange for everything it takes?"[27]

What follows are the figures for education, health, and industry, all resoundingly low, and all described in the same sardonic voice. The text continues, looking at the tourist industry in the old colonial capital of San Cristóbal de las Casas. Marcos gives us the number of hotel rooms as compared with the number of hospital beds (7 hotel rooms per 1,000 tourists as compared to 0.3 hospital beds for each 1,000 Chiapanecos), condemning the racist infrastructure that welcomes foreigners and supports mestizo business while summarily discriminating against the local indigenous population.

The second chapter begins again with a picaresque epigraph:

> Which narrates facts of the governor, apprentice of the viceroy, of his heroic combat against the progressive clergy, and of occurrences with the feudal lords, of cattle, coffee and commerce, and which narrates other facts equally fantastic.[28]

Mention of the viceroy—the colonial-era governor who represented the interests of the Spanish Crown in the New World—again brings us back to the Age of Discovery, and what followed soon on its heels, the Age of Enlightenment. While Mexico and all of the Americas were plundered—in fact, *because* of the plunder, the wealth of gold and of "information," the sense of adventure and possibility that exploitation of the

New World promised—Europe saw the advent of an age of science and knowledge, art and leisure, the likes of which had never been witnessed before. "The Southeast in Two Winds" harks back to the satirical travel tales that came after *Don Quixote* as the world opened up to European eyes, the most widely known of which are Jonathan Swift's *Gulliver's Travels* and Voltaire's *Candide*.

In these moralistic Enlightenment tales, an individual traveler, through contact with the general perversity and depravity of institutions of church, state, and common morals, finds himself at odds with the beliefs and attitudes of the time. By echoing these well-known and still stubbornly relevant works of Enlightenment literature, Marcos assumes a disingenuous voice that performs several functions at once.

At the level of the text, the writing invites the sympathy of the reader with its false naiveté and humor. The reader is intended to assume the underdog position relative to the "beast" of global capitalism. We sympathize with the impoverished, the miserable, and the exploited. At another level, that of the reproduction of other texts—that is, by mimicking Cervantes and Swift—Marcos invites the heady sympathy of the intellectual class, a move that will prove crucial as the Zapatista movement gains ground. He reveals himself as an intellectual, displaying a sharp wit and a deeply informed playfulness that places him outside of the cardboard cut-out caricature of the "rebel bandit," and assures, early on, that the motives behind the Zapatista uprising are treated as "serious," if not by the political class in Mexico then at least by its academics and intelligentsia. He takes his stand as spokesman and, without revealing his identity, makes it more-or-less clear where he is "coming from." He also makes it clear that he has both ideology and facts at his disposal.

The highly stylized prose, heavy with allusions to world literature, foregrounds the historical context of the uprising, making it clear that this is neither the first nor the last movement for popular liberation. Simultaneously, by echoing the form of *Candide* and Gulliver, Cervantes and Sir Walter Raleigh, by bringing the histories of indigenous exploitation and European colonization together in the present moment, Marcos issues a challenge to the political and intellectual classes to confront these histories head-on.

The Sleep of Reason Breeds Nightmares

During Europe's Age of Enlightenment, human reason—as opposed to faith or piety, for example, or unbridled passion—was held up as the key to liberty, and liberty was pronounced to be the highest aspiration of man (*sic*). It was the golden age of colonialism, when the great beast of European capitalism was just sinking its claws firmly into the shanks of Latin America, Asia and Africa, when the global indigenous population was stabilizing after the ravages of conquest and disease and becoming, along with the enslavement of Africans, the richest source of free labor and production that the world had ever seen.[29] The play on Enlightenment literature and colonial discourse in "The Southeast in Two Winds" reminds us, viscerally, that the repression of the 1990s is a consequence of the colonial expansion of the 1790s, that this is not an isolated moment in the history of an isolated "third world" state, but a problem intrinsic to the colonized world, a problem known today as globalization.

The colonial origins of the global era produced an abundance of utopian visions—dreams of a just, prosperous, and enlightened future constructed in the virgin wilds of an unknown continent. Accompanying these dreams were visions of unlimited riches at home built upon the spices, textiles, fuels, foods, medicines, and labors of the New World harvest. Soon after the opening of the New World and the quaint burlesque ruminations of Cervantes came the scientific advances that led to the Industrial Revolution. Francis Bacon developed the scientific method and the mandate to examine every living thing under the proverbial microscope; Descartes described the universe as a machine ordered and driven by reason; Sir Isaac Newton unveiled the mechanical laws of that universe, making it clear that, with human reason, all things could be understood and thus brought under control.

These budding mythologies were made possible largely by the leisure to think —"I think, therefore I am" —afforded by new imports of minerals and hardwoods, dyes and foodstuffs, not to mention slaves, serfs, and servants. And this exploration and exploitation, from the landings at Jamestown, Massachusetts Bay, and Cape Anne south to Veracruz, Yucatán, Hispaniola, the mouth of the Orinoco and all the way to Tierra del Fuego, with its mad search for El Dorado and the Fountain of Youth, hardly reflected the rational order that was so fashionable among Europe's greatest thinkers. In fact, as is now common knowledge (though only as of late, it would seem), it was a bloodbath and a baptism of fire. But, despite the presence of several million indigenous inhabitants and the slavery and genocide necessitated by European exploration, the myth of utopia persisted, and "reason," as such, won out over the wretched life of the heathen savages.

Edward Said, among many others, has demonstrated that this apparent contradiction—the meeting of Western "reason" and the "darkness" (à la Joseph Conrad) of the "sad tropics" (à la Claude Levi-Strauss)—was, in fact, the substrate upon which "modernity" thrived. He cites the British mystic poet William Blake: "The Foundation of Empire is Art and Science. Remove them or Degrade them and the Empire is No More. Empire follows Art, and not vice versa as Englishmen suppose."[30]

In any case, the missionaries of reason and enlightenment managed to propagate savagery and to spread disease. Ibé Wilson, a Kuna man from the San Blas archipelago off of Panama refers sarcastically to the "syphilization" of his culture.[31] When Gandhi was asked what he thought of Western civilization, he replied: "It would be a good idea." It is this same joke that resonates behind the texts of Marcos and the resurgence of ancient voices in Chiapas.

"The Southeast in Two Winds" is Marcos's first attempt to give the Zapatista uprising historical context. This context has several dimensions. There is the indigenous history of the region, a history characterized by uprisings and resistance, as native peoples sought to free themselves from colonial oppression. There is the history of the Mexican Revolution and the Institutional Revolutionary Party (PRI), which dominated Mexican national politics since the founding of the modern state with the Constitution of 1917, and whose trajectory toward political monopoly led ultimately to the marginalization, exclusion, and oppression of large segments of the Mexican population. And there is the history of the outgrowth of corporate capitalism from the free market and its foster parent, the nation-state, characterized most recently and most dramatically by the passing of NAFTA and the consequent ravaging of the Mexican Constitution.[32]

Through this historic tale runs a metaphor of wind and tempest which, while it mirrors human torment in the play of natural phenomena—another trick of Renaissance literature, most famously seen in Shakespeare's *Tempest*, a play about colonialism and utopia, about reason and resistance—also sets up the action of the natural world in the context of indigenous vision. We get the inexorable sense from this narrative that Mother Earth is seeking her revenge for centuries of abuse and crimes against nature.

Marcos speaks of two winds, the wind from above and the wind from below, and the voice that is carried on each wind. It is the meeting of these two winds that will cause the storm to arise.

> But not everyone listens to the voices of hopelessness and conformity. Not all allow themselves to be carried away on the toboggan of powerlessness. Most, the millions, continue without hearing the lukewarm voice of power, they don't manage to hear; they are deafened by the weeping and the blood that, through death and misery, cries in their ears. But when there is a moment of rest, which there are still, they hear another voice, not that which comes from above, but that which is carried by the wind from below and which is born in the indigenous heart of the mountains, that which speaks of justice and liberty, that which speaks of socialism, that which speaks of hope … the only hope in this earthly world. And the oldest among the old in the community tell of a man named Zapata who rose up for his people, and his voice more than shouted, it sang, "Land and Liberty!" And these ancient men tell that Zapata never died, that he will return. And the oldest of the old people tell that the wind and the rain and the sun tell the *campesino* when he must prepare the earth, when to plant and when to harvest. And they tell that hope is planted and harvested also. And the old people tell that the wind, the rain and the sun are speaking in their own way to the earth, that after so much poverty they cannot continue harvesting death, that it is time to harvest rebellion. So say the old people. The powerful don't listen, they don't manage to hear; they are deafened by the stupefaction of the cry of the world powers in their ears. "Zapata" repeat the cries of the young and the poor. "Zapata," insists the wind, the wind from below, our wind.[33]

The talk of winds and rain, of the old people and the planting and the harvest, is directed as much to intellectuals in Mexico City as to *campesinos* in their villages. It is a rhetoric carefully crafted to strike at the heart of Mexico's troubled relation with its indigenous heritage, and undoubtedly the rhetoric of a man who has lived for many years with *campesinos*. The metaphor of wind bears the millenarian tone of repentance, of apocalyptic justice. It carries the mythic implication that the struggle of the Zapatistas is the true and right and *natural* path, that the darkness and misery of the past centuries have been an aberration, as much a historical error as a natural disaster, and that the forces of nature are stirring to reclaim and redeem justice and history. Through his rhetoric, Marcos aligns the EZLN with the forces of nature, proclaiming an impending overthrow, by nature herself, of depredatory capital. To that extent, Marcos's poetic gesture suggests that the forces of nature will be embodied by the EZLN.

Karl Marx is supposed to have said, "history repeats itself, the first time as tragedy, the second time as farce."[34] In an amazing instance of this dictum, a full sixteen years after Marcos penned "The Southeast in Two Winds," an article appeared in the *New York Times* travel section entitled "Frugal Mexico." The writer, a New Yorker whose profession is to travel frugally and advise others on how to do the same, selected Chiapas as his destination of choice in Mexico, because "for not much more than $50 a day, mildly adventurous travelers have unfettered access to lovely colonial towns and indigenous cultures (Indians make up a fifth of the state's 4.3 million people), to the ancient Maya ruins at Palenque, Bonampak and beyond, to lush, isolated rain forests, to good coffee, to quirky and affordable hotels, and even to the shadowy Zapatistas themselves."[35] The wonderful coincidence of low prices and abundant, colorful Indians was treated without irony, but with great satisfaction. It is, after all, the Indians' job to offer thrifty tourists the reward of a few photos and a glimpse of their exotic culture. Making a mockery of history and brushing aside nearly two decades of daily work invested in the construction of autonomous infrastructure, the *Times* cited the "the failed revolution," which, today, "is below a simmer, invisible except for the occasional tortilla shop named '1 de enero,'" adding that "Subcomandante Marcos, the pipe-smoking balaclava-clad EZLN spokesman, is an object of interest mostly to backpackers and idealists who might find Che Guevara too mainstream."

That the *New York Times* should offer up Chiapas as a tourist package, rather than as "news," is little surprise. It is the nature of the media to exploit, and the nature of tourism to further exploit. What is shocking is the echo of Marcos's joke: "Suppose that you decide to get to know the Southeast of Mexico, and suppose that in the Southeast you decide to travel to the state of Chiapas." What is shocking, too, is the impunity of the frugal traveler in the face of poverty, misery, and humiliation. To Marcos's question, "What does the beast leave in exchange for everything it takes?" the frugal traveler responds, "As little as possible, thank you very much."

Old Antonio's Dream

> In the voice of Old Antonio—or of his medium, Subcomandante Marcos—speaks the transcendent historical conscience of the community, the deep voice of the people embodied in the elders.
>
> —Armando Bartra[36]

The force of history, memory, myth, and ancient wisdom—"the deep voice of the people"—is embodied in Marcos's writing by a figure who first appears in "The Southeast in Two Winds" and then proceeds to walk through many of the communiqués and to create his own myth, which takes on its own sustained and familiar life throughout the tales. Speaking with the voice of earthy authority, the voice of the elders and of the aged prophet, Old Antonio guides Marcos on his path and, repeatedly, corrects his misguided notions. Here is Antonio's first appearance:

> Antonio dreams that the earth he works belongs to him, he dreams that his sweat is paid for with truth and justice, he dreams that there is a school to cure ignorance and medicine to frighten away death, he dreams that his house has light and that his table is full, he dreams that his land is free and that his people have the

> right to govern themselves, he dreams that he finds peace with himself and with the world.... He dreams and he awakes ... now he knows what to do and he sees his wife, squatting, rekindle the fire, he hears his son cry, he sees the sun greeting the East, and, smiling, he sharpens his machete.
>
> A wind comes up and everything is thrown into the air, he rises and walks out to meet with others. Something has told him that his desire is the desire of others and he goes in search of it.[37]

Through the tales we see the history of struggle in Antonio's bent back as he walks to the *milpa*[38] each morning; we witness Antonio discerning the voice of change on the wind; and we see in his posture that, already, he carries the weight of the coming rebellion. Old Antonio represents at once the ancient past and the near future, the crossroads of the two where the wind rises up. In the mythos of the writer Subcomandante Marcos, beside and behind the main character, who is also Marcos, we constantly see the figure of Old Antonio.

As we will see in "The Story of the Questions," which follows, the allegories of Old Antonio generally take the form of dialogues between Marcos the young mestizo guerilla leader and Antonio, the old sage. Scholar Carlos Montemayor notes:

> Old Antonio ... is the image with which we see Marcos learning to listen. Learning from Old Antonio, he can hear the ancient and profound heart of the Mayas saying that it continues living in times that we might not be able to situate clearly on occidental calendars.[39]

From their content and context, these talks between Marcos and his mentor could be true tales. Antonio could be a real person, his village a real village, these meetings real meetings carefully scribed by Marcos and culled for their mythic content. Marcos acknowledges this in conversation with Yvon Le Bot: "Old Antonio died in 1994, in June, and I met him in 1984."[40] Chiapan historian Jan de Vos, too, maintains a belief about the veracity of the man upon whom Old Antonio is based:

> Their place of first encounter would not have been a romantic jungle settlement in the Lacandon, but a prosaic house in the Ch'ol town in the municipality of Huitiupán. There is a possibility that Old Antonio in reality is named José Antonio, and was the father, not only of young Antonio, but also of Ana Maria who was, for more than ten years, Marcos's companion.[41]

Yet, however real Old Antonio may be, one is forced to assume that Marcos developed the character in the interests of literary creation. The allegory is too direct, the mise-en-scène too strategic, Antonio, with his hand-rolled cigarettes and his huaraches and his shaman-like qualities, too much an archetype, the Marcos character too naïve, too much a rookie. The stories are too perfect as propaganda to be absolutely true. But, as we've seen and will see again, this is how myths are made.

Of course, as we speak of invented characters it is key to keep in mind that Marcos himself—not just his portrayal of himself in the *relatos*, but the "real" Marcos—is a fiction as well.

The stories of Old Antonio partake in a narrative structure built on dialogue, a traditional form of Mayan stories. These dialogues are a kind of oral performance, where the teller of the tale is accompanied by another person who responds at frequent intervals by affirming the speakers' statements or making brief comments or questions. In *The Mythology of Mexico and Central America*, John Bierhorst presents a short version of this type of oral performance found on the Yucatán:

> "Let's hunt."
> "My rifle's broken."
> "Where are the parts?"
> "I burned them."
> "Where are the ashes?"
> "Eaten by a falcon."
> "Where's the falcon?"
> "Went to the sky?"
> "Where in the sky?"
> "Fell."
> "Then where did it fall?"

"Went in a well."
"Where's the well?"
"Disappeared."
"Where'd it disappear?"
"Into your belly button."
"True."[42]

In this case magical events are reported by the teller and affirmed through dialogue with his partner. In the Old Antonio stories, Marcos the author presents Marcos the character in dialogue with Antonio. Together, they weave a story that invites the reader to sit in.

Bierhorst also notes that these traditional Mayan tales often include the teller —as Marcos includes himself. Even in stories of gods and heroes the storyteller may step in, as if to break the barrier between the enchanted world and the real world, the world of myth and the world of history:

> If the story ends with an unresolved problem, the teller can say, "When I passed by, they were still trying to save him," or, "If I had been there, I would have saved him myself." Such storyteller's tricks have been reported from the vicinity of Chichen Itza in Central Yucatán State and also from the Chorti Maya of Eastern Guatemala.[43]

Thus, by chance or by design, the Old Antonio tales ring of traditional Mayan storytelling techniques, where true and false, gods and humans, characters and speakers mix and mingle, opening a portal between the world we live in day-to-day and another world that we see through the character of Old Antonio as if through a glass darkly.

Voice of the Wind, Voice of the People

Antonio dies soon after the January uprising, but he is a character whose presence is stronger even in death than in life; as prophesied, he has disappeared in order to be seen, and he has died in order to live. From a communiqué published in *La Jornada* on May 28, 1994:

Old Antonio has died. I met him ten years ago in a community deep in the jungle. He smoked like nobody else I knew, and when he was out of cigarettes he would ask me for some tobacco and would make more cigarettes. He viewed my pipe with curiosity, but the one time I tried to loan it to him he showed me the cigarette in his hand, telling me without words that he preferred his own method of smoking. Two years ago, in 1992, I was traveling through the communities attending meetings to decide whether or not we should go to war, and eventually I arrived at the village where Old Antonio lived. While the community was discussing whether or not to go to war, Old Antonio took me by the arm and led me to the river, about one hundred meters from the center of the village. It was May and the river was green. Old Antonio sat on a tree trunk and didn't say anything.

After a little while he spoke: "Do you see? Everything is clear and calm. It appears that nothing will happen…" "Hmmm," I answered, knowing that he wasn't asking me to answer yes or no. Then he pointed to the top of the nearest mountain. The clouds lay gray upon the summit, and the lightning illuminated the diffuse blue of the hills. It was a powerful storm, but it seemed so far away and inoffensive that Old Antonio rolled up a cigarette and looked uselessly around for a lighter that he knew he didn't have. I offered my lighter. "When everything is calm here below, there is a storm in the mountains," he said after inhaling. "The mountain streams run strong and flow toward the riverbed. During the rainy season this river becomes fierce, like a whip, like an earthquake. Its power doesn't come from the rain that falls on its banks, but from the mountain streams that flow down to feed it. By destroying, the river reconstructs the land. Its waters will become corn, beans, and bread on our tables here in the jungle.

"Our struggle is like this," Old Antonio told me. "It was born in the mountains, but its effects won't be seen until it arrives here below." To my question about whether he believed the time had come for war, he responded by saying, "Now is the time for the river to change color…"[44]

American indigenous bodies of myth and history are animated by the elements, by the nonhuman beings that fly, swim, crawl, and walk on four legs, and by the forces of nature. Passed on orally down the generations and only recently brought into print as languages and peoples are extinguished, one role of native stories is to bring to life the spirits that animate all things. Rivers and birds speak, coyotes and rabbits and jaguars have meetings and make plans and play jokes on one another, winds bring messages from across the earth, the dead return to life. Invoking this tradition, the *relatos* of Old Antonio are animated by squalls and tempests, by metaphors of mountains and of rivers, are inhabited by the jungle and the night. The rain and winds that move through Marcos's tales serve both to foreground the indigenous communion with the natural world, and to reflect the living circumstances of the writer and the tens of thousands of people for whom he serves as spokesman.

The indigenous people of Chiapas, and especially the *guerilleros* of the EZLN in their clandestine and nomadic vocation, live exposed to and dependent on *the elements* in a way that urban or suburban residents of the "first" world rarely do. This, as much as any ideological character, is substructure to the superstructures of *difference* between the indigenous rebels and the state establishment. For rural, agrarian people, every rain, every wind has its voice and its meaning. Marcos simply lifts this trope—the animation of natural phenomena that is integral to the Mayan worldview—and gives it global scope and a political referent. The war that the Zapatistas are to make two years after the writing of "A Southeast in Two Winds" is, in Marcos's (and Old Antonio's) version, the natural response to centuries of oppression, just as the raging river is the natural accumulation of rain in the mountain streams.

As the extended metaphor goes, the war that the Zapatistas are forced to make is a war to redistribute resources and reconstruct social relationships—"By destroying, the river reconstructs the land"—and its results will be justice, equality, even abundance—"Its waters will become corn, beans, and bread on our tables here in the jungle."

In the usual historical schema, taken for granted as "history" in the Western world, capitalism is the "natural" economic system. Though Marx may have been the first to formulate the theory, it has become as common in the Western mind-set as Darwin's *Origin of Species*: capitalism evolved from primitive accumulation much the way humans evolved from apes, and it could hardly be any other way. The stories of Marcos reverse this scientific formula, suggesting that the old ways, reflected in wind and rain, are the natural ways; neoliberal capitalism, in this formula, is an insult to the natural world and the proper order of things. It is, quite simply, an abuse, and it has gone on too long. Marcos plays on both indigenous symbolisms and contemporary ecology when he invokes the powers of the earth to rise up and overthrow the "unnatural" and "superimposed" abuses of industrial capitalism.

Marcos's positioning of himself *as author*, by way of Marcos *the character* that moves through the Old Antonio stories, offers a significant clue to his relationship, as a *ladino* (white man), with the indigenous movement and its history. While in many other communiqués he speaks as "we," in a way that associates himself directly with the indigenous people ("we are the product of 500 years of struggle"), in the Old Antonio tales he distinctly positions himself as an individual, a mestizo, and one who is a newcomer to these dark jungle villages. In "The Story of the Questions," for example, Marcos the character is essentially an outsider, characterized by his clumsiness and his lack of knowledge of the ways of the jungle. These stories are the clearest case of *relatos* in which Marcos pointedly demonstrates the cultural difference between the wise old Indian and the bumbling ladino. In so doing, their narrative verges on essentialism—portraying both Indians and "whites" in strongly stereotypical portraiture. Arguably the purpose of this overly simplistic rendering is to demonstrate the cultural difference at work here, and to highlight difference itself as a positive value.

Clearly, if Antonio stands as Marcos's stock representation of *indigineity*—Indian-ness, the proverbial *Indio con plumas*, or Indian with feathers trotted out to represent entire panoplies of cultures—he is a crude sketch. A look at the ethnic and cultural make-up of the EZLN reveals, as is so often the case, that these are not story-book Indians, home-grown in a pristine setting and trapped in time as if they were on a movie-set. Historian Antonio García de Leon asserts that "Today, the Zapatista army is composed mainly of the mass of marginal, 'modern,' multilingual young people with experience in wage labor. Their profile has very little to do with the isolated Indian that we imagine from Mexico City."[45] While it is tantalizingly easy to reverse the historic notion that says the Mayan people have "disappeared" by conflating these Maya with their ancestors who walked the same territory, we are talking in actual fact about a people who have been displaced, exiled across borders, forced to adapt "modern" ways, and who have over centuries adopted customs and habits and languages and skills and in many cases families and bloodlines that differentiate them from any image of pure, unadulterated "Indian-ness."

This is due in large part to what *has*, in fact, disappeared: the Lacandon rainforest, which once stretched for some 30,000 square kilometers, has been reduced to roughly 300 square kilometers centered around the Montes Azules Biosphere Reserve, which is, in principal at least, off-limits to all but a few ethnic Lacandon communities.[46] When we talk about the Zapatistas living in the Lacandon jungle, most of the territory in question is in fact, second-growth forest, pasture, or "marginal land." In the jungle of southeastern Mexico, scarcely 1 percent of the original forest remains.[47]

The loss of their historically inhabited territory and the adulteration of their bloodlines does not diminish the Zapatistas claims to land and liberty and collective rights or the fact that the Zapatista struggle is as much a demand for justice as an assertion of ethnic identity. It does, however, disturb the notion that at this late date in history we can draw lines of race and ethnicity in such simple terms as "Indian" and "white."

In some sense, this is the territory that Marcos is playing in with the Old Antonio stories. By pushing the "real" Marcos toward a caricature of bumbling self-conscious whiteness and the "real" Antonio toward a caricature of "sage Indian-ness," he turns up the volume on the question of ethnic identity and very real conditions of historical possession and dispossession.

Guardian and Heart of the People

As the voice of the elders is embodied in Old Antonio, the wind and tempest raised against the arrogance of neoliberalism come to be embodied by a mythic figure, at once god and man, who first appears in a speech given by Marcos on Independence Day, September 16, 1994, and who will appear in subsequent communiqués as the spirit of the revolution and the rebirth of two ancestral voices in one figure. He is Votan-Zapata, "guardian and heart of the people."

> Votan-Zapata, guardian and heart of the people, returns to sing his war chant for the smallest sons of these lands, the drum of the battle in the heart and mind of the true men and women sounds again, in the word that walks by night, that lives in the mountain.[48]

In "The Story of the Questions," Old Antonio, serving as intermediary between past and present, between gods and humans, narrates the origins of Votan-Zapata, hero of these lands, guardian of the spirit of the Zapatistas. This is the first meeting of Marcos and Old Antonio:

> **The Story of the Questions**[49]
> The cold in these mountains tightens your bones. Anna Maria and Mario accompany me in this exploration, ten years before that January dawn. The two have only just joined the guerillas and I, an infantry lieutenant then, get the job of teaching them what I have just been taught: how to live in the mountains. Yesterday I met Old Antonio for the first time. We both lied. He, saying that he was going to tend his *milpa*, and I, saying that I was out hunting. We both knew we were lying and we both knew that we knew. I left Anna Maria to follow the route of our exploration, and I returned toward the river to see if, with the clinometer, I could locate on the map the high hill before me, when again I ran into Old Antonio. He must have had similar thoughts as I had, because we ran into each other at the exact spot of our earlier encounter.
>
> Like yesterday, Old Antonio sits on the ground, lying back on a seat of green moss, and begins to roll a cigarette. I sit across from him and light my pipe. Old Antonio begins:
>
> "You're not out hunting."
>
> I respond: "And you are not going to your *milpa*." Something brings me to use a formal tone with him, to speak with respect to

this man of infinite age and a face creased like cedar bark, who I am seeing now for the second time in my life.

Old Antonio smiles and adds, "I've heard of you and your *compañeros*… In these canyons they say you are bandits. In my village, the people are restless because you are walking around here."

"And do you believe we are bandits?" I ask. Old Antonio lets loose a great puff of smoke, he coughs and shakes his head no. Pleased, I ask him another question: "And who, then, do you think we are?"

"I would prefer to have you tell me," responds Old Antonio, sitting still and looking me in the eyes.

"It is a very long story," I say, and I begin to tell of the times of Zapata and Villa and the revolution and the land and the injustice and hunger and ignorance and disease and repression and everything. And I end with "and so we are the Zapatista Army of National Liberation." I await some signal in Old Antonio's face, which hasn't stopped watching me during the length of my talk.

"Tell me more about this Zapata," he says after a puff of smoke and a cough.

I begin with Ananecuilco, I continue with the Plan de Ayala, the military campaign, the organization of the villages, the treason at Chinameca. Old Antonio keeps watching me as I finish the story.

"It wasn't like that at all," he says to me. I make a gesture of surprise and manage to blurt out "No?" "No," insists Old Antonio. "I am going to tell you the true story of that Zapata."

Getting out tobacco and a paper, Old Antonio begins his story, which unites and confuses old and new times, as the smoke of his cigarette and my pipe join and curl together rising into the jungle air.

"Many histories ago, when the first gods, those who made the world, were still wandering in the night, two gods spokc who were Ik'al and Votan. The two were only one. The one turned to reveal himself to the other, the other turning to reveal himself to the one. They were opposites. The one was light, like a May morning at the river. The other was dark, like a night of cold and caves. They were the same. The two were one, because the one made the other. But they didn't walk, they always stayed still without moving, these two gods who were one, without moving. 'What do we do then?' asked the two. 'It is sad this life, just being like this, the way we are,' and they were saddened, the two who were one in there, just being there. 'The night doesn't pass,' said Ik'al. 'The day doesn't pass,' said Votan. 'Let's walk,' said the one who were two. 'How?' asked the other. 'Where to?' asked the first. And they saw that like this they moved a little, first by asking how, and then by asking where. The two who was one became happy when he saw that they moved a little. They wanted the two to move at the same time but they couldn't. 'How do we do it then?' And they approached, first one and then the other, and they moved another little bit and they realized that if one first, and then the other, then, yes, they could move, and they came to an agreement and nobody remembers who was the first to begin to move because they were very happy that they were moving at all, and, 'What does it matter who moved first if we're moving?' said the two gods, who were the same and they laughed; and the first agreement they made was to have a dance, and they danced, one little step the one, one little step the other, and they danced awhile because they were happy that they had found each other. Then they grew tired of so much dancing and they saw what other things they could do and they saw that the first question of 'how to move?' brought the answer 'together but separate in agreement,' and this question didn't matter much to them because when they realized the question, well, now they were moving, and then came the other question when they saw that there were two roads: the one was very short and reached to there and no further and it was clear that there, very close, the road ended, and the pleasure of walking that filled their feet was so much that they quickly said that they didn't much want to walk that road and they agreed to walk the long road and there they went to begin to walk when the answer of taking the long road brought them the other question of 'where does this road take us?' They delayed in coming up with an answer and the two who were one suddenly got it in their head that only if they walked the long road would they know where it took them because like this, how they were, they would never know where the long road would take them. So, the one who were two said, 'Well then, let's walk it then,' and they began to walk, first the one and then the other. And right there they realized that it took a lot of time to walk the long road and then came the other question 'how are we going to manage to walk for a long time?' and they remained thinking a good little while and then bright Ik'al said that he didn't know how to walk in the day and Votan said that at night he was afraid of walking and they cried for awhile and then after the fit ended and they came to an agreement and they saw that Ik'al could walk well by night and that Votan could walk well by day and like this they came up with the answer to walk all the time. Since then the gods walk with questions and they never stop, they never arrive and they never leave. And, so, the true men and women learned that questions are for walking, not for just standing there. And, since then, the true men and women, to walk they ask questions. And when they arrive, they say farewell and when they leave they greet each other. They are never at rest."

I stay chewing on the now-short-little-tip of the pipe waiting for Old Antonio to continue but he seems not to have the intention of doing so. With a fear of breaking something very precious, I ask: "And Zapata?"

Old Antonio laughs: "Now you've learned that to know and to walk you've got to ask questions." He coughs and lights another cigarette that I don't know when he made and, between the smoke that drifts from his lips words fall like seeds to the soil:

"This Zapata appeared here in the mountains. He wasn't born, they say. He just appeared, just like that. They say he is Ik'al and Votan, who never stopped walking until now, and to not scare the people, they turned themselves into one man. Because now after a lot of of walking together Ik'al and Votan learned that they were the same and that they could become one in the day and the night, and when they arrived here they became one and they called themselves Zapata, and Zapata said he had come all the way here and here he was going to find the answer to where the long road would take him and he said that at times there would be light and at times darkness, but that he was the same, Ik'al Zapata and Votan Zapata, the white Zapata and the black Zapata and that the two were the same for the true men and women."

Old Antonio pulls a little plastic bag from his pack. Inside there is a very old photo, from 1910, of Emiliano Zapata. Zapata has his left hand holding a sword at the level of his waist, and in the right he holds a carbine, two bands of bullets across his chest, a two-colored band, black and white crossing from left to right. His feet are of someone standing still or walking and in his look there is something like "here I am" or "there I go." There are two stairways. In the one, which comes out of darkness, more Zapatistas are visible with brown faces, as if they'd arrived from the bottom of something; in the other stairway, which is lighted, there is nobody and you can't see where it goes or from where it comes. I would be lying if I said I noticed all these details. It was Old Antonio who called my attention to them. On the back of the photo are the words:

Gral. Emiliano Zapata, Jefe del Ejercito Suriano
Gen. Emiliano Zapata, Commander-in-Chief of the Southern Army
Le General Emiliano Zapata, Chef de l'Armee du Sud
C. 1910. Photo by: Agustin V. Casasola

Old Antonio says to me, "I have asked many questions of this photo. This is how I arrived here," he coughs and tears up the stub of his cigarette. He gives me the photo. "Take it," he says to me. "So you learn to ask questions ... and to walk."

"It is best to bid farewell on arriving. That way it doesn't hurt so much when you go," Old Antonio says extending his hand toward me to say that he is leaving, that is, that he is arriving. Since then, Old Antonio greets me upon arriving with an "*adios*" and he bids farewell extending his hand and heading off with "I'm here." Old Antonio gets up. So do Beto, Toñita, Eva and Heriberto. I take the photo from my pack and show it to them.

"Is he going to go up or down?" asks Beto.

"Is he going to walk or to stand still?" asks Eva.

"Is he taking out or putting away the sword?" asks Toñita.

"Did he just shoot or he is about to begin shooting?" asks Heriberto.

I do not cease to be surprised by all these questions that this eighty-four-year-old photo brings up and which, in 1984, was given to me by Old Antonio. I look at it for the last time before deciding to give it to Ana Maria and the photo brings out of me one more question: "Is this our yesterday or our tomorrow?"

Now in this climate of questioning and with surprising coherence for her four-years-completed-beginning-five-or-is-it-six, Eva lets out "My gift then?" The word "gift" provokes identical reactions in Beto, Toñita, and Heriberto; that is to say they all beging shouting "And my gift, then?" They have me corralled and at the point of sacrificing myself when Ana Maria appears who, like almost a year ago in San Cristóbal but in other circumstances, saves my life. Ana Maria has brought a big giant bag of candy, I mean really big. "Here is the gift that the Sup brought you," she says while she throws me a look of "What-would-you-men-be-without-us-women?"

While the children make a decision—that is to say, they fight—to share out the sweets, Ana Maria gives me a military salute and says:

"Report: the troops are ready to leave."

"Good," I say, attaching the pistol to my hip. "We will leave as the law dictates: at dawn." Ana Maria leaves.

"Wait," I say to her. I give her the photo of Zapata.

"And this," she asks, looking at the photo.

"It's going to help us," I respond.

"For what?" she insists.

"To know where we're going," I respond while I check my carbine. Above, a military airplane circles.

We take our leave of you all. I am at the end of this "letter of letters." First I have to throw the kids out...

> And finally, I will respond to some questions that, there is no doubt, you will raise:
>
> "Do we know where we're going?" Yes.
>
> "Do we know what awaits us?" Yes.
>
> "Is it worth the trouble?" Yes.
>
> Good, then.
>
> Can whoever answers yes to the three questions above stay still without doing anything and not feel that something inside has broken?
>
> Good. Health and a flower for this tender fury, I believe it is well deserved.

"The Story of the Questions" is a myth of origin. In it, there is a story that teaches about the beginning of the world and the beginning of the gods and humans that populate the world. It also teaches of the origin of the EZLN and a thing or two about their beliefs and ideology. And it teaches of the common origins of Zapata, a figure from modern Mexican history, and Votan, a god-hero from ancient Mayan legend.

By aligning Zapata with Votan, the myths of modern Mexico and the local indigenous history are fused. The modern Mexican nation has its origin in the Revolutionary Constitution of 1917, fought for and won by Zapata and his army of Zapatistas. By drawing together the origins of the Zapatista uprising of 1994, the origins of modern Mexico in 1917, and the origins of the world—the story of Marcos and the story of Antonio—the EZLN uprising is drawn into the world of sacred events. In a word, it is *mythologized*. Similarly, by describing the gods' acts of questioning, their consensus-decision-making, and recognizing that this is the way the Zapatista communities work together and forge their decisions, the ideology of the Zapatistas becomes aligned with the old Mayan gods. In this tale of origins, the basis of revolutionary mythistory is established.

Antonio is not a ranking official in the EZLN command, but an old man from the village. His authority doesn't rest on military order, but on his simply being "one of the wise ones, the ones who know." Marcos comments that Old Antonio is "the only man who can breach all of the Zapatista checkpoints and enter wherever he wants without anyone impeding his passage."[50] In this ability to move where he pleases, he possesses a storied attribute of tricksters, coyotes, shamans, thieves and revolutionaries—the ability to cross borders with ease. It is an ideal that the Zapatistas hold in high esteem.

Antonio embodies the ancestors and through them, we suppose, he has a direct line to the gods. By listening to the words of Antonio, by channeling this voice into his own military authority, Marcos portrays his actions and those of the EZLN as enacting the ancestral will of the people. By equating the ancestral will of the people with contemporary political demands, popular history is reclaimed, reenacted, and the goals of the revolution become articulated in their most profound form: a return to the values that made us human in the first place.

"The Story of the Questions" contains elements that run through many communiqués: the dialogue between Marcos and Antonio accompanied by the ritual of smoking; the children Beto and Toñita, Eva and Heriberto; Ana Maria, who for a time figured in many communiqués as Marcos's *compañera*. The operative moment in the story, its crux, is the moment when Old Antonio commandeers the tale of Zapata from the *subcomandante*:

> "It wasn't like that at all," he says to me. I make a gesture of surprise and manage to blurt out "No?" "No," insists old Antonio. "I am going to tell you the true story of that Zapata."

The story illustrates the value of questioning, of cooperation and of duality, of a world made up of many worlds. Like the earlier wind born of two histories colliding, this story is built around the meeting of two histories: the indigenous history as told by Antonio, with its atemporality and enchanted blending of characters, and the mestizo or "modern" history, prosaic and expository, as spoken by Marcos. Marcos, the narrator, displays himself as the well-schooled historian, understanding the roots of struggle, the whys and wherefores of Mexican history. But he is made to look a fool when Antonio, the better storyteller, lifts the tale from his educated grasp and retells it in a way that *includes myth*. Suddenly there is more than one truth at play. The two histories are irreconcilable, but they both speak of the origin and history of a single, historic figure —Emiliano Zapata—and so are forced to coexist.

Looking at the divergent histories, the "Indian" history with its aspect of "myth" and the "ladino" history with its assured air of "fact," we can begin to see the very roots of the struggle between the two worlds, the indigenous world and the mestizo world, as embodied by divergent understandings of historical reality. This is the struggle played out by the EZLN in its bid to reclaim history. Marcos here positions himself as the allegorical outsider (in Tzeltal, he would be called *kaxlan*, one who is only passing through, generally one with European blood) who can only begin to understand the different history personified in the figure of Old Antonio. To the revolutionary slogan of Zapata, "The land is for he who works it and liberty is for he who takes it," add a third imperative: history is for those who tell it. And we see the prosaic, historicist version of Marcos—a temporal and rational history which gives rise to the founding conceptions of capitalism as well as Marxism (progress, evolution, competition, dialectical materialism, etc.)—give in to the indigenous mythistory with its magical occurrences, divine dimension, and eternal returns or cyclical perspective: "Because now after a lot of walking together Ik'al and Votan learned that they were the same and that they could become one in the day and the night, and when they arrived here they became one and they called themselves Zapata."

Antonio's version of events, indeed his entire way of being, is at odds with the Eurocentric version, down to the details: "Old Antonio greets me upon arriving with an 'adios' and he bids farewell extending his hand and heading off with 'I'm here.'" The characteristics of the indigenous people, vilified by the mestizo state for their "intransigence" and "superstition" and frequently portrayed by the Western anthropologist's eye as "a primitive animism," are drawn by Marcos as the comic wisdom of Old Antonio, contradicting or doubling over the common ways of all things Western. Humor is a constant in indigenous American narratives, both north and south of the Rio Bravo—another nod to the indigenous roots of Marcos's storytelling—and Antonio here is a kind of trickster figure, with Marcos, as Antonio's foil, playing it straight. As a trickster, though, Antonio is gentle, and wise, and seems to always act from a profound set of beliefs.

The actions and words of Antonio, imparted to Marcos under the gaze of the reader, give a "spiritual" dimension to the Zapatistas' struggle, while revealing that the indigenous cannot live under the same law as the "white" or *ladino* because they are, in fact, different. At the same time, Antonio's history, where Votan and Ik'al join together, (light and dark, day and night), to become Emiliano Zapata (modern and ancient), a direct genealogy is established that runs from "the true men and women"—the *tojol winik* in Tojolabal, the language Old Antonio would speak—to the modern revolution of the history-bound Zapata. This genealogy has less to do with biology and historical events than it does with a mythic yet deeply embodied relation to the ancestors. Here this genealogy—this relation with the ancestors, to which the EZLN's ethical struggle is bound as a kind of prayer—is confirmed by the magical fusing of Votan, Ik'al and Zapata.

Who is Votan? José Rabasa explains:

> Votan, "guardian and heart of the people," is a pre-Columbian Tzeltal and Tzotzil god, names the third day of the twenty-day period in the Mayan calendar and is the night lord of the third *trecena* (thirteen twenty-days periods) of the *Tonalamatl* ("count of the days," the Mesoamerican divinatory calendar)....[51]

John Bierhorst writes of him:

> The old Tzeltal hero called Votan is said to have come from the East. He was a lawgiver and promoter of religious worship. In addition he taught hieroglyphic writing, the art of sculpture and the cultivation of corn. When his work was complete, he entered the underworld through a cave.[52]

Victoria Bricker mentions Votan in *El Cristo Indigena, El Rey Nativo*, again, as "the cultural hero of the highlands of Chiapas, recognized as the sovereign of the *teponaztli*.... a musical instrument which, to this day is associated in [the Chiapan highland village of] Zinacantán with the magical act of producing rain."[53]

As bringer of rain, Votan returns us to the storm and the prophecy of Marcos. Going back to the earth from his underworld cave, Votan brings the wind and rain from below that will wash the earth of the oppression that came with conquest and colonization. Antonio Garcia de Léon, one of the foremost chroniclers of indigenous histories in Chiapas, reveals a history of Votan in an essay examining the significance of indigenous calendrical dates and their relation to historic moments in the Mayan struggle against colonization:

> That 12 of October of 1974, the turn of the *Katún*,[54] two opposite and complementary occurrences were celebrated: one sun and the other moon, one eagle and the other jaguar, one fire and the other water, one day and the other night, one male, the other female, one flame and the other ember. In sum, one exposed and the other hidden. The one were the 500 years since the birth of Fray Bartolomé de las Casas, the first bishop of Chiapas, defender of Indians from the abuses of *encomenderos* [generally, ladino plantation owners] and ranchers, expelled from the diocese by a mob of angry merchants and landowners, and whose sin had consisted in denying confession to the exploiters, and in believing that all the human race was of one stock. His example, which shines like the sun over the course of centuries, illuminates to this day the steps of those simple Christians who continue to live here. The other occurrence was the third day in the Tzeltal calendar—that which the Yucatecan Mayas called *ak'bal*, night, known here as *Vo'tan*, the heart of the pueblo, the heart of the mountain, the heart of the people beating in the depths of the mountain (called *tepeyolotl* by the Nahaules), lord of the *teponaztle* [wooden drum], and—as even the Tzeltales will tell you—the first man that God sent to share out land among the Indians, he who defended them from his oracular parapet in the long colonial night which still hasn't seen the dawn. He who put treasures in a sealed jar, or in a coffer, and put blankets in a dark cave with guardian protectors to secure them. The jaguar god of darkness, he of the celestial spots which mask him like the stars of the night sky, watchman in the pre-dawn dark, the number seven, defender of the true word—the *tojol ab'al*,[55] the Mayan word, the mother tongue. He of the nocturnal thought shining in the mountains, he of the feminine force

capable of engendering men and worlds, of bearing the pain of death, of sacrifice and of birth. Lord of the day Night, lord of the day Moon, he who comes riding over the hill mounted on a dark tapir, there near the town of Yajalón. The same who in these days of October, 20 years ago, began to melt, in the eternal memory of the *campesinos* of Chiapas, with the other heart of the people with the profound gaze like water, like night: Votan-Zapata....[56]

Fusing Zapata with Votan effects the rebirth of Mayan cosmology through the living history of revolutionary Mexico. If the Zapatistas are defined both as *indigenas* and *campesinos*, the figure of *Votan-Zapata* is the historical symbol par excellence, combining the features of both groups. As Votan is guardian and heart of the true people, Zapata is the bearer of justice for the peasant farmer, the protector of land and liberty whose integrity was never shaken by temptations of power. In the figure of Zapata, the history of modern Mexico is reiterated, and in the figure of Votan the origins of the indigenous world are called forth. The affirmation is made that the two are one, that Mexico has never existed apart from the gods who created the true people, that the enchanted world, "a world extended and reiterated in gestures and symbols [and made up of] masked figures, warriors, clothing, fog, forest, stories of the night, and nocturnal ceremonies" has always existed behind and beneath the modern world.[57]

This structure of "The Story of the Questions," where the textbook history meets the indigenous mythistory and irrupts into a new understanding encompassing both, mirrors the trajectory of Marcos and his companions' work with the indigenous populations in the Chiapas jungle. In an outline of this history detailed in Yvon Le Bot's 1996 interview with the *subcomandante* in *El Sueño Zapatista*, a handful of Marxist/Maoist youth form the Fuerzas de Liberación Nacional (FLN) and journey to the jungle with the idea of implementing a campaign to begin the overthrow of the national government.[58] Their training, both ideological and tactical, comes from years of study of Mexican revolutionary politics from Zapata to Lucio Cabañas,[59] as well as from visits to Nicaragua and Cuba. They subscribe to the *foco* theory of revolutionary action developed in the Cuban revolution and detailed in the writings of Che Guevara and

Regis Debray, where a few well-trained leaders initiate guerilla war in a remote area of the territory, gathering popular support from peasants as well as urban sectors, striking when and where possible until finally they achieve victory and overthrow the state-party.[60]

Marcos and his *compañeros* of the Fuerzas de Liberacion Nacional began their campaign in the Mexican Southeast largely on this model of revolution. But what eventually happened, Marcos explains in his interview with Yvon Le Bot, was not the expected route of the *foco.* After some years developing their campaign among the remote indigenous communities of Chiapas, the revolutionaries found that the indigenous people had their own sophisticated ways of organizing and their own understanding of revolutionary struggle. The indigenous revolutionary effort into which these urban socialists had fallen was based on 500 years of resistance and a conceptual understanding of history as engrained in their culture as the cultivation of *maiz.*

The Twin Heroes

> And then the hearts of the lords were filled with longing,
> with yearning for the dance of Hunahpu and Xbalanque,
> so then came these words from One and Seven Death:
> "Do it to us! Sacrifice us!" they said. "Sacrifice both of us!"
> said One and Seven Death to Hunahpu and Xbalanque.
> "Very well. You ought to come back to life. After all, aren't
> you Death?"
>
> —Popul Vuh[61]

Votan-Zapata, representing the duality of the divine and the terrestrial, the world below and the world above, is an archetype of one of the classic themes of pre-Hispanic Latin American literature. The principle of duality—beginning with an ancient understanding of god as the first mother-father—is extremely common, embodied in characters such as the twin heroes who march through the early days of the world fooling the gods and making the world safe for humanity. For the Quiché Maya, the twin heroes, whose games with death result in their immortality, are Hunahpe and Xbalanque, the first children of *maiz*, protagonists of the

Popul Vuh. For the people of highland Chiapas, these twin heroes are present in the characters Votan and Ik', the Tzotz, or people of the bat, who live in darkness but see light.[62]

In the Popul Vuh, the twin heroes Hunahpe and Xbalanque journey to Xibalbe, the underworld, to play ball with the Lords of Death. Before the game begins, the lords put the two boys through a set of trials. They are given a series of challenges, but through wit and playfulness they manage to throw off death's oppression and ultimate finality. The boys are imprisoned in a house of darkness, a house of knives, a house of jaguars, and a house of bats. With their clever tactics, the boys outwit the lords of death and survive each test. They go on to win the ball game as well.

In a final attempt to outsmart the lords of death, the heroes show how they can kill a man and bring him back to life. The lords, excited by the show, ask if the boys can do it to *them*. The boys carry out the lords' wishes, but quit halfway through the sacrificial performance, failing to bring the lords back to life. They thereby defeat the lords of death and rise into the sky to become immortal in the form of the sun and the moon.

Here is Marcos's version of the story:

> **A Light, a Flower, and a Dawn**[63]
>
> The eldest of the elders of our communities say that our very first ones were living in rebel struggle even then, because the powerful had already been subjugating and killing them for a long time. The powerful becomes so because he drinks the blood of the weak. And so the weak become weaker and the powerful more powerful. But there are weak ones who say, "Enough is enough! *¡Ya basta!*" and who rebel against the powerful and give their blood not to fatten the great but to feed the little ones.
>
> And that is how it's been for a long, long time.

The tale goes on to tell of the Popul Vuh's seven houses of punishment, "for anyone who wouldn't passively accept his blood fattening the powerful," and then introduces the twin heroes:

> A long time ago, there lived two rebels, Hunahpe and Xbalanque, they were called, and they were also called the hunters of the

dawn. Evil lived in a deep hole named Xibalbe, out of which you would have to climb very high to reach the good earth. Hunahpe and Xbalanque were rebels against the evil gentlemen living in the great House of Evil. One day those evil gentlemen ordered that Hunahpe and Xbalanque be brought to them through a trick, so they would come down into their evil dwelling.

And through trickery, the hunters of the dawn arrived, and the evil gentlemen shut them up in the House of Darkness, and they gave them a torch and two cigars for light. They told them that they must pass the whole night inside the House of Darkness, and on the following day, deliver the torch and the two cigars back whole. And a guard would watch all night to see if the light from the torch and from the two cigars ever went out. If the torch and cigars weren't whole the next day, then Hunahpe and Xbalanque would die.

The two hunters of the dawn were not afraid, no. Seeming content, they said to the evil gentlemen that what they proposed was fine, and settled into the House of Darkness. And then they used their thinking and they called the macaw, the bird that guarded all the colors, and asked him to lend them red, and with it they painted the end of the torch so that from far off it looked as if it were burning. And Hunahpe and Xbalanque called the fireflies and asked two of them for their company, and they ornamented the ends of the two cigars with them so that from far off it really looked as if the two cigars were lit.

And dawn came and the guard informed the evil gentlemen that the torch had been lit all night long, and that the two hunters of the dawn had been smoking their cigars the whole time. And the evil gentlemen were happy because this would give them a good excuse to kill Hunahpe and Xbalanque, because they wouldn't be able to fulfill their agreement to deliver the torch and the cigars whole. But when the two hunters of the dawn left the House of Darkness and handed over the torch and the two cigars whole, the evil gentlemen became very angry because they no longer had a good excuse to kill Hunahpe and Xbalanque. So, they said to each other: "These rebels are quite intelligent, very intelligent. Let's look, then, for another good excuse to kill them."

"Yes," they said, "Let them sleep now in the House of Knives, that way they will surely die, since it will cut off their understanding."

"That's not enough," said the other gentleman of evil, "because these rebels have so much understanding, they must be given a much harder task, one they won't be able to carry out, so that if the knives don't kill them, we will have another good excuse to do away with them."

"That's good," said the evil gentlemen. And they went to where Hunahpe and Xbalanque were, and said to them:

"Now you must go rest, so we will talk again tomorrow, but we are telling you now quite clearly that tomorrow at dawn you are to give us flowers." And the evil gentlemen laughed a little, because they had already warned the guardians of the flowers not to let anyone approach during the night to cut flowers, and if someone were to approach, to attack and kill them.

"Fine," said the hunters of the dawn, "And what colors do you want these flowers to be that we must give you?"

"Red, white, and yellow," responded the evil gentlemen, and they added: "We should make it quite clear to you that if you don't give us these red, white and yellow flowers tomorrow, we'll be greatly offended and we shall kill you."

"Don't worry," said Hunahpe and Xbalanque. "Tomorrow you'll have your red, white, and yellow flowers."

In Marcos's iteration of the Popul Vuh story, the two hunters of the dawn then go to the House of Knives and say "Let's talk." The twin heroes offer a gift of meat to the knives to let them escape, "and that is why, since then, knives have been used for cutting animal flesh, but if a knife cuts human flesh, then the hunters of the dawn pursue it to make it pay for its crime."

Next, the heroes set off to cut the flowers as requested, but rather than risk their lives, they ask a band of leafcutter ants to do it as a favor, "for the evil gentlemen want to kill our struggle."

> On seeing the flowers, Hunahpe and Xbalanque became very happy, and this is how they spoke to the cutting ants:
>
> "Thank you very much, little sisters. Although you are small, your power is great, and because we are so grateful to you, you shall always be many, and nothing big will ever be able to attack you." And that is why they say that ants always resist, and no matter how big their attackers are, they can't be defeated.
>
> The next day the evil gentlemen came, and the two hunters of the dawn gave them the flowers that they wanted. The evil gentlemen were surprised to see that the knives hadn't cut them, but they were even more surprised when they saw the red, white, and yellow flowers Hunahpe and Xbalanque gave them, and then those evil gentlemen grew very angry and set about looking for more excuses to do away with the rebel hunters of the dawn."

For the modern Zapatistas, the heroic twins—now in the guise of Votan and Zapata—have returned from their underworld journey to illuminate the dark night of the second 500 years of war in Mesoamerica. The evil gentlemen of the ancient tale, are, in fact, the *mal gobierno* (the bad government, or evil government, in Zapatista parlance) of modern Mexico. In typical timeless Mayan history, the two exist in the same age; the ancestors are present as always, and their past and their present are one as the dead and the living are one. And in typical Mayan cosmogeography, the Zapatistas signal the presence of two distinct, but united, worlds: the aboveground world, where we, the living, dwell by day, and the *inframundo* or netherworld where the ancestors, the spirits and the planets live at night.

Central to this tale is the fact that the twin heroes did not resist their captors by means of violence, but rather through acts of intelligence and a profound engagement with the natural world, the world of the senses. As one of the original ancient stories of the Mayan people, the story of the twin heroes exemplifies values embraced and embodied by that culture: natural intelligence, fortitude, wit, and harmony in social relations. By retelling this story, and by embedding in it an understanding that the "rebels"—the Zapatistas—are our heroes, Marcos suggests that these same values infuse the modern indigenous rebellion.

The twin heroes of the Popul Vuh are intermediaries between the living world and the *inframundo* of *Xibalbe*. Similarly, Votan and Zapata are intermediaries between the past and the present, the ancient and the modern. It is their ability to cross between worlds—like the trickster abilities of the Zapatista rebel herself, ready at any moment to make the shift from an armed and masked warrior to a simple peasant tending her family garden plot—that gives Zapatista military strategy its edge and its continuity with centuries of indigenous guerilla struggle.

As we will see, parables of sacrifice resonate throughout the communiqués. From the descent of Marcos and his comrades to the deep jungles of southeastern Mexico, to the death masks worn by Zapatista warriors, to the suggestion of an *inframundo* beneath this world, we see the myth of the underworld journey and the ethics of sacrifice drawn upon again and again in Zaptista mythology: "We are those who have died in order to live," they say repeatedly. Their penchant for self-sacrifice allows the twin heroes to travel to the underworld and back; similarly, the sacrifice of individual desire and identity for cultural unity and the collective good permits the indigenous struggle to continue down the generations.

From the perspective of the movement's strategic messaging or "public relations," it would likely be mistaken to assume that the average mestizo or white spectator would immediately and consciously "get" the symbolism at work here, though many in Mexico, for whom this cultural vocabulary is deeply embedded, certainly would. But as one among many keys to the Zapatista mythos, this tale from the Popul Vuh exerts the ancient power of story—the ability to unlock the imagination and bring us into a profound communion with a shared imaginary, a collective unconscious.

Eternal Returns

> Struggles, conflicts, and wars for the most part have a ritual cause and function … Each time the conflict is repeated, there is imitation of an archetypal model.
>
> —Mircea Eliade, *The Myth of the Eternal Return*[64]

If revolution is about returns, the Maya with their cyclical understanding of time and its events have a predisposition toward revolution.

Rather than an affinity for "progress," the linear, evolutionary concept that is one of the predominant mythic underpinnings of Western industrial society, the Mayan people of Chiapas have a sense of history that celebrates the past, that welcomes the emergence of eternity into time's fabric, and that understands that the past and the future are like two ends of a woven strand in a *huipil*: if you tug on either end, you feel the pull.

Mexican historian Adolfo Gilly writes:

> The Chiapan conflict takes place in a "right now;" Zapatismo legitimates itself in a "back then," a "time before." The communities live these two times as the timelessness of myth. Time and again the discourse takes up these timeless myths as the signs of identities of the communities. This mythic thought is not a literary recourse or a nostalgic romance about the past. It exists—it lives in the Indian community, inextricably woven into the rationality with which that community has to confront the world of the state and the market.[65]

The essence of the conflict, Gilly notes, is in the surging forth of an indigenous consciousness, replete with symbolism, meanings and codes, that exist and *have always existed* behind and beneath the "modern consciousness," whose modus operandi is to negate the value—and the very existence—of this "other world." "At the most profound level," Gilly writes, "my hypothesis is that with an unprecedented crisis of *values* and of *security* closing in on Mexican society [and by extension, the entire industrial "first" world] in a veritable end of the regime, the words and deeds of the Indian rebellion strike the chord of what I call the enchanted world."[66]

There is something undeniably *romantic* in Gilly's phrase "the enchanted world," something that smacks almost of "othering." But this is, or has proven to be, nearly inescapable in discussing the divergence of these particular cultures, the "Indian" and the "white," as well as the temporal senses they each evoke, the "ancient" and the "modern." To deny that we are looking at cultures with different symbolic orders and different logics is to deny a basic truth. To approach the problem from this side—the "modern," "first world," disenchanted side—of the cultural fence, is to enter a necessarily subjective realm where we are forced to define the "other" world by its most salient characteristics. Gilly chooses the mythic character of the indigenous cultures—animist concepts, a mystical relation with historical cycles, and a communal order that springs from spiritual or ethical values as much as from economic necessity.

Like all subaltern orders at large within colonial schemes, the mythic relationship to the world—what is called the cosmovision—of the indigenous communities of Chiapas, only makes itself fully apparent to the colonizers, when, due to dire circumstances threatening its existence, it bursts forth into public view demanding acknowledgment. Implicit in this surging forth is the demand to be approached with the respect due to all human subjects in a world that assigns value to people a priori rather than as a condition of their place in the market. For the Zapatistas, one word sums up this demand, a word that ripples through Marcos's communiqués and gives endless trouble to the politicians and mediating bodies whose purpose is to interpret the obscure intentions of the Indians: the word is *dignity*.[67]

An important function of the communiqués is their ability to translate the concept of dignity—a concept that lies at the very heart of their struggle—through different narrative instances. That is, to tell stories about dignity so that we, foreigners that we are, can begin to grasp what it means. In a communiqué dated April 10, 1995, Marcos traces the roots of dignity back to Votan:

> The powerful with all their money don't understand why Votan-Zapata doesn't die, they don't understand why he returns and rises from his death alive in the words of the true men and women. Brothers, they don't understand our struggle. The power of money and pride cannot understand Votan-Zapata. They cannot because there is a word which does not walk in the understanding of the great sages who sell their intelligence to the rich and the powerful. And this word is called dignity, and dignity is something that doesn't walk in people's heads. Dignity walks in the heart. [68]

In a historical order that goes back to the gods themselves, says Marcos, dignity resides in historical memory, in the knowledge that certain ethical codes are in place which were established, generations ago, by the *tojol winik*—the first humans—in a covenant with the gods.

We will return later to dignity.

Mircea Eliade, in *The Myth of the Eternal Return*, looks at the cyclical view of history in ancient cultures, making the point that this cyclical view of history is based on repetitions of the archetypal events that occurred at the beginning of the world. Thus, every historic action is, to some extent, a ritual reiteration of earlier events, and history is itself sacred: "The archaic world knows nothing of 'profane' activities: every act which has a definite meaning—hunting, fishing, agriculture, games, conflicts, sexuality—in some way participates in the sacred." He continues: "The only profane activities are those which have no mythical meaning, that is, which lack exemplary models. Thus we may say that every responsible activity in pursuit of a definite end is, for the archaic world, a ritual."[69]

This reiteration of ancient events and revisiting of the ancient gods points to the belief that, in the beginning, there was justice. One of the objects of resistance and revolutionary struggle is to return society to that original state. Not to turn back time, but to shepherd the cycle of history on its return to a more just society. John Berger, writing from his experience living for decades among French peasants, explains one of the central dynamics of peasant rebellion:

> The peasant imagines an un-handicapped life, a life in which he is not first forced to produce a surplus before feeding himself and his family, as a primal state of being which existed before the advent of injustice. Food is man's first need. Peasants work on the land to produce food to feed themselves. Yet they are forced to feed others first, often at the price of going hungry themselves. They see the grain in the fields which they have worked and harvested—on their own land or on the landowner's—being taken away to feed others, or to be sold for the profit of others. However much a bad harvest is considered an act of God, however much the master/landowner is considered a natural master, whatever ideological explanations are given, the basic fact is clear: they who

> can feed themselves are instead being forced to feed others. Such an injustice, the peasant reasons, cannot always have existed, so he assumes a just world at the beginning. At the beginning a primary state of justice towards the primary work of satisfying man's primary need. All spontaneous peasant revolts have had the aim of resurrecting a just and egalitarian peasant society.[70]

Zapata Vive, La Lucha Sigue

Every social movement has its icons, and the rebirth of the martyred Emiliano Zapata as the icon and namesake of the indigenous rebels of Chiapas is as brilliant as it is self-evident. The primary people's leader who propelled the Mexican Revolution of 1910–1919 to overthrow the Porfiriato, the brutal, feudal, decades-long regime of dictator Porfirio Díaz, and establish the Carta Magna, the founding document of modern Mexico, Zapata is a figure whose presence is everywhere in Mexico, and whose name is attached to everything from barbershops and taco stands to agricultural unions to rebel armies. By evoking Zapata, a claim is laid for the "true" meaning of the Mexican Revolution, a struggle for a united peasantry and for the practical ideals of land and liberty. Of all of the Latin American leaders of the twentieth century, perhaps the only ones who maintain the status of popular legend across classes are Emiliano Zapata, Pancho Villa, and possibly Che Guevara. There is a clear reason why this might be the case:

> Lenin, Mao, and Tito have been knocked off their pedestals in recent years, while [Villa and Zapata] have not only retained their positions, their power has multiplied. The reason for their continued relevance, and also that of Che Guevara, springs from, among other things, the fact that they were foreign to power. In other words, it is not enough for an individual to embrace popular causes, it is crucial that they maintain distance from that which contaminates whoever touches it: power and its symbols.[71]

The icon of Zapata as a symbol of *ongoing* revolution is particularly potent in Chiapas, because, as has been noted extensively, if simplistically, the Mexican Revolution and the reforms it gained *never quite arrived* in

Chiapas. The original Zapatistas, the revolutionary army of the South led by the horse-trader-cum-rebel General Emiliano Zapata, waged a campaign throughout Zapata's home state of Morelos and the neighboring regions of Oaxaca, Michoacan, and Guerrero, but neither the rebel army nor the agricultural reforms carried out largely in the 1930s under President Lazaro Cardenas arrived in the villages of the Chiapan *altiplano* or the *Selva Lacandona*, where *caciquismo* (the law of the jungle) and the system of *encomenderos* (large land-holdings owned by ladinos, or whites), have persisted to the present day.[72] For the rural indigenous population of Chiapas, the figure of Zapata sustains, in this sense, too, the quality of myth.

For the better part of the twentieth century, Zapata was associated with peasant uprising and not, strictly speaking, with *indigenous* uprising. It is only with the growth of the indigenous movement —a movement based in cultural values that emerged with the end of the Cold War, when class ideologies began to give way, the world over, to cultural ideologies—that Zapata becomes an indigenous hero. And his image grew so closely linked to the rebel movement in 1994 that, that same year, the Mexican government removed Zapata's image from the ten-peso note. This action is indicative both of the PRI's crisis of legitimacy—it could no longer credibly claim that its ideology descended from the "liberator of the South"—and of its need to distract attention from the Zapatistas in Chiapas. The war of symbols had extended itself to bank notes.[73]

In an analysis of Zapata's mythic presence, Enrique Rajcheneberg and Catherine Héau-Lambert write:

> Nothing is more exemplary than the photograph of Zapata and Villa sitting in the presidential chair in 1914 when their peasant armies took Mexico City. At the side of a Villa who laughs at the pomp and circumstance, though undoubtedly somewhat pleased, we see a Zapata clearly uncomfortable and with an urge to be done as quickly as possible with the part of the carnival in which the poor take the place of the powerful.... Maybe it is for this reason, beyond the horse and the bandoliers of bullets crossing his chest, that Marcos is so strongly identified with Zapata: a poet, he said on one occasion, would make a terrible legislator.[74]

Like the other photo of Zapata that Old Antonio carries with him, this one is a well of answers, or rather, questions.

Mexican scholar Carlos Montemayor, too, draws the figure of Zapata into the realm where Mexican historical reality and indigenous mythistory coexist:

> For the occident, the calendar of history is obvious: we believe that what happened once happened only in this moment, and that it has nothing to do with the subsequent moment. For indigenous culture, time has another nature, another speed, and is one of the secrets of the cultural resistance and combative capacity of these people. For them, the past is found in another dimension that continues coexisting with the present. The indigenous memory is a process of revitalization of the past. The festivals, dances, prayers, the oral tradition, are the force of a memory that communicates with this other dimension in which things remain alive. This is why, when they speak of Emiliano Zapata (or of heroes from the remote conquest, from the independence or from the nineteenth century), they are speaking of a living force.[75]

The indigenous sense of eternal returns, of history as living myth, is voiced every time an impassioned crowd bellows out the slogan "*Zapata vive, La lucha sigue!*" —"Zapata Lives, the struggle continues!" The living presence of Zapata, clashing with the collective awareness that native and peasant cultures are being relegated by the forces of the market and the state to some primeval mythic past, spells resistance, and evokes an ever-recurring mythic present. "Indian communities," Adolfo Gilly writes, "cannot accept taking themselves as 'the past' of Mexican society's present, nor even the present of that future that awaits them."[76] Consequently, they invoke the revolutionary past to give voice and currency to their demands. By aligning themselves with the *Zapatistas* of the nation's founding, these "neo-zapatistas," as they've been called, lay claim to the gains of the previous revolution, asserting that their demands are nothing unheard of or extreme, but merely the same justice, dignity, and liberty that all Mexicans are granted by the constitution of 1917. In fact, to the charge of "*neo-zapatismo,*" Marcos has countered, to paraphrase, "We are

not 'neo,' we are the continuation of the revolution of 1910." "*Zapata vive!*" they continue shouting. "*La lucha sigue!*"

Marcos the public figure, who is also Marcos the performer, goes so far as to pose in the guise of Zapata, to invoke that hero's image in his own:

> Marcos surprised everyone when he made his appearance on horseback, his chest crossed with bandoliers. For Mexicans, this appearance was not merely a surprise, but the awakening of a collective memory that had been stuffed into a corner, practically entombed by neoliberalism, on the verge of falling into oblivion. The image of Marcos immediately invoked another, more distant image: that of Emiliano Zapata on horseback, dressed in a cavalier's finery, with his wide sombrero and his chest crossed by bandoliers: this unforgettable photo which served as a model for innumerable Mexican cinematographers went on to become the archetypal image of the good revolutionary. From the identity of Marcos, hidden behind the ski mask, remained only the symbolic identity of an agrarian revolutionary hero. This surprising apparition from the remote past was more eloquent than all of the speeches. The emblematic figure of the defender of the people who died for his ideals was reborn.[77]

The Aguascalientes

In the summer of 1994, when it was clear that the Zapatista rebellion had attracted the world's attention, Zapatista strategists saw fit to use the international attention that they had garnered to draw a circle of protection around themselves and make it clear that their struggle was national, international, and universal. They called for a convention, known as the National Democratic Convention, that was convened in the summer of 1994 and that would be the first in a series of meetings held inside rebel territory. Invitees included the press, politicians, dignitaries, celebrities and activists from all walks of life, and, of course, indigenous supporters from across Mexico and the world. The Zapatistas chose to name the convention center Aguascalientes, after the city where Emiliano Zapata and Pancho Villa forged their revolutionary alliance, one of the key events that led to the formation of the modern Mexican nation. Carlos Montemayor explains:

> The Second Declaration of the Lacandon Jungle ... took as its its epigraph part of the speech given by Paulino Martinez, a Zapatista delegate, at the sovereign Revolutionary Convention on October 27, 1914 in the city of Aguascalientes. This convention, the reader should recall, in the central years of the Mexican Revolution marked the rupture between the forces of Zapata and Villa, on one side, and the constitutionalists of the government of [Venustiano] Carranza, on the other....
>
> Eighty years later, the EZLN reclaimed this vision of the forces of Villa and Zapata to construct, in the area surrounding the village of Guadelupe Tepeyac, the site of another convention that also received the name "Aguascalientes"....[78]

By using the name "Aguascalientes" for their convention center, the Zapatistas assert their claims to the Mexican revolutionary Constitution, thereby proclaiming at once the populist, democratic nature of their project, their loyalty to traditional Mexican patriotic ideals, and their status as heirs to the patrimony of the first Mexican revolution. By insisting on the patriotic and populist nature of their revolution, and by embedding this history in the name of their convention center, the Zapatistas succeed in frustrating the ability of the state-owned media to discredit or vilify them.

Soon after this first *encuentro*, the Mexican military destroyed the Aguascalientes and occupied the village of Guadelupe Tepeyac. But shortly after the first was destroyed, five more Aguascalientes were constructed. Overnight, five villages throughout the Zapatista-controlled zone of conflict became Aguascalientes—symbolic and real centers of resistance, with meeting rooms, public amphitheaters, command structures, and guest lodging. The proliferation of the Aguascalientes became, in itself, symbolic of *Zapatismo*. "If you throw an ear of corn to the ground," a Zapatista insurgent told me after the murder of his *compañero*, "the seeds will take root and more corn will grow. This is how we are."[79]

Marcos described the occurrence in the long series of communiqués known as "The Thirteenth Stella" (through which, in July, 2003, he announced the "death" of the Aguascalientes):

> If anything characterizes the Zapatistas, it is tenacity ("that would be necessity," more than one might think). So it was that not a year had gone by when new Aguascalientes appeared in different parts of rebel territory: Oventik, La Realidad, La Garrucha, Roberto Barrios, Morelia. So, yes, the Aguascalientes became what they were intended to be: spaces for meeting and dialogue with national and international civil society. Beyond being the home to great initiatives and *encuentros* on memorable dates, on a daily basis they were the places where civil society and the Zapatistas met up.[80]

Once the EZLN's historical, pro-democracy stance became embedded in the fabric of Mexican discourse through their explicit association with the first Mexican revolution, it would cost the government a great deal in terms of public relations to discredit them. In fact, among a fluctuating majority of Mexicans (or so it would seem), the rhetorical strategy of the Zapatistas served to discredit the state's counter-revolutionary campaign and contributed to a profound crisis of confidence then overtaking the ruling party, the PRI, which led to its eventual and inevitable demise. This crisis of confidence—manifested in the rapid devaluation of the peso, the establishment of a middle-class resistance movement *(*El Barzón*)*, an entrenched student strike at the UNAM, Latin America's largest public university, and finally in the defeat of the PRI in the 2000 elections—was precipitated to a great degree by the strategy of symbolic warfare carried out through the EZLN communiqués.

In a successful strategy that descends from a long indigenous tradition of warfare through the clever manipulation of signs, the mask of liberal democracy was torn away from the face of Mexican politics. Once torn away, it could not be easily recovered, and the hypocrisy of the state was revealed at every turn. As critics of the modern Mexican state are fond of noting, the eternal flame that once burned in the Monument to the Revolution in Mexico City had been extinguished for a long time.

The Inverted Periscope: Assault on the Colonial Mind

We can see from histories of Mexican agrarian revolt, and the almost continuous guerilla warfare fought in Mexico since the conquest, that agrarian inequality and the hegemony of ruling elites are the bread-and-butter issues behind the Zapatista revolt. At the same time, the rebellion of the Zapatistas is a response to the collision of two wholly different worlds, the colonial and the indigenous, the world where kinship relations are dominant and the world where relations of production dominate. "On the side of oblivion are the multiple forces of the market," wrote Marcos. "On the side of memory is the solitary reason of History."

The Zapatistas' struggle is not "anti-colonial" in the conventional sense of a colonized nation struggling to throw off a foreign power; theirs is a struggle against *internal colonialism,* in which the indigenous cultures are forced to play a subaltern role within a dominating state.[81] Whatever we call it, the assertion made throughout Zapatista literature is that indigenous history has not been supplanted, but has continued to exist throughout the 500 years of "the encounter of two worlds." Which leads us to:

The Story of the Buried Key[82]

They tell that the very first gods, those who gave birth to the world, had a very bad memory and they tended to easily forget what they were doing or saying. Some say that it was because the greatest gods had no obligation to remember anything, because they came from when time had no time, that is to say, there was nothing before them, and if there was nothing, then there was nothing to have a memory of. Who knows, but the fact is that they used to forget everything. This ill they passed on to all those who govern the world, and have governed it in the past. But the greatest gods, the very first ones, learned that memory is the key to the future and that one should care for it like one cares for one's land, one's home and one's history. So that, as an antidote for their amnesia, the very first gods, those who gave birth to the world, made a copy of everything they had created and of all they knew. That copy they hid underground so that there would be no confusion with what was above ground. So that under the world's ground there is another identical world to the one here above ground, with a parallel history to that of the surface. The first world is underground.

I asked Old Antonio whether the underground world was an identical copy of the world we know.

"It was," Old Antonio answered me. "No longer. And it's that," he explained, "the outside world began to get messy and disorderly as time went by. When the very first gods left, no one in the governments remembered to look down below in order to put in order what was getting out of place. So that each new generation of bosses thought that the world he inherited was simply that way and that another world was impossible. So that what is underground is identical to what is above ground, but it is so in a different way."

Old Antonio said that's why it is a custom of the true men and women to bury the newborn's umbilical cord. They do it so the new human being may take a peek at the true history of the world and learn how to struggle so he or she may be put back in order, as it should be.

So that down below not only is the world, but the possibility of a better world.

"And the two of us are also down there?" asks a sleepy Sea.

"Yes, and together," I answer.

"I don't believe you," says the Sea, but she discreetly turns on her side and peeks through a little hole left by a small pebble on the ground.

"Truly," I insist, "if we had a periscope we could take a look."

"A periscope?" she whispers.

"Yes," I tell her, "a periscope. An inverted periscope."

The modern, neoliberal Mexican state and the corporate order, it appears, would prefer to believe that the "dirty," "superstitious," and "primitive" world of indigenous cultures has died off, given way to the free market and the relations of advanced, industrial capitalism, but Marcos asserts that the ancient history continues to exist, underground, and that it is merely the ignorance and short-sightedness of the "bosses" that proclaims the disappearance of this world. Gilly writes:

> We cannot think about the globalization of communications and exchange as a linear and successive process; rather, it presents itself as an arborescent reality in which the unlimited hybridization of both worlds continues unrelentingly. The modern world subverts and disintegrates traditional societies. But in the process of doing so, it internalizes them as well, unknowingly receiving their practical and silent forms of critique; and this presence alters the modern world's manner of being.[83]

It is amply demonstrated in the anthropological literature—and is obvious to anyone visiting deep Mexico[84] and many other parts of Latin America—that the beliefs and practices of the indigenous were never wiped out, as the conquerors intended, but rather syncretized with the dominating culture in a way that thoroughly reconfigures both. As historian Serge Gruzinski notes in his reflections on religious syncretism among the Maya: "Nostalgia often dressed up an ever-present past, and to the consternation of the missionaries (for they were not all fools) these images of yesterday were uncomfortably close to contemporary life."[85]

This is nothing new. However, in bringing indigenous demands to the attention of international society, the Zapatistas have challenged global capital's assertion that, since the fall of communism, it is the sole mode of relations between and among people(s). In dressing the Zapatistas' demands in the fabular language of indigenous histories, Marcos demonstrates the continued presence of an indigenous worldview that raises a profound challenge to both the nation-state as a locus of identity and to the free market economy that circumscribes, defines, and delimits modern social relations.

In this sense, perhaps the most crucial moment in "The Story of the Buried Key" comes when Marcos makes direct reference to the indigenous practice of burying the newborn's umbilical cord, relating it to the sustained vision of the "true history of the world." This practice, along with countless other traditional practices, is a fact of indigenous life, as inherent to the culture as planting corn in time for the rains. By emphasizing the healing nature of the practice and by associating it with an understanding of history, Marcos makes it clear that a living vision of the "true" indigenous history is essential to the millenarian, revolutionary project of the Zapatistas, assuring that each individual "may be put back in order, as it should be."

Images of the underground world, the buried key that is memory, bring us back to Xibalbe and the twin heroes, whose journey through the underworld allowed them to conquer death. By returning to the *inframundo*, the world of the ancestors, the Zapatistas conquer temporal death by (literally) planting the hope that their children and their cosmovision, will survive into the future.

Carlos Montemayor elaborates on the evolution of the indigenous presence within Mexican national culture:

> In the sixteenth century, the religious conversion of the Indians marked their destruction as a people and their Christian "rebirth"; in the seventeenth and eighteenth centuries their real marginalization and historic rebirth were consummated. But the Indian that was rescued was an idea, a concept from the past. Since then, those of us who are not indigenous believe that this culture is ours, that it belongs to all Mexicans. And we appropriate from this culture without any agreement with the real Indians of flesh and blood.[86]

The project of the Zapatistas, as put forth in the communiqués, is to reclaim the status of the indigenous not only as possessed of flesh and blood, of human dignity and culture, but as the legitimate founders and builders of the Mexican nation. As "the first postmodern, post-communist revolutionaries," their aim is not merely to enter history as actors in the drama of political machination. It is to manifest a different history altogether.

Liberation of the Enchanted World

> In 1992, Virgins bathed in rays of light were seen at Ixthuacan and Teopisca, closer to the Bishop's bailiwick. The year 1992 marked five hundred years of indigenous resistance to the European invasion of the Americas, and among the Mayans of eastern Chiapas the appearances of

> Virgins and Niños and glowing lights seem to coincide with moments of maximum Indian rage.
>
> The *altos* and the jungle of Chiapas have never lacked for prophets in the way they have lacked for bread and land and liberty.
>
> —John Ross[87]

The historical ties of indigenous resistance struggles to the Catholic Church have been well documented, going back to the early, heroic intervention of Archbishop Bartolomé de las Casas who argued, in the Valladolid debate of 1550, that the Indians had souls. Over the last several decades popular adherence to the version of liberation theology espoused by the Diocese of San Cristóbal de las Casas and its Bishop Samuel Ruiz, has had a good deal to do with creating the conditions for the growth of the social movement.[88] Zapatista pre-history reaches back to a number of social organizations that emerged after the infamous 1968 massacre at Tlatelolco, the crisis that birthed a thousand clandestine movements; one of the largest peasant organizations in the *cañadas* of Chiapas, K'ip Tic Talekumtasel, or Quiptic (Tzeltal for "We unite our forces to progress,") emerged from a nationwide meeting of the National Indigenous Congress organized by Biship Ruiz in 1974. Quiptic, which underwent several transformations by the late eighties, served as an important organizing base for the EZLN.[89] Perhaps due in part to this history, a majority of the communities that came to join the Zapatista movement profess devotion to the Catholic faith.

But another spirituality, masked by Catholicism, is clear in the communiqués and in the actions of the rebels. Marcos and the EZLN are not the first to invoke indigenous spirituality in the name of revolution. Indeed, the blending of occidental religions and native spiritual traditions, like other blendings, is a thread throughout popular uprisings since the establishment of modern Mexico, most famously, perhaps, in the Guadalupana, the cult of the Virgin of Guadalupe.

These uprisings have often had as their prime motivator the apparition of the Virgin, the rebellious actions of a local hero who comes to represent the Christ figure, or some other act of divine intervention exhorting the people to rise up in arms. In 1850, a cross magically appeared engraved in a tree in the town of Santa Cruz—the Holy Cross—in Yucatán. The cross began to speak, advocating indigenous independence and leading to the War of the Castes that lasted more than half a century until it was finally quelled, for a time, by the federal government. Elsewhere in Mexico, in 1893 and 1894 in the Sierra Tarahumara in Chihuahua, a young prophetess, the Doncella de Cabora, began to perform miracles while espousing a vision of justice and liberty for the embattled poor; divine forces called for class war.[90]

This syncretism of Catholic mysticism, native animism, and popular insurrection has been a characteristic of virtually all Mayan uprisings since the eighteenth century. Between 1697 and 1730, there occurred various indigenous religious movements in the highlands of Chiapas, all of them marked by divine revelations; several resulted in armed uprisings. The stories are well known in Chiapas of the Virgin of Candelaria whose appearance in 1712 inspired an army of 3,000 Tzeltal *campesinos* to arm themselves with machetes and farm implements and launch a reign of terror against priests, tax collectors, and agents of the crown. This rebel army established, for a brief moment, an autonomous holy land known as the "Republic of the Tzeltales."[91]

And there are the famous green stones that fell from the sky in 1868 at Tjazaljemel, near San Juan Chamula, which is just outside of San Cristóbal de Las Casas.[92] When the stones began to speak against the colonial authorities and the church, another rebellion ensued. Throughout the history of the Mayan regions in Mexico, indigenous leaders like Jacinto Canek in Yucatán and Juan Gómez and Sebastien Gómez in Chiapas led their people to rise up against the ladino overlords in the name of the Father, the Son, and the Holy Ghost. Their prophecies are engrained in the history of the region, their redemptive mythologies echoing through time.

By invoking the figure of Old Antonio and the old gods Votan, Ik'al and the others, and by speaking in the mythic tone of voice about the *tojol winik*, the true people, Marcos is adding his voice to the long line of prophets who invoke the ancient religion or the Holy Trinity to spark righteous anger, leading toward open rebellion. For the Zapatistas, reclaiming history is an act of faith, as much "spiritual" as it is "political." Indeed, for much of the population of the Zapatista zone of conflict, there is no distinction between the spiritual and the political, between redemption and revolution; history—time itself—is sacred, and includes all of human and nonhuman experience; reclaiming time, for the Zapatistas, is a fundamental revolutionary act. In contrast, the thrust of modernity secularizes history and disarticulates it, causing a radical break between past, present, and future; a rupture occurs, too, between the individual, cast into secular time absent of its sacred, ritual function; the community, which struggles to articulate itself in the absence of a historically based identity; and the natural (and supernatural) world, which is, at best, the hastily assembled stage on which the *telenovela* of history plays out.

By building a mythology of *Zapatismo* rooted at once in the ancient indigenous past and in the agrarian struggle of modern Mexico, and by making that mythology central to a popular and political discourse with the state, the press, and civil society, the Zapatistas define their movement as a reassertion of mythistorical reality and a redefinition of the relation of indigenous history to occidental history. By invoking the mythic history and by donning the magical insignia of the ski mask, which we'll examine next, the Zapatistas assert their continuity with the past and proclaim a historical, moral, and spiritual imperative for justice with dignity.

Interregnum: A Dream of Paradise Lost

The mythopoesis that Marcos invokes and transmits like a telepathic signal, attracting legions of "revolutionary tourists" to the Mexican southeast to dig ditches and take photos and cart away revolutionary souvenirs, is a subterranean voice that has been invoked time and again from the earthen vaults of deep Mexico. In *The Plumed Serpent*, D. H. Lawrence wrote fantastically of a European tourist drawn ever deeper into a pre-Christian religion, a cult of the plumed serpent Quetzalcoatl, whose drums leavened the Mexican night with a perfumed mystery and whose traces revealed a shadowy uprising of natives threatening to overturn the rule-bound modernity of Mexico. The violence that encompasses Mexican society—indeed, in Lawrence's view, the violence of the world—was rooted in that clash of ancient autochthonous spirits and modern technocratic civilization.

There is a danger to this vision, and not of the earthen psycho-sexualized variety that concerned Lawrence. The Nobel Prize–winning, French author J. M. G. Le Clézio submits to the danger when he equates Mexico with the idealized perception of Tahiti promoted by the nineteenth-century post-impressionist painter Paul Gauguin—a virgin oasis where spirits dwell on earth compelling the mystical poets of Europe to make it a site of pilgrimage. Le Clézio writes:

> It was the discovery of the ancient magic of the conquered peoples that gave new value to the contemporary indigenous world and which has enabled the Mexican dream to be perpetuated. The dream of a new land where everything is possible; where everything is at the same time very ancient and very new. The dream of a lost paradise where the science of the stars and the magic of the gods were as one. Dreams of a return to the very origins of civilization and knowledge.[93]

The danger is that of essentialism, of orientalism; of leaving behind the awareness that, mingling like a drift of copal smoke among "the ancient magic of the conquered peoples" is the fact of hunger; the fact of misery; the fact of disappearances and of torture and of low-intensity war. The romance of the revolutionary tourist draws a scrim over the quotidian suffering of this "lost paradise."

Certainly Mexico was a favored destination of the surrealists, and for precisely this reason. The French dramatist, poet, and madman Antonin Artaud arrived there in 1936; in an article written that year called "What I came to do in Mexico," the poet dismissed Europe as "a frightful dusting of cultures," called the Orient "decadent," accused the United States of "multiplying the vices of Europe," and came to the following conclusion: "All that is left is Mexico and its subtle political structure, which, after all, has not changed since the time of Montezuma. Mexico, that precipitate of innumerable races, is like the crucible of history. It is from that precipitate, that mixture of races, that it must derive a unique product from which the Mexican soul will emerge."[94]

Artaud came to Mexico seeking what he called "the new idea of man," which is strangely echoed thirty years later by Che Guevara's call for "a new man," emerging from colonial subjugation, and thirty years after that by the Zapatistas' storied reinvention of the world. But Artaud's fascination, layered as it was with opiate visions of a Mexico that had not changed since Montezuma, came to ruin. After writing of Tarahumara dances and of a "mountain of signs" he discovered in the barren Sierra of northern Mexico, and after "an exhaustion so cruel that I can no longer believe that I was in fact not bewitched, or that these barriers of disintegration and cataclysms I had felt rising in me were not the result of an intelligent and organized premeditation, I had reached one of the last places in the world where the dance of healing by Peyote still exists." Artaud was forced to abandon Mexico for the asylums of decadent Europe. As Le Clézio writes, Artaud's vision was "so powerful that it seemed to completely erase the daily reality of Mexico."[95]

Yet Artaud's vision, like Lawrence's, had a draw that could not be denied. He wrote, "I believe in a force sleeping in the land of Mexico. It is for me the only place in the world where dormant natural forces can be useful to the living. I believe in the magical reality of these forces, as one might believe in the healing and beneficial power of certain thermal waters."[96] Artaud's pilgrimage prefigured that of André Breton who, upon arrival in 1938, declared Mexico "the most surrealist country in the world." The poet Benjamin Perét emigrated there in 1942; Spanish surrealist filmmaker Luis Buñuel followed in 1946.

Without doubt there is something there that calls to poets and revolutionaries, and to deny this "magic" is, perhaps, to make the world a little duller. But a cautionary note: where so many poets and visionaries tread, it can become a puzzle to untangle the materialist roots of struggle, and one may easily engage in a facile indulgence that may, as in the case of Artaud, lead to madness—or at the very least, completely erase the daily reality of Mexico. While the Zapatistas have kindled an ancient flame, and have invited poets, artists, and visionaries from around the world to visit their jungle villages and participate in their *encuentros*, sharing without hesitation their aura of myth, they urge at the same time that rather than vanish into the mists of a disengaged poetic reverie, visitors to their communities engage in critical encounter with them in order to establish lasting and meaningful bonds of solidarity and shared resistance. They urge, again, that the meeting of worlds occur in mutual respect and dignity, and that any path forward be wrought collectively, by asking questions while walking.

III
Of Masks, Mirrors, and Metamorphoses

> To be sure, the torturer's desire is prosaic: to acquire information, to act in concert with large-scale economic strategies elaborated by the masters of finance and exigencies of production. Yet there is also the need to control massive populations, entire social classes and even nations through the cultural elaboration of fear.
>
> That is why silence is imposed.
>
> —Michael Taussig[1]

A Poetics of Liberation

If the torturer's desire is prosaic—the desire to serve money and power in all their merciless guises—then the desire of the liberator is itself poetic, a voice against torture and against the closed chambers, metaphorical or real, where torture takes place. Torture and terror have been instrumental in the colonial campaign against the indigenous throughout the Americas since the time of conquest. The struggle to wrest the body politic from the torturers—with their surgical bombs and their secret police, their flesh-eating dogs and their work camps—is a struggle to restore a social order that terror has all-but destroyed. In the case of the Zapatistas, this order involves an attention to pre-conquest forms of governance and means of socializing, accompanied by experiments in grassroots democracy, and a continual cry of resistance alongside the centuries-long echo of the grief of conquest.

Anthropologist Michael Taussig, writing of the collision of cultures that is our America,[2] describes "the space of death where the Indian, African and white gave birth to a New World."[3] The Zapatistas, product, as they say, of 500 years of misery and oppression, consciously inhabit this "space of death" through its invocation in their symbols and their language. Death is a constant presence in the communiqués and the writing of Marcos; the presence of death is evoked, too, by the ski masks donned by Zapatista warriors. These masks signify resistance, and they signify those who have died and those who will die in this struggle. In a sense, the ski masks call forth all the dead and, for the one who wears a ski mask, the mask creates a warrior persona, in the same way that war paint means war. However, for the Zapatista warrior, battle, the field of struggle, may not necessarily mean armed confrontation, but rather any public appearance—even on film or video—because the battlefield is the arena of public space. Suddenly, guerilla war is declared every time a ski mask appears in public in Mexico. When the Zapatistas and their sympathizers wear ski masks in public, or in print, they are carrying their struggle into the open. They are saying, "*Aqui estamos. Resistimos.*"

The Story of the Ski Masks

Immediately after the appearance of the EZLN in 1994, the ski mask bloomed like a dark flower across the cultural landscape. In December 2000, when the Zapatistas declared that they would march to the capital of Mexico to speak before Congress, the chief concern among opposition leaders was not that the rebels would bear arms, but that they would wear masks. An almost pathological terror of the masks has been evident among the ruling class, mirroring, in its way, the fetish that surrounds the masks among youth and the left.

In a letter to historian Adolfo Gilly, Marcos himself wrote: "The case is that the ski mask is a symbol of rebellion. Just yesterday it was a symbol of criminality or terrorism. Why? Certainly not because we intended it to be."[4] Innumerable journalists in Mexico and around the world became fascinated with the ski masks when they first appeared and for years after. They make for great photo-ops. As with the appearance of Votan-Zapata, we can find in the literature instances of myth to help us interpret the manifold meanings of the *pasamontañas*, the ski masks, both for those who wear them, the Zapatistas, and for those who confront them in the streets and the press photos. This leads us to:

The Story of the Ski Masks[5]

Toñita with the tiny hands comes in to ask for a story. Toñita has decided to adopt a corncob and get rid of the ungrateful rabbit that never learned how to live in the mud. She comes in to ask me for a story. Obviously it doesn't bother her in the least that I am writing and she sits with her corncob—excuse me, her doll—in her arms. I begin to think of an excuse but Toñita appears to be disinterested in anything but a story. I sigh and light the pipe to buy some time. Between puffs of smoke, I tell her:

"Night, rain, cold. December of 1984. Old Antonio looks at the light. The campfire waits in vain for the meat of a whitetail deer that we had gone to hunt with flashlights in the dark, without success. In the fire, the colors dance, they speak. Old Antonio watches the campfire, listening. Dragging it out of himself, barely disputing the sound of crickets and the murmur of the flames, in the words of Old Antonio a story of long ago is woven, when the oldest were very ancient and the old of today were still tumbling in the blood and silence of a campfire on a night like this one, a hundred, a thousand, a million nights ago without deer, cold, rainy, without anyone to count the hours: In the beginning was the water of the night. All was water, all was night. The gods and the people walked around like mad people, tripping over one another and falling down like old drunks. There was no light to see one's steps, there was no earth to rest on for weariness and for love. There was no earth, no light, the world was no good.

Then the gods, in the night, in the water, went and ran into one another and they became angry and they spoke strong words and the anger of the gods was great because the gods themselves were great. And the men and the women, all ears, all Tzotz, bat men and women, hid themselves from the sound of the great anger of the gods. And then the gods were alone, and when their anger passed they realized that they were alone and they were ashamed to be alone, and in their repentance they cried and their weeping was great because without men and women the gods were alone. Tears upon tears, weeping and more weeping, and more water joined the water of the night and there was no remedy, and the night and the water continued filling with more water of the sorrowful weeping of the gods. And the gods grew cold, because when you are alone it is cold, and even colder if everything is water and night. And they thought of making an agreement that they would do away with their loneliness, that they would bring the bat men and women out of their caves and they would bring light to illuminate the path and bring the earth to rest and to love. And so the gods agreed to dream together in their hearts, and to dream of light and of land. They set themselves to dreaming of fire and, grabbing the silence that wandered there, they dreamed a fire, and in the middle of the silence of the water-night filling everything in the middle of the gods, a wound appeared, a little crack in the water-night, a little word, this big, which danced and grew big and shrank and stretched and was fat and skinny and began to dance in the center of the gods who were seven because now they could see they were seven and they saw themselves and began to count and went up to seven because they were the seven greatest gods, the first gods. And the gods quickly began to make a little house for the word that danced among them, which danced in the silence. And they began to bring other little words near it, which came from their dreams, and "fire" they called these little dancing words and together they talked and they began to bring the earth and the light to the fire and the bat men and women left their caves to peek out and see each other, to touch each other and love each other, and there was earth and light and now they could see their steps and now they could lie down in love and in rest, in the light, in the earth. And the gods didn't see them because they went to make a general assembly and they were in their hut and would not come out and nobody could enter because the gods were meeting and coming to an agreement. In the hut, the gods came to the agreement that the fire would not die out because there was too much water-night and very little light and earth.

And they made the agreement to take the fire up into the sky, so that the water-night would not reach it. And they sent word to the bat men and women to stay in their caves, because they were going to raise up the fire, up to the sky, they said. And they made a circle around the fire and began to discuss who would take the fire up and die below in order to live above, and they could not agree because the gods did not want to die below, and the gods said that the whitest god should go because he was the most beautiful and that way the fire up above would be beautiful, but the white god was a coward who didn't want to die in order to live, and then the blackest and ugliest of the gods, ik', said that he would take the fire up, and he grabbed the fire and burned himself and turned black then gray then white then yellow then orange then red and then he became fire and he went chattering away until he reached the sky and there he stayed round and sometimes yellow and sometimes orange, red, gray, white and black, and "sun," the gods called it and more light came to help see the path, and more earth came and the water-night stood to one side and the mountain came. And the white god was so ashamed that he wept a great deal and, for so much weeping, he couldn't see his path and he tripped himself and fell into the fire, and so he also rose up to the sky but his light was sadder because he wept a lot for being such a coward, and a sad pale ball of fire the color of the white god stayed there alongside the sun, and "moon," the gods called this white ball. But the sun and the moon just stayed there and went nowhere and the gods looked at each other and were very ashamed, so they all threw themselves into the fire, and the sun began to walk and the moon followed behind, to ask its forgiveness, they say. And there was day and night, and the bat men and women came out of the caves and made their huts near the fire and they were always with the gods, day and night, because in the day they were with the sun and in the night they were with the moon. Everything that happened after was not an agreement by the gods, because they had already died … in order to live.

Old Antonio pulled from the fire, with his bare hands, a half-burned log. He leaves it on the ground. "Watch," he says. From red, the log traveled the reverse order of the black god in the story: orange, yellow, white, gray, black. Still hot, Old Antonio's calloused hands took it and gave it to me. I tried to pretend it didn't burn me, but I dropped it almost immediately. Old Antonio smiled and coughed, picked it up from the ground and doused it in a puddle of rain, a water-night. Once cold, he gave it to me again.

"Here ... remember that a face covered in black hides the light and the heat that the world lacks," he said, and looked at me.

"Let's go," he adds as he collects himself, saying, "Tonight the whitetail deer will not come, the feeding ground shows no tracks."

I made to put out the fire, but Old Antonio said to me, now with his sack over his shoulder and his musket in hand, "Leave it... with this cold even the night appreciates a little warmth..." Both of us left, in silence. It rained. And, yes, it was cold.

Another night, another rain, another cold. November 17, 1993. Tenth anniversary of the formation of the EZLN. The Zapatista General Command gathers around the fire. The general plans have been made and the tactical details worked out. The troops have gone to sleep, only the officers ranking above Major stay awake. There with us is Old Antonio, the only man who can breach all the Zapatista checkpoints and enter wherever he wants without anyone impeding his passage. The formal meeting ends and now, between jokes and anecdotes, we review plans and dreams. The issue of how we will cover our faces comes up again, whether with bandanas, or veils, or carnival masks. They all turn to look at me.

"Ski masks," I say.

"And how will the women manage that with their long hair?" asks Ana Maria.

"They should cut their hair," says Alfredo.

"No way man! What are you thinking? I say they should even wear skirts," says Josue.

"Your grandmother should wear skirts," says Ana Maria.

Moisés looks at the roof in silence and breaks up the discussion with "and what color should the ski-masks be?"

"Brown... like the cap," says Rolando. Someone else says green. Old Antonio makes a sign to me and separates me from the group. "Do you have that charred log from the other night?" he asks. "Yes, in my backpack," I respond. "Go get it" he says and walks toward the group around the fire. When I return with the bit of wood everyone is quiet, looking at the fire, as does Old Antonio, like that night of the white-tail deer. "Here," I say, and place the black wood shard in his hand. Old Antonio looks at me steadily and asks, "Remember?" I nod in silence. Old Antonio puts the log on the fire. First it turns gray, then white, yellow, orange, red, fire. The log is fire and light. Old Antonio looks at me again and moves to disappear into the fog. We all stay watching the log, the fire, the light.

"Black," I say.

"What?" asks Ana Maria.

I repeat without taking my eyes from the fire, "Black. The ski masks will be black..." No one opposes the idea...

"The Story of the Ski Masks" is another myth of origin that grows out of a dialogue between Old Antonio and the character Marcos. In the dialogue between Marcos and Antonio, the ski masks come to take on a poetic significance; as in "The Story of the Questions," notions of collectivity and of sacrifice predominate. And again, as in "The Story of the Questions," the meaning of the masks reaches back to the first gods, grounding the origin of the EZLN in the origin of the world.

In the story, "the blackest and ugliest of the gods, Ik', said that he would take the fire up, and he grabbed the fire and burned himself and turned black"; thus, the sacrifice of the Zapatistas is traced back to the sacrifice of the god Ik', who volunteered "to die below in order to live above." The black color of the masks, we are told, harks to the sacrifice by fire of "the blackest and ugliest of the gods." By tracing the origin of the ski masks back to the mythic origin of the world, the masks take on a ritual function. To don the mask is to participate in that original sacrifice.

The masks, and the myths that sustain them, more than serving to cover the faces of combatants, reinforce values fundamental to Zapatista ideology. Like the god Ik', whose name in Tojolabal means "black," the Zapatista warriors are those who have died in order to live, both in the real sense of giving their lives to the common struggle, and in the symbolic sense of disappearing behind the mask in order to demand the human dignity that, for them, defines their humanity.

In the process, we see the gods working out their problems in the collective, proto-democratic way by which the Mayan people typically govern themselves. As in "The Story of the Questions," everything is done by common agreement. In displaying this, Marcos again sets forth the political values and methodologies of the indigenous communities, grounding them, at once, in a pre-Columbian spirituality and in pre-Columbian forms of traditional authority. We see the gods coming to the decision to invent the sun through discussion and dissent. Typically, as we'll see in other stories, the gods argue and debate and sometimes forget what they were arguing about, or make bad decisions and have to fix their mistakes. They are far from all-powerful, or always right, or perfect. In fact, they are very human, very like the true men and women who live below. It was from these gods, we suppose, that the true men and women learned their way of governing. Later, we see the guerilla leaders in the process of deciding how they'll cover their faces in the uprising that is only six weeks away; after first witnessing how the gods come to a decision, we now get a glimpse into the dynamics of decision-making among their latter-day descendents, the Zapatistas. The argument reflects Marcos's position as leader, but shows the process, the dynamic, of executive decision-making. When Ana Maria and the men go at it over whether or not the women should wear skirts and long hair, the argument also reveals a tension between traditional gender roles and the new gender roles announced in *la ley revolucionaria de las mujeres* (the revolutionary women's law) and made mandatory—with great popularity—among the Zapatista communities. There is no illusion here that decisions are made harmoniously, or that everyone is happy with the arrangements. But there is space for discussion and argument.

When it comes to settling on the color of the ski masks, it is clear that the others defer to Marcos. But his authority does not rest on military strength or *caudillismo* (bullying); it resides in the doctrine of *mandar obedeciendo*, to lead by obeying—a guiding ethic of *Zapatismo* that we'll explore in depth further on. That is to say, his authority—at least as we have it in his own fictionalized account—resides in his deference to Old Antonio. There we see his role as *representative* of the indigenous demands. In his own version of events, Marcos has achieved the status and rank of a leader largely due to his humble posture toward the elders.

The Story of December 30, 1993

What I have called "The Story of the Ski Masks" is just one bit of a long communiqué from late 1994 that bears the title "The Long Journey from Despair to Hope." And there is more to the story. We left off where Marcos decided that the ski masks would be black like the burnt log, like the blackest and ugliest of the gods, Ik'. We take it up again two nights before the New Year's uprising, with Marcos and his troops on the road to San Cristóbal preparing for their pre-dawn raid on the town.

> Another night, another rain, another cold. December 30, 1993. The last troops begin their march to take position. A truck has gotten stuck in the mud, and the combatants are pushing it out. Old Antonio approaches me with an unlit cigarette in his mouth. I light it for him, and light my pipe with the opening face down, a trick the rain helped me invent.
>
> "When?" asks Old Antonio.
>
> "Tomorrow." I respond, and I add: "If we arrive on time..."
>
> "It's cold..." he says and he pulls his old wool jacket closed.
>
> "Mmmmmh," I respond.
>
> I roll another cigarette, and he says to me, "This night could use some light and some warmth."
>
> I show him the black ski mask and he smiles. He takes it in his hands, he examines it, and he gives it back.
>
> "That charred log?" he asks.
>
> "It burned up that night... there's nothing left," I tell him, a little embarrassed.
>
> "That's the way it goes," says Old Antonio in a weakened voice.
>
> "Dying to live," he says, and he gives me a hug. He wipes his eyes with his sleeve and he murmurs, "It's raining a lot, it's getting my eyes all wet."
>
> The truck is freed from the mud and they call me. I turn to say goodbye to Old Antonio, but he's gone...
>
> Toñita gets up to go. "Where's my kiss?" I say.
>
> She comes up to me, shoves the corncob against my cheek, and runs away.
>
> "What's that?" I protest.

She answers, laughing, "It's your kiss… the story was for the doll, so now she gave you your kiss." And she runs away…

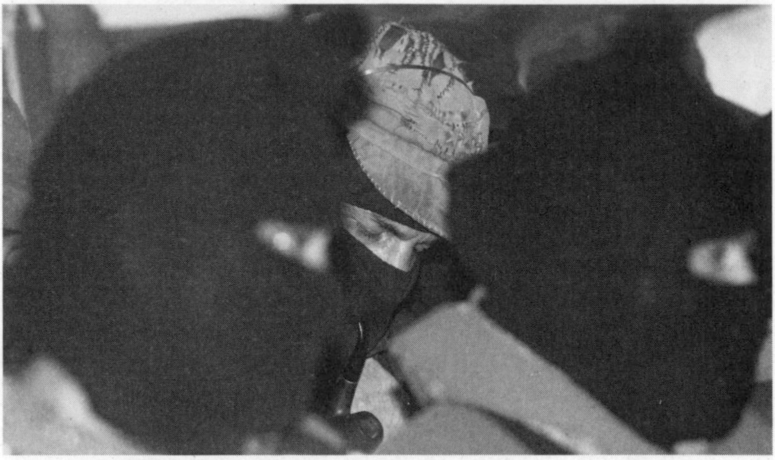

Metamorphosis

Masks are generally associated with bank robbers and other "common" criminals, as well as with terrorists or freedom fighters, all of whom have something to hide because they are breaking the moral, ethical, and legal codes of their societies. The mask covers the face to protect the identity. Simple enough, this pragmatic function of the mask works as well for the insurrectionary (whether fundamentalist or freedom fighter, Palestinian defender of the intifada or Korean student protestor) as the highway robber.

This is, of course, the case for the Zapatistas as well. They keep their faces covered in order to protect their identities. But for the Zapatistas, the ski mask also initially served a second, consummately pragmatic function, almost too simple to mention, made apparent in this last bit of the story, with Antonio's plea for warmth. On New Year's Eve in the high mountain town of San Cristóbal de las Casas, at 2,700 meters elevation, the wind burrows into your bone marrow, whips your face and freezes your eyebrows. It's *cold*. In winter in the *altiplano* of Chiapas, late at night and in the early morning hours, it is common to see people wearing ski masks to protect against frostbite.

What's not so common is to see people wearing ski masks, brown shirts, black pants, brown caps with little red five-pointed stars, and carrying assault weapons, rifles, and hand-carved, imitation wooden guns. The practical aspects of the masks—for covering the warrior's face, protecting her from recognition and from the cold—do not belie their more profound, ritual functions. Commenting on the use of masks in the Sandinista revolution in Nicaragua, Salman Rushdie wrote: "The true purpose of masks, as any actor will tell you, is not concealment, but transformation. A culture of masks is one that understands a good deal about the processes of metamorphosis."[6]

Rushdie is referring to the masks often worn by some Sandinista guerillas in Nicaragua in the 1980s, "masks of pink mesh with simple faces painted on them." The Sandinista masks are the same masks used by the indigenous of Nicaragua to satirize the Spanish conquistadores in the ritual drama called the Güegüense. Tania Solís Rubí, a former Sandinista now working for the Nicaraguan government says, "This drama originated in Diriamba and also in Masaya and Monimbó, which are centers of national folklore. So, when the struggle against Somoza reached these cities, the *guerrilleros* used these same masks for two fundamental reasons: to represent the anti-imperialist spirit just as they had hundreds of years before against the Spaniards, and to hide their *guerillero* identities."[7]

Throughout Mexico and the indigenous Americas, the use of masks is common in dance, ritual, and warfare, to bring about metamorphoses in indigenous ritual drama.[8] In "Masks and Shadows: From the ritual concept to the quotidian practice of anonymity," Juan Anzaldo Meneses traces the history of masks from the Aztec dance of the *quetzals*[9] and the *voladores* of Papantla[10] through spectacular representations of the return of Quetzalcoatl, the plumed serpent, to Mixtec dances invoking rain, and reenactments of the fall of the Mexica king Cuauhtemoc, son and heir to Moctezuma, in battle against Cortés's conquering army. Masks are worn in Hopi Kachina ceremonies, Zuñi dances, and other traditions of more northern peoples.

The Plains Indians of the nineteenth century were known to wear elaborate buckskins adorned with feathers and to paint their faces, invoking a warrior identity before engaging in battle. After the Ghost Dance religion swept the Plains during the latter part of the century, these buckskins took on a special power. Ghost Dance shirts, invested with the sacred power of Wovoka, the Western Paiute prophet who announced the Ghost Dance, made their wearers invisible and impervious to bullets. The Ghost Dance itself, which would invoke the ancestors and bring the dead back to life to form an army to wipe out the white invader, gave the Indians a primordial power to resist. In similar fashion, the Zapatistas bring the ancestors back to life through their communal mythology, and invoke an army of the dead by donning the ski masks.

All of these rituals have a common element, according to Meneses: "The dance and the dancers acquire another dimension. They are no longer common men and women, but rather they represent and personify creative forces capable of invoking a divine equilibrium."[11] Further, "The dancer, during the dance, ceases to be an individual and is converted into a collective instrument, a reflection of the will of the people to reach another manner of communicating with the cosmos and the natural world." He continues:

> Reclaiming this indigenous tradition of hiding the face to represent an interest no longer individual but rather collective, today this element of the mask has surfaced with great force, attracting the attention of the entire nation and even the whole world.... Pundits and sincere investigators have argued this matter of the EZLN's ski masks from the points of view of terrorism and banditry. Effectively, in occidental society, covering the face means hiding one's identity for anti-social ends—dark glasses are worn when one wants to avoid revealing one's intentions—this custom is used equally by criminals, police, security agents and politicians. But, on the popular front, the bandana, and now the ski mask, has represented a symbol of insurgency, and it revitalizes and actualizes the indigenous concept of the loss of individuality of each in favor of the collective.... The ski mask thus acquires the value of an insignia, of a symbol wherein the subject ceases to be an individual and is reborn as a collective agent.[12]

Symbolically, this is concordant with the collectivist rhetoric of the Zapatistas: "Everything for everyone, nothing for us." The mask brings about a metamorphosis from collective silence to collective insurgency.

"The Long Journey from Despair to Hope" is a long, rolling communiqué written in sections with Cervantean epigraphs and titles like "Mexico, Between the Dream, the Nightmare and the Awakening," and "The Women: Double Dream, Double Nightmare, Double Awakening." The communiqué opens with a poem by Paul Eluard, French surrealist, communist, populist, and emblematic poet of the French anti-Nazi resistance. Again, by invoking Eluard, Marcos aligns the Zapatista struggle with twentieth-century struggles against totalitarianism. By turning to Europe, Marcos invokes a modern history, solicits the support of a European modernism, and communicates that, though this is a local, indigenous, Mexican struggle, it is also part of the larger history of global struggle against silencing regimes. Before Eluard's words, apparently translated from French by Marcos, is a dedication to a fellow combatant:

> To señor Ik', Tzeltal prince, founder of the CCRI-CG of the EZLN, fallen in the battle of Ocosingo, Chiapas, January 1994 (wherever he is…)

Señor Ik' was the nom de guerre of one Francisco Gómez, also known as Comandante Hugo.[13] He was a Tzeltal from the *ejido* of La Sultana, one of many who died in the massacre at Ocosingo in the first days of the uprising. Bearing the name of the god who brought fire to the sky, the blackest and ugliest of the gods, Señor Ik' himself becomes a symbol of those who have died in order to live. In death, Señor Ik', a.k.a. Comandante Hugo, once again becomes Francisco Gómez, when his name is immortalized as the name of the autonomous municipality in his home territory.

The Mask and the Mirror

The ski masks figure in many communiqués, giving life to the symbol in all of its dimensions, from the pragmatic to the mythic to the comic. In one account, from an early communiqué dated January 20, 1994, Marcos offers a slap in the face to civil society for its failure to see beneath the culture of masks:

Epilogue: "About ski masks and other face masks"[14]

Why all the scandal about the ski mask? Isn't Mexican political culture a "culture of covered faces?" But, to end the growing agony of some who fear (or wish) that some "Kamarrada"[15] or Boogie el Aceitoso[16] is the one who, in the end, is behind the ski mask and the "pronounced nose" (as *La Jornada* calls it) of the "Sup" (as the *compañeros* call me) I propose the following: I am willing to take off the ski mask if Mexican society takes off the mask that foreign desires have already been imposing for many years. What would happen? The predictable: Mexican civil society (excluding the Zapatistas, because they know it perfectly well in image, thought, and deed) would realize, not without disillusionment, that "Sup Marcos" is not a foreigner and that he is not as handsome as he was purported to be by the public record of the Attorney General's office. But not only that, by taking off its own mask, Mexican civil society will realize, with a stronger impact, that the image it has sold itself is a forgery, and that reality is far more terrifying than it thought. Each of us will show our faces, but the big difference will be that "Sup Marcos" has always known what his real face looked like, and civil society will just wake up from a long and tired sleep that "modernity" has imposed at the cost of everything and everyone. "Sup Marcos" is ready to take off the ski mask. Is Mexican civil society ready to take off its mask? Don't miss the next episode of this story of masks and faces that reaffirm and deny themselves (if the airplanes, helicopters, and olive-drab masks allow it).

Marcos refers to a political culture in which the intentions of the actors are constantly hidden behind the veneer of "popular will" or "the good of the people," where elections are held every six years and every six years the PRI—the party that had been in power since 1932—wins; where nationalism and patriotism are operative words while the economic structure of the nation is underwritten by the World Bank and the International Monetary Fund, Chase Manhattan and Georgia Pacific; where a U.S.-sanctioned and funded War on Drugs is fought in the press while the real drug lords dominate entire communities and pass with impunity through the halls of power. A nation implementing "vast democratic reforms" while the national media is owned by the PRI, and whose population suffers from a rate of poverty and illiteracy higher than it was in 1968, and a nation which prides itself on its indigenous heritage while systematically destroying the native cultures which form its fundament. Political scandals have wracked Mexican society in recent years and throughout its history, to the extent that a profound crisis of confidence exists in the nation, and corruption is taken as a given. Events such as the 1988 presidential elections, when the power went out in Mexico City with progressive Cuauhtemoc Cardenas in the lead for president and then came back on to find the PRI candidate Carlos Salinas de Gortari ahead by a landslide, and the disappearance of relief money after the catastrophic 1985 earthquake, caused widespread protests and rioting throughout the country. The notorious corruption of the police force and common knowledge that torture, bribery, and extortion are semi-official practices, while each party claims honesty and the government espouses its democratic reforms, all lead to the charge that this is a "culture of masks."

In referring to the culture of masks, Marcos harks back to one of the seminal texts of the critical life of modern Mexico. *The Labyrinth of Solitude: Life and Thought in Mexico,* written by Octavio Paz in the late 1940s, is an examination of some of the central myths of modern Mexico, a kind of psychoanalysis of the Mexican national character. Paz looks at the indigenous roots of modern Mexico and examines the mestizo society that has grown out of these roots. He takes as a point of departure the sophistication of the pre-Colombian cultures, and their survival in contemporary cultural forms: "Any contact with the Mexican people, however brief, reveals that the ancient beliefs and customs are still in existence beneath Western forms."[17] This is now a commonplace, as we have seen, though its implications for public policy are still violently contested.

In an entire chapter devoted to "the culture of masks," Paz refers to the "harsh solitude" lived by each Mexican behind a mask of machismo or deference to authority. In a sort of high literary style indicative of the era, infused with a psychoanalytic passion, Paz suggests that the Mexican character is one of deception, dissimulation: "The Mexican, whether young or old, *criollo* or mestizo, general or laborer or lawyer, seems to me to be a person who shuts himself away to protect himself; his face is a mask and so is his smile."[18]

Paz's critique is personal, suggesting that the Mexican character is one of deception, even self-deception, which expresses itself on an individual level. In keeping with psychoanalysis, Paz addresses a national trait as a kind of personality disorder, in what must have been an outrageous statement at the time. "His face is a mask and so is his smile." Paz paints the national character as suspicious, guarded, and distrustful.

Marcos gives his *paisanos* more credit, launching his critique specifically at the political culture. It is not the individual who is guilty of deception, but rather a political culture that feigns democracy while robbing the ballot box[19] and poses alongside a portrait of Zapata while writing Zapata's most important contribution to Mexican politics, Article 27 (based directly on Zapata's Plan de Ayala*)*, out of the Constitution.[20] For Marcos "the Mexican character" is not to blame, but "civil society," which has deceived itself with images of modernity and democracy: "Mexican civil society will realize, with a stronger impact, that the image it has sold itself is a forgery, and that reality is far more terrifying than it thought."

Searching for the roots of this "culture of masks," Paz takes a look at what he imagines to be the indigenous character, and he defines something like a tendency to disappear into the background, to *become* the background even:

> The Indian blends into the landscape until he is an indistinguishable part of the white wall against which he leans at twilight, of the dark earth on which he stretches out to rest at midday, of the silence that surrounds him. He disguises his human singularity to such an extent that he finally annihilates it and turns into a stone, a tree, a wall, silence and space.[21]

Paz paints a portrait of the indigenous character *as perceived* by the mestizo, and particularly an elite mestizo, in 1950—the year *The Labyrinth of Solitude* was first published. But the image here may be more a part of the problem—the pejorative, not to say racist, mestizo perspective on the indigenous tendency to "turn into a stone, a tree, a wall"—than it is any kind of profound or empathetic or learned understanding of cultural characteristics. At the same time, it is a demonstration of the perceived facelessness of the indigenous culture—"The Indian blends into the landscape"—that gives rise to the need of "the Indian" to rise up behind the magical insignia of the mask in order to be recognized. It is this facelessness—and the racist neglect that accompanies it—which gives rise to the "Enough already!" of the Zapatistas.

At the same time, this apparent ability to disappear as an individual—to "disguise his human singularity"—is a trait that transcends diverse native cultures, at least *as perceived from outside*. As well, it is a trait that can serve, perhaps, as a form of protection. Within a milieu of ongoing insurrection, whether in a phase of passive resistance or of armed uprising, a veil of anonymity—the ability to be mistaken for any of the countless others of your kind, class, or color—has its purposes. It is this "facelessness," this "loss of individuality" which allows the "enchanted" army of masked, uniformed warriors to come into existence and to draw the curiosity of the entire world. Paz's reductionist—not to say profoundly ignorant—interpretation of the indigenous character has as its flipside the truly transcendent cultural characteristics embodied by indigenous mass movements when they demand to be recognized collectively, through collective land rights (the right to territory), collective human rights (the right to have legal norms applied to peoples, not just to people), and collective cultural rights (the right to maintain and protect sacred sites, cultural artifacts, languages, and religious practices). The Zapatista warrior dies in order to live in the collective memory; he hides his face in order to be recognized as a people. He puts on his ski mask, picks up his wooden gun, stands out from "the white wall against which he leans at twilight" and says, "*Aqui estamos. Resistimos*"—"We are here. We resist."

Addressing the delicate question of the breaking of stereotypes within which they have been cast for centuries, Marcos (consciously identifying himself as a mestizo, as apart from the native army he serves), says of his Zapatista *compañeros*:

> They are indigenous rebels. As rebels, they break the traditional scheme that, first from Europe and then from all of those who

> dress in the color of money, was imposed on them as a way to see themselves and be seen by others.
>
> It's like this that the "diabolic" image of people who sacrifice humans to please the gods doesn't fit them comfortably, nor does that of the indigent Indian with hands outstretched begging for charity from those who have everything, nor that of the noble savage perverted by modernity, nor that of the infant who makes adults laugh by babbling, nor that of the submissive peon of all the haciendas that scar the history of Mexico, nor that of the skilled artisan whose products adorn the walls of the same people who disdain him, nor that of the ignoramous who shouldn't venture opinions about anything further than the nearest geographical horizon, nor that of one who fears gods both celestial and earthly.[22]

And it's like this that, donning his mask in order to be seen, the Zapatista rebel fails to be comfortable blending into the landscape until he is an indistinguishable part of the white wall against which he leans at twilight.

We Who Have Died in Order to Live

A crucial moment in the drama of the ski masks comes during the National Democratic Convention at the first Aguascalientes of Guadalupe Tepeyac in August 1994, when Marcos, speaking before a crowd of hundreds of Mexican intellectuals, students, professionals, *campesinos,* and left-of-center politicians, offers to remove his mask. Carlos Monsivais describes the moment:

> "If you want, I'll take it off right now. You tell me." And the crowd, happy beneath the sun, unites: "NO! Don't take it off! NO!" The scene is marvelous in its metaphorical confirmation. Marcos without the ski mask is not admissible, is not photographable, is not the living legend. The mood and the symbol melt beneath the patriotic inhalation.[23]

Marcos commented early on that one function of the masks was to "prevent *caudillismo*"—a word that translates as something like "bossism." The mask serves to equalize, to unite all in the struggle as one. That sacrificial ethic is at work: "we are those who have died in order to live."

With the notion of sacrifice in mind, of the surrender of the individual life for the life of the community, we'll look at another tale in which Marcos, through the character of Old Antonio, narrates a second symbolic history of the ski masks. This one, like the previous stories, is a tale of the first gods and the creation of the world; and like the previous stories, it draws a direct link between a primordial ethics represented by the gods and the myth of the world's origin, and the Zapatistas' contemporary struggle for social justice.

The Story of the Night and the Stars[24]

Many nights ago everything was night. The sky was an enormous ceiling of shadow and sad was the song of the men and women. The gods were hurt by the sad singing of men and women, and they got together to make an agreement. The gods always got together to come to an agreement to do work, and so our elders learned and so we ourselves learned. We learned to get together to make agreements on how to work. The gods made an agreement to get rid of the ceiling of night, so that the light that was above would fall over the men and women so that their song would not be so sad. And they got rid of the whole ceiling of night and all the light, which was a lot, came down, because the night was long and covered everything from the river to the mountains and there was very much light which had been held back by the enormous roof of the night. The men and women were blinded by so much light and the eyes never rested, and besides they worked all the time because it was always light. And the men and women complained because so much light did them harm, because they were bat men and women. And the gods realized that they had made a mistake, because they were gods, but they weren't stupid and they understood enough to see that their agreement had been bad and they got together again and came to a new agreement to put back the night sky while they came to a new agreement. And they delayed in making the agreement and the long night went on and on and it was then that the men and women of the bat learned to walk by night, without light, because the gods took a very long time in resolving the problem of the great ceiling of night. And then after the gods finished making their agreement they went to the place where the men and women were and they asked for volunteers to resolve the problem. And the gods said that the volunteers would be bits of light that they would sprinkle in the ceiling of the night so that the night wouldn't be so long. "You will be stars," said the gods. And they wanted to be stars and they no longer wanted to be men and women and everyone was made into stars and they splashed the whole ceiling of the long night and now there remained not even a little piece of the ceiling of night and everything was light again and the problem was not resolved. No, it was worse because now they had torn the great roof off the night and there was no way to cover the light that entered from all sides. And the gods didn't realize because they were sleeping very happily after they had resolved the problem and so they felt fine and so they slept.

And then the men and women of the bat had to resolve their problems themselves, the problems that they themselves had made. And then they made like the gods and they got together to make an agreement and they saw that it doesn't work if everyone wants to be stars, that if some are going to shine, others have to put out their light. And so began a great discussion because nobody wanted to put out their light, everyone wanted to be a star. But then the true men and women, those with a heart the color of earth, because corn comes from the earth, said that they would put out their light, and so they did, and like this the night stayed as it is, the night, because there was darkness and there was light, and so the stars could shine because there was darkness to shine against—if not, we would still be blind. And the gods woke up and they saw that it was night and there were stars and that the world was beautiful like this, how they had made it, and they left, and they believed that they, the gods, had resolved the problem. Really, it was the men and women who came to a good agreement and who resolved it. But the gods were not aware because they were asleep and they slept thinking that they had fixed everything,

> poor little gods, who never knew how it came to be that the stars were truly born in the night sky that is the ceiling over the true men and women. And this is how the story goes: some have to put out their lights so that others shine, but those who shine do it for those who have no light. If it weren't like this, well, nobody would shine.

This tale appeared in early October 1994, during the EZLN's formal evaluation of the National Democratic Convention. A lot of questions were in the air about how to build a popular movement based on the common will of civil society and not on the commands of a handful of revolutionaries. The question of what it means to "*mandar obediciendo*," to lead by obeying, as Zapatista ethics obliged, became increasingly challenging as the EZLN became a force in national politics. Who would lead and who would follow? What sacrifices must be made, and by whom?

Although there is no direct reference to the masks, the visual symbolism of a light which goes dark to allow other lights to shine, echoing the image in the previous story of the god Ik' leaping into the fire invokes at once the image of the ski masks and the purpose they serve in obscuring the face and establishing the warrior persona.

Typical of the Old Antonio stories, this is a fable ending with a moral: "some have to put out their lights so that others shine, but those who shine do it for those who have no light. If it weren't like this, well, nobody would shine." Again we see the collectivist rhetoric of the Zapatistas invoked by the voice of the autochthonous gods. And again we see a representation of the indigenous mode of collective authority founded in ancient tradition.

As in "The Story of the Ski Masks," we are shown a vision of the gods coming together to make decisions, the same way the true men and women, guided by a spirit of collectivism, come together to make decisions. The repeated narration of the process of decision-making serves at least two functions. First, it counters the Mexican government's explicit and implicit claims that the indigenous people cannot govern themselves. This has been one of the foundations of the state's approach to indigenous cultures for hundreds of years, in Mexico as in the rest of the Americas, based on a racist perception of these cultures. This vision has justified, at worst, genocidal policies, and, at best, a sort of paternalism that masks itself as enlightened benevolence.

According to the paternalist view, indigenous peoples are incapable of self-determination, so when they rise in rebellion against the state and the landowners, they are naturally being manipulated by "outsiders." In this version of the story, these outsiders include Marcos and his mestizo companions—Mexicans, yes, but educated Mexicans from the north of the country—as well as Guatemalan and Nicaraguan *ex-guerilleros* who were initially assumed to be behind the uprising. While this assumption was quickly proved wrong, the Mexican national press continued to demonize foreigners, leading, by early 1998, to the summary expulsion of hundreds of international human rights observers, solidarity workers, and tourists. These outsiders were expelled from the country on charges ranging from "inciting rebellion" and "destabilizing Chiapas" to "establishing parallel authority within Mexican territory."[25] All of these charges, as much as they may have been upheld in the Mexican courts, carry the basic assumption that the indigenous communities, if not giving up their self-determination to the Mexican state, are giving it up to foreign visitors.

The second function of Marcos's narration of the traditional style of governing by consensus is to demonstrate that Zapatista ideology, while ringing of classic leftist dogma (Marxism/Maoism/Guevarism/ Bakuninism), is in fact largely informed by ancient collectivist notions belonging to the indigenous cultures themselves. It shows that not only are outsiders not "behind" the rebellion, the ideas central to the rebellion are not the Marxist ideas that have predicated many other Latin American insurgencies, from the Cuban Revolution to the Sandinistas to the Shining Path of Peru. They are native ideas. And in fact, these native ideas, mostly unacknowledged, often inform the ideologies of the outsiders who show up to "incite rebellion."

Indigenous modes of social organizing have long been taken into account by left social theorists, most famously by Marx and Engels, whose interest in the Iroquois confederacy is made explicit in Engels's *The Origins of Family, Private Property and the State*[26] and by Benjamin Franklin, Thomas Jefferson, and the other architects of early U.S. government, who borrowed the Iroquois political structure of a loose federation of states, independent but bound by similar laws, in forging the Declaration of Independence and the U.S. Constitution. The influence of native ideas on Jeffersonian democracy was not lost on Ricardo Flores Magón, one of the great voices of the first Mexican Revolution, as he faced trial in the United States for his international political activities.[27]

Flores Magón, an anarchist journalist of Mazatec heritage who tirelessly promoted resistance to the regime of Porfirio Díaz and who died in Leavenworth prison, grounded his ideas of national liberation as much in internationalist labor ideology as in the indigenous traditions of his native Oaxaca. "It is clear," Flores Magón said, "that the Mexican people are apt to arrive at communism, because they've practiced it, at least to an extent, for centuries."[28]

In *Magonismo y Movimiento Indigena en Mexico* (*Magonism and Indigenous Movements in Mexico*), the authors assert that:

> Numerous actions of the Partido Liberal Mexicano [the Mexican Liberal Party associated with Flores Magón] are intimately tied to the thought and the forms of struggle of the Indian peoples. In proclamations, circulars, articles, programs, and mobilizations, the indigenous claim is present, as is the reclaiming of communal forms of living as a possible organizing principal for a new Mexican society. The socialist ideal of the Magónists recognized representation by assembly, community work, and common ownership of land as ancient forms [of social organizing] of the Indian peoples, all of which represented a revolutionary alternative.[29]

It was also clear to Flores Magón that these traditions were not limited to the indigenous, but were the practice of mestizo *campesinos* as well: "the mestizo population, with the exception of the inhabitants of the large cities and some of the larger towns, enjoyed communal lands, forests, and waters, just like the indigenous. Mutual aid was the rule; houses were built collectively; money was almost unnecessary because there was barter."[30]

It has been suggested that Magónismo, the brand of native anarchism associated with him, and which was crucial to the gains of the Mexican Revolution of 1910, is the closest thing to the real ideology behind *Zapatismo.* In the new Zapatista geogaphy, in which established territorial boundaries are redrawn and municipalities are renamed, Ricardo Flores Magón figures, along with Che Guevara and Gandhi, as the name of a reclaimed Zapatista municipality.

Sustaining the notion of sacrifice, both fables of the ski masks point us toward pre-Columbian ritual. In *The Flayed God: The Mythology of Mesoamerica, Sacred texts and Images from Pre-Columbian Mexico and Central America*, Roberta and Peter Markman discuss Aztec death masks and their relation with sacrificial rituals: "At Tlatilco," they write, "ritual masks appear often in burials, perhaps suggesting a conceptual relationship between ritual and funerary masks, a relationship that might well have been derived from the idea that the deceased was involved in the ritual movement from one state to another in a way very similar to the comparable movement of the shaman, whose 'death' enabled him to travel to the world of the spirit."[31]

From this analysis, we can draw a connection between the death masks of the Mexicas (one of the groups within the Aztec nation at the time of conquest) and the notion of the Zapatistas as "the dead of forever who have died in order to live." In the quest to understand the indigenous roots of the current revolution and ongoing political crisis, we must appreciate the fact that, in every previous Mayan rebellion against Spanish, British, French and U.S. imperialists, features of traditional Mayan religion have been evident. Among its other meanings, the ritual use of ski masks is a resurgence, in a new form, of the funeral masks worn by the ancient Mayan priest "whose 'death' enabled him to travel to the world of the spirit." The individual dies and is reborn in the collective. She puts out her light in order that others may shine.

The Markmans' discussion of the use of masks carries things even further into the realm of the metaphysical:

> The practice of ritual masking carries with it certain fundamental mythic assumptions. Wherever and whenever the ritual mask is worn, it symbolizes not only particular gods, demons, animal companions, or spiritual states but also a particular relationship between matter and spirit, the natural and supernatural, the vis-

> ible and the invisible. The mask, a lifeless, material thing, is animated by the wearer, and this is, of course, precisely the relationship between men and the gods—human beings are created from lifeless matter by the animating force of the divine, and their life can continue only as long as it is supported by that divine force.[32]

The Markmans draw further connections between funerary masks and the mask donned by a priest to invoke the presence of a particular god of the ancient Mexicas, Xipe Totec, "Our Lord the Flayed One:"

> Very late in the period of the village cultures in the nearby Valley of Teotihuacan, at about the same time that the first evidence of the construction of the monumental architecture characteristic of the later high civilization is apparent, there begin to appear curious figurines with absolutely smooth, featureless faces containing three indentations, one defining a mouth and the others two eyes. These faces are often ringed with a band and at times have another band stretched across the forehead, giving the impression of a mask, and in this case a very particular mask. Anyone familiar with the later art of the high cultures of central Mexico will see immediately in these figurines the portrayal of a ritual performer wearing what was known among the Aztecs as the mask of Xipe Totec, Our Lord the Flayed One, a "mask" that was the skin flayed from a sacrificial victim, then donned and pulled taught by the living performer, whose eyes and lips, in later representations, can be seen through the slits in the skin that had earlier revealed the eyes and mouth of the still-living victim.[33]

Although the mask of Xipe Totec has a graphic brutality not quite achieved by the ski masks, it is easy to see in this image distant echoes of the Zapatista rhetoric of sacrifice, "the already dead who have died in order to live." As if in some form of historical return, the masks described as "absolutely smooth, featureless faces containing three indentations, one defining a mouth and the others two eyes" bears an uncanny resemblance to the image of the ski mask. In this gruesome depiction of a ritual death mask made of the stretched skin of a sacrificial victim, we can see an echo of the sacrifice of Ik', the god who dives into the fire to become the sun. In thinking about ancient sacrificial rituals, as strange and difficult to comprehend as they may be to us, we can find some mythic sense when we recall "The Story of the Night and the Stars."

Questions of sacrifice are undoubtedly quite different for the Mayan people and for the Mexicas, who had divergent cultural practices. But they are more distinct, still, for occidental cultures, for whom the will of the individual comes almost unquestionably before the good of the community, and for whom social harmony does not depend on any sort of sacred understanding of history, time, social relations, or the natural world. Mythologists have demonstrated that a common thread running through Mayan stories of the creation of the world is the understanding that after the gods created life, it became the responsibility of humans to maintain it. By undergoing ritual sacrifice, a covenant is established between the natural world of humans and the supernatural world of the divine, which maintains social and natural equilibrium and gives meaning to human actions. Without a sense of the sacred—an attentiveness to and respect for the supernatural—there is a distinct absence of a sense of the related notion of sacrifice.

This sense of sacrifice, as we've seen, lies at the heart of the Zapatista worldview. In the case of the Zapatistas, it would be difficult to claim that the divine element, while it is drawn out in these creation stories and used by Marcos as a rhetorical strategy, is absolutely central. Still, the combined logic of dialectical materialism—the historical cycles of power and loss which are undoubtedly present in Marcos's thinking—with the earth-based spirituality of an agricultural society—show that meaning is ultimately constructed through human action. And this human action, to a greater or lesser degree, whether a simple act of daily toil or an extraordinary act of bravery in warfare, is analogous to the ancient Mayan notion of sacrifice.

Sacrifice of the individual will for the collective good is, of course, not unique to emancipation struggles; indeed, it is a salient feature of fascism as well. The distinction lies, perhaps, in the ends toward which the collectivity is guided—whether toward emancipation or toward domination—and in the particular ethics that drive the movement overall. While a collective or mass driven toward ends of domination might practice an ethic that sanctions torture and brutality, a collective driven toward liberation, and whose tactics are coherent with its goals, will eschew violence to the extent possible while pursuing the path toward the greater good.

We Are the Dead of Forever

In "Culture of Terror, Space of Death," Michael Taussig suggests that "the space of death" produced by terror is precisely the terrain where terror becomes most bold: "This space of death is preeminently a space of transformation: through the experience of coming close to death there may well be a more vivid sense of life; through fear there can come not only a growth in self-consciousness but also fragmentation of self conforming to authority."[34]

When the Zapatistas tell us "we are the dead of forever, who have died in order to live," they are invoking the ancestors, speaking through the voice of the ancestors, or letting the ancestors speak through them. They are also warning us that death for them is not the place where they end but the place where they begin. The dead are not only the grandfathers and grandmothers, the Old Antonios and Emiliano Zapatas, but also the *compañeros* who die in prison or in battle day by day, and the children who die of malnutrition and diarrheal disease. And they are warning us that terror, the terror of death, has become so commonplace that they have transcended it. They have transformed terror into resistance.

The ritual ski mask invokes the space of death—invokes death itself and admits the dead into *our* world, the world of the living. It is also in this space where the Zapatistas' war is fought, and where the poetics of death and the poetics of resistance gain their power. From the beginning, the Zapatista army had little hope of military victory; Marcos and other military leaders of the January 1 uprising have admitted that they saw their mission as almost suicidal. But what they lack in might and in arms they account for in strength of words and tactics: the armaments that add up to what we might call the magic war, where the spirit, which cannot be killed, may emerge victorious over mere bullets. By entering upon a suicidal mission, the space of death is evoked and terror is transformed from something paralyzing to something catalyzing, a force which propels action.

Taussig writes of "the history of terror and atrocity ... wherein the intimate codependence of truth on illusion and myth on reality was what the metabolism of power, let alone 'truth,' was all about." A war between very different cultural factions involves the manufacture of beliefs about or prejudices toward the enemy. The Spanish Catholics at the time of the conquest promoted the belief that the indigenous people were "savage heathens" and "bloodthirsty cannibals." The few soldiers, mercenaries, missionaries, and traders who first made the journey from Spain perceived the inhabitants of New Spain as "savages" and sold that belief to the Crown and all of Europe. This belief allowed for the inhuman treatment, the tortures, massacres, and slave economy that formed the base of early colonization. Similar beliefs continue to justify the theft of lands, cultural traditions, "intellectual property," and "genetic resources" to this day. Undoubtedly, European perceptions of the indigenous cultures were tied to horrific tales of human sacrifice, nudity, and godlessness as much as to economic necessity (the quest for gold and spices, etc.), which justified slaughter.

For their part, the indigenous have their own beliefs about the Spaniards. In the township of San Juan Chamula in the highlands of Chiapas, for example, it is said that the Spaniard is the product of the fornication of an Indian and a dog.[35] Throughout villages in Chiapas there is a belief that "gringos"—meaning specifically U.S. Americans—eat human children. With or without television, in remote areas of southeastern Mexico it would be difficult to learn otherwise but that rich white foreigners from the North are, occasionally, also bloodthirsty cannibals. And indeed, a caricature of the gringo cosmovision—the relentless consumption of the natural resource base without regard for the needs of future generations—could be viewed, metaphorically, as a kind of cannibalism. The literalizing of these kinds of beliefs grows out of "the history of terror and atrocity"—a natural fear of outsiders which may take on fantastic proportions, but which is based on a very real history. These kinds of beliefs, on both sides, generate power to dominate or to resist.

At the same time, this is how the state and corporate powers fight *their* "magic war"—by using the media apparatus in such a way that ideological beliefs based on versions of history—"myths" —are perceived as realities. Like a few hundred Spanish adventurers and priests proliferating the image of the first Americans as "ignorant savages" in the sixteenth century, a few corporate media outlets can portray them as terrorists at the end of the twentieth century and these images will tend to take hold in the popular imagination. Lacking faith in the Catholic God, the indigenous were "heathens." Looked at through the lens of a culture founded on material excess and a political economy built on industrial production and thriving on values of "growth" and "progress," the indigenous communities of Chiapas, made up largely of subsistence farmers and day laborers, are "backwards." But the occidental approach, from a native perspective, is equally backwards.

Paula Gunn Allen, a native writer with her roots in Laguna Pueblo, speaks from the U.S. side of the fence when she writes, "Native Americans are entirely concerned with relations to and among the physical and nonphysical and various planetary energy-intelligences of numerous sorts. The idea of expending life-force in oppression and resistance strikes most Indians, even today, as distinctly weird."[36]

But this idea, "distinctly weird" as it is, has achieved dominance in Mexico as it has in the United States and other neo-colonial New World nations. The ideology of progress, expansion, growth, and mastery of the natural world that gives rise to the oppression of which Allen speaks is enforced and reinforced in advertising and education, movies and television, news and entertainment.

In invoking the terror that has become part and parcel of native identities, the turn of phrase, "we are the dead of forever who have died in order to live," has had resonance far beyond the mountains of southeastern Mexico. Other native resistance movements in the Americas have taken up the poetic outfitting of *Zapatismo* and in turn made it their own. Colombian organizer and activist Manuel Rozental, who works closely with *la Minga Indigena*, Colombia's native uprising, says, "When the Zapatistas said 'we cover our faces in order to be seen, we die in order to live,' we took this and we developed the saying, 'We wear our chains in order to be free.' In 2008, we held a march and we put on chains to symbolize our struggle for liberty, and we carried this saying with us to show our suffering, to make it visible."[37]

The Mask of the Other

A final aspect of the masks, important to their poetic and their function as propaganda, is their ability to conjure a sort of "radical otherness." As Octavio Paz poignantly described, "The Indian blends into the landscape until he is an indistinguishable part of the white wall against which he leans at twilight, of the dark earth on which he stretches out to rest at midday, of the silence that surrounds him." Like Ralph Ellison's Invisible Man, he is dismissed because of his otherness, arriving at a point where he must disappear in order to be seen. This is where the ski mask comes to signify the very identity of the "other," the subaltern, the darkness of mystery, "the dark earth" that is a trope for everything indigenous, everything native, everything non-European.

The mask became the symbol of all of those whose identities are dismissed by the dominant culture. Anonymity, facelessness, is claimed with a ferocity and an intelligence that turns it from a deficiency into a source of power and a threat. In a classic *detournement,* the ski mask becomes the symbol of the underclass—the social majorities—rising up to confront the dominant power structure.[38] For the Mexican neoliberal establishment and the international powers supporting it, the mask invokes a terrifying vision, a sort of Frankenstein's monster confronting his creator: "You made me what I am. Now look at me!"

The Zapatistas are defined and define themselves repeatedly as "*Los hombres sin rostro*"*:* the men without faces. By covering their faces, they have claimed their status as *other*, as the invisible. By giving themselves the distinguishing characteristic of the mask of the bandit, the mask of ritual sacrifice, they establish a subject-position from which they can speak with authority. By establishing a collective identity, the wearer of the ski mask achieves, perhaps, one of the main symbolic victories of subaltern rebellion: she disdains and dismisses the class which had previously disdained and dismissed her. She is no longer the other.

In *The Conquest of America: The Question of The Other*, Tzvetan Todorov examines what he calls "the semiotics" of conquest and colonization, specifically examining the relations that Columbus, Cortés, Diego Durán, and Bernardino de Sahagún sustained with the indigenous "other" during the first encounters in the New World, and takes these relations as models for the subsequent development of relations between the colonizers and the colonized. He examines ways in which indigenous culture was given an identity—the delineation of "specific features of the Indian society"—in order to more easily subvert and dominate it, or, put less gently, to justify its genocidal destruction. He cites the Spanish conquistador Ginés de Sepúlveda:

> Concerning the kingdom and the king's duties, the greatest philosophers declare that such wars may be undertaken by a very civilized nation against uncivilized people who are more barbarous than can be imagined, for they are absolutely lacking in any knowledge of letters, do not know the use of money, generally go about naked, even the women, and carry burdens on their shoulders and backs like beasts for great distances.[39]

The indigenous culture is defined by its lack of "occidental values." In other words, it is defined by an *absence* of specific features—clothes, money, writing, beasts of burden, and Christian ritual—rather than by an active *presence* of constituted characteristics. For the next five hundred years, as the indigenous cultures are destroyed or assimilated, they are given value, either positive or negative, only in terms of "absence." They are defined not by what they are, but by what they lack from the perspective of Catholic, occidental culture. The great argument, pursued by the first Bishop of Chiapas, Bartolomé de las Casas, is whether or not the Indians have a soul. With the absence of a soul they are, of course, not human, and are treated as beasts to be enslaved for gain, raped for sport, and tortured and killed for fun. It is not until the 1950s that indigenous people are allowed to walk the same streets as ladinos in San Cristóbal de las Casas. By understanding the terms of this absence and inverting its sign, the Zapatistas subvert the entire relationship by asserting their *presence*. There is something of the damned in the image presented by the masks, something of the undead. The ski mask, while playing on the trope of absence, of the disappearance of the individual, of the mysterious terrestrial darkness of the unknown other, becomes the established symbol of mass presence. *Aqui estamos,* they say. *Resistimos.*

The Other as Icon: Little Dolls Bearing Little Guns

Small armies are gathered in the wide doorways along Real de Guadalupe and Avenida Insurgentes in San Cristóbal de las Casas. They are dolls of the rebel forces dressed in wool coats and ski masks, carrying little wooden rifles, each with the trademark red bandana of the Zapatistas around its neck. Some sit astride horses, others are gathered in trucks as if heading into battle; still others hang delicately from key chains and hair ribbons. The women and girls sitting among these armies call out to every passerby: "Buy a Zapatista!"

At the slightest sign of interest, the woman stands, flattening out her black wool skirt, and holds forth a handful of the dolls: "Buy one! This is Marcos," presenting one on a horse, "This is Tacho," presenting one with a hat. "This is Ramona," presenting one with a white blouse and skirt. "Buy one," she insists, "Anna Maria, David, Marcos," intoning the names of the Zapatista command. Ask her if she knows the Zapatistas and she might giggle and turn shy, looking away, but she will continue in her insistence—she works long and hard making these dolls from the scraps of clothes she weaves—"Buy one! Buy one!"

San Cristóbal is home to countless battalions of dolls, a monument to that New Year's Day when the Zapatistas flooded the town and tore apart the town hall. The Zapatista combatants have long since disappeared into their villages to tend their fields, to resume life under the threat of siege. But the dolls remain vigilant. Of course, there are plenty here who are not entirely in favor of the indigenous movement. The owners of the town, the bankers, the businesspeople are haunted by the dolls—to them these diminutive figures must be hobgoblin terrorists threatening the security of their investments. During the height of the conflict, federal police and intelligence agents were a constant presence here, looking beyond the dolls in search of the real actors in the struggle. But like the dolls, the Zapatistas are everywhere. There are more of them than can be counted, and they blend in with the fields they tend, working with a bent back over a hoe or sitting on the ground in a stall in the artisans' market, weaving. Of course the huge army presence, the Humvees and troop transports, the soldiers walking the streets with their guns, cause the rebels to blend in that much more. Hiding in plain sight, they are invisible because they are everywhere.

A phenomenon congruent with the ski masks, and representative of the vast presence of Zapatista supporters throughout Chiapas and throughout Mexico, these dolls invoke the presence of the Zapatista warriors themselves. But where the ski masks, as uniform, announce the identity of an actor who is truly present, and link her identity with the mass movement, the dolls, for their mysterious ubiquity and their nature as icons, serve to invoke *the magical presence* of the warriors. I'll explain:

In terms of military strategy, after the first week of January 1994, the Zapatistas never have the upper hand. Although their local popular support is estimated in the tens of thousands, the number of *insurgentes*—the guerillas with guns and ski masks living in the mountains with the potential to carry out a consistent military campaign against the government forces—are estimated at between 300 and 1500 at most. They are poorly equipped, poorly fed, and forced to constantly adapt their strategy to changing conditions. In contrast, in 1994 the number of government troops in Chiapas is reckoned at 15,000, and they are well fed, well armed, and well trained, with air support and the assurance of a massive military aid package from the United States under the guise of the War on Drugs. And yet, after eleven days of armed struggle in early 1994, the EZLN managed, in the words of border artist Guillermo Gómez-Peña, "to determine the terms of the cease-fire, to force the government to sit and negotiate in their own territory, to introduce into the spectrum of Mexican political force a new vision of the future of the country, and above all, to create a new political mythology in a time when most political mythologies are bankrupt."[40]

By 1996, the number of troops rotated through Chiapas has increased to 45,000, and by early 1998 to 60,000—a full third of the Mexican army.[41] As Yvon Le Bot noted in late 1996, almost three years after the uprising, "Although it is probable that their capacity to mobilize to combat is much less than it was during the uprising, the Zapatistas might easily be prompted to new desperate actions."[42] The key word here is "desperate": four years into the uprising, while the Zapatistas had created a new political mythology, they had also been effectively quarantined in their communities, hostage to a low-intensity war that erupted into frequent fire fights and village occupations. They had conquered territory, but by 1998 they were largely confined to it, international attention notwithstanding.

Given their weakened strategic position, the war of symbols, the media war, the magic war, becomes that much more crucial. As the ski masks represent the historical otherness of the indigenous people, the dolls mark the historic ability of the Mayan people to defend themselves, and serve as a reminder that the struggle continues. Like the ski masks, the dolls are both symbolic and declarative. More than mere tokens, more even than icons, the dolls are magical warriors whose very presence invokes the possibility of revolution. *Swoosh.*

As you pass by this doorway in San Cristóbal and you see this bent over, tiny old woman holding up a handful of the dolls for you to purchase, she names them again, one by one: "This is Marcos! This is Maria! This is Tacho! This is Ramona!" The woman is insistent—*these are the real thing*, her voice demands, these are the people you read about in the papers, these are the heroes of the revolution. Does her urgency simply reflect her need to earn the five pesos you'll pay her for the doll, or is she doing a service to the revolution by exporting still another magical Zapatista warrior? One wonders about the trajectory of each doll after the tourist purchases it, making its way to New York, Paris, Barcelona, Rome. Is this a simple, totemic way of ensuring that the struggle lives, of spreading the revolution across the globe? Does the woman selling these dolls to the tourist from some northern country think of the life that her creation will take on in that country, of the chain of sympathetic events that may be loosed by the arrival of Zapatistas on the other shore of the Atlantic? In the manner of Hopi Kachinas, are these dolls magical, inhabited by spirits? In the manner of Guatemalan worry dolls, are the dolls vessels, servants, protectors? In the cyclical time inhabited by the Mayan people, the vivid, living history where the past and the future are one, and are never very distant from the present, do the dolls perhaps exist equally as reminders of the uprising and as warnings that another such uprising is perpetually imminent?[43]

Of course, such appreciation of the dolls would appear to be sorely compromised by the fact that they are for sale. Further, there exists the profound irony that, according to local lore, many of the women who make and sell Zapatista dolls are from the village of San Juan Chamula, an entrenched enclave of *PRIistas*, beholden to a kind of adventurist capitalism, not at all friendly to Zapatistas or *Zapatismo*. The exploitation of the Zapatista fetish by the reactionary women of San Juan Chamula might be seen as a cynical commodification, the market coopting the Zapatista image. After all, what difference is there between marketing Marcos, marketing Che, and marketing, say, Coca-Cola?

But, from a fetishist or symbolic perspective it doesn't matter who sells the dolls. From a perspective beyond ideological concerns, the pittance of loose pesos that go to the Chamula weavers serve to allay the hunger of indigenous families barely subsisting in the market economy—no matter which side they are on. But more than that, the fact of their creation and proliferation—their mere presence—is, arguably, the implicit source of their power.

And then, returning from a "spiritualist" approach to an appreciation of the dolls based more in direct experience, there is the way in which the dolls uphold and stimulate native pride. A Tzotzil woman named Xunka' López Díaz, a Zapatista sympathizer, tells how she came to produce the dolls:

> In January 1994, when the Zapatistas came, my parents told me I couldn't go out. After a while I went, but I didn't sell my crafts in the park that day because I was afraid. The policemen told us we shouldn't be there. When I finally saw the Zapatistas, I was surprised to see they were indigenous like me. My girlfriends weren't afraid. They even went to talk with the Zapatistas. We decided

> to make dolls that were like the Zapatistas, and we sold them in the park. This is how we started to make Zapatista dolls, because we were impressed by these people. The dolls sell very well with the tourists.[44]

In a market where images of native people and native icons are perpetual tourist knick-knacks, diminishing with each sale the value of the living culture, here is an icon that not only represents the living culture, but represents it in its most ferocious and contemporary aspect. Rather than an image that portrays a misty-eyed vision of a mysteriously vanished culture, emptied of social power and political underpinning, the Zapatista doll is an image that says, yet again, "*Aqui estamos, resistimos.*" We are here, we resist.

Violence as Symbol

If the ski masks are symbolic of the twin mysteries of otherness and of death, and if the dolls represent, or actualize, these mysteries and their iconic presence in the living culture, then we begin to see a more complete picture of a war whose effect, fought by means both symbolic and material, occurs on more than merely an earthly plane. This of course is not new. Like all social technologies, war has its aspect of materiality and its aspect of symbolic effect, both being essential to its realization in practice. Beyond the daily struggle to construct autonomy in their villages, the battle fought in public by the Zapatistas is fought almost entirely with symbols, or icons. There is little "real violence" on the part of the EZLN, especially relative to the ground gained in public relations regionally and internationally. It might even be said that the violence itself takes on a largely symbolic quality, and that this quality of violence-as-symbol is what gives the Zapatistas an edge, morally, militarily and in terms of popular support, over the government forces.

Traveling back several hundred years, we can look at an instance of violence used in the first moments of conquest. By going back to the battles waged by Cortés (conqueror of the Valley of Mexico), by Diego de Mazarriegos (conqueror of Chiapas), and by Pédro de Alvarado (conqueror of Guatemala) against the indigenous, we can look at the currency of the responses. Coming from the "enchanted world" of the indigenous, we might be tempted to believe that a symbolic or "magical" violence is a quality engineered by the Indians. Looking at the following passage from Tzvetan Todorov, we see that this is not necessarily so:

> Throughout the campaign, Cortés shows a preference for spectacular actions, being very conscious of their symbolic value. For example, it is essential to win the first battle against the Indians; to destroy the idols during the first challenge to the priests, in order to demonstrate his invulnerability; to triumph during a first encounter between his brigantines and the Indian canoes; to burn a certain palace located within the city in order to show how irresistible his advance is; to climb to the top of a temple so that he may be seen by all....
>
> The very use Cortés makes of his weapons is of a symbolic rather than a practical nature. A catapult is constructed which turns out not to work; no matter: "Even if it were to have had no other effect, which indeed it had not, the terror it caused was so great that we thought the enemy might surrender."[45]

This use of "symbolic violence" becomes crucial to the Zapatistas in their response, five hundred years later, to the conquest. The ski masks give the Zapatista army a symbolic appearance as an "army of the other" and the dolls represent the ubiquity of the Zapatistas and give them unlimited presence, declaring their complete infiltration of the territory (whether or not this is, in fact, the case). The uprising itself, scheduled for the day of the coming-into-effect of NAFTA, "the death sentence for the indigenous people," has the effect of alerting the Mexican nation—and the Mexican people—to their complicity in the structural violence of poverty. The EZLN's occupation of several cities, the burning of land records, the attack on the Mexican military headquarters outside of San Cristóbal, the public reading of the First Declaration of the Lacandon Jungle (first in Tzotzil, recall, and then in Spanish), the liberation of prisoners from a state correctional facility, the takeover of several ranches in the highlands and the jungle, and the strategic destruction of roads and bridges to prevent reprisal: all was carried out over the course of two days by a force numbering less than 2,000, many of whom, for lack of real weapons, carried imitation rifles carved out of wood, giving them the symbolic and strategic presence of soldiers, though they were incapable of inflicting real violence of any sort.

Here, the wooden guns served the same purpose as the ill-made catapults of Cortés. The presence of armed Indians itself is enough to throw the power structure of Mexico into a panic. It is the gesture of violence, rather than the number of dead, that brought about an immediate response: the violence of the state apparatus followed, two weeks later, by a cease-fire and the establishment of negotiating teams; the international outcry for peace and human rights; the collapse of the peso and subsequent signal that Mexico, in the throws of its transformation into a "democratic," "first world" nation, was neither truly "democratic" nor truly "developed" (in the illusionary economic/humanist sense of the word where economic reform and political reform are reciprocal, "as if the status of the consumer were equivalent to that of the citizen"[46]). The movement of solidarity with the Zapatistas spread immediately from Chiapas to the universities in Mexico City to urban centers across the world. It is easy to imagine that, had their strategy been less symbolic and more truly violent, the movement would not have gained such immediate popularity.

Certainly, there was violence. The storming of the Rancho Nuevo military facility and the protracted battle of Ocosingo left uncounted tens or hundreds dead and wounded. To say that all of the violence that occurred in these weeks was on the part of the government forces reacting to the uprising would be false. The Zapatistas planned and carried out violent actions and engaged in battle in several cities. However, these acts of violence, extremely limited in scope (in accordance with the available armaments) served intentionally and specifically as a wake-up call to civil society and as a symbolic action that served to foreground the subsequent non-violence and the deference to civil society to resolve the conflict. Even detractors of the Zapatista cause make note of the fact that they have never caused harm to civilians. In *El Sueño Zapatista,* Yvon Le Bot writes:

> The force of the Zapatistas is rooted in nonviolence; their originality resides in the new relation between violence and nonviolence.

> The problem consists in maintaining this tension without becoming absorbed in violence. The growth of a contained and repressed violence over the course of decades, or centuries, announces itself in a strategy of armed nonviolence in the service of the production of meaning, of a symbolic and political invention.[47]

It is in this tension "between violence and nonviolence" where we find the symbolic significance of the use of political violence by the Zapatistas. By displaying their willingness to die for the cause alongside their rhetoric of "peace and justice with dignity," their real weapons become largely symbolic of the struggle, inviting the sympathy of civil society for those who have been driven to desperate measures, and displaying at the same time the true nature of both institutional and revolutionary violence.

As a military force whose primary goal is to capture and defend territory, the EZLN's key role is to enact something akin to the kinds of direct action strategies that labor movement activists call "interventions at the point of production," such as sabotage, road blockages, and occupations. But winning the public relations victory necessary to maintain this territory requires additional intervention *at the point of assumption.*[48] U.S.-based organizer Patrick Reinsborough elucidates:

> Point-of-assumption actions operate in the realm of ideas and the goal is to expose pathological logic, cast doubt, and undermine existing loyalties. Successful direct action at the point of assumption identifies, isolates, and confronts the big lies that maintain the status quo. A worthy goal for these types of actions is to encourage the most important act that a concerned citizen can take in an era defined by systematic propaganda—*questioning!*[49]

It is in this sense that the Zapatistas' approach to military strategy partakes of questioning the very logic behind militant action. Part of the symbolic aspect to their use of arms rests in their declaration, "We are soldiers so that after us no one will have to be soldiers."

The sudden appearance of a new guerilla army, the EPR—the Popular Revolutionary Army—in the summer of 1996, threw this tension between violence and nonviolence into even greater relief. At a time when the Zapatistas were pursuing a strategy of peaceful negotiations—and even considering a transformation into a civil political force—the violent eruption of the EPR throughout Guerrero, Oaxaca, and the Huasteca border between Hidalgo and Veracruz made the Zapatistas look even more like "the good guys." A contentious public exchange between Marcos and the EPR highlighted the differences between the two rebel groups, even brooking the subject of whether or not poetry was a proper vehicle for revolution. When the EPR, following the strict Marxist/Leninist line, accused Marcos and the Zapatistas of a soft approach, as voiced in the flowery language of the communiqués, the Sup referred to the Salvadoran poet and martyr Roqué Dalton, whose revolutionary credentials are without question. In a letter to the EPR leadership, Marcos shot back:

> When Roqué Dalton wrote that it was possible to arrive "at the revolution by way of poetry," the leaders of the El Salvadoran ERP planned the assassination of the guerilla poet for "being misguided" and an "enemy agent." Today the old "revolutionary" leadership of the ERP makes alliances with the criminal right wing of El Salvador, while from the tomb Roqué continues cursing Power and walking towards the revolution on the path of poetry. Is there any similarity here? It seems that, for being just a handful of poets, we've given plenty of problems to Power, no?[50]

Marcos is acutely aware of the tendency for leftist guerilla groups to revert to reactionary violence in order to keep a firm grip on power (however minimal that power may be), and his rhetoric consistently affirms the EZLN's goal of opening a space for democracy, pointing to an ideal future when the revolutionaries will lay down their weapons once and for all. In the meantime, however, armed struggle is the only road left open to them. In an echo of the famous quote of Mexican revolutionary Praxedis Guerrero, "better to die on your feet than live on your knees," the Zapatistas have said that they carry guns because they would prefer to be killed in public in a spectacle of violence for all to see than to die of gastrointestinal diseases in their remote jungle villages.

As always, there are historical echoes. Frantz Fanon, the Martinique-born psychologist, insurrectionist, and proponent of pan-African revolution whose book *The Wretched of the Earth* inspired generations of militancy against colonial oppression, argued that brutal violence, rather than enlightened civilization or the rule of law, was the defining characteristic of colonialism, thus revolutionary violence was an essential way to turn the tools of the colonist against him in the struggle for liberation. When Fanon died, the Martinican poet Aimé Césaire eulogized his former student, writing, "His violence, and this is not paradoxical, was that of the non-violent. By this I mean the violence of justice, of purity and intransigence. This must be understood about him: his revolt was ethical and his endeavor generous."[51]

Marcos, having largely renounced violence as an effective strategy following the initial uprising, cannot be said to be an adherent of Fanon's particular revolutionary legacy, though Cesaire's words certainly apply. What Roqué Dalton, Aimé Césaire, and Subcomandante Marcos have in common is not only the belief that one can arrive at the revolution by way of poetry, but that the poetry of words must, at times, be accompanied by a poetics of action in the form of tactical violence: the liberatory word accompanied by the fire of arms, the fire lending weight and tactical primacy to the word.

In *Witness to War*, Charles Clements, a Vietnam vet who left the front disgusted and later worked as a physician in rebel territory in El Salvador in the 1980s, reports the words of one Salvadoran:

> You gringos are always worried about violence done with machine guns and machetes. But there is another kind of violence that you must be aware of too.... To watch your children die of sickness and hunger while you can do nothing is a violence to the spirit. We have suffered that silently for too many years. Why aren't you gringos concerned about that kind of violence?[52]

The Zapatistas ask the same question. Having seen the failure on the part of most outsiders to understand the violence of poverty and cultural destruction—the neglect and silent oppression which are forms of violence as intolerable as open combat—they choose combat. To be clear, they choose combat both for its tactical ends—to fight is the only option—and for the spectacle, the attention it wins them. (Combat, too, it might be suggested, is a form of public relations.) When they raise their weapons in defense against the torture of hunger they reveal the nature of institutional violence and state terror, announcing time and again that they are not the purveyors of violence, but the victims of violence who have been driven to this pass by necessity.

In fact, the bearing of arms by the Zapatistas carries with it the very real risk that, aside from attracting the attention of the media, they invite invasion, occupation, and obliteration. As Marcos has said, "Our army is very different from others, because its proposal is to cease being an army. A soldier is an absurd person who has to resort to arms in order to convince others, and in that sense the movement has no future if its future is military. If the EZLN perpetuates itself as an armed military structure, it is headed for failure."[53]

In the same interview, Marcos continues: "The EZLN has reached a point where it has been overtaken by *Zapatismo*. The 'E' in the acronym has shrunk, its hands have been tied, so that for us it is no handicap to mobilize unarmed, but rather in a certain sense a relief. The gun-belt weighs less than before and the military paraphernalia an armed group necessarily wears when it enters dialogue with people also feels less heavy."[54]

Armed Diplomacy

In Elia Kazan's classic movie *Viva Zapata!*, (incidentally written by John Steinbeck, that great literary defender of the poor and landless), Marlon Brando plays the wily and untrusting rebel, General Emiliano Zapata. The Liberating Army of the South has just achieved victory, and Zapata and his men are in the office of Francisco Madero, the new president of Mexico. Madero's officers remove the portrait of Porfirio Díaz, the hated dictator who has just fled the country. When Madero offers Zapata a piece of land—a sweeping green valley between two streams—as his reward for service to the *patria*, Zapata flies into a rage. He curses at Madero, "I did not fight for a ranch. The land I fought for was not for myself."

Madero tries to placate him, urging Zapata to stay calm, but he explodes, "What are you going to do about the land I *did* fight for?"

Madero tells him that it takes time, new laws must be made, justice must be upheld. Zapata tells him, "Tortillas are made from corn, not from time. We cannot eat time." But Madero insists. And he asks Zapata to disband his army, so that the new government can go to work.

But Zapata will not trust the new president until his people have gotten their lands back. He asks, "Who will enforce the laws once we have them?"

Madero answers, "The regular army, and police."

Zapata explodes again: "They are the ones we just fought and beat!"

He takes his rifle and aims it, point blank, at Madero, sitting behind his oak desk.

"Give me your watch," demands Zapata. "Give it to me!" he shouts again.

Madero hands it to him.

Zapata turns the gold pocket watch over in his free hand. "It's a beautiful watch. Expensive." He pauses. "Now take my rifle."

Zapata flips the rifle around and shoves it into Madero's hands. The gun is pointing at Zapata.

"Now you can have your watch back," he says. "But without the rifle, never."

The Zapatistas have said time and again that their goal is not to take state power but to "open a space for democracy." Many times they have extended an invitation to "global civil society" to meet, debate, and generate visions of "a world in which many worlds fit." They talk repeatedly of "walking by asking questions." Yet amid the question marks is a single exclamation point demanding that the questions be taken seriously: the fact that the Zapatistas carry guns, and do not put them down lightly.

In Mexico, as in much of Latin America, the spectacle of men with guns—even automatic weapons—is extremely common, though usually it is the police, the military, or the private security men hired to protect the banks, the McDonalds and Kentucky Fried Chickens, and the shopping malls. But peasants with guns? You see it less, but you certainly hear tell of it. Any time things turn especially bad for *el pueblo*, when the balance of power and the land base shifts too much into the hands of the few, students in universities and men in bars and cantinas begin to talk of "going to the mountains," of taking up arms to defend their collective rights. If there is anything "new" in the Zapatistas' use of armed propaganda, it is not in their handling of weapons so much as in their explanations of why they carry them, and the media by which this discourse travels.

Gustavo Esteva, a Mexican intellectual, was an adherent of Gandhian nonviolence in 1994 when the Zapatistas unleashed their shock wave of rebellion. Upon being asked to act as an advisor to the EZLN—a role he maintains to the present day—he rushed to reread Gandhi's ideas on the subject of violence:

> There is an interview with Gandhi and he talks with his son. There has been an attempt against Gandhi. And his son asks Gandhi, "Father, what should I do if there is a guy trying to kill you, comes against you and tries to kill you? Should I preach non-violence? Should I passively observe the situation? Or should I use my violence against him to stop the killing?"
>
> Gandhi smiled and said, "Well, the only thing you must *not* do is to do nothing, because if non-violence is the supreme virtue, to be cowardly is the worst of vices and you must not be a coward. You must do something. Passive resistance is not the best. Perhaps

> it is the only resource of the weak but the weak also have violence and they can use the violence as the last resource if they are the weak."
>
> "Non-violence is for the strong," said Gandhi. "It would be criminal if I preach non-violence to a mouse on the point of being devoured by a cat. If I am preaching non-violence to the Hindu it is because I don't see why 300 million people are afraid of 150,000 British. Because they are strong, they should use non-violence."[55]

Looking back at Gandhi's remarks to his son, Esteva says, "the same rule applies perfectly to the case of the Zapatistas. They clearly were the weak. They were dying like flies … but then they became the strong because of our support. When we had millions of people in the streets and great massive support, even international support, immediately they became the strong and they became the champions of nonviolence. This is one of the most paradoxical elements of the Zapatistas. They are an army that is the champion of nonviolence in Mexico."[56]

After the initial uprising, the EZLN adopted the strategy they call "offensive ceasefire," effectively practicing nonviolence in the midst of constant low-intensity conflict. They have not fired their weapons offensively since the eleven-day war in January 1994, when they first declared war on the Mexican state. Without doubt, since 1994, the red soil of Chiapas has seen many violent deaths, tens of thousands of internally displaced people, numerous massacres, several political assassinations, and countless disappeared, tortured, arrested, and expelled. There have been uncounted confrontations between Zapatista communities and military and paramilitaries, as well as, in the early days of 1994, a good deal of gunfire exchanged between the EZLN and the Mexican army (when the EZLN attacked the Rancho Nuevo military base outside of San Cristóbal to eliminate the military threat and liberate a cache of weapons; when soldiers bore down on EZLN insurgents in the Ocosingo marketplace for two days; and at scattered ranches throughout Chiapas when ranchers fought to defend their land against Zapatista occupancy). But even in those battles, most of the blood that ran was Zapatista blood, and if anything was proven it was that armed struggle could not be sustained, let alone emerge victorious on any significant scale. Only one incident—

a firefight in which EZLN troops allegedly returned government fire in the village of El Bosque in 1998—calls into question the EZLN's track record of offensive ceasefire in their fifteen years of public struggle.

This strategic nonviolence is not so much evidence of a pacifist ideology as it is a recognition that every shot fired at the Mexican military may be answered by massacre with impunity. This denouncement of arms, whether tactical or philosophical, is part of what has made the Zaptistas approachable, despite the EZLN being a military force. At the same time, their refusal to take a militant stand has left many supporters and allies disillusioned. When Mexican military police raided the city of Atenco in 2006, raping, beating, and jailing people with impunity, while Marcos was holed up in nearby Mexico City and declared a Red Alert in Zapatista Territory that effectively brought all public activity to a halt, the Mexican left awaited a militant response in vain. Soon after, when the city of Oaxaca was in flames as striking schoolteachers were violently repressed, resulting in several extrajudicial killings, including the unvindicated slaying of Brad Will, an American independent journalist, the EZLN maintained their cease-fire.

Of course, this failure to use their arms, as it is sometimes perceived, is often harshly criticized. Gustavo Castro, Director of the Chiapas-based NGO Otros Mundos and a longtime fellow traveler of the EZLN, tells of entering the community of Morelia and witnessing the changing of the guards:

> Several insurgents shoulder their arms, stand in formation, and draw a bullet into the chamber to fire a salute, but the rifles are so rusted that they're locked up tight and the insurgents are there screwing around with the guns trying to get them to fire, looking like parodies of soldiers. This is the famous EZLN, defenders of the rights of people everywhere?[57]

Nonetheless, the symbolic aspect of their bearing of arms, though perhaps with time it's force is drastically reduced, remains potent. The Zapatistas challenge the rules of engagement by using "symbolic warfare" of masks and words, by appealing to allies outside of their national boundaries, and by opposing force with nonviolence.

Unfortunately for the EZLN and the communities they defend, the state also breaks the rules of engagement by committing low-intensity warfare (burning crops, dismantling water systems, destroying autonomous infrastructure, engaging in shows of military force through low overflights, parading troops through autonomous villages, etc), with the effect of deepening the structural violence of hunger, poverty, illiteracy, want, and terror. The state also breaks the rules of engagement by employing paramilitaries, in a strategy often described as hammer-and-anvil: the military is the hammer, engaging in strategic violence when conditions allow, and the paramilitaries are the anvil, always present and ready to strike when above-board military action is not prudent.[58] And while the Zapatistas have often succeeded in casting a circle of protection around themselves by creating a visual spectacle and maintaining a strong public appearance and media presence, the state has in many cases done precisely the opposite—acting in secret, through the use of paramilitaries, while publicly minimizing "the problem of Chiapas," and denying that the war even exists. President Fox, for example, took a magical realist approach, boasting that he could solve the conflict in fifteen minutes, and reducing the indigenous struggle to the need for "*vocho, changarro, y tele*" (a Volkswagen, a small business, and a television).

The "symbolic" nature of violence is, of course, not unique to the Zapatista movement—it may be seen as no more than a manifestation of a kind of propaganda that is all too common in global politics. When the U.S. State Department uses this tactic in seeking to establish "meaningful dialogue" with its enemies, be they in Iran, Panama, or North Korea, it calls this aggressive display "armed diplomacy." The Zapatistas simply engage in armed diplomacy on a much smaller scale, arguably for legitimate self-defense, and without the authority of the nation-state to justify their cause. Even as they stand silent, their guns have served them well in attracting media attention and, indeed, in bringing about opportunities for meaningful dialogue.

For the Zapatistas, bearing arms is largely about survival, but it carries with it a powerful message of defiance to state authority and an ethical demand for collective rights that echoes every Latin American historical call to "go to the mountains." By carrying weapons, the Zapatistas present themselves as subject to no law but their own.

It is the privilege of the nation-state to make the laws, and to enforce the laws. The defenders of the national order—the armed forces—carry weapons and are authorized to use them. In defending the national order, the effect of the weapons is intended to be preventive: latent violence as prophylaxis. So, when we see police with guns, we may not perceive the latent violence (unless of course we are criminals, insurgents, homeless people, indigents, or otherwise fit the profile of lawlessness, perhaps for reasons of race, ethnicity, class, or culture). Even soldiers with guns, if they are not fighting, should, one supposes, give us a sense of "security" rather than instilling fear. They are protecting the public interest, serving the public good.

But when we see images in the news of rural insurgents with guns, they are not, apparently, protecting the public interest. They represent violence and instill fear of lawlessness. If an army kills to protect the national interest it is, of course, duty-bound—certainly not "nonviolent," but perhaps not violent either, in the sense that it is upholding the "rule of law." But if a private citizen of the state, or a group of them, raises arms in defense of what she perceives as her "rights" or interests, she will be accused of violence, for she has transgressed the authority of the state. It is not the bearing of arms that is seen as violent—certainly the men guarding the Kentucky Fried Chicken, not to mention state actors like Mexico's elite Federal Preventive Police, are just doing their job. It may not even be the effect of the arms that constitutes violence. The charge of violence ultimately lies in the challenge to state authority.

This brand of armed diplomacy is a challenge to the nation-state itself, (that is, to the very concept of a nation-state imbued with inalienable authority), as well as to the established (nationalist) view of history. All nations, with varying degrees of punitive response, forbid this challenge. Virtually all have armed forces at their disposal to enforce the prohibition.

Though the Zapatistas might never use their arms, they would still be perceived as a threat for bearing them in the name of autonomy and resistance.

Every morning the Mexican National Army stationed in Military Post #1, the National Palace in Mexico City, marches forth in strict formation onto the central plaza—a huge sweeping flagstone plaza that was once the center of the great Aztec city of Tenochtitlan and is now the center of the Mexican Republic—and raises the nation's flag, the huge red, white and green tricolor bearing the ancient Aztec image of the eagle devouring the serpent. The soldiers, in fatigues and silver helmets polished to a solar luminescence, march in precise formation, following a complex pattern across the flagstones like bees or ants traveling on extrasensory pathways, until they arrive at the flagpole and undertake the ritual flag raising. Watching this spectacle, one is overwhelmed by the drama and the precision of the soldiers, the discipline and the devotion to the *patria*, the fatherland. Resonating with shades of Roman legions or the Nazi spectaculars of Albert Speer, it is the choreography of fascism declaring "*Patria o muerte!*": the fatherland or death. Ironically, the same slogan wraps up the Zapatista Hymn, the official *corrido* of the uprising "*Vivamos por la patria, o morir por la dignidad*"—Let's live for our country or die for our dignity.[59]

Both "*patrias*" are Mexico, but one is the Mexican state, with its supposedly fixed laws and its historically established boundaries, and the other is Mexico *profundo*, a Mexico from below redolent of the native earth and constructed at the hands of peasant labor. Mexican anthropologist Gilberto López y Rivas elucidates a crucial distinction:

> It is important to distinguish two complementary concepts: state and nation. While the first one derives from judicial and administrative necessities and from the monopoly on violence that is required for a society to survive, the nation is a social/historical construction which, on the one hand gives the state its identity, but on the other hand is betrayed by being made up of subjects whose identity is negated by the hegemony of state power.[60]

The Mexican federal army carries guns to protect the nation-state, and the Zapatistas carry guns to challenge it, but both sides claim to defend the *patria*. Both, bearing arms to display their legitimate claim to the law of the land, are carrying out armed diplomacy.

Recall the First Declaration of the Lacandon Jungle, sounding through the rebels' voices in the pre-dawn chill of January 1, 1994, making the EZLN perhaps the first Latin America guerilla to take up arms demanding to be included in the Constitution:

> As our last hope, after having exhausted every option to exercise the legal rights in the Carta Magna, we return to her, our Constitution, to apply Article 39, which says, "national sovereignty resides essentially and originally in the people."...Thus, in keeping with our Constitution, we issue the present declaration of war against the Mexican federal army..."

As we'll explore further on, ultimately the distinction between the Zapatistas' bearing of arms and the government's bearing of arms may lie not only in their differing relationships to power—the fact that one side has power and the other does not—but also in their different *attitudes* to it; as George Orwell wrote, "the distinction that really matters is not between violence and non-violence, but between having and not having the appetite for power."[61]

A Jovial Image: The Revolutionary Ethics of Good Humor and Good Sportsmanship

Firearms aside, the chief weapon of the Zapatistas remains the word, and in some cases, more precisely, the wisecrack. From the beginning the Zapatistas have been tricksters, ridiculing everyone, even themselves. When it was noted that their takeover of San Cristóbal on the day NAFTA went into effect began "a few minutes after midnight," Marcos commented, "We were late as usual." Many of the stories Marcos has written take the form of comic fables, and many of their gestures serve to turn revolution into a battle of wits. A typical Marcos joke from the mid-nineties looks like this:

> **The Story of the Hot Foot and the Cold Foot**
> Once upon a time there were two feet. The two feet were together but not united. One was cold and one was hot. So the cold foot said to the hot foot, "You are very hot." And the hot foot said to the cold foot, "You are very cold." And there they were, fighting

> like this, when Hernán Cortés showed up and burned them both alive.[62]

Marcos is addressing the question of infighting on the left, a problem that has plagued the Zapatistas no less then it has any social movement or political organization since the beginnings of time. Even here, by introducing Cortés, and thus setting his parable at the moment of the conquest, Marcos makes the point that the same divide and conquer strategy that, in the sixteenth century, set the Tlaxcaltecas against the Mexicas, resulting in the sacking of Tenochtitlán, is at work today. More importantly, though, he makes his point through a kind of Aesop's fable with a Tom and Jerry twist.

Some of the most beloved and original early communiqués feature the famous beetle Durito—little tough guy. Durito takes offense at Marcos's big clumsy boots and his simplistic analysis of globalization, and takes it upon himself to lecture (repeatedly) about neoliberalism and war, ultimately suggesting that the Zapatistas are fighting for nothing because the capitalists are so stupid they will run themselves into the ground of their own accord. As we'll discuss later, Durito takes on the persona of Sherlock Holmes to Marcos's Watson and of Don Quixote to Marcos's Sancho Panza, injecting a shock of profound literary humor and giving historical context and intellectual weight to the Zapatista cause—Marcos as Mister Magoo. At the same time, the use of humor disarms and delights, further reinforcing the sense of these ski masked, gun-toting rebels as sympathetic characters.

Speaking of Tom and Jerry, Marcos's wit is such that he sees fit to use the trope of cartoon violence, where the cartoon kitty cat may be bludgeoned to death any number of times by the cartoon mouse and still return to chase the mouse another day, in:

> **The Story of the Kitty Cat and the Little Mousy[63]**
>
> Once upon a time, there was a very hungry little mousy who wanted to eat a piece of cheese from the kitchen. The mousy went with great confidence into the kitchen to take the cheese, but suddenly a kitty cat appeared and the mousy was very frightened and ran away and had to abandon the cheese. So the mousy thought

about how to get the cheese from the kitchen, and he thought and thought and this is what he said:

"I know, I'll put out a little bowl of milk and then the kitty cat will stop to drink the milk. When the kitty cat is drinking his milk unawares, I'll run to the kitchen and eat the cheese. Veeerrrrry good idea!," the mousy said to himself.

So he went to get the milk but it turned out that the milk was in the kitchen, and when the mousy went to get it the kitty cat appeared and the mousy was very frightened and ran away and had to abandon the milk. So the mousy thought about how to get the milk from the kitchen and he thought and thought and this is what he said:

"I know, I'll throw a big fish very far and then the kitty cat will run for the fish. When the kitty cat is eating the big fish unawares, I'll go to the kitchen and grab the milk and put out a little bowl and then, when the kitty cat is drinking his milk unawares, I'll run to the kitchen and eat the cheese. Veeerrrrry good idea!," the mousy said to himself.

So he went to get the big fish but it turned out that the fish was in the kitchen, and when the mousy went to get it the kitty cat appeared and the mousy was very frightened and ran away and had to abandon the fish.

Then the mousy realized that the cheese he wanted, along with the milk and the big fish were all in the kitchen and he couldn't get them because the kitty cat was in the way. So then the little mousy shouted "ENOUGH ALREADY!" and he grabbed a machine gun and blew the kitty cat to smithereens. Then he went to the kitchen and saw that the big fish, the milk and the cheese had all gone bad, so he returned to get the kitty cat and dragged it into the kitchen and made a big barbecue. He invited all his little friends and they made a big party and ate barbecued kitty cat and sang and danced and lived happily ever after. And so the story went....

Beyond the Tom and Jerry joke, and the bravado of Marcos at using the trope of cartoon violence to invoke the very real bearing of weapons by the rebels, this little parable illustrates the Zapatistas' belief in the importance of framing the debate, of changing the terrain of struggle—not just winning the struggle, but defining the terms. Rather than continuing to scurry around the kitty cat, the parable tells us, there comes a time when every little mousy must cry "*Ya basta!*" and take matters into his own hands.

Of course, one of the characteristics of the trickster is that he sometimes gets snared in his own devices.[64] That is to say, not everyone finds Marcos funny.

In December 2000, Fernando Baltasar Garzón Real—the Spanish judge responsible, on the one hand, for arresting former right-wing dictator Augusto Pinochet of Chile on charges of murder and human rights abuses, and on the other for issuing indictments against members of the extreme left-wing, Basque separatist group Euskadi Ta Askatasuna (ETA)—challenged Subcomandante Marcos to a debate. Marcos accepted, but demanded that he set the terms:

> Señor Baltasar Garzón…
>
> I am informing you that I accept the challenge and (as mandated by the laws of knight-errantry), given that I am the man challenged, it is up to me to set the conditions of the meeting…
>
> FIRST. The debate will be held in the Canary Islands, more specifically on Lanzarote,[65] from April 3 to 10, 2003.
>
> SECOND. Señor Fernando Baltasar Garzón Real shall secure the necessary and sufficient guarantees and safe-conduct, from the Spanish government as well as from the Mexican, so that the knight who has been challenged and six of his gallants can attend the duel and return home safely.[66]

Following these opening salvos, Marcos lays out a series of demands that amount to calling for a truce between the Spanish government and the Basque separatists. Marcos does not reserve his strong words for Garzón and the Mexican government, but takes ETA to task for having recently engaged in violent actions that resulted in the deaths of several innocent civilians: "Subcomandante Insurgente Marcos shall, in addition, address the ETA, asking them for a unilateral truce of 177 days, during which time the ETA shall not carry out any offensive military actions."

Without doubt, foreign affairs of this sort are none of Marcos's business, and ETA apparently found the entire missive offensive in itself. But it went further. After asking ETA for a truce—a bold and unprecedented move for an armed revolutionary on the global stage—Marcos set the terms of victory and defeat:

> If Señor Fernando Baltasar Garzón defeats Subcomandante Insurgente Marcos fairly and squarely, he will have the right to unmask him once, in front of whomever he wishes. Subcomandante Insurgente Marcos shall, in addition, publicly apologize and will be subjected to actions of Spanish justice so that they may torture him (just like they torture the Basques when they are detained)....
>
> If, on the other hand, Señor Fernando Baltasar Garzón Real is fairly defeated, he will commit himself to legally advising the EZLN on the charges which—as perhaps the last peaceful Zapatista recourse, and in front of international legal bodies—will be presented in order to demand the recognition of indigenous rights and culture, which, in violation of international law and common sense, have not been recognized by the three branches of the Mexican government.
>
> Charges will also be pressed for crimes against humanity by Señor Ernesto Zedillo Ponce de Leon, responsible for the Acteal killing (perpetrated in the mountains of the Mexican southeast in December of 1997), where forty-five indigenous children, women, men and old ones were executed....
>
> Charges will similarly be presented against the heads of state of the Spanish government who, during Señor Zedillo's administration in Mexico, were his accomplices in that, and other, attacks against the Mexican Indian people.[67]

Of course, the debate never happened, but by publicly engaging the well-known and controversial judge with his barbed wit, Marcos reveals the hypocrisy of a human rights discourse that allows the state to perpetrate violence (as in Acteal and the Basque country) while condemning the violence of "extremists" such as ETA and the EZLN. And by turning the debate into a duel and the discourse of human rights into a question of honor between knights errant (invoking again Spanish literature's great dreamer, fool, and madman, Don Quixote), Marcos turns revolution into postmodern slapstick comedy. Using humor, literary allusion, and a well-calibrated ethical compass, Marcos saw in the challenge a grand public relations opportunity—and came off looking like a clown.

While several important messages may have come through the diatribe, looking like a clown didn't serve Marcos well in the eyes of ETA, Judge Garzón, the Mexican government, the Spanish government, the human rights establishment, or virtually anyone else. Mexico's grand literary lion Carlos Fuentes accused Marcos of abandoning the Indians and compared him to Colonel Kurtz, the jungle-explorer-turned-madman around whom Joseph Conrad's *Heart of Darkness* revolves. Mexico's intellectuals, among them longtime supporter Carlos Monsivais, began to drop away from Marcos's orbit.

Then again, this is not a group who could be expected to take a joke.

In a more recent bout of global sportsmanship, the EZLN accepted a challenge to play a match against an Italian soccer team. In a letter to Massimo Moratti, President of the Milan International Football Club, dated May 25, 2005, Marcos writes:

> Don Massimo,
>
> I'm letting you know that, in addition to being spokesperson for the EZLN, I have been unanimously designated Head Coach and put in charge of Intergalactic Relations for the Zapatistas football team (well, in truth, no one else wanted to accept the job)....
>
> Perhaps... I might suggest that, instead of the football game being limited to one match, there could be two. One in Mexico and another in Italy. Or one going and one on return. And the trophy known the world over as "The Pozol of Mud"[68] would be fought for.
>
> And perhaps I might propose to you that the [revenue from the] game in Mexico ... would be for the indigenous displaced by paramilitaries in Los Altos of Chiapas.

> Rushing headlong now, we might play another game in Los Angeles, California, the United States, where their governor (who substitutes steroids for his lack of neurons) is carrying out a criminal policy against Latin migrants. All the receipts from that match would be earmarked for legal advice for the undocumented in the USA and to jail the thugs from the "Minuteman Project." In addition, the Zapatista "dream team" would carry a large banner saying "Freedom for Mumia Abu Jamal and Leonard Peltier."[69]

As in the letter to Judge Garzón, Marcos uses the terms of sport to describe the playing field of global justice, and the occasion of a sporting duel to level a critique at the abuses of a foreign power, in this case the United States. By avoiding the kind of rhetoric normally associated with "vanguard revolution," "popular uprising," or "anticapitalist resistance," Marcos gets beyond narrow ideologies to appeal to a universal sense of ethics that speaks not only to anarchist revolutionaries, but also to *futbol* fans (who no doubt represent a far larger constituency than the aforementioned anarchist revolutionaries). Ever the strategic populist, Marcos goes to great lengths to show that he is not just an elite literary scholar and student of revolution, but a man of the people and an all-around sporting kind of guy whose struggle is broad enough to include immigrant rights, political prisoners, and Italian soccer stars.

IV
So That the True Tongue Is Not Lost, or The Story of the Words

> The national government will need to eliminate the Zapatistas to demonstrate their effective control of the national territory and of security policy.
>
> —Chase Manhattan Bank, in a note to President Carlos Salinas de Gortari, January, 1994[1]

The Language of the True Men and Women

The Story of the Words[2]

An illustrious banker, outstanding member of the most powerful social sector, criminal and cynic of the history of humanity, that is to say of financial capital, let the words escape as if spitting:

"The problem with the Mexican economy is called Subcomandante Marcos.'

The death sentence is pronounced. Money begins seeking the price of the bullet that will eliminate this "problem." At the same time that the illustrious banker pronounces the dictum, young Antonio shivers beneath the rain and the cold of the mountains of southeastern Mexico. Young Antonio trembles, but he has no fear; he trembles because there is no fire tonight to scare off the cold, to hold back the water, to illuminate the night. Marcos approaches young Antonio and comes to sit by him.

"It's cold," he says.

Young Antonio sits in silence. Beneath the black plastic that makes another nocturnal roof beneath the roof of rain and cold sit the two men who are the same man. There is no fire, it's true. But now Old Antonio is approaching with another source of heat in his hands: the word. Old Antonio puts the word on the ground, between the three men, and begins to speak, begins to share heat and advice with words that embrace like friends, like *compañeros*. The warmth reaches the chest and the eyes, and young Antonio and Marcos doze beneath the night and the cold of a Chiapas December.

Old Antonio speaks to guide their dream. His voice leads young Antonio and Marcos by the hand to an earlier time. History flies backwards, until it arrives ten years before this cold, this night and this light sleep. Time retreats until it arrives at…

The Story of the Words

The night seizes them as they speak. "My flashlight has no batteries," young Antonio says, losing hope. "I left mine in my backpack," says Marcos looking at his watch. Old Antonio leaves and returns with leaves of *watapil*. Without saying a word he begins to build a little tent. Young Antonio and Marcos help. With vines and sticks cut to a Y-shape, little by little a sort of lean-to takes shape. Then they go off to find firewood. The night and the rain have been brothers for a little while now. From between the hands of Old Antonio grows, finally, a little flame that becomes a fire. Marcos and young Antonio make themselves comfortable however they can, resting on their sides by the fire. Squatting, old Antonio speaks and lulls the night with this story, with this inheritance…

"The true tongue was born with the first gods, those who made the world. From the first word, from the first fire, other true words were formed, and they were degrained, like maize in the hands of *campesinos*, to make other words. The first words were three, three thousand times three gave birth to another three, and from them others formed, and in this way the world was filled with words. A giant stone was walked along all the steps of the first gods, those who gave birth to the world. After so much walking, the stone became very smooth, like a mirror. Against this mirror the first gods threw the three first words. The mirror didn't give back the same words it received, but rather it gave back three different words. The gods passed awhile this way, throwing words at the mirror so that others would surface, until they grew bored. Then they had a giant thought in their heads, and they pushed another stone in their walking way and another mirror was polished and they put it in front of the first mirror and they threw the three first words at the first mirror, and this mirror gave back three times three different words which threw themselves, with their pure force, against the second mirror, and this gave back, to the first mirror, three times three the number of words it received and like this more and more different words were thrown by the two mirrors. This is how the true language was born. It was born from mirrors.

"The first three of all the words and of all the languages are 'democracy,' 'liberty,' and 'justice.'

"'Justice' is not punishment, it is giving back to each that which is deserved, and each one deserves that which the mirror gives back: himself. He who gives death, misery, exploitation, arrogance, pride, deserves to walk with a good bit of shame and sadness. He who gives work, life, struggle, he who acts as a brother, has as reward a little light that forever illuminates his face, his breast, and his steps.

"'Liberty' is not each one doing whatever each one wants, it is being able to choose the road which appeals to him to reach the mirror, to walk with the true word. Whatever road as long as you don't lose sight of the mirror, as long as the road doesn't bring you to betray yourself, your people, the others.

"'Democracy' means that all thoughts arrive at a good agreement. Not that everyone thinks the same, but that all ways of thinking or the majority of ways of thinking arrive at a common agreement that is good for the majority without eliminating the minority. That the word of the leader obeys the word of the majority, that the scepter of authority holds the collective word and not a solitary will. That the mirror reflects everything, the walkers and the road, and that it be, in this way, a motive for thinking inside of oneself and outside in the world.

"From these three words all words come, to these three are chained the lives and deaths of the true men and women. This is the inheritance that the first gods brought, those who gave birth to the world, to the true men and women. More than an inheritance it is a heavy load, a load that some abandon in mid-stride and lay aside as if it were nothing. Those who abandon this inheritance break the mirror and walk blind forever, without ever knowing who they are, where they come from and where they are going. But there are also those who always carry the inheritance of the first three words, they walk hunchbacked from the weight on their backs, like when the load of maize, coffee, or firewood points your eyes at the ground. Always small because of so much to carry, always looking down from such a heavy load, the true men and women are giant and they look upwards. It is said that the true men and women watch and walk with dignity.

"But, so that the true tongue is not lost, the first gods, those who gave birth to the world, said that the first three words must be taken care of. The mirrors of language might break one day, and then the words they gave birth to would break just like the mirrors and the world would remain with words to speak or be silent. Like this, before dying in order to live, the first gods delivered these three words to the men and women of maize to take care of. Since then, the true men and women take it as their inheritance to watch over these words. So that it is never forgotten, they walk, they struggle, they live...."

When the two awoke, Old Antonio was preparing to cook a tepescuintle. In the fire the wood burned and dried at the same time, because it had been wet before with the rain and the sweat of Old Antonio's back. Dawn came and, on waking, young Antonio and Marcos felt that something weighed on their shoulders. Since then they search for a way to relieve themselves of this burden... To this day they are doing it....

Young Antonio wakes up and despairs. He shakes Marcos who, sitting at the foot of an ocote pine, slept with his pipe between his lips. The helicopters and the barking of hunting dogs frighten the morning and the dream. They must keep walking... They must keep dreaming....

The three words that are the first words are a direct link to the first gods, the story tells us; throughout the tales Antonio suggests to Marcos that it is crucial to maintain this link to the creation in order to walk with dignity. Language is what gives humans the ability to communicate, to reason, to argue out decisions like the decision to walk in the night until reaching the dawn, and thus the ability to transform the world. The majority of the communiqués end with an invocation to *democracy*, *justice*, and *liberty*, as if the continual presence of these words, like a mantra, will invoke their essential qualities.

Anthropologist Gary Gossen looks at the role of language and the sacred:

> Mayas (indeed, most MesoAmerican Indian communities) link language and dialogue to the dawn of consciousness in their creation narratives. In time present, as in time past, language, with its range of rhetorical, poetic, and musical embellishments, has served as a sacred symbol which allows humans to share qualities with, and communicate with, gods. In effect, beautifully executed speech and song are the only substitutes the human body can produce that are accessible to and worthy before divine beings. Ritual speech, prayer, song, and sacred narrative performance share with other sacramental substances—such as liquor, incense, tobacco, fireworks, aromatic leaves, and flowers—the quality of metaphorical heat. They all produce "felt" intensity of message (i.e., heat) that is essence, not substance.[3]

The true men and women are the Tojolabales, the people who live on the southern and eastern edge of the remaining Lacandon rainforest, the people with whom Marcos has lived for most of his career as a *guerillero*.[4] The name is derived from their words "*tojol*"—true—and "*abal*"—language or tongue: *tojolabal*. Gossen explains that: "*tojol* represents a way and not a possession of property. It is offered to everyone on the condition that they remain free of the arrogance which implies a shutting out of the rest. We ourselves can achieve the *tojol* or lose it. It depends on us, on our commitment."[5]

The Tojolabales, then, are the people who speak the true word; it is their guardianship of the word that gives them their sense of humanity, their sense of duty to sacred tradition. Along with the struggle for land and liberty, the indigenous Zapatistas struggle to maintain their guardianship of the word.

In *Los Hombres Verdaderos* (in English, the title might translate as *The True Men and Women*), Carlos Lenkersdorf looks at the Tojolabal language and finds the concept of dignity built into the very structure of the syntax, into the fabric of speaking.[6] He describes the way the language works and finds implied in it the specific signs of relation between the individual speaker and the larger community.

"In Tojolabal," he writes, "we have two subject-agents, (I) and (You). Each of them performs an action that corresponds to them. The first *spoke* and the second *listened*. In regards to the thing spoken or the thing heard nothing is said. In fact, it is implied in the verbs."[7] So, whereas in English (and the Indo-European languages) we can say "I speak" and have only "I," the single subject, existing apart from the action taken, "speak," in Tojolabal there are multiple subjects implied by the verbs, so that one says "I speak you hear." Or "She speaks we all hear." In addition, the "I" and the "you" are inflected —they have an extra syllable attached to them—to codify the kinship relation between speaker and listener. So a sentence in English as simple as "I speak," in Tojolabal is more along the lines of "I speak to you my brother, you my brother hear me." Lenkersdorf calls this action of the language "intersubjectivity." He goes on to suggest that intersubjectivity in the Tojolabal language implies both individual agency and responsibility toward the community; the language, he suggests, is structured to be inclusive, or egalitarian, or "horizontal."

A prevalent trend in linguistics suggests that our language shapes our thought, that the syntax and structure of language serve to reinforce and define the perceptions and beliefs of the speaker. In this view, language is not merely descriptive but prescriptive—that is, creative: the word and the deed are one. As Lenkersdorf says, "The language is not separate from the way we view the world; rather it manifests our cosmovision."[8]

The Tojolabal language is predicated, Lenkersdorf suggests, on the notion of dignity—a concept central to Tojolabal culture. And, he adds, dignity in this sense is *not* central to European culture, as reflected in the subject-verb-object structure of most European languages. That is to say, in a simple English sentence like "I speak to you," the direction of communication is one way—from the active subject (I) to the passive object (you). "Communication … in Indo-European languages is a unidirectional relation. The subjects speak or announce their words so that the non-subjects receive them."[9] In Tojolabal, by contrast, both you and I are active.

Lenkersdorf further asserts, "Intersubjectivity informs the cosmovision of the Tojolabales and subject-object relations inform the cosmovision of the speakers of Indo-European languages."[10] This is not to say that speakers of European tongues are *incapable* of dignity in the sense discussed here; simply that it is not reflected in daily communications and thus, perhaps, is not embedded in the European view of the world in the way it is in Tojolabal. Indeed, "The Story of the Words" shows Old Antonio, a Tojolabal, telling Marcos, a mestizo, of his sacred duty to protect the true tongue—and passing this responsibility on to Marcos, though he is, in essence, a foreigner.

In general, the different cosmovisions—indigenous and European—give rise in turn to different modes of communication.

> This is what happens, for example in the so-called "communications" media, above all in the news. The subjects of these programs select and interpret the themes that are considered suitable for putting on the news. The listener-objects have the liberty of listening to what they say. In fact, looked at from the Tojolabal perspective, we can say that the communications media don't do what their name indicates. They would be better called media of information, because that already implies selection, different types of censoring, interpretation, etcetera.[11]

Lenkersdorf goes on to suggest that the denial of subject-status—dignity—to the indigenous peoples violates their very concept of social relations, leading inevitably to a deep rupture of cosmic understandings. The misunderstandings that have plagued negotiations and communications between the Zapatistas and the Mexican government, this line of reasoning suggests, are not simple misreadings of each others' intentions, but cultural differences which, when accompanied by the government's cynicism and the Zapatistas' deference to community consensus, are nearly impossible to bridge.

Like many indigenous peoples, the Tojolabal traditionally have a sense that they are profoundly responsible for the harmony of social and cosmic relations. In order to reestablish the cosmic order and the social balance that have been disrupted by conquest and colonization, periodic restructurings must occur. On the level of the larger society, these take the form of social uprising and open rebellion.

Like the three talking stones that fell from the sky near San Juan Chamula heralding rebellion throughout the highlands,[12] the three words *liberty*, *justice*, and *democracy* are denoted in "The Story of the Words" as precious objects to be guarded by the first people. By equating *liberty*, *justice*, and *democracy* with the first words, the roots of language, Marcos suggests a primordial responsibility to protect them, to pronounce them. They are the crucial values that connect the future with the past, the values that make us human. They all have to do with responsibility for ourselves and our social order. They all imply dignity.

A life lived in dignity, in the Tzeltal language, is *lekil kuxlejal*. The phrase might also be translated as "the good life," or "a life in balance." Investigator Antonio Paoli equates *lekil kuxlejal* with peace, with silence, with accords made and kept within the group, within the family, and within the community-of-communities. "*Lekil kuxlejal* is not a utopia because it does not refer to a non-existent dream. No, *lekil kuxlejal* existed, and has been degraded but not extinguished, and it is possible to recover it. And, it does not only refer to this world, but also to the world beyond."[13]

Paoli devotes an entire book to the concept, showing how *lekil kuxlejal* acts as an ethical compass and motivating force in Tzeltal society as demonstrated in community education, in the way authority is understood, in the practice of agriculture, in the stability of marriage and family life. A complex notion, *lekil kuxlejal* is described variously throughout Paoli's book; one of the most striking examinations of its resonance is in the words of a man identified as Manuel, a human rights promoter in Ocosingo:

Lekil kuxlejal is found in every arrangement of the family or the community. There are agreements made within the community that must be treated with reverence, because nobody else will make these arrangements, nobody that comes from somewhere else, they won't happen just because the state government sends someone to do it. It is here, in the community, that we agree on how to do things the right way. There are agreements that say somebody should not harass others, that certain things should not be done in such and such a way; this is what we tell each other in our assemblies, and these agreements from the assemblies have to be obeyed. The word that comes from each assembly is the only way to seek the right path for our lives.[14]

Pardon?

In a communiqué written soon after the uprising, on January 18, 1994, called by Carlos Montemayor "one of the most eloquent communiqués in the history of Mexican armed movements,"[15] Marcos responds to the government's offer of pardon by articulating some of the key elements of *Zapatismo* and giving voice to a question that is central to the understanding of subaltern insurrections:

> For what do we have to ask pardon? For what are you going to pardon us? For not dying of hunger? For not shutting up in our misery? For not having humbly accepted our gigantic historic cargo of neglect and abandonment? For having risen in arms when we found all other avenues closed? For not having deferred to the Chiapas penal code, one of the most absurd and repressive in memory? For having demonstrated to the rest of the country and the entire world that human dignity still lives, and that it lives in the world's poorest inhabitants? For being conscious and well prepared? For having carried rifles into combat, rather than bows and arrows? For having learned to fight before doing battle? For being all Mexicans? For being mostly indigenous? For calling all Mexicans to struggle, by any means possible, for what belongs to them? For struggling for liberty, democracy and justice? For not following the patterns of earlier guerrillas? For not surrendering? For not selling ourselves? For not betraying ourselves?…
>
> Who should ask for pardon, and who can grant it?[16]

The question touches on the very definition of the indigenous cultures by the colonizing state. As we've acknowledged, the authority of the Mexican state rests on its nation status—its claim to be the only body that can legally arbitrate justice and legitimately use violence within its claimed boundaries. With regard to the indigenous communities, this authority rests, tautologically, on the state's promotion of violence to maintain control. That is, as in any colonial situation, the colonized population has not willingly accepted the authority of the dominant state, but is the victim of coercion. Symptomatic of the violence of the state toward the colonized subject, is that the state wins the right to define the other's culture on its own terms, and, likewise, to arbitrate the dialogue (if it can be called that) between the two entities. In fact, one of the historical approaches to "the Indian problem" in Mexico has been the desire on the part of the state to absorb the indigenous populations, eliminate any traces of independent culture, including their languages, and to create, in liberal terms, an "integrated Mexican culture."

Of course, the indigenous have never been consulted on this issue, and the result has been periodic uprisings and armed conflicts like the current one. While the state, using the language of power that it inherits as part of the package of modern statehood, defines the opposing group as "hostile," "intransigent" and "rebellious," or in more patronizing terms, "ungrateful," "backwards" and "subject to manipulation," the indigenous communities, without the badge of statehood and therefore without access to the mechanisms of international law, are silenced. It is no wonder they are seen as "backwards," when they are given no opportunity to speak. Questions like "What is it the Indians want?" proliferate, while little attempt is made to understand their speaking position. So, when the Mexican government, backed by tremendous military and economic strength, offers the rebels a pardon, the rebels, not ready to back down, ask, "Who should ask for pardon, and who can grant it?" The problem is not that they have committed a crime of which they need to be pardoned—this assumes that they are a consenting part of the dominant society. The problem is that they fail to recognize the authority of the state.

"What the Indians want," among other things, is to be allowed to speak, and to be heard, to explain, in their own words, "what the Indians want." Fundamental to this right is what they repeatedly refer to as "dignity." In this case, dignity can be defined as a speaking position and a respectful audience. The effect of the guns, the ski masks, the communiqués, and the strategic takeovers of towns and cities, is to force the state to listen.

It may appear paradoxical, then, that the most prominent speaking voice of the uprising belongs to Marcos, who is not indigenous. We will return to this question further on; for now, suffice it to say that the EZLN's use of Marcos as their primary voice is a strategic decision based on his unique ability to translate, to act as a bridge across cultures.

Still, some concepts, it appears, are untranslatable. Perhaps one of the greatest jokes of the Zapatista rebellion was when Marcos, in the postscript to a communiqué dated June 10, 1994, discussed the Mexican government's offer that the Zapatistas surrender in exchange for an amnesty:

> In the committee we were arguing all afternoon. We looked for the word in our languages to say 'surrender,' but we didn't find it. It has no translation in Tzotzil or in Tzeltal, and nobody remembers

if this word exists in Tojolabal or in Chol. We spent hours trying to find some equivalent. Outside, the rain continued and a cloud came to lie down among us. Old Antonio waited until everyone was quiet, and only the sound of rain drumming on the metal roof remained. In silence, he approached me and with a tubercular cough he spoke into my ear:

"This word does not exist in the true tongue. This is why our people have never surrendered and prefer to die, because our dead tell us that words which do not walk must not be given life."

He walked over to the fire to frighten off the fear and the cold. When I tell Ana Maria what he said to me, she looks at me with tenderness and reminds me that Old Antonio is dead...[17]

Beyond demanding a voice and demanding to be heard (manifesting politically as the Zapatistas' insistence on equal representation of indigenous cultures in the nation's congress), they demand that the party in power "learn how to speak to them." Scholar José Rabasa writes:

> The impossibility of speaking and the eminent folklorization that has haunted the discourse of the Zapatistas at every stage of their dialogue with the government—exchanges that could very well be understood as colonial encounters caught in a struggle to the death—do not manifest subalterns who "know far better" and "say it well," but a clear understanding that the possibility of their call for justice, liberty, and democracy resides paradoxically in the impossibility of being understood. The point of departure is not that "subalterns speak very well," but that they "cannot speak" and "choose not to learn how"—indeed, they demand that the discourse of power "learn how to speak to them." This position is, perhaps, nowhere better exemplified than in Comandante Trinidad [a woman of over sixty years of age] who, at a session with the government, chose to address the official representatives in Tojolabal and then asked them in Spanish if all was clear.[18]

Like the uprising itself, the joke of Comandante Trinidad is a response to a relation established early in the conquest. Five hundred years after the discovery, the indigenous people of Chiapas are demanding a forum where they can attempt to dialogue in their own language.

The document that first established the rights of the Spanish *conquistadores* over the culture and territories of the natives of the Americas was known as the *Requerimiento*, or *Requirement*. Written in 1514 by a royal jurist under the auspices of the Spanish Crown, the *Requirement* is a text born of the need to regulate the hitherto chaotic process of conquest and colonization. Beginning in 1514, Spanish conquistadors are required to read this text *en voz alto*—aloud—before unleashing their reign of terror on the savage natives.

The text includes a brief history of humanity from the perspective of the Church, culminating in the appearance of Jesus Christ, "Master of the human lineage." It goes on to tell how Jesus transmitted his power to Saint Peter, and Saint Peter to the popes who followed him. One of the last popes bestowed the American continent on the Spaniards and the Portuguese (divided down the middle, more or less), and so, in the name of Jesus Christ, these lands and peoples belong to the Spanish crown. If the native peoples submit to this belief, they will come under the benevolent protection of the crown. If however, they do not, the *Requerimiento* dictates their fate in no uncertain terms:

> If you do not do this, and wickedly and intentionally delay to do so, I certify to you that, with the help of God, we shall forcibly enter into your country and shall make war against you in all ways and manners that we can, and shall subject you to the yoke and the obedience of the Church and of their Highnesses; we shall take you and your wives and your children, and shall make slaves of them as their Highnesses may command; and we shall take away your goods, and we shall do all the harm and damage that we can as to vassals who do not obey and refuse to receive their lord, and resist and contradict him.[19]

If this injunction were not sufficiently despicable, the fact that it was read with no interpretation into the native languages makes the wholesale slaughter that followed all the more arbitrary.

Remembering that the conquerors rarely, if ever, spoke the language of the natives, we can assume that there was no understanding of the text that was read. Looking at a report from 1550 by Pedro de Valdivia after his war on the Arawaks, the pre-Hispanic inhabitants of modern-day Chile, Todorov comments:

> We do not know in just what language Valdivia's messengers expressed themselves and how they managed to make the contents of the *requerimiento* intelligible to the Indians. But we do know how in other cases the Spaniards deliberately neglected resorting to interpreters, since such neglect ultimately simplified their task: the question of the Indians' reaction no longer came up.[20]

So we see that Comandante Trinidad's joke is a mirror of the cruel joke played on her people over the course of 500 years, and the linguistic underpinning of colonial antagonism is made clear. The basis of the colonial power's misunderstanding of the indigenous demands is in their unwillingness to learn the language—both literally and figuratively—and their insistence on speaking over top of them. And the Zapatistas, in order to have their language heard and their demands attended to, resort to another language, the language of violence. Still, their demands are not respected, and the government strategy is to create the appearance of dialoguing with the rebels while steadily increasing the military presence in the state, arresting presumed Zapatistas and vilifying them in the press. José Rabasa, in looking at the gulf of understanding between the Zapatistas and the state, stresses the cultural differences between the two parties. But rather than citing "lack of civilization" or "backwardness" on the part of the indigenous, as the state regularly does in its concerted attempt to marginalize the rebels, he suggests that the incapacity is in the other camp: "The Zapatistas attribute the incapacity of the government—as well as of intellectuals—to address their demands as a mixture of moral ineptitude (cannot understand what dignity means), racism (cannot dialogue with Indians on an equal basis), and intellectual torpidity (cannot understand the terms of a new communist revolution)."[21]

Be that as it may, due to the balance of power, the burden of communication still rests with the Zapatistas. In order to come to an understanding with occidental society and the world of market relations, party politics and consumer culture, the Zapatistas must to some degree achieve fluency in the languages and media of the dominant society.

Social Netwar on the Information Superhighway

> The army is well positioned to assault and defeat the EZLN in its home base, though this remains politically inadvisable because of the transnational netwar dimensions.
>
> —*The Zapatista "Social Netwar" in Mexico*, Rand Corporation, 1998[22]

Mexico is a nation where most of the mass media is either owned and controlled by the government or is in the hands of wealthy oligarchs with vast economic interests. Independent journalists, especially on the left, run a great risk in expressing their point of view. Maite Rico and Bertrand de la Grange, in their book *Marcos, La Genial Impostura* [*Marcos, the Genial Imposter*] (which, while it paints Marcos as an egomaniac and follows the racist-state party line that Marcos and other "outsiders" manipulate the indigenous people, still does not fail to reveal the corruption of the Mexican government), note that:

> The state is the principal, and sometimes the only, source of income of the news agencies, by way of institutional publicity, paper subsidies, free credit, contracts, and corruption. Free trips, secret

> envelopes given to editors and columnists (known as *chayotes*) and other favors are the press's daily bread. They are considered expenses for services rendered. And despite the great efforts made to guard these secrets, nobody is being fooled, at least in the political class.
>
> Of the twenty-three periodicals published in the capital, no more than seven or eight have a real readership, and only two or three that would survive without official support. The majority are the mouthpieces of the different groups in power. [23]

With the exception of the Mexico City daily *La Jornada*, and a few small, local papers and alternative news magazines—notably *El Tiempo*, a San Cristóbal weekly edited for thirty years by Concepción Villafuerte and her late husband Amado Avandaño (who was voted Rebel Governor of Chiapas in 1994 before a near-fatal "accident" removed him from public life)—all of the major media, when they couldn't black out news about the Zapatista uprising, simply reported the government line: this was a violent insurrection confined to four municipalities in Chiapas where a handful of foreigners—professional revolutionaries from Cuba, Nicaragua, and Guatemala—had manipulated the indigenous population in an attempt to overthrow state and federal authorities. This line of propaganda descended directly from the colonial power's historical view of the indigenous people as passive and incapable of organized resistance, and from the popular mythology that portrays Latin American social movements as power struggles waged by self-interested, bloodthirsty bandits.

But the EZLN was prepared for such treatment by the media. The Zapatista high command was careful during the January 1 uprising to court international media attention. And the international media, given a fast-breaking, sexy story, responded. Interviews were conducted with Subcomandante Marcos and other rebels, which managed to give some perspective to their point of view. Over the course of the first years of the rebellion, international media moguls, literati and stars—from Oliver Stone to Jose Saramago to Kevin Costner to the editors of *Vogue*, *Vanity Fair* and so on ad nauseam—trekked to the jungle to act as messengers of the word.

But inside Mexico, the real story was consistently obscured. After a time *La Jornada,* a paper with international distribution and a distinct leftward slant, took to publishing entire communiqués (a practice it continued for over a decade until around 2008, when the paper began offering only partial communiqués in print and making the rest available online). The leftist weekly news magazine *El Proceso* offered cogent political analysis, and alternative 'zines like *La Guillotina* appeared on news stands throughout Mexico offering feature articles about *neo-Zapatismo* alongside countercultural material such as photo-essays on sadomasochism and translations of William S. Burroughs. Later, with the emergence of the Other Campaign in 2005, the magazine *Rebeldía* served to amplify the voice of *Zapatismo*. But these media are largely inaccessible to the general population, and even, in many cases, to those who seek them out. *La Jornada* has a habit of mysteriously disappearing from newsstands, or even more mysteriously, never showing up.[24]

Since 1994, the one generally reliable source of information directly from the Zapatistas and those who visit them has been the Internet. If the movement had not coincided with the explosion of Internet technology, it might have remained isolated from the rest of Mexico and from the world. But, coming as it did in 1994, just as personal Internet use was booming in the United States, Europe and Latin America, links were immediately established which made news of the war in Chiapas available across the globe. The masked figure of Subcomandante Marcos became an international symbol of open rebellion and the cause of indigenous human rights entered world consciousness and the global political spectrum like it never had before. With the help of international solidarity groups, nongovernmental human rights and development organizations, and activist collectives who translated and disseminated the news and communiqués, the indigenous people of Chiapas were able to make their voices heard. The Zapatista army had won a forum in which to speak, and achieved a public relations coup that no previous rural insurgent group could have imagined.

Harry Cleaver, in an early essay on the use of Internet technology in the Zapatista rebellion, explains:

> Even after the cease-fire when the emphasis of the Zapatista offensive shifted from arms to words, the commercial media over-

> whelmingly refused to reproduce the striking and often eloquent communiqués and letters sent out by the EZLN. With the distribution of *La Jornada*—which did continue to publish Zapatista material in full—sharply limited, especially outside of Mexico City, this refusal of the world's media was a serious blockage to the ability of the Zapatistas to get their message out.
>
> For those in Mexico who read those messages and found them accurate and inspiring, their blockage was an intolerable situation which had to be overcome in order to build support for the Zapatistas and to stop the government's repression. What they did was very simple: they typed or scanned the communiqués and letters into e-text form and sent them out over the Net to potentially receptive audiences around the world. Those audiences included, first and foremost, UseNet newsgroups, PeaceNet conferences, and internet lists whose members were already concerned with Mexico's social and political life; secondly, humanitarian groups concerned with human rights generally; thirdly, networks of indigenous peoples and those sympathetic to them; fourthly, those political regions of cyberspace which seemed likely to have members sympathetic to grassroots revolt in general and fifthly, networks of feminists who would respond with solidarity to the rape of indigenous women by Mexican soldiers or to the EZLN "Women's Revolutionary Law" drafted by women, for women, within and against a traditionally patriarchal society.[25]

A loosely organized network of Zapatista supporters was quickly established in cities throughout the world— Mexico City, Los Angeles, San Francisco, Austin, New York, Montreal, Paris, Madrid, Barcelona, Rome, etc. A handful of people in each city would receive the news from the front by email, translate it appropriately and post it on the World Wide Web or various listservers. New NGOs and collectives were formed—the Comité Emiliano Zapata, the National Commission for Democracy in Mexico, Acción Zapatista, Enlace Civil—and existing ones sprang into action or developed programs to do work with, for, or about the Zapatistas. In this way, a global network was formed which could respond immediately to the news from Chiapas by marching to Mexican consulates, writing to legislators, performing in the streets, or, most directly, setting up aid and support networks to send people and supplies to the Zapatista zone of conflict. This response, propagated by the Zapatistas' request that everyone, everywhere, get involved in whatever way possible, prompted perhaps the first truly global response to the global crisis of corporate power (in the form of NAFTA), and resulted in the establishment of a new kind of war, dubbed "social netwar" by tactical thinkers inside the U.S. government.

In late 1998 the Rand Corporation, the long-lived tactical think tank, released a report on the war in Chiapas entitled *The Zapatista "Social Netwar" in Mexico*. This report, which runs to 170 pages, takes as its focus the challenges that Zapatista "network-style" organization and media strategy posed to traditionally hierarchical structures of social organization (namely, the military-industrial complex). In naming and analyzing this "social netwar," the report asserts that the media strategy carried out by the EZLN and the nongovernmental organizations and individuals representing civil society has had direct strategic effects.

The Rand report says:

> The netwar has obliged the army to devote much increased attention to public affairs, psychological operations, relations with NGOs and human-rights issues.... This new focus has entailed efforts to cultivate better relations with the media and has extended to mounting a number of psychological operations, including "sky-shouting" from helicopters with bullhorns, as well as leafleting. More importantly, the pursuit of an integrated information strategy spurred the Mexican government to form a joint intelligence apparatus that is supposed to put an end to the proprietary, baronial practices that have characterized its competing intelligence operations throughout the twentieth century. Above all, the information strategy is being keyed to a need to show respect for human rights.[26]

This new "respect for human rights" on the part of the Mexican military, however, has not necessarily resulted in fewer human rights violations. Rather, it has given way to a strategy on the part of the local and federal governments to allow human rights violations—the burning of crops, the murder of civilians, rape, death threats, and disappearances—to be carried out by government-trained paramilitary death squads while the military remains at a safe distance from the killings. Rather than reducing the violence, international media attention has caused the violence to be redirected. From direct assault—the initial reaction of President Carlos Salinas de Gortari in the "twelve-day war" of early 1994—the strategy shifted to low-intensity warfare, or what was known in Vietnam and the Central American conflicts of the 1970s and 1980s as a war of attrition. Nonetheless, it remains clear that the netwar undertaken by international civil society has brought increased attention to human rights, and has forced the Mexican military and the Mexican federal government to continually develop strategies in response.

The report continues, "it can be said that hierarchies have difficulty fighting networks. It takes networks to fight networks—indeed, a government hierarchy may have to organize its own networks in order to prevail against networked adversaries."[27] The "networks" referred to here are not simply the communications networks established by the then-brand-new Internet technology. The "networked adversaries" are, at root, the widely spread villages of the Chiapas highlands and canyons, the traditionally non-hierarchical Mayan institutions of local cooperative government, and the Zapatista National Liberation Army, whose guerilla structure developed partially in response to the need to support and protect the loosely bound and decentralized base communities.[28]

In another passage, the Rand report notes, "in sum … the federal government, its national security apparatus, and the military had to try to transform themselves to respond to this social netwar. Yet this transformation has never been complete, and there has been a constant tension and interplay between, on the one hand, learning to treat the Zapatista movement as an information-age social netwar and, on the other hand, wanting to treat it as a traditional insurgency."[29] This "tension and interplay" mirrors the tension and interplay of the EZLN's form of armed diplomacy—which is, in fact, a hybrid of traditional insurgency and social netwar.

What the Rand report called "social netwar" is not limited merely to the realm of communications—it is not simply hacking, nor is it limited to "social networking." Social netwar is about emergent forms of organizing and collective action. The example given in the Rand report is "terrorist" cells, which are organized in a decentralized fashion that allows them to perform rapid, remote actions and disperse quickly. A document published by the Chiapas think tank CIEPAC (Centro de Investigaciones Económicas y Políticas de Acción Comunitaria) in 2002 analyzes the netwar concept: the paper, called "Notes on Ants and Steamrollers,"[30] offers additional examples of successful network-style organizing, the most famous being the decentralized and ultimately very successful organizing that shut down the World Trade Organization meeting in Seattle in 1999.

> But there are other examples. A very studied case of network-based struggle was the world campaign against landmines. From being the concern of just a few people, the campaign expanded through civil society organizations which later organized themselves into networks, to create a massive, global movement and created the pressure needed to forge an international treaty against landmines. The treaty initially encountered tremendous opposition from the government of the United States; but the U.S. was forced to give way to the intensity of the campaign, and the movement ended up winning the Nobel Peace Prize in 1997.[31]

The author then gives an example from Chiapas, concurrent but distinct from the Zapatistas' own network-style organizing:

> In Chiapas not long ago there was a victory of civil society organizations that exercised a network-style struggle and managed to detain a biopiracy project, called ICBG-Maya, which joined the University of Georgia, the British company Molecular Nature Limited, the College of the Southern Border [Colegio de la Frontera Sur], and various federal agencies of the United States government. Thanks to an alert spread by the COMPITCH Network (the Council of Traditional Indigenous Healers and Midwives of Chiapas), the indigenous communities of Chiapas learned about ongoing biopiracy activities, and, together with other networks

in and beyond Mexico, they developed a media campaign with enough pressure to force the cancellation of the project.[32]

"Notes on Ants and Steamrollers" goes on to point out some pertinent features of netwar: the actors are usually decentralized organizations, small groups, and individuals who communicate, coordinate, and realize their campaigns without any central authority; they maintain flexible structures whose actions can be determined spontaneously by needs as they arise, often by consensus; they are able to unite and disperse quickly, often ceasing to exist between actions; they are united by a common discourse that reflects not only identity and belonging, but the shared experiences and values which originally brought members of the network together; and, perhaps most importantly, the functioning of the network depends to a great extent on mutual respect, shared experience, friendship, and trust.

Given the widely dispersed nature of the civil society organizations in question, it would seem strange that these networks should depend on "friendship" and "trust"; yet what this reveals, perhaps more than anything, is that this emergent network-style organizing is built not on dogma or doctrine, which tend to displace or replace trust as the glue in social relations, but on a dynamic and inclusive set of ethics. In ways that we see throughout our narrative, the messages embodied by the Zapatistas and voiced in the communiqués of Marcos, speak directly to this particular set of ethics.

The March of Progress: A Dying Colonialism

> Marcos: "'Don't tell me you have a computer!"
> Don Durito: "'Of course, insolent villain! Us knights errant have to keep modernizing in order to better carry out our labor." [33]

It is perhaps surprising that an army of indigenous subsistence farmers struggling to maintain their cultural heritage would so readily adopt global information technology. The irony is apparent. But there are many ways to look at the EZLN's relation to the new high technology.

In *A Dying Colonialism*, Frantz Fanon looks at the relation of the Algerian people to different technologies throughout the course of the Algerian war of independence from France, and the way the demands of the war brought about technological change in a manner that would not have happened otherwise. Fanon focuses on communications' technology when he notes that, before 1945, ownership of radio receivers in Algeria was almost entirely limited to the European colonial population. He attributes this largely to the fact that the off-color remarks and suggestive humor of the announcers was inappropriate to the strictly orthodox Algerian Muslim family, and he examines the breaking of this taboo over the succeeding years in light of the struggle for national liberation. Elucidating the changing meaning of the radio as a cultural artifact over the course of the war, he writes:

> Almost magically—but we have seen the rapid and dialectical progression of the new national requirements—the technical instrument of the radio receiver lost its identity as an enemy object. The radio set was no longer a part of the occupier's arsenal of cultural oppression....[34]
>
> After 1954, the radio assumed totally new meanings. The phenomena of the wireless and the receiver set lost their coefficient of hostility, were stripped of their character of extraneousness, and became part of the coherent order of the nation in battle.[35]

Fanon explains how, by 1957, ownership of a radio set by an Algerian became illegal under the colonial government, where previously it had been "a part of the occupier's arsenal of cultural oppression." This signals a 180-degree turnaround in the relation of the colonized to communication with "the world-at-large." A similar shift occurred in regards to the French language. Before the war, the Algerian nationalist refused to speak the colonial language, in an attempt to negate domination and maintain traditional cultural practice. However, during the course of the war, the ability to speak French became essential to the Algerian nationalist's survival and his revolutionary identity. Both in order to communicate and in order to blend in, the adoption of the French language and the use of radio technology became revolutionary strategies. So, whereas before the war, in the early 1950s, the Algerian nationalist might be identified by his lack of high-tech skills and his refusal to speak French, by 1957 he could be identified by exactly the opposite characteristics.

The Zapatistas' adoption of Internet technology—participating in the kind of high technology that threatens to overwhelm their own tradition in the first place—can be looked at in the light of Fanon's reading of the Algerians' use of radio and the French language. In order to win some advantage within the colonial scheme, the colonized is forced to adopt the technologies of the colonizer. In the case of the indigenous of the Americas, the list of adopted technologies is endless, beginning with horses and firearms and ending, of course, with the latest electronic gadgetry. It is arguable whether the early acceptance of the colonial technology in fact gives the colonized an advantage, or simply places her further in the shadow of colonial dependency; in fact, it does both. But in the short-term crisis of a war of liberation, the contradictions of modernization are a constant foil. Historian Walter Mignolo, speaking on a parallel development throughout the indigenous Americas, points out, "The social movements in Bolivia use methods of organizing that emerge from centuries of Aymara culture, such as the community assembly and informal consensus process—and they communicate on cell phones."[36]

At the same time, it is something of an exaggeration to speak of "the Zapatistas' use of Internet technology." The majority of the indigenous population, after all, has not adopted this new technology. It is true that, thanks to the flood of international support, certain members of the Zapatista command, and later the Juntas de Buen Gobierno, are now in possession of laptop computers, GPS satellite direction finders, two-meter band radios, and other advanced technologies, and that these tools have some bearing on the tactical strategy of the guerilla. At the same time, the general level of technology available to the average *campesino* has changed only slightly. Most of the technology brought to Zapatista communities by international solidarity is more on the order of piped water and latrines, and in some cases low-watt electricity and portable video cameras. As Harry Cleaver noted in 1995, "despite all the media hype which came with the discovery of the role of cyberspace in circulating Zapatista words and ideas, Subcomandante Marcos is not sitting in some jungle camp uploading EZLN communiqués via mobile telephone modem directly to the Internet. Zapatista messages have to be hand-carried through the lines of military encirclement and uploaded by others to the networks of solidarity."[37]

In the early years of the uprising, and now on a continuing basis, computers and video cameras have been brought by international solidarity workers to villages which had previously never seen a telephone or television, let alone a fax machine, and which, further, have only the most basic health clinics, schools, and stores. Contrary to the popular imagination, however, these computers have mostly not been used to access the Internet. Hard as it is to imagine from the wealthy northern latitudes, most of these villages are without running water and electricity. The relatively few computers that have made it into the hands of villagers in the remote Mexican Southeast are charged by automobile batteries or the intermittent electricity that arrives, and are used as word processors, mainly for writing human rights reports and recording daily events in the villages. These reports may then be incorporated into denunciations and declarations to be broadcast over the Internet by human rights NGOs in San Cristóbal, but until very recently, were not uploaded to the Net by web-surfing *campesinos*. In the fifteen years since the uprising, digital technology has permeated more broadly through the Zapatista communities, and many do enjoy the use of computers and even Internet connections, but they continue to be the vast minority.

This is indicative of the general state of affairs. Armand Mattelart, in *Networking the World, 1794–2000*, notes that, "according to ... the MIT experts, on the eve of the third millennium barely 2 percent of the world population was connected in one way or another to a world information network."[38] While a considerable population of urban intellectuals, university students, and solidarity groups have become informed about the Zapatista struggle via Internet, this does not signal the vast global shift in communications that we sometimes imagine.

It is more the case that the Zapatistas have provided a flood of information for *everyone around them* to circulate on the Internet; rather than abandoning their *milpas* and their struggle on the ground to journey into cyberspace, they have, for the most part, made extraordinarily savvy use of the solidarity groups, human rights organizations, sympathetic media outlets, collectives, and individuals who pick up the news they offer and send it onward. This ability to avail themselves of others' use of information technology simultaneously created a web of protection around the Zapatista villages and caused a radical shift in the strategy of the Mexican military and federal government. War always engenders overwhelming technological change in the cultures involved, and it can be said that the advance of the Zapatista rebellion has brought innumerable new technologies to the Mayan villages—from paved roads and cooperative associations to Western medicines, electricity, and increasing Spanish literacy.

The effect of Internet technology on the communities themselves is hardly the most far-reaching of the changes that the indigenous people in Chiapas are undergoing. The appearance of indigenous Tzeltales, Tzotziles, Choles and Tojolabales in cyberspace probably affects the perception *of* them more than it affects the communities themselves. In this sense, the more radical shift is on the part of the observers—those of us who have learned about the indigenous movement largely by way of the Internet—than in the Zapatista villages. A global society which, five years earlier, might have known of an Old Antonio or a Comandanta Ramona only through the anthropological literature or through the medium of *National Geographic*—as curiosities of a primitive or exotic culture—must now confront them as speaking subjects themselves.

These new technologies and modes of communication, of course, do not simply replace the old ways. It is in the melding of autochthonous tradition and the electronic world that the Zapatistas' adoption of these technologies signals a new vision and, at best, gives them some measure of control over the process of cultural and political change. Just as the indigenous peoples of Chiapas use Western medicine alongside divination and other shamanic practices, they find no contradiction in using Internet technology to preserve territory and traditional values.

Constant adaptation to new technologies and social structures imposed from the outside has been a strategy of indigenous resistance since the conquest. The tale of the Surui tribe in the Brazilian Amazon is emblematic: the Surui had not been contacted by outsiders before 1969; over the ensuing three decades, the 5000-member tribe was driven nearly to extinction. As a measure of last resort, the tribe not only used the Internet to communicate their struggle against logging, mining, agricultural, and other development interests; they engaged in a partnership with Google to map their territory. The partnership benefited both parties: Google's humanitarian mission gained hero status, giving the company the kind of legitimacy that acts as a highly valued brand-booster; and the Surui gained their continued existence. Google's project literally put their villages on the map, resulting in protection of the last forested swath of their remote territory. Speaking of the pure pragmatism of using cutting-edge technology to save his people, the tribe's chief, Almir Narayamoga Surui, is matter-of-fact, with perhaps a hint of wry humor: "When people ask us, 'Isn't the Internet dangerous for you?' we say, 'What isn't?'"[39]

Vilma Almendra, a native Nasa woman who spearheads communications for Colombia's Minga Indigina as part of the "Weaving of Communications and External Relations for Truth and Life," calls the Internet "a window to the outside."

> At first our elders were against the use of Internet. In 2005 there were assaults by the FARC[40] in Toribio for almost twenty hours. One of our *compañeros* was trapped in a *telecentro*. The phones were cut, the radio didn't work, and he couldn't get out. By Internet he sent me a message, from Toribio to Santander—at that time I didn't even know how to write—and we sent it on to friends in Canada, and they published it. Next thing we knew, everyone knew the assault was happening, and solidarity started arriving. This was a key moment when our elders realized that these technologies were not just for nothing, but that they had a strategic use for us.[41]

In a confluence of the "pre-modern" and the postmodern, where the enchanted world of spirit relations and disenchanted world of the market collide and collapse upon one another, the Zapatista movement demands that pre-colonial values be acknowledged in a post-colonial context. The appearance of the Zapatista voice on the Internet signifies the eruption of indigenous voices into global debate. As the state-owned media is bypassed, the cultural forces that generally silence indigenous voices are subverted by the heterodox power of Internet communication.

This new position, as a political subject speaking the language of the colonizer or using his technologies, poses its own difficulties. Remembering that language is itself a technology, and one whose adoption causes a radical shift in perception and worldview on the part of its user, we can see a similar situation posed at a different historical juncture: the adoption of the Roman alphabet by Mexico's indigenous populations in the first century of the conquest.

Speaking the Master's Tongue

When the Spanish landed at Hispaniola and later at Veracruz in 1519, marching from the coastal lowlands to the Valley of Mexico to overtake Tenochtitlán, the person who served as translator for Cortés and his army was the native woman who became his concubine, La Malinche.[42] Subsequently, it fell to the natives to learn the language of the conqueror if they were to achieve any understanding of the culture that overtook them, and any status within that culture—a relation that has remained current to the present day. Along with the massive genocide and enslavement of indigenous peoples and the destruction of their lifeways, they were forced to adopt a new mode of expression—which they did with surprising skill and amazing rapidity.

Looking at the first official statement of the Mexican government subsequent to the Zapatista uprising, Carlos Montemayor notes:

> This perspective of the local government during the first hours demonstrated the long tradition of racism in Chiapas.... The statement accentuated the "monolingual" status of the rebels not so much to demonstrate any linguistic fact about the groups involved as to demonstrate their distance from the "civilized" world of Spanish speakers. In this moment, to consider the EZLN insurrection as an indigenous movement was to disqualify the movement itself. This racist vision of the government neglected that on our continent the majority of monolinguals are not the Indians: the average Mexican is monolingual, speaking only Spanish, like the average North American who speaks only English. Indigenous

> Mexicans, besides speaking their own language, tend to speak a neighboring indigenous tongue as well as Spanish.[43]

French historian Serge Gruzinski has traced the history of the adoption of alphabetic writing by the conquered *indigenas:*

> According to the friars, learning reading and writing did not pose major difficulties. The experience began at Texcoco about 1523, where the Franciscan Pedro de Gante taught the young nobles "to read and write, to sing and to play musical instruments, as well as Christian doctrine." The undertaking extended progressively to the children of the nobility of Mexico-Tenochtitlan (1524–5) and the environs, to the regions of Tlaxcala (1527) and Huetjotzingo (1525), while the first Franciscans undertook the alphabetization of the Nahuatl language.[44]

During the conquest, the indigenous peoples of Mexico produced books, several of which remain in existence. As far as we know, all of them are currently in collections in Europe or the United States—rather than in the possession of the people to whom they rightly belong—and they are named according to the city where they reside: Dresden Codex, Madrid Codex, Paris Codex, Vatican Codex, etc. All of them, written in the sixteenth century, make use of Roman letters rather than Mayan or Mexica glyphs to convey their messages. Similarly, the style of painting that accompanies the text—replacing the earlier pictographic script in which the painting *is* the text—is highly influenced by renaissance perspective, brought by the conquerors from Europe.

The presumption among anthropologists and historians, including Gruzinski, is that the indigenous people took rapidly to learning the colonial language, both spoken and written, in order to preserve their cultural traditions. The native peoples were aware that their cultures were being systematically destroyed, and the books were written not for themselves, but for the colonizers. Again, if any cultural memory was to be preserved, the language of the conquerors had to be adopted to preserve it.

Gruzinski examines some of the differences between pre-conquest modes of expression—pictographic, cyclical, painterly—and the linear and detached form of expression characteristic of alphabetic writing, suggesting that the difference involves "a question of the implicit basis for any representation of reality."[45] The adoption of European, Christian modes of expression formed a fundamental barrier between the indigenous cultures and their past, putting a new and vast distance between the present of these cultures and their ancestral heritage. "But this distance," Gruzinski notes, "was also a recomposition, to the extent that alphabetical writing imprinted its linear continuity, its one-way reading on the story, marked necessarily by a beginning and an end." He continues, "By accommodating it to an exotic means of expression practiced by acculturated Indians, thus subjected to a Christian and European education, alphabetic writing assumed an ambiguous, surreptitious function: it ensured the safeguarding of "antiquities" at the expense of an imperceptible transformation that was also a colonization of expression."[46]

The "antiquities" would be preserved, but they would be preserved as antiquities, as relics, and not as embodiments of living culture. The past and the present were surgically and permanently divided. One of the effects of alphabetic writing, he suggests, was to drive the individual mind inward and away from the collective expression that had characterized pre-conquest life. Another effect was to change the perception of time from cyclical—seasonal, the time of eternal returns—to linear. Gruzinski refers to these kinds of changes as "the colonization of the imagination." One particularly poignant moment in this colonization was the distribution, at the end of the sixteenth century, of a special survey:

> From 1578 to 1585, throughout the New Spain of the period, the *corregidores* and the *alcaldes mayores* convened the responsible officials of the Indian pueblos. For they had to complete a questionnaire developed by the chronicler and cosmographer of the king, Juan López de Velasco, in 1577.... It was composed of 50 sections, themselves subdivided into several questions, which together tackled almost all aspects of the colonial world. Physical geography, toponymy, climate, agricultural and mineral resources, botany, languages, political history, population, diseases and business are some of the numerous themes touched on by these questions.[47]

Whether or not the survey was useful in collecting data, and whether or not it was truthfully answered by the *indigenas*, it "imposed a conception of knowing which was perhaps not that favored by the Indians.... It projected on to the Indian world an approach to society, politics, religion and economy; in other words, it imposed a cut-out of reality with its infrastructure, its presuppositions, its explicit and implicit logic, its tacit axioms, its unconscious organization.... For the first time, all the Indian *pueblos* were invited to describe themselves and to do so in the language of the rulers."[48]

From that day forth, the "Indians" were to be understood by the colonizing population and the future generations of mestizo Mexicans only insofar as the colonial language allowed. But, Gruzinski notes, despite the perception of the *indigenas* by the conquerors, and although the indigenous cosmovision was unalterably compromised, there was no lack of attempts on the part of the *indigenas* to sidestep the questions and remain true to themselves and their heritage:

> Far from remaining passive, some informants knew how to turn aside and exploit these riddles to highlight the distant past, without idols, with a view to diverting attention from the presence of an embarrassing paganism. In other words, if it imposed on indigenous memories acrobatics and often impoverishing exercises, the Spanish survey neither paralyzed nor stifled them.[49]

There was resistance on every level of the imagination. Speaking the language of the rulers in the sixteenth century, like the use of Internet to communicate with global civil society in the twenty-first century, allows certain advantages. One of these advantages is that, though nothing is preserved in whole cloth, the cultural perceptions of the *indigenas* force their way into the vocabularies and worldviews of the colonists. This is seen in the many ways that values and knowledge from the native cultures worked their way not only into the culture, but also into the mythic and even legalistic underpinnings of modern Mexico. The heroes of the Mexican War for Independence all had close ties with native tradition: Miguel Hidalgo spoke Otomí; Jose María Morelos developed his political ideas among the Purepechas; Vicente Guerrero marched with an army almost wholly made up of Indians and blacks. At the height of the War for Independence an anomymous "citizen of Xidalgo" wrote and published the first call for the political organization of a federal republic, *Contratos de Asociación para la República de los Estados Unidos del Anáhuac* (*Articles of Association for the Republic of the United States of Anahuac*), which makes a clear case for the institution of common land stewardship as historically practiced by the original inhabitants of these lands.[50] A similar ideal was written into Emiliano Zapata's Plan de Ayala, one of the principle documents of the Mexican Revolution a century later. Hundreds of years after the initial conquest, the ancient indigenous voices can still be heard, and as the Zapatistas have made evident, both directly and through the intercession of Marcos and other interlocutors, these voices refuse to be silenced.

PINGUINO
APATISTA

V
Tilting at Windmills

> In fine, having quite lost his wits, he fell into one of the strangest conceits that ever entered the head of any madman; which was, that he thought it expedient and necessary, as well for the advancement of his own reputation as for the public good, that he should commence knight-errant, and wander through the world, with his horse and arms, in quest of adventures, and to put in practice whatever he had read to have been practiced by knights-errant, redressing all kinds of grievances, and exposing himself to danger on all occasions; that by accomplishing such enterprises he might acquire eternal fame and renown.
>
> —Miguel de Cervantes, *The Ingenious Hidalgo Don Quixote of La Mancha*[1]

Enter Don Durito de la Lacandona

In 1994, year of first appearances, first appeared an ornery beetle named Durito, or "little tough guy," in the fables of Marcos. Durito began, innocently enough, as a character in a letter Marcos wrote to a child, as a vehicle for demonstrating that these newly emerged guerilla warriors had their soft side. The brave guerilla leader wrote stories for children! The beetle appears in the spring of 1994, asking Marcos for a pinch of tobacco and demanding that the rebels step lightly in the jungle to avoid crushing him. And so it happens that Marcos, ever humble in the role of servant, begins to receive lessons in political economy from a bug. After a year or so, Durito appears again, introducing himself as Don Durito de la Lacandona, a knight errant, the animated insectoid equivalent of Don

Quixote de la Mancha, the famous fool of Cervantes. Commanding and imperious, Don Durito appoints the Sup to be his faithful shield-bearer Sancho Panza:

> "Dawn, my battered squire! This is exactly the hour when night arranges its vestments to leave and day sharpens its thorny Apollo's mane to appear to the world! It is the hour when knights-errant ride off seeking adventures that elevate their prestige in the absent gaze of the lady that prevents them, even for an instant, from closing their eyes to seek oblivion or rest!"
>
> I yawn and let my eyelids bring me oblivion or rest. Durito becomes irritated and raises his voice:
>
> "We must go out to despoil maidens, take advantage of widows, come to the aid of bandits and incarcerate the penniless!"
>
> "That menu sounds like a government program," I tell him with my eyes still closed.[2]

Durito brings levity to the communiqués and demonstrates a widely ignored fundament of literature and politics—that revolutionary multitudes like to laugh. Combining parody, literary allusion, and semi-serious political analysis, the Durito tales serve as a vehicle for Marcos to ridicule everything from presidential politics and mass media to the pretensions of a guerilla warrior and popular hero (i.e., himself). Durito, tough on the outside and soft underneath, is the essence of guerilla machismo. As a beetle, he invokes Kafka's pathetic and doomed insect, Gregor Samsa, whose *Metamorphosis* recalls to us the horrors of bourgeois life and, indeed, life. But Durito, an intellectual—and an insurgent intellectual at that—has escaped from the dull reality of a beetle on the jungle floor by undertaking that most noble of professions: knight-errantry.

Durito represents "*los de abajo*," those from below, the little people. A mythological figure, the scarab of ancient Egypt is both a sun god and a funerary figure representing transformation, resurrection, and renewal. *The Book of Chilam Balam of the Mayas* depicts the scarab as the filth of the earth, in both material and moral terms, destined to become divine.[3] In Nahua, the language of the Aztecs, and still the most widely spoken native language in Mexico, the dung beetle is called *mayate*, a word that has entered modern Mexico City slang to refer pejoratively to both homosexuals and people of African descent.[4] The scarab dung beetle Durito, then, is the underdog, or, rather, the underbeetle, destined, perhaps, to take his place at the vanguard of history. At the same time, as Canadian scholar Alex Khashnabish points out, the Durito tales are "conduits for expression that need not conform to the discourse of the Zapatista declarations and communiqués," speaking powerfully "to the ways in which the transnationalized imagination of *Zapatismo* has sought to provoke a (re)shaping of the terrain of political struggle."[5] Durito's role is, essentially, to lecture Marcos, and us, on the vagaries, inconsistencies, and indeed, traps, of neoliberalism. And, while the Old Antonio stories serve to invoke native mythistory and put the old gods in the daily news, the Durito tales work at an opposite pole of the literary canon, building a mock-heroic pastiche of Western literary figures and contemporary pop symbols in order to undermine inherited cultural narratives.

In his first appearance, in a letter Marcos writes to a little girl on the anniversary of Zapata's assassination, April 10, 1994, the beetle castigates Marcos for leading an army of giants through his home, with the imminent danger that he'll be crushed beneath a combat boot. Marcos, for his part, apologizes, making it clear that the Zapatistas have no choice. And he warns Durito that more soldiers are coming. After establishing their roles with one another, the two make a pact of peace:

> April 10, 1994[6]
> To: Mariana Moguel:
> From: Subcomandante Insurgente Marcos
>
> Subcomandante Mariana Moguel:
> I greet you with respect and congratulate you for the new rank acquired with your drawing. Permit me to tell you a story which, perhaps, you will understand someday. It is the story of…
>
> **Durito**
> I am going to tell you a story that came to me the other day. It is the story of a small beetle who wears glasses and smokes a pipe. I met him one day as I was looking for tobacco to smoke, and could

not find any. Suddenly, on one side of my hammock, I saw that a bit of tobacco had fallen and formed a small trail. I followed it to see where my tobacco was, and to see who the hell had taken it and was spilling it. A few meters away, behind a rock, I found a beetle sitting at a small typewriter, reading some papers and smoking a diminutive pipe.

"Ahem, ahem," I said, so that the beetle would notice my presence, but he paid me no heed.

Then I said: "Listen, that tobacco is mine."

The beetle took off his glasses, looked me up and down, and told me, quite irritatedly: "Please, Captain, I beg you not to interrupt me. Don't you realize that I am studying?"

I was a bit surprised and was going to give him a kick, but I calmed myself and sat down to one side to wait for him to finish studying. In a little while, he gathered up his papers, put them away in his desk, and, chewing his pipe, said to me:

"Well, now, what can I do for you, Captain?"

"My tobacco," I responded.

"Your tobacco?" he said to me. "You want me to give you a little?"

I started to get pissed off, but the little beetle handed me the bag of tobacco with its little foot, and added: "Don't be angry, Captain. Please understand that tobacco cannot be found here, and I had to take some of yours."

I calmed myself. I liked the beetle, and I said to him, "Don't worry about it. I have some more over there."

"Hmm," he answered.

"And you, what is your name?" I asked him.

"Nebuchadnezzar," he said, and continued, "but my friends call me Durito. You can call me Durito, Captain."

I thanked him and asked him what it was that he was studying.

"I'm studying neoliberalism and its strategy of domination for Latin America," he told me.

"And what good is that to a beetle?" I asked him.

He replied, very annoyed: "What good is it? I have to know how long your struggle is going to last, and whether you are going to win. In addition, a beetle should care enough to study the situation of the world in which it lives, don't you think, captain?"

"I don't know," I said. "Why do you want to know how long our struggle will last and whether we are going to win?"

"Well, nothing has been understood," he told me, putting on his glasses and lighting his pipe. After exhaling a mouthful of smoke, he continued: "To know how long we beetles are going to have to take care that you do not smash us with your boots."

"Ah!" I said.

"Hmm," he said.

"And to what conclusion have you come in your study?" I asked him.

He took out the papers from the desk and began to leaf through them. "Hmm... hmm," he said every so often as he looked through them. After having finished, he looked me in the eye and said, "You are going to win."

"I already knew that," I told him. I added, "But how long will it last?"

"A long time," he said, sighing with resignation.

"I already knew that, too....Don't you know exactly how long?" I asked.

"It cannot be known exactly. We have to take into account many things: the objective conditions, the ripeness of the subjective conditions, the correlation of forces, the crisis of imperialism, the crisis of socialism, etcetera, etcetera."

"Hmm," I said.

"What are you thinking about, Captain?"

"Nothing," I answered. "Well, Mr. Durito, I have to go. It was my pleasure to have met you. You may take all the tobacco you want, whenever you like."

"Thank you, Captain. You can be informal with me if you like."

"Thank you, Durito. I am now going to give orders to my *companeros* that it is prohibited to step on beetles. I hope that helps."

"Thank you, Captain. Your order will be of much use to us."

"Whatever happens, take much care, because my young men are very distracted, and they do not always look where they are putting their feet."

"I will do so, Captain."

"See you later."

"See you later. Come whenever you like, and we will talk."

"I will," I told him, and went back to the headquarters.

That is all Mariana. I hope to know you personally someday and be able to trade ski masks and drawings.

After this story, Durito begins to appear in Marcos's discourse with regularity, establishing a presence as the Zapatista mascot. Before long he is on T-shirts and in pop songs. In the stories, Durito is always a little unsettled, a little pissed-off, and he never ceases in his studies of "the objective conditions, the ripeness of the subjective conditions, the correlation of forces, the crisis of imperialism, the crisis of socialism, etcetera, etcetera." Durito is a foil for Marcos's ego, a reminder that beneath the underdog is another underdog. He also brings to life the animal forces of the Lacandon jungle, and gives voice, again, to that animating influence present in all things. Beyond that, the little tough guy, being particularly vulnerable as a member of the fragile and threatened jungle ecosystem, is the perfect spokesman on the evils of unchecked, free-market capitalism. Throughout tale after tale—and often in the middle of serious discourses—Durito lectures on neoliberalism, revealing, in a light-hearted way, the essence of what the Zapatistas are struggling against.

Like a Saturday morning cartoon pretending to educate, Durito appears in each episode in the persona of a different fictional character: Don Quixote, Sherlock Holmes, Blackbeard the pirate. His trusty steed is a turtle named Pegasus. Like Don Quixote, Marcos, and every Zapatista insurgent, Durito has two names (at least). Just as Don Quixote is the nom de guerre of "one of those old gentlemen, who usually keeps a lance upon a rack, a lean horse, and a greyhound for coursing," and whose real name is perhaps Quesada or Quixada, and as Marcos is the nom de guerre, allegedly, of a certain former university professor, Durito is the second name of a certain beetle named Nebuchadnezzar. Nebuchadnezzar itself is a name that rings with meaning: the biblical king of Babylon at the height of its glory, responsible for the defeat of the Egyptians and the sacking of Jerusalem, Nebuchadnezzar eventually went mad, losing both his kingdom and his mind.

And so we see that Durito is not just any old beetle, but a shape-shifting character with royal blood coursing through his tiny veins. As a serious researcher and an investigator into the mysteries of the contemporary political scene, Durito is perhaps best as Sherlock Holmes, starring in:

Stupid Improvisation Directs the Cabinet[7]

Toward the West, the Moon lowers itself down between the parted legs of two mountains and rests its cheeks on their belly, where the river stirs up its sex, dripping a serpentine rumor. Some excited clouds stroke the trees with their moisture. In the East there is lightning and tremors, the crickets pipe up with their alarms, and now only a few scattered stars will be surprised by the storm that announces itself to the South. The watchful airplane purrs its threat and recedes into the distance.

Another daybreak of waiting and tobacco. Everything calm. An excellent occasion for the uninvited (as usual) appearance of …

Durito VI (Neoliberalism: The Catastrophic Political Management of Catastrophe)

A glow-worm is shining on Durito's shoulder. A stack of newspaper clippings serves as a bed-chair-desk-office for my master, the illustrious Don Durito of the Lacandon Jungle, maximum representative of the noblest profession that any human being has ever practiced: knight-errantry.

Through the smoke of his pipe, I observe and guard the last and greatest righter of wrongs, the famous knight for whose security I pass a watchful night, and for whom I keep myself alert and ready in case … y-a-a-a-a-awn.

"Yawning again, knave!"

Durito's voice interrupts a blink which, he says, lasted for hours.

"I wasn't asleep!" I defend myself. "I was thinking…." I look at my watch and I notice that….

"It's three o'clock in the morning! Durito, can't we sleep?"

"Sleep! Thou thinkest only of sleep! How canst thou aspire to achieve the supreme station of knight-errantry if thou dost occupy the most opportune hours in sleep?"

"Right now, I only aspire to sleep," I say as I yawn and curl back up against the backpack that serves as my pillow.

"Do so, then. I, until Apollo scratches the skirt of the night with his golden knives, I will devote myself to thoughts of the highest and most dignified lady that any knight has ever chosen for his flag and desire, the one and only, the best, the one without equal, the ... are you listening to me!?" I hear Durito shout.

"Mmmmfg," I respond, knowing that I don't need to open my eyes to notice that Durito must be standing on his stack of newspaper clippings, with Excalibur in his right hand and his left hand on his heart, and the other right hand on his belt, and the other fixing the armor of the other ... Actually, I don't remember how many arms Durito has anymore, but he has enough, more than enough for the gestures he has to make.

"And what keeps thee up, my sluggardly shield-bearer?" Durito asks, with evident will to keep me awake.

"Me? Nothing, if it weren't for your midnight speeches and studies ... Really, what is it you were studying?"

"The governmental cabinet," Durito responds, returning to his papers.

"The governmental cabinet?" I ask with surprise, doing what I didn't want to do — opening my eyes.

"Of course! I have discovered why the members of the cabinet contradict each other, why each one takes off in his own direction, apparently forgetting that the boss is...

"Zedillo!" I say, losing interest in the talk.

"Error! It isn't Zedillo," says Durito with satisfaction.

"No?" I ask at the same time that I feel around in my backpack for the little radio that I use to listen to news. "Did he resign? Did they get rid of him?"

"Negative," says Durito, enjoying my sudden activity.

"There it is, just where we left it yesterday."

"So?" I ask, now completely awake.

"The boss of the governmental cabinet is a character who, for the sake of convenience and discretion, I will now call, 'Character X'."

"Character X?" I ask, remembering Durito's enjoyment of mystery novels. "And how did you find him out?"

"Elementary, my dear Watson."

"Watson?" I manage to stammer out, upon noticing that Durito has turned the cactus shell that he uses as a helmet, and I see that it looks like a rapper's cap (although he insists that it is a detective's deerstalker hat). With a magnifying glass, Durito examines his papers. If I didn't know him better, I'd say he isn't Durito, but …

"Sherlock Holmes was the Englishman who learned from me to assemble apparently unimportant details, to unify them into a hypothesis and to look for new details that would confirm or refute it. It's a simple exercise of deduction like those which my pupil Sherlock Holmes practiced when we were out drinking in the bad neighborhoods of London. He would have learned more from me, but he went off with some Conan Doyle who promised to make him famous. I never heard about him since."

"He got famous," I say lazily.

"I don't suppose he became a knight errant?" asks Durito with some interest.

"Negative. My dear Sherlock became a character in a novel and got famous."

"Thou dost err, my dear big-nosed Watson, fame only arises in knight-errantry."

"O.K. let's leave this and get back to all this about the governmental cabinet and this mysterious 'Character X.' What's going on with this?" Durito begins to review his magazine and newspaper clippings.

"Mmmmh … Mmmmh … Mmmmh!" exclaims Durito.

"What? Did you find something?" I ask on account of the last "mmmmh."

"Yes, a photo of Jane Fonda in Barbarella," says Durito with a look of ecstasy.

"Jane Fonda?" I ask-lift-myself-up-stir.

"Yes, and *au naturel,*" he says with a prolonged sigh.

Durito then launches into a Sherlock Holmesian exercise in deductive reasoning:

> Suppose that we have some country whose name is accented on the antepenultimate syllable and which happens to be located, unfortunately enough, beneath the empire of the chaotic stars and stripes. And when I say, 'beneath,' I mean just that, 'beneath.' Suppose that this country is struck by a terrible plague. Ebola? AIDS? Cholera? No! Something more lethal and more destructive … neoliberalism!

He explains that neoliberalism is the project of "a generation of junior politicians applying the only lesson they ever learned: 'act like you know what you're doing,'" and that it is, at bottom, "the chaotic theory of economic chaos, the stupid exaltation of social stupidity, and the catastrophic political management of catastrophe."

> "But there's something that gives coherency to all of this governmental incoherence. I've been analyzing several different clues. I read all of the cabinet's declarations, I classified all of its actions and omissions, I contrasted their political stories, I analyzed even their most minute acts, and I arrived at a very important conclusion."
>
> Durito stops, sucks in air to give himself importance and lengthen the pause so I will ask, "And what is the conclusion?"
>
> "Elementary, my dear Watson! There's an invisible element in the cabinet, a character which, without making itself evident, gives coherence and a systematic quality to all of the government team's braying. A boss under whose command all are subject. Zedillo included. That is to say, 'X' exists, the real governor of the country in question …"
>
> "But who is this mysterious 'Mr. X?'" I ask, unable to hide the shiver that runs up my spine as I imagine that it might be …
>
> "Salinas? Something worse…," says Durito, putting away his papers.

"Worse than Salinas? Who is he?"

"Negative. It's not a 'he;' it's a 'she'," says Durito, blowing smoke from his pipe.

"A 'she?'"

"Correct. Her first name is Stupid, and her last name is Improvisation, and note that I say, 'Stupid Improvisation.' Because you ought to know, my dear Watson, that there are intelligent improvisations, but this isn't the case here. 'Ms. X' is the Stupid Improvisation of neoliberalism in politics, neoliberalism made a political doctrine; that is to say, Stupid Improvisation administering the destinies of the country ... and of others ... Argentina and Peru, for example.

"So you're insinuating that Menem and Fujimori are the same as...?"

"I'm not insinuating anything. I'm affirming it. It's enough to ask the Argentine and Peruvian workers. I was analyzing Yeltsin when my tobacco ran out."

"Yeltsin? But wasn't it the Mexican cabinet you were analyzing?"

"No, not only the Mexican one. Neoliberalism, as you should know, my dear Watson, is a pestilence that plagues all of humanity. Just like AIDS. Of course, the Mexican political system has an enchanting stupidity that is difficult to resist. But nevertheless, all of these governments that are depopulating the world have something in common: all of their success is based on lies, and therefore, it's base is only as solid as the bench you're sitting on."

I jump up instinctively and examine the bench of sticks and creepers we've constructed and make sure it's firm and solid. Relieved, I tell Durito, "but suppose, my dear Sherlock, that the bad guys are able to maintain their lie for an indefinite period of time, that this false base remains solid and they keep having successes." Durito doesn't let me finish. He interrupts me with a shout of ...

"Impossible! The basis of neoliberalism is a contradiction: in order to maintain itself, it must devour itself and, therefore, destroy itself. That's where we get the political assassinations, the blows under the table, the contradictions between the statements and the actions of all levels of public functionaries, the squabbles between 'interest groups,' and all of those things that keep the stockbrokers up at night."

"It kept them up at night. I think they're getting used to it already, because the stock market is going up," I say with some skepticism.

"It's a soap bubble. It will burst before too long. Mark my words," says Durito as he smiles with a know-it-all air and continues, "What keeps the system going is what will bring it down. It's elementary. All you have to do is read Chesterton's three horsemen of the apocalypse to understand it. It's a police story, but as is well known, life ends up imitating art.

"Sounds to me like your theory is pure fanta..."

"I wasn't finished talking."

As I sat down on the bench of sticks, it fell down with the muffled sound of my bones hitting the ground and my not so muffled cursing. Durito laughs as if he's about to suffocate. When he calms down a little bit, he says:

"You were going to say that my theory is pure fantasy? All right, as you can appreciate from your current low position, nature proves me right. History and the people will also give their help."

Durito ends his talk there and lies back against his newspaper clippings. I don't even try to get up. I pull my backpack over and lie down against it again. We fall silent, watching how in the East, a wheat and honey colored light pours through the space between the legs of the mountain. We sigh. What else could we do?

Farewell, good health, and may neither history nor the people wait long.

"El Sup" with a tender pain in his flank.

Tilting at Windmills

What is this mysterious note full of mixed metaphors, star-crossed literary allusions, pseudo-erotic innuendo, non-sequiturs, and poetical babble? Who is this tough-skinned little beetle animating and illuminating the long night of indigenous struggle, and what does he know about neoliberalism? If anyone is improvising, it would seem to be the Sup, concocting this collage of images (Jane Fonda? Sherlock Holmes? Fujimori?), and gluing it all together with the character of a cartoon beetle.

Durito the knight-errant is the character that reveals the quixotic nature of the Zapatistas' war. Like Don Quixote tilting his lance at phantasmagorical giants who are really inanimate windmills, the Zapatistas—"a ragtag army of Mayan Indians" as described by the *New York Times*—must be under some spell, some illusion, when they point their wooden guns at the military-industrial complex defending global capital. Don Quixote, righter of wrongs, is the consummate representation of the naïve struggle for justice in a hostile and unjust world. He is a fool, but an admirable fool; one whose strength of will and imagination allows him to create a safety net around himself while performing the most ridiculous actions in the name of "doing the right thing."

Probably the best-known scene from Cervante's burlesque romance is the windmill scene, in which the knight-errant mistakes windmills for giants and launches into them with his lance:

> As they were thus discoursing, they perceived some thirty or forty windmills that are in that plain; and as soon as Don Quixote espied them, he said to his squire:
>
> "Fortune disposes our affairs better than we ourselves could have desired; look yonder, friend Sancho Panza, where you may discover somewhat more than thirty monstrous giants, with whom I intend to fight, and take away all their lives; with whose spoils we will begin to enrich ourselves for it is lawful war, and doing God good service to take away so wicked a generation from off the face of the earth."
>
> 'What giants?" said Sancho Panza.

Unconvinced by his squire that the imagined giants are, in fact, windmills, Don Quixote leaps to the attack:

> Setting his lance in the rest, he rushed on as fast as Rosinante could gallop, and attacked the first mill before him; and running his lance into the sail, the wind whirled it about with so much violence that it broke the lance to shivers, dragging horse and rider after it, and tumbling them over and over on the plain, in very evil

> plight. Sancho Panza hastened to his assistance, as fast as his ass could carry him; and when he came up to him, he found him not able to stir; so violent was the blow he and Rosinante had received in falling.[8]

This is the inevitable end of the foolhardy warrior who mistakes windmills for giants. Our knight-errant, living in a world of enchantment and not of technology, sees the windmills in their evil guise: they are monsters. But perhaps what Quixote is seeing is the monstrous aspect of the windmills as they threaten his very way of life—they are the modern face of technology, the unyielding machines of progress and industry. In Cervantes' tale, Quixote is an anachronism, a throwback to a time of different values—he is reliving the now-obsolete pastime of slaying enchanted beings and rescuing damsels in distress. Milan Kundera writes in "The Depreciated Legacy of Cervantes":

> As God slowly departed from the seat whence he had directed the universe and its order of values, distinguished good from evil, and endowed each thing with meaning, Don Quixote set forth from his house into a world he could no longer recognize. In the absence of a Supreme Judge, the world suddenly appeared in its fearsome ambiguity; the single divine Truth decomposed into myriad relative truths parceled out by men. Thus was born the world of the Modern Era....[9]

So it is easy for Quixote to see the windmills as agents of the enemy. They are the prosaic forces of scientific production, the advance guard in the industrial revolution with its textile mills and paper mills, and the "dark satanic mills" of William Blake. Or, in Kundera's reading, they are harbingers of a mechanistic, disenchanted world where meaning is relative (and, perhaps, based on production quotas rather than codes of honor, on value rather than virtue.) Whatever they are, in them Quixote sees only trouble. And by tilting his lance at them he is asking for trouble. He attacks them and he gets knocked off his nut. And yet, four hundred years later, the battle continues.

Power Against Power

> People's attachment to nations depends on their belief that the nation is the relevant arbiter of their private fate. This is less and less so. Political languages which appeal to us only as citizens of a nation, and never as common inhabitants of the earth, may find themselves abandoned by those in search of a truer expression of their ultimate attachments.
>
> —Michael Ignatieff[10]

Cervantes's windmills and the dark, satanic mills of Blake were tropes for the disenchanted world of the industrial revolution and (for romantics like Blake and Cervantes) the rationalist nightmare of the Enlightenment. This nightmare—the end of centuries of peasant life, marked by what critic Raymond Williams has called "loving relations between men actually working and producing what is ultimately, in whatever proportions, to be shared,"[11]—was embodied on the British agrarian frontier as the enclosure of the commons. The fencing off of common farming and grazing land to make way for the pre-industrial production of wool for textiles heralded the encroaching era of privatization which has endured to the present, an incipient form of corporate globalization. It was during this storied moment in the early history of capitalism that the modern state developed, many argue, in order to protect the merchant class that was, just then, bringing unheard-of wealth to Mother England from her outlying colonies. The state, this line of historical reasoning suggests, exists to protect the capitalist class, and thus to wrest common resources from the social majorities and transfer them to capitalist elites. This state, profoundly subservient to economic elites, is the form of governance that has dominated the world for centuries.

So, centuries later, scanning the horizon for forms of social organization that may be less arbitrary and less destructive to both the natural environment and the social fabric, it seems reasonable to ask the question: can some form of non-coercive, nonviolent governance exist within, or apart from, or alongside, the modern state? These forms have likely always existed; it is equally likely that they have always collided, catastrophically, with coercive power. This collision is the Zapatistas' wind from above and wind from below meeting and building a storm front; in a concrete sense, it is the Zapatistas' autonomous municipalities developing their own grassroots democratic governance structures which tend to last until they are violently uprooted by the Mexican military or undermined by paramilitary intervention.

If "opening a space for democracy" without taking state power is the explicit goal of the Zapatistas, then we are talking about a shift in how power is arbited, and where in the social fabric it resides. John Holloway has focused his theoretical work on the question, inspired by the Zapatistas, of transforming the world without taking state power. "Power," he reminds us, "is usually associated with control of money or the state."

> The left, in particular, has usually seen social transformation in terms of control of the state. The strategies of the mainstream left have generally aimed at winning control of the state and using the state to transform society. The reformist left sees gaining control of the state in terms of winning elections; the revolutionary left (certainly in the Leninist and "guerillero" traditions) thinks of it in terms of the seizure of state power. The classic controversies between reformists and revolutionaries have been about the means of winning control of the state. The actual goal of taking state power is generally taken as an obvious prerequisite for changing society.
>
> The attempts to transform society through the state (whether by reformist or revolutionary means) have never achieved what they set out to do. So many historical failures cannot be accounted for in terms of "betrayal" of the revolution or of the people. The failure of so many attempts to use state power suggests rather that the state is not the site of power. States are embedded in a worldwide web of capitalist social relations that defines their character. States are incapable of bringing about radical social change simply because the flight of capital which any such attempt would cause would threaten the very existence of the state. The notion of state power is a mirage: the seizure of the state is not the seizure of power.[12]

Recognizing that control of the state no longer need be the end goal of social struggle, Holloway goes on to suggest that "The revolutions of the twentieth century failed because they aimed too low, not because they aimed too high."[13]

It would appear strange that, at a moment when, in stark contrast to the wave of dictatorships that controlled most of Latin America deep into the 1980s, progressive governments are in power in Venezuela, Bolivia, Brazil, Ecuador, Argentina, and Chile, the Zapatistas would continue their insistence that state power is not the prime mover for a politics carried out "from below." Yet, speak to many social movement actors from these countries, and the common thread you will find is precisely the sense of "betrayal" of which Holloway has spoken. Certainly, the road the Zapatistas have traveled—abandoning their fight for constitutional reform to strengthen their own autonomous structures—reveals an attempt to work through the state giving way to efforts to build power independent of it.

While social movements, in general, tend to struggle for progressive or radical changes to national policy—think of the U.S. civil rights movement, or the suffragist movement—indigenous-led movements tend toward constructing power outside the framework of the state. The Zapatistas, practicing a hybrid strategy by pushing constitutional reform above while simultaneously building autonomy below, do both.

By 2006, when Marcos was invited to attend the inauguration of Evo Morales as president of Bolivia, he declined, saying, "We don't have relations with governments, whether they are good or bad. We have relations with the people."[14] Indeed, *Zapatismo* recognizes that legitimate power never resides in one individual, regardless of how responsive, ethical, or just she or he may be; power is held in the community assembly and the organized multitude. Legitimate power, for the Zapatistas, is never static and singular but always plural, collective, and dynamic.

The invitation to attend Morales' inauguration came in 2006, when Marcos was holding day-long meetings with grassroots groups as part of the Otra Campaña. Referring to these meetings, Marcos said, "Our way is more like what we are doing right now. That is how we have achieved all that we have won. There might even be sometimes a candidate that wins with a good program. But as long as the problem of the system is not solved, the problems will repeat over and over again."[15]

This problematic has been addressed in numerous communiqués, and has become one of the de facto understandings of *Zapatismo* as a political philosophy. Nonetheless, it bears illustration. In a 2002 communiqué called "Chairs of Power and Butterflies of Rebellion," Don Durito offers a parable—directed toward his fellow revolutionaries—about how the true revolutionary approaches the seat of power:

> **Chairs**
> Well, it's about how the attitude human beings have about chairs defines them politically. The Revolutionary (like that, with a capital R) scorns ordinary chairs and says to others and to himself: "I don't have time to sit down, the heavy mission commended to me by History (like that, with a capital H) prevents me from distracting myself with nonsense." He goes through life like this until he runs into the chair of Power. He throws off whomever is sitting on the chair with one shot, sits down and frowns, as if he were constipated, and says to others and to himself: "History (like that, with a capital H) has been fulfilled. Everything, absolutely everything, makes sense now, I am sitting on the Chair (like that, with a capital C) and I am the culmination of the times." There he remains until another Revolutionary (like that, with a capital R) comes by, throws him off and history (like that, with a small h) repeats itself.
>
> The rebel (like that, with a small r), on the other hand, when he sees an ordinary chair, analyzes it carefully, then goes and puts another chair next to it, and another, and another, and soon it looks like a gathering because more rebels (like that, with a small r) have come, and then the coffee, tobacco, and the word begin to circulate and mix, and then, precisely when everyone starts to feel comfortable, they get antsy, as if they had ants in their pants, and they don't know if it's from the coffee or the tobacco or the word, but everyone gets up and keeps on going the way they were going. And so on until they find another ordinary chair and history repeats itself.

> There is only one variation, when the rebel runs into the Seat of Power (like that, with a capital S and a capital P), looks at it carefully, analyzes it, but instead of sitting there he goes and gets a fingernail file and, with heroic patience, he begins sawing at the legs until they are so fragile that they break when someone sits down, which happens almost immediately. *Tan-tan.*[16]

The metaphor of the seat of power is a clear reference to the famous photograph, visited earlier in our narrative, showing Pancho Villa, Emiliano Zapata, and a cadre of their supporters in Mexico's National Palace. Stories about this historic photo are legion, but the operative myth is in the interplay between Villa and Zapata. One version of the story serves:

> At the Zocalo the entire army was reviewed by [President] Eulalio Gutiérrez, but Villa and Zapata themselves treated Gutierrez with contempt and swept past him into the presidential palace. There, as a joke, Villa sat in the presidential chair, then motioned to Zapata to take his turn. Humor was never Zapata's strong point, and his response was po-faced: "I didn't fight for that. I fought to get the lands back. I don't care about politics. We should burn that chair to end all ambitions." However, Villa did persuade his comrade to pose for a photograph with him. The famous image shows a euphoric Villa alongside a surly Zapata. As Enrique Krauze remarks, Zapata is on edge, "always wary of a bullet perhaps springing out of the camera instead of the flash of a bulb."[17]

The image forms the basis of one of the crucial myths of Zapata and the Mexican Revolution, offering a whole-cloth representation of Zapata as the selfless warrior for the poor, free of personal ambition, and devoted not to the struggle for power, but to the struggle *against* power. This is the Zapata that has endured as a revolutionary icon, fiercely beloved by *los de abajo*. It is also the Zapata who was assassinated a few years after, and whose revolution, in failing to take state power, essentially failed.

Each state grows its own history, distinct and distinguished by unique conditions, but all national histories are constructed, at least in part, on the power relation between wealthy elites and the rest. In Mexico, the Revolution of 1910–1917 did not distribute land equitably among all of Mexico's poor as Zapata had hoped; it did, however, give peasants "status and specific rights as peasants, not simply as citizens,"[18] "a status built upon the expectation of protection by the state in exchange for their obedience to the ruling elite."[19] As Lopez y Rivas argues, "The construction of the Mexican nation, above all in its formal aspects (judicial, economic, administrative, territorial, and political), has been undertaken by a reduced sector composed largely of the descendents of the colonizers. The indigenous and *campesino* sectors—that is, the great majority—have been thus permanently excluded, denying them political and cultural rights.[20]

The Mexican peasantry and, above all, the indigenous peasantry, marginalized from any meaningful political participation, has long had a relationship of institutionalized paternalism with the state. This relationship served as the basis of power for the PRI, the century's longest-running single-party dictatorship, while simultaneously splintering the peasantry along lines of party loyalty. It is this paternalism itself—the carrot—and not merely its more repressive aspects—the stick—against which the Zapatista concept of resistance is built. Based on long historical experience, paternalism itself is recognized by the Zapatistas as a form of state violence.[21]

As Wixarica lawyer Santos de La Cruz Carrillo, echoing the voice of Zapata and the neo-Zapatista resistance, has said, "Power wants to make us complicit with money, with lies, with violence. We will not be complicit."[22] Consequently, *Zapatismo*, as the living embodiment of Zapata's rejection of power, does not merely reject the current seated government of the contemporary ruling elite, but the notion of the state itself. Examining the why's and wherefore's of this rejection of the state, John Holloway makes the point that:

> States function in such a way as to reproduce the capitalist status quo. In their relation to us, and in our relation to them, there is a filtering out of anything that is not compatible with the reproduction of capitalist social relations. This may be a violent filtering, as in the repression of revolutionary or subversive activity, but it is

> also a less perceptible filtering, a sidelining or suppression of passions, loves, hates, anger, laughter, dancing.[23]

Strategically, the movement, especially early on, struggled for constitutional reform in order to protect, defend, and expand indigenous rights. But, at the same time, the terms of the communiqués, the efforts toward autonomy, and the revivifying of culture at the heart of *Zapatismo* show that their struggle is for something at once less tangible and more immediate than mere political control.

In its explicit rejection of the goal of state power, the Zapatista project carries with it a notion that there is, perhaps, another locus of power rarely taken into account either by the state or by the traditional leftist opposition. In reviving national symbols, rebirthing native beliefs, reinhabiting a narrative of history that includes a future as yet unwritten, and galvanizing civil society not at the voting booth but in the streets and schools and fields and factories and prisons, *Zapatismo* affirms that power—and especially the transformative power that guides the *realpolitik* of social change at the grassroots—lives not in the halls of government but in the fabric of culture. In the poetic terms of a famous graffito, "Our dreams don't fit in your ballot box!"

Successful movements for radical social change have always combined the strategy of exerting pressure on the state with myriad forms of popular empowerment and cultural liberation. The civil rights movement in the United States would have been unimaginable without innumerable bold exertions of direct, everyday empowerment accompanied by the chorus of "We Shall Overcome" and the hand-clapping, foot-stomping gospel, blues, jazz, and rock 'n roll that kept it moving, and which it, the movement for black liberation, conversely fostered. Salvador Allende's brief socialist experiment in Chile would not have occurred without the popular movement he fronted, and would have been greatly diminished without the songs of Victor Jara, Violetta Parra, and Inti Illimani, not to mention the poetic substrate woven into the Chilean national identity through decades of poetry by the great Pablo Neruda. The struggle against apartheid in South Africa was both a "political" struggle waged through militant force, direct action, and global solidarity, and a cultural one—a generations-long gambit to rebuild the politics of the nation by bringing about fundamental change in the culture itself. Examples are infinite: culture is power (like that, with a small p). And by culture, I do not mean merely "the arts," but the bulk of unaccounted-for activities in the collective life of everyday—all the ways in which we construct a collective vision of a bearable world.

To Lead by Obeying

What Don Quixote, Sherlock Holmes, and our character Subcomandante Insurgente Marcos have in common is their apparently foolhardy pursuit of justice at any cost, a preference to die on their feet rather than live on their knees. Like Zapata himself, they are visionaries, dreamers whose dream is at odds with the overwhelming forces of imperial history. *Zapatismo* signals a utopian politics, bound by a code of ethics with its feet set firmly in historical struggles, the births and deaths of gods and heroes, the dates, the names and places of defeats, insurrections, massacres, and meetings whose moments portended change, at least. At most, a world in which many worlds fit.

Don Durito's conclusion, that the guiding principle of neoliberalism is "stupid improvisation," is a conclusion that has been reached by indigenous people throughout the centuries when confronting the brutal insensitivity of imperial capital. Don Durito's revelation should be looked at in the light of *Zapatismo*: an ethical stance with roots in the *terra firma*, rather than in the shifting politics of the market economy. It has been noted by indigenous scholars that a government built largely on a personal power that changes every four or six years is, by nature, incapable of long-term vision, and practices, by virtue of its fly-by-night composition, a politics of improvisation.[24] Neoliberalism is the perfect culmination of this politics of improvisation, especially as it is practiced in the "developing world," where government policies are often the tail of the dog whose body is the free market and whose head is the tripartate multilateral financial institutions: World Trade Organization, World Bank, and International Monetary Fund.

Indigenous visions, on the other hand, despite genocide, forced migration, assimilation, and other indignities, have tended to remain more constant over the course of centuries. While the occidental view shows free market capitalism to be an enduring force, with steady growth over its long 400 year history, in the light of indigenous cosmovision, based in a striving toward social harmony, and confined by clearly recognized ecological limits, Western politics reveals itself to be, as our beloved Don Durito tells us, "the Catastrophic Political Management of Catastrophe." We can recall Mircea Eliade discussing the creation of meaning through ritual interaction with the sacred: "The only profane activities are those which have no mythical meaning, that is, which lack exemplary models. Thus we may say that every responsible activity in pursuit of a definite end is, for the archaic world, a ritual."[25] And we may say, to the contrary, that the irresponsible pursuit of profit at the expense of the greater good of social harmony is stupid improvisation. As Durito says, "That lesson is always the same: 'Act like you know what you're doing.' This is the fundamental axiom of power politics under neoliberalism."

Durito—that is, Sherlock Holmes—refers to the generation of politicians in charge of contemporary Mexico as being ignorant of history, hitching their wagon to the speeding trainwreck of globalization: "Suppose now that a young generation of 'junior politicians' has studied abroad how to 'save' this country in the only way in which that generation conceives of its salvation, that is to say, without knowing its history and annexing it to the tail of the fast train of brutality and human imbecility: capitalism." Our hero is referring specifically to former Mexican presidents Ernesto Zedillo, a Yale economist, and Carlos Salinas de Gortari, a graduate of Harvard. Both politicians developed social and economic programs designed to attract foreign capital at the expense of their nation's social safety net, and both treated *Zapatismo* as a foreign element to be ridiculed in the press and crushed on the ground, while at the same time making an occasional bow to "human rights" in order to further encourage foreign investment. And both presidents, beholden to the *patria* in their rhetoric, left Mexico for greener pastures at the end of their six-year terms—the former for an executive position with Union Pacific Railroad in New York and the latter in search of political asylum abroad after his family was implicated in the assassination of a political rival. No better word can describe their presidencies than "schizophrenic."

Zapatismo, on the other hand, is a movement whose logic is not based in some utilitarian cost-benefit analysis, but rather in human ethics. For the huge conglomerate of social groups worldwide confronting an alienated existence dominated by capital and marching under the broad banner of the so-called "anti-globalization movement," the global justice movement, *globalphobicos* (a delightfully arbitrary term proudly coined by Zedillo), *altermundialisme*, or whatever it may be called, the Zapatistas' proposed and enacted conquest of dignity has offered something of a compass by which to navigate away from an overarching and improvisatory politics of destruction.

Throughout the 1990s and at the beginning of the twenty-first century, the recuperation of politics by ethical demands has replaced the rote recourse of the international left to dogmatic vocabularies of Marxist-Leninist ideology. Furthermore, these ethical demands have been transformed into concrete proposals for an alternative power base in the short term, such as the opening of markets for fair trade products, the demand for citizen control over the big financial powers (for example, the taxing of junk bonds, the outcry against free-trade zones, and the demand to end structural adjustment conditions placed on loans from the World Bank and the IMF), and the defense of economic, social and cultural rights like employment, health, education, agrarian reform and access to basic services. But the principal achievement of the global justice movement—visible on all continents—is the struggle toward an effective democratization that seeks the empowerment and direct political engagement of everyone.

The phrase "*Para todos todo, para nosotros nada,*"—Everything for everyone, nothing for us—first appeared in February 1994[26] and was repeated consistently in the following months, becoming one of the most recognizable early slogans of *Zapatismo*. It is, essentially, a moral or ethical pronouncement suggesting that they (the EZLN and the base communities) are willing to sacrifice all for the greater good. As the Second Declaration of the Lacandon declared, in an unleashing of another cogent formulation of Zapatista ethics, "We will resist until he who commands, commands by obeying."

In many cases the Zapatistas have denounced a politics—whether right, left, or somewhere in between—in which the ends are supposed to justify the means. Marcos has exchanged harsh words with the neoliberal establishment for sacrificing human dignity for short-term economic gain. He has criticized NATO for its indiscriminate bombing of Yugoslavia, because in the Zapatista ethic it is wrong to use massive firepower against a population center, even in order to bring down an oppressive regime. He has exchanged harsh words with the EPR for basing their struggle on the will to power. He has criticized the long-enduring Colombian guerillas of the FARC and ETA, the Basque independence movement, for their use of violence against civilians as a means of advancing their struggle. And he has ceaselessy lambasted Mexico's mainstream progressive left, represented by the Partido de la Revolución Democratica (Party of the Democratic Revolution, or PRD) in terms equally harsh. At the same time, Marcos has praised individual activists like Mumia Abu Jamal and Leonard Peltier, whose steadfast persistence in the face of decades of imprisonment heightens the dignity of their struggles. In these distinctions, we see that the Zapatistas' is an ethical struggle, but also a struggle for identity—for an identity which is unique to them at the same time as it expands outward to include all of "the many," "the social majorities," those who in postcolonial theory are called "subalterns" and in current neo-Marxist language, "multitude." The "*nosotros*" in "*para nosotros nada,*" might refer to the EZLN as a revolutionary organization, to the Zapatistas as a movement, to indigenous peasant farmers, or to a much broader and more inclusive social movement base.

Ultimately, this *nosotros*, this we, is dynamic and expandable. Major Ana María, opening the International Encuentro in July 1996, said to the crowd, "*Detras de nosotros estamos ustedes.*" The phrase, which later became the title of a volume of communiqués, has no ready translation because of its clever and intricate misuse of Spanish pronouns; but we might translate it as, "behind us we are you." The fact is, we don't need to know exactly who the "us" is: whoever they are, they are standing on the moral highground and holding up a mirror in which we—whoever "we" are—may see ourselves. Behind them, we are us.

The Zapatistas attempt to make no distinction between means and ends: the principle goal is the way forward itself; the road, as they say, is made by walking, and the steps forward are guided, in principal, by the notion of *mandar obediciendo*, to lead by obeying. As Antonio Paoli writes, "Whoever leads must lead by respecting the community will, and must be *p'ekel, ma'stoy sba* [humble, not overbearing or arrogant], must be the first to begin the appointed work on the appointed day. This attitude is a fundamental principle of [Tzeltal] social organization, and has been translated as "*mandar obediciendo,*" to lead by obeying."[27]

Mandar obediciendo is a riddle, a paradox, because the words themselves, *to lead* and *to obey*, carry such moral weight and cultural baggage. *Mandar*, to lead, to tell others what to do, to boss around, to be in charge. The word itself carries a charge of *caudillismo*—again, bossism—of singular male power. To command. "*Si, patron!, yes boss!*" Similarly, "to obey:" One bows down before authority, follows the leader, stays in line, does what one is told to do. "Obey!"

So, written into the language itself, this lead by obeying is at once a challenge to authority as it is constituted in occidental societies—certainly to the chafing, traditional authority of the landowner over the serf, the priest over the Indian, the police officer over the urban poor, the domineering husband over the subservient wife, and so on—at the same time, stretching and twisting the language to make room for an unfamiliar concept. *Mandar obediciendo* challenges the authority of the language to tell us what to think. As signaled in another communiqué of 1994, it is the root concept of Zapatista democracy: "The word, 'democracy', was given to this road on which we walked even before words themselves could walk."[28] We'll explore this further on, as we examine, from the Zapatista perspective, what democracy looks like.

We Are All Marcos

> The essence of revolution is not the struggle for bread; it is the struggle for human dignity. Certainly this includes bread.
>
> —Frantz Fanon

As a student at the National Autonomous University, Rafael Guillén begins his thesis with this quote from the French philosopher Michel Foucault: "Discourse is not simply that which translates struggles or systems of domination, but that for which and by means of which struggle occurs."[29] Guillén is the disappeared university professor pegged by the government of Ernesto Zedillo as the man behind the mask—the figure who disappeared to become Marcos. One of the clues to his identity is his thesis, which, being about the power of discourse in revolutionary politics, admittedly rings of Marcos.

It is understood from the outset that the struggle is undertaken both for the ability to speak—a goal of the revolution is for the population in resistance to establish a speaking position—and by means of an ongoing articulation of the established position. The Zapatistas declare their indigenous identity—"We are the product of 500 years of struggle"—and with it they present their demands and their history. And yet, there persists the paradox that the principal speaking voice is that of a highly educated, middle-class intellectual, whose specialty, it turns out, is the study of discourse as power.

Naming is both a means and an end of revolution. One of the *consignas* or slogans of the Zapatistas which took on immediate currency throughout Mexico, a cry heard at rallies from the *zocalo* in San Cristóbal to the *zocalo* in Mexico City was the now famous "*Todos somos Marcos*": We are all Marcos. A definitive statement of the populism of the movement and of the idolatrous, almost fanatical support that Marcos initially received as a revolutionary leader and cultural hero, the affirmation accompanies the ubiquity of the ski masks and the aura of anonymity, mystery, and otherness they convey. In the rhetoric of the government reacting to the January 1 uprising, the leaders of the movement were branded "intransigent," "professionals of violence," and routinely declared to be foreigners. Marcos, identified by his green eyes and tall stature, was conjectured to be Spanish, Cuban, French, Italian—anything but Mexican, in a strategic othering that has had a certain success among some sectors. It is preferable for the ruling class to believe that the revolutionaries come from outside, and it is certainly preferable for them to convey this idea to the nation. Simultaneously, the offensive of the government, from the outset, was aimed at eliminating the leadership; psychologically, proving them foreign was one way to eliminate them.

In what is known as the "February Offensive," on February 19, 1995, a military offensive was launched against Zapatista-held territories, its aim to capture Marcos and the other leaders. The offensive failed to achieve this goal, though it succeeded in winning back large areas of the jungle for the government forces and establishing a military presence to wage the low-intensity war over the ensuing years. A few presumed

Zapatista leaders were rounded up in other areas of Mexico and arrested. Accompanying the strategic retaking of jungle territories, President Zedillo accounced Marcos's true identity: he was ex-philosophy professor Rafael Sebastián Guillén. By revealing his identity, the Zedillo government hoped to remove his magic aura of invincibility and, with it, the entire mystique surrounding the movement.

In this, too, the government failed entirely. Days after the February offensive, tens of thousands gathered in the Zocalo in Mexico City to denounce the government's action. They affirmed their support with the rallying cry "*Todos somos Marcos!*" Marcos himself declared, in true populist revolutionary form, that if he were captured, others would spring up to replace him; that Marcos was not a person but an ideal, that he was, again, "the dead of forever who had died in order to live." You can kill the person behind the mask, said the Zapatista spokesman, but you cannot kill what the mask represents.

Without ever revealing if President Zedillo has correctly identified him, Marcos has stated on numerous occasions that the name "Marcos" is that of a *compañero* who was killed years earlier, in the early days of the EZLN, when it was composed of less than a dozen urban intellectuals and was known as the Forces of National Liberation (FLN). It is the custom of individual Zapatistas to have a public name and a private name, a given name and a Zapatista name. It is not unique to Marcos, but rather a security measure taken by the entire Zapatista leadership. At the same time, the Mayan people, like many ancient peoples, have a deep sense of the power of naming. In their essay "The Land Where the Flowers Bloom," on the worldview of Guatemalan novelist Miguel Angel Asturias, Luis Harss and Barbara Dohmann explain: "For the Indian, even today, words capture the essence of things. To be able to put an exact name on something, says Asturias, means to reveal it, to bare it, to strip it of its mystery. 'That's why in the villages of Guatemala all the men answer to the name of Juan, all the women to the name of Maria. Nobody knows their real names. If a person knew the name of a man's wife, he could possess her, in other words, snatch her from her husband.'"

We can surely see this function in the tactic of double naming that is an essential characteristic of Zapatista identity. By declaring "We are all Marcos," the popular movement announces at once its understanding of the power of naming, its support for the man who had become the recognized "leader" of a non-hierarchical movement, and its contempt for the government agents who maintain the simplistic belief that by rounding up a handful of revolutionary leaders they can asphyxiate an entire movement.

At the same time, an inversion on the phrase "*Todos somos Marcos*" (We are all Marcos), leads to the reciprocal formula, "*Somos todos Marcos*" (Marcos is all of us).

In one of the most oft-cited early communiqués, whose frequent reproduction speaks to its power and appeal, Marcos wrote, "Marcos is gay in San Francisco, a black person in South Africa, Asian in Europe, a Chicano in San Isidro, an anarchist in Spain, a Palestinian in Israel, an indigenous person in the streets of San Cristóbal, a gang-member in Neza, a rocker on campus, a Jew in Germany," and so on.[30] While the point of this list is to say that Marcos—and by extension the Zapatistas—are aligned and identified with underdogs everywhere, it has the equally important effect of inferring that Marcos (and *Zapatismo*) is whatever (and whoever) you want it to be. As he affirmed to Yvon Le Bot, especially in regard to the need for international support, "the lack of definition of Zapatismo is particularly important."[31] We are all Marcos, Marcos is all of us. This lack of definition, and the ability of *Zapatismo* to be, at some point, all things to all people, would become both a strength of the movement and one of its most persistent weaknesses.

The name Marcos itself has many mythic origins. In 1996, Marcos told Yvon Le Bot that it was the name of a comrade fallen in arms,[32] and Jan de Vos confirms that this comrade was one Alfredo Zarate, alias Marcos, killed February 14, 1974, during the very early days of the FLN.[33] In an earlier interview, Medea Benjamin suggested (and Marcos denied) that the name came from the initials of "Movimiento Armado Revolucionario Comandante Obispo Samuel" (referring to Bishop Samuel Ruiz) or from the names of the communities occupied during the seven-days war of January 1994: Margaritas, Altamirano, Rancho Nuevo, Comitan, Ocosingo, San Cristobal.[34] The Subcomandante himself makes a Shakespearean (and indeed, very Mexican) double entendre of his name; "*marco*" in Spanish means "frame," as in a picture frame or a window frame. Marcos serves as a window through which to view the changes afoot in Mexico and the world; an aperture onto the communities he serves as sub-commander.

In a speech given in Tepoztlán, Morelos during the Caravan for Indigenous Dignity, March 6, 2001, Marcos says, "Marcos doesn't exist. He is not. He is a shadow. He is the frame of a window. If you are seeing that behind me are my comrades, commanders, and bosses, you better get on the other side, the side of the communities, and you better realize that when we look at them it is exactly the reverse, they come before us."[35] Throughout the speech he returns to the word *marco*, frame, and its metaphor of windows. "[Marcos is] more than anything a window. We call it the frame of a window that we hope will serve to help you understand what we are, what is behind me and behind our *comandantes*: the indigenous people. And the whole situation that there has been, of injustice and poverty and misery, and above all sadness, that there has been in the indigenous communities."[36]

At a certain point, leaving aside comparisons to great historical figures or even literary personages, Marcos announces that he is, in fact, an actor. In "The Thirteenth Stella," of 2003, he refers to himself (in jest, needless to say), as "the one they say is the leader, one Sup Marcos, whose public image is more like Cantinflas or Pedro Infante than Emiliano Zapata or Che Guevara."[37] Like Cantinflas and Pedro Infante,[38] both heroes of the golden age of Mexican cinema whose fame as cultural icons is unrivaled by the characters they played on screen, Marcos is better known for *who he is* than for who he pretends to be.

For Marcos to "not be, not exist," as he claimed in his speech in Tepoztlán, he'd have to mask not just his face, but his person, his personality as well. He'd have to be, not Sup Marcos, a.k.a. Delegado Zero, aka Rafael Sebastián Guillén, the genius behind what *Newsweek* magazine called "the Marcos Mystique,"[39] but Joe the Plumber or Bartleby the Scrivener, the silent majority or the invisible man, Franz Kafka's K or Samuel Beckett's Krapp. But, to the detriment of his everyman argument, his personality comes through the mask, and we do not doubt that he, as an individual, has an exceedingly large personality. Through his public persona we can know, for example, that Marcos is vain, clever, pushy, egotistical, a lover of children and animals (at least kitty cats, mou-sies, chickens, beetles, and penguins); that he is no doubt an "alpha male," that he has a passion for justice, that he is "a natural leader," etc. That is to say, Marcos does not disappear in order to be seen, in part because his personality, and his ego, get in the way. Yet, like a Hollywood celebrity whose job it is to continually be someone else, and yet whose celebrity rests on his "real" self, it is this paradox that ensures his public allure.

The character or persona of Marcos is, in fact, deeply paradoxical: poet and a military commander, urban mestizo and voice of indigenous *campesinos*, avowed feminist and loud-mouthed, boastful *machista*, leader and subordinate, public wit and clandestine, armed revolutionary. As literary theorist Kristine Berghe notes:

> Marcos's self-portrait has much of the anti-hero; it is fragmentary and built of contradictions. Marcos is indigenous but at the same time he's not, he plays a role that is subordinate but at the same time he has an enormous influence; he's Sancho Panzo but he's also Don Quixote; he's a useless figure in the jungle, and the military leader of the EZLN. In other words, he's a figure whose characteristics change according to the political moment and the exigencies of the war.[40]

Like opposing magnetic forces, these contradictions generate electricity. But they also generate controversy, disillusion, and, in a movement that prizes transparency and horizontalism, more than occasional disdain. In fact, by late 2008, Marcos's *protagonismo* (a Spanish word widely used by Mexican activists to refer to those who take up too much space, dominating the discourse and alienating the rest) had offended so many people within the movement that, returning to the heart of darkness in colonial literature, he continued to invite casual comparisons to Joseph Conrad's Colonel Kurtz.[41]

While criticisms of Marcos the man are increasingly barbed, and, in the spirit of *auto-critica* (self-criticism), are necessary if the movement is to retain its transparency and democratic underpinnings, there is something else at work, which is revealed, rather than hidden, by the paradox of Marcos: Marcos the figure is much more than an individual icon, and in fact comes to embody, perhaps as much as any individual can, the collective agency that is at the core of the Zapatista ethic, and of the Zapatistas' designs for transformation of the world, the nation state, or at least the Mexican southeast. When he says, "through my voice speaks the voice of the EZLN," he is not merely stating that he represents the interests of the Zapatista Army, but, perhaps, acknowledging the possibility of a multiple speaking position, or a collective agency. As Comandante Tacho pronounced in the ceremony of the Seven Messages, "Now you are not you, now and forever you are us."

Marcotrafficking in the Age of Digital Storytelling

Returning to an aspect of the ski mask overlooked earlier, Marcos with his wit has surely been aware of the mask's ability to evoke comic book superheroes. By combining the ski mask with the bandaliers and horse of Zapata, he becomes the postmodern Mexican superhero, a cross between Zapata, Zorro, and Superman. The effect on Mexican youth is immediate, identifying him as "cool" and recognizing him as part of the "*banda*," the gang.

The effect is equally strong on the women of the nation, and of the press. Nick Henck, author of *Subcomandante Marcos: The Man and the Mask*, the only English-language biography of Marcos, summarizes:

> Anne Louise Bardach, a reporter for *Vanity Fair*, wrote that "he looked the very stuff of myth," and described "his good features" and "his manner—one of palpable gentleness," all of which ensured that in her eyes "there could never be a convincing imitation of this unique creature." Nor was she alone. Alma Guillermoprieto, no stranger to the guerilla scene, was clearly impressed with Marcos when she met him, writing that he was "more articulate, cosmopolitan, humorous, and coquettishly manipulative than any guerilla leader of El Salvador or Nicaragua who ever locked horns with the press." Likewise, *La Jornada*'s reporter, Eva Bodenstadt, was led to ask herself, "Why does this man motivate an almost irrational sexuality?"[42]

Henck describes a scene in which reporter Bill Weinberg encountered Marcos, at home in La Realidad, entangled with a gaggle of adoring female hangers-on, and then adds, "Other women are merely content to worship him from afar. The ex-wife of former Mexican president José López Portillo (1976–82) has written him effusive poetry."[43]

The *subcomandante*'s machismo is both heightened and tempered by his righteousness, and a sort of guerilla chic overtakes Mexico in the months following the uprising, and lasts for years. Suddenly the standard fantasy of the women of Mexico as projected by the mass media is to be carried into the jungle on the back of Marcos's stallion. Magazines appear on the newsstands in which ski-masked Marcos mimics performing sexual acts with barely clad, pale-skinned, and made-up models: "The Kama Sutra According to *el Sup*." Years later, in another farcical repetition of history, a version of this image is repeated on the cover of Marcos's own book of erotic poetry.

Revolution undeniably has a certain sex appeal—an appeal presided over by Che Guevara's ubiquitous image, Errol Flynn's Hollywood Robin Hood, James Dean's to-die-for rebel without a cause; but the heroic bravado of Marcos, combined with his poetic language, his humor, and his mysterious disguise, raise this to a new level. He becomes an icon, or, beyond an icon, a fetish, the embodiment of guerilla chic—"the very stuff of myth"—and so is ensured, at least as long as he can maintain his invisibility, his ubiquity, and his mythic status, a safe haven among the icons of civil society. His image appears on balloons and T-shirts, cigarette lighters and buttons, bumper stickers, clocks, pencils, and anything else that can be sold for a few pesos at a street-side post or a rock concert. The Marcos fetish—known in Mexico as Marcotrafficking—is a significant element of what has kept the Zapatista struggle in the public eye; early interviews and photo spreads in *Time* ("Zapata's Revenge"), *Newsweek* ("The Marcos Mystique"), *Vanity Fair* ("Mexico's Poet Rebels"), *Esquire* ("On the Zapatista Trail"), and so forth, continue to resonate. The same phenomenon, of course, serves as well to obscure and confuse the real issue behind the ski mask: self-determination of the indigenous people. As Manuel Rozental of Colombia's Minga Indigena told me:

> We admire Marcos, just as we admire Ramona and all the rest of the Zapatistas. We admire Marcos as a figure who symbolizes the struggle. In our point of view, Marcos is not the protagonist—the

> protagonist is the process itself, the struggle. I think that people with a mature understanding get this. What we don't like is that this world wants merchandise—bandanas with pictures of Che, products with the picture of the man with the pipe, and so on—and this leaves people confused. Just like Che, Marcos becomes about merchandise.[44]

Marcos himself has recognized the deep contradictions in the question of how he is portrayed and how he represents the movement. In an interview by Julio Scherer Garcia, broadcast by Televisa from Milpa Alta in Mexico City on March 10, 2001, upon the Zapatistas' arrival in the capital with the March for Indigenous Dignity, he said, "We believe they've constructed an image of Marcos that doesn't correspond to reality, but that has to do more with the world of the communications media."[45] When probed about his charisma, he offers this explanation:

> There's an emptiness in society, a space that has to be filled one way or another. The space that [newly elected President Vicente] Fox filled, in the political arena, doesn't mean what it apparently could or should be. The same occurs with Marcos.... The image of Marcos responds to some very romantic, idealistic expectations. That is to say, a white man in the role of the Indian; the closest comparison that the collective unconscious has is to Robin Hood, Juan Charrasqueado, etc.[46]

With the Other Campaign, launched in 2005, the problem of Marcos "filling an empty space" becomes increasingly problematic, as it becomes clear that no other figure on the Mexican left can fill his ski mask. In an interview with Laura Castellanos in 2008, Marcos states: "If there's anything that I would go back and do differently, it would be to play a less protagonistic role in the media."[47]

Speaks the Gray-Eyed Indian

> The victory of literature: thanks to his undeniable rhetorical and theatrical talents, Subcomandante Marcos has won the battle for public opinion.
>
> —Octavio Paz[48]

In discussing the speaking voice of this insurrection, the question remains: if this is an indigenous rebellion in which the Mayan people of Chiapas claim their own history and their own voice, how is it that the man who speaks for them is not indigenous?

As far back as the beginning of the conquest, Spanish soldiers periodically abandoned the Crown and "went native." Known in Latin America as "gray-eyed Indians," the first of these characters—real people whose strange histories have given them the status of myths—is Gonzalo Guerrero, a soldier of Cortés whose ship wrecked on the Yucatán Peninsula in 1511. Guerrero was captured by Yucatec Maya and quickly became sympathetic to their cause. His captors spared his life, and he joined the Mayan struggle against Spanish domination. When Cortés sent troops to rescue him, they found him bearing facial tattoos and leading a troop of natives into battle. He was unwilling to be saved. Another gray-eyed Indian is Alvar Nuñez Cabeza de Vaca, who, like Guerrero, washed up on the shore of present-day Florida when his ship wrecked in a storm in 1528. In his peregrination across what is the now the southern part of the United States, Cabeza de Vaca was befriended by the Indians and trained in the arts of shamanic healing. Unwilling and uncooperative at first, Cabeza de Vaca gave in to the local culture, going so far as to become a medicine man, curing diseases using indigenous science.

As an urban warrior in the age of information, Marcos—like thousands of other "white" Zapatistas—follows in the footsteps of Gonzalo Guerrero and Cabeza de Vaca, choosing to fight his battle on the side of the land's most ancient inhabitants. In the long history of war in the Americas, the indigenous have never been the ones to reject respectful accompaniment by those of European descent. Marcos, as noted previously, receives the rank of "subcomandante" or "subcommander" because, being non-indigenous, he cannot be an equal member of the Clandestine Committee of the Indigenous Revolution-General Command (CCRI-CG). However, his is a privileged position: as one of the founders of the movement, his commitment to the indigenous cause has been demonstrated over many years of living in the jungle. His role as military strategist, if we believe the various speculative biographies available, evolved from training in Cuba and Nicaragua, and his facility in Spanish, French and English gives him a clear advantage as spokesperson. Paradoxically, as spokesperson his primary task is to listen: "We had to learn to listen, not just to speak. For this reason, when we are asked what we are, we don't know what we are, we are a hybrid, a result of reality."[49]

It is this hybridization, as much cultural as political, that makes the EZLN a viable organization in national and global politics, and it is this hybridization—a meeting of neo-Marxist or social anarchist intellectuals and indigenous communities—that allows Marcos to be the mouthpiece for a native insurrection. From the beginning the movement has been an inclusive one. In an early interview, he said, "You can't put too much emphasis on the old traditional discipline—the you're-with-us-or-you-are-dead school of thought. You can't raise the step so high that nobody can climb it; you have to make room for all the people to participate to the best of their abilities and so you are always in the process of looking for what unites people."[50]

With this strategy at work, by the turn of the millennium, *Zapatismo* had expanded to embrace movements across the globe. Marcos, with his great capacity for generating communiqués, letters, speeches, articles, and stories has served to focus the energy of the indigenous movement and the global movement and to establish the terms on which this movement makes change in the world, at best without falling into "the you're-with-us-or-you-are-dead school of thought."

Still, a cult of personality quickly came to surround Marcos. In the communiqués, he is both narrator and protagonist, and the international press has consistently (and unsurprisingly) focused more on "*el Sup*" as an icon or leader than on the issues behind the uprising or the ongoing struggle of the Zapatista communities. If this has led some to question his role as spokesman, where the cult of personality eclipses both the issues and the collective agency he represents, this can be attributed to the nature of the press, with its need to paint in black and white, to create heroes and villains, and to commodify dissent. It can also be attributed to the need of civil society for a mouthpiece on which to focus. Marcos has played into this role perfectly, and while his relationship with the indigenous communities is based on deep trust and service, his handling of the press has made him appear at times cynical, manipulative, and clever. While his role originated as spokesman for the indigenous movement, he has been transformed into a representative—unwilling perhaps—of the entire struggle against corporate globalization.

Throughout the communiqués, Marcos generally makes no distinction between himself as culturally mestizo and the indigenous army for which he speaks: "We are the dead of forever," "We are those who have disappeared in order to be seen," "We are the people the color of the earth, demanding our place on the earth." He assumes in his writing the voice and symbolism of the indigenous past and present, essentially counting himself as one of the "Indians."

According to Marcos himself, the language in the First Declaration deliberately situated the speaker as indigenous, but, at the same time, manifested a desire to represent the struggle as including, potentially, all Mexicans and all the marginalized peoples of the world:

> In the First Declaration the expression "we are products of 500 years of struggle" left no doubt that this was an indigenous uprising. But the *compañeros* insisted strongly, in the discussion about the First Declaration, that it had to be made clear that this was not merely a war of indigenous people, but a national war. They said, "it can't be that non-indigenous people do not feel included. Our call has to be broad, for everyone."[51]

While enemies of the movement may indulge themselves in criticizing Marcos for eliding his ethnic identity, ultimately one should ask, why should this even be a concern? Marcos is not indigenous from Chiapas, Che Guevara is not a *campesino* from Cuba—etcetera. Indeed, Marcos's very identity demonstrates the possibility, and the urgency, of fighting for a cause that is not, according to an oversimplified view, "one's own." Marcos the gray-eyed Indian belongs, in this sense, to that dignified tradition of internationalists, class and race traitors, shape-shifters, renegades, border crossers, and trickster types who, due to ethical conviction, willingness to live outside their own inherited law and culture, and the ability to act as conduits for cross-cultural narratives, abandon bourgeois virtue to not only speak for, but also to work tirelessly on behalf of, *los de abajo*. While his status as an outsider opens him to constant criticism, that criticism generally comes from those who would likely sling racial epithets at the Zapatistas as a whole were Marcos not present as a target. More often than not, it is unbelieving *ladinos,* or whites, who deny that one of their own can authentically join the struggle for indigenous liberation. More often than not, those who argue that a mestizo like Marcos has no place speaking for the indigenous people are those who, consciously or not, would prefer that the indigenous people have no speaking voice to begin with. There is nothing strange, nor should there be, in a mestizo devoting himself to the indigenous cause, any more than it should be strange for white people to struggle for black liberation, for heterosexuals to support gay rights, or for men to vociferously demand equal rights for women.

In looking at Marcos's profound integration into the indigenous struggle, Nick Henck suggests, "Subcommander Marcos represents the most advanced stage so far in the evolution of the revolutionary—a

Homo sapiens in a world of Neanderthals."[52] This may be going a bit far. But then, it may not: it may be, at the least, an apt metaphor for an individual capable both of speaking for the collective and of listening on behalf of them, of taking fearless action on behalf of the powerless without himself seeking power. It is certainly refreshing to think that what we have in Subcomandante Marcos and his message is a figure agile enough to step over deeply entrenched barriers of color, culture, race, and ethnicity, and powerful enough to reveal the tremendous failure of the modern world in constructing these barriers in the first place.

Hybridity and Resistance

> The function of literature is to renew the language of the tribe.[53]
>
> —Stéphane Mallarmé

The Zapatistas, and more specifically, their communications strategies, are repeatedly labeled "postmodern." The communiqués, as a sort of hybrid literature that is not either-or but rather both-and, put forth a multi-centric, multi-dimensional vision—a world in which many worlds fit. Certainly these characteristics meet the academic criteria for postmodernism. But aren't the Zapatistas, as peasant farmers seeking to escape the dominion of the nation-state and the industrial civilization it presupposes, also pre-modern, or even anti-modern?

From the perspective of the villages of remote rural Chiapas—where there may be electricity and running water (hallmarks of modernity) or there may not (premodernity?); where children regularly die from diarrheal disease in the presence of Coca-Cola and the absence of safe water (postmodernity in extremis?); where cell phones exist alongside medieval Catholic mystery plays and timeless agricultural rituals—the question is of course moot. Decades ago, Octavio Paz, one of the foremost voices of literary modernism in Mexico, who, beyond his own country, knew well both the impoverished misery of India and the furnished urbanity of Europe, wrote, "Our century is a huge cauldron in which all historical eras are boiling and mingling"[54]—an observation perhaps even truer now than then.

If anything, the Zapatista project redefines modernity (and therefore postmodernity) by framing what it means to be modern (or postmodern) from the perspective of those who have been, in very real historical terms, dispossessed by all of it. As the Mexican Revolution of the 1910s just barely reached Chiapas through land reform in the 1940s, so too did Chiapas miss the benefits of the boom years of capitalism from the 1960s onward until decades later, when capitalism began to fall recognizably into decline. So, a more interesting question than whether the Zapatistas belong to one or another subcategory of cultural studies, perhaps, is how the Zapatistas, through their use of strategy and symbol, are engaged in redefining modernity; how the message they project and the ways in which they have chosen to represent the world prefigure emerging conceptions of the world itself at the dawn of the twenty-first century—conceptions that are increasingly mirrored in the construction of popular movements, social structures, and even the emergence of new forms of the nation-state itself.

Considered as literature, the communiqués do not fit any clear genre. Between fiction and non-fiction, essay and chronicle, epistle and manifesto, the writing is a hybrid of forms that places it squarely outside of all literary canons. What is more, despite Marcos having been nominated for a number of literary prizes, some literary analysts have proffered the radical suggestion that "to read Marcos's writing as a practice of literature is to challenge 'universal' theories of aesthetics."[55] At the same time these very characteristics—its quality of pastiche, its recombinant bricollage of multiple voices from multiple speaking centers—place much of the writing squarely within the camp of what is considered "postmodern," and "postcolonial," or "border writing." From a critical perspective, this is not to say that Marcos is "a postmodernist" or sets out to produce postmodern literature; nonetheless, much of his literary output can be read in this way. It is this same hybrid form that initially grabbed the attention of readers in 1994, making apparent that this was no ordinary guerilla.

Many of the communiqués have been written as letters addressed to a particular reader—"To Civil Society," "To the Mexican People," "To the governments of the world," "To Bill Clinton," "To our indigenous Brothers and Sisters," "To Mariana Moguel," etc. Carlos Fuentes,

Mexico's most celebrated literary figure, gushed, in his correspondence with Marcos, "to you … is owed the reactivation of the tradition of sending letters."[56] By constructing manifestos in the form of letters, Marcos opens up the possibility that he, as the voice of the EZLN, is not speaking to an anonymous audience, but addressing particular sectors and encouraging a response: sending a letter, one hopes for a reply. This suggests a desire for an exchange of ideas; an exchange that has become essential to the construction of the epistemological armature of *Zapatismo*: a voice in which speak many voices. In a note written December 13, 1994, entitled "Letter from Marcos to correspondents who still haven't received answers," Marcos writes:

> I always intended to respond to all and every one of the letters that came to us. It seemed to me, and it continues seeming to me, that it was the least I could do to correspond with so many people who took the trouble to write some lines and took the risk of including their name and address in order to receive an answer. A reinitiation of the war is imminent. I should suspend indefinitely the saving of these letters, I should destroy them, in case they fall into the hands of the government, they could cause problems for many good people and not so many bad people.[57]

In many cases—at least in the cases of sympathetic readers such as Carlos Monsivais, John Berger, José Saramago, and famously, in the case of Mariana Moguel, the ten-year old girl in Baja for whom Marcos wrote the first Durito story—Marcos did respond, and dialogue was initiated. Thus, from the beginning, communication has been two-way—a fact which indeed challenges theories of aesthetics, where literature has been, until the advent of postmodernity, understood principally as a one-way conversation directed outward, from author to reader. At the same time, there is a certain subgenre of outlaw literature—the ransom letter, the note to the bank teller demanding that she hand over the money—which is by nature call and response.

It is of no small import that the early Durito stories, among other communiqués, were addressed to children—a clear route to propaganda victory. Speaking with Yvon Le Bot, Marcos suggests that Durito was a character he'd dreamed up "during the epoch of the solitary guerilla, when there were only eight or ten of us," and that, during the February offensive of 1995, he brought Durito back to life, " to try to explain, from the heart, concepts that generally go to the head."

> I had to find a way to explain, without repeating the same old mistakes, what we wanted and what we thought. And Durito was a character, like Old Antonio, or the Zapatista children that appear in the stories, that permitted an explanation of the situation in which we found ourselves, that would be felt before it would be understood.[58]

Elsewhere, Marcos suggests that Durito "chose as his interlocuter first the child which we all have inside and which we've forgotten along with our shame."[59]

Thus, the audience(s) for the communiqués are multiple; like the best children's cartoons, some are ostensibly directed toward children while speaking on multiple levels to adults; others are directed toward government officials while in fact addressing civil society; others, like the stories of Durito, are generally embedded in stories of Marcos playing with the children Heriberto and Toñita, or like the Old Antonio stories, are embedded in narratives of the EZLN's strategic planning sessions—which themselves are embedded within longer communiqués with multiple narratives and narrative intentions. This story-within-a-story form bears the hallmarks of postmodern fiction—open-ended, self-contradictory, betraying its own narrative structure; at the same time, the form mimics the discursive way in which information travels at the community level: around the campfire, late into the night, one thing simply leads to another.

The postscripts that follow many of the communiqués serve to further hybridize them, to give them, on the one hand, the form of intimate letters, while simultaneously subverting the epistolary form and multiplying the meanings. In some cases, the postscripts are multiple and contain more information than the body of the letter, even entire stories. The postscripts themselves are one of Marcos's recurrent jokes, in effect saying, on the one hand, "there may not be much time, I've got to get everything into this letter and send it off," and on the other denoting the fact that these words-as-weapons, like the struggle itself, may well be endless.

While there are countless examples of this hybridity among the communiqués, the search for one that perhaps speaks directly to the "literary" quality—which is of course, also an anti-literary quality—inevitably leads us to:

The Story of the Bay Horse

Once upon a time there was a bay horse who was bay like a pinto bean and the bay horse lived in the house of a *campesino* who was very poor, and the poor *campesino* had a very poor wife and they had a very skinny chicken and a lame pig. And then one day the very poor woman said to the very poor *campesino*, "Now we have nothing to eat because we are so poor, so it will be good if we eat the skinny chicken." And then they killed the skinny chicken and they made a thin broth of skinny chicken and they ate it. And then they were okay for a while but hunger came again and the very poor *campesino* said to his poor woman: "Now we have nothing to eat because we are so poor, so it will be good to eat the lame pig." And then the little lame pig's turn came and they killed him and made a lame broth of lame piggy and they ate it. And the bay horse's turn came but the bay horse didn't wait for the story to end and he took off for another story."

"Is that the whole story?" I ask Durito, unable to hide my confusion.

"Of course not. Didn't you hear that the bay horse left for another story?" said Durito as he prepared to leave.

"And then?" I ask, exasperated.

"Then nothing, you have to go look for the bay horse in another story," he says, adjusting his sombrero.

"But Durito!" I say, protesting in vain.

"Not one more word! You tell the story as I told it. I can't because I have to go on a secret mission."

"Secret? And what's the nature of it?" I ask, lowering my voice.

"Deceitful insolent! Don't you understand that if I tell you what its nature is then it will no longer be secret...." Durito manages to say as he scurries beneath the door.[60]

The tastelessness of a little story that could as well be called "the one about the poor *campesino*, his poor wife, the very skinny chicken, and the lame pig" is moderated by Marcos's speaking position, and certainly self-mockery and ridicule of one's sorry lot is a hallmark of *campesino* humor. The joke about the horse escaping to another story is, itself, a kind of postmodern literary device—the story undermining its armature by calling attention to itself as story. In so doing, Marcos engages in one of his literary-political games, which is the calling into question of narrative itself, especially grand narratives.

By turning Quixote into a spoof (not that Marcos is the first to have done so, for Cervantes himself intended it this way), by pushing "revolution" with a small "r," by directing timeless "mythic" stories of the time-before-time to six-year-olds with corncob dolls, and by alternating such stories with tales of chocolate bunny rabbits and cat-and-mouse cartoons, the communiqués serve to undermine the kind of totalizing theories of history known to sociology as "metanarratives." Skepticism toward metanarratives is a basic tenet of postmodernism since the French philosopher Jean-François Lyotard declared it so in *The Postmodern Condition* of 1979. Marxism, one of modernity's grand historical narratives, and one that weighs especially heavy on the international left as it struggles to construct an emancipatory vision, received parodic treatment by Marcos at the Festival de la Digna Rabia in early 2009 when Marcos told a story of a woman quoting "Carla Marx." "I believe its Carlos Marx," the Subcomandante told her, to which she replied, "That's only because it's always men who talk about these things."

The joke makes the point that, for those who've been silenced for too long by dominating voices—stories of the hunt told not by the lion, but by the hunter—the effort to dismantle the grand narratives has a practical function beyond merely tearing at the fabric of the overdetermined world of modernity; it makes space for the stories, myths, and foundational beliefs of marginalized peoples. It makes way for living history.

As far as the question of postmodernity goes, one might suggest that the Zapatistas practice a postmodern form of discourse grounded in real-world grassroots organizing; they engage in narrative resistance using all the techniques of twenty-first-century aesthetics while all the time building a deep and broad social movement base, holding territory, and developing forms of governance that reflect a solid ethical and ideological position. As elsewhere, the answer to the question is another set of questions. When Marcos was asked to give his opinion about whether or not the Zapatistas are postmodern, he gave a typically feisty response: "these attempts at cataloguing sooner or later break down. We are very slippery—so slippery we can't even explain ourselves to ourselves. But fundamentally, because we are a movement, we are always moving."[61]

The Zapatista March for Dignity

The caravan of buses is miles long, draped with banners, painted with political slogans, packed with people from the poorest and most distant corners of Mexico—people the color of the earth, as they say—but also filled with people from dozens of other countries who find common cause here. The roads are lined with crowds, cheering, waving shirts and white flags of sheets and toilet paper, flashing victory signs and shouting: "*Zapata vive! La lucha sigue!*" Police accompany the caravan, helicopters circle above, news teams and film crews race from the front of the caravan to the back, and in every town the newspaper headlines shout their arrival: "The Zapatistas are coming!" In the lead bus, faces peer out at the crowds—but the faces are covered, hidden from view behind black ski masks. Not long ago, these masked figures were barred from leaving their villages; even now they represent a real threat, though they bear no arms and have committed no crime.

The caravan follows a circuitous route through the country's indigenous heartland, etching a snail-shell spiral on the rugged topography of Mexico, beginning in Chiapas to the far south; proceeding west through Oaxaca; north through Puebla, Tlaxcala, and Hidalgo; west again through Queretaro, Guanajuato, and Michoacan; south to Guerrero; east and north to Morelos; and then, finally triumphantly over the Sierra de Chichinautzín and down into the urban heart of the country in the Valley of Mexico.

The march lasted thirty-seven days (from February 24 to April 2, 2001), covered 6,000 kilometers and thirteen states, comprised seventy-seven public acts, and culminated with one of the largest demonstrations Mexico City's Zocalo had yet seen, followed by the Zapatistas' previously unthinkable visit to the congress of the nation. The route from Chiapas to the Federal District was historical, built on a fundament of poetry; the caravan traced a spiral path around the capital, circumscribing the heart of the nation in a symbolic journey that was said to take not five weeks, but five centuries. The indigenous Zapatistas, together with their massive international following, drew a conch shell, Mayan symbol of renewal and eternal life, over the map of Mexico—a conch shell to sound the call to indigenous Mexico and civil society. In Nurio, Michoacan, the Zapatista command took part in the third National Indigenous Congress, with the idea of establishing a nationwide consensus among indigenous nations as to their demands of the government. Continuing on to Morelos, the caravan passed through Ananacuilco—birthplace of Emiliano Zapata—and Chinameca—where he was assassinated—before following Zapata's own road over the mountains and into the federal capital.

In every city and many smaller towns, the caravan of motley vehicles stopped and emptied its cargo of ski-masked Zapatistas, Italians uniformed in white overalls (the famous Tutti Bianchi, or all whites, a.k.a. Monos Blancos, or white monkeys), and sympathizers of all descriptions—young, old, brown, white, yellow, and red; university professors and union organizers; punks and hippies; grandmothers and young children. The *encapuchados*—the men and women without faces—spoke to the crowds about democracy, liberty, justice; they told jokes and offered metaphors about a wind from below, about a window frame through which to look onto a better world, about an unstoppable force the color of the earth. They said, we are not here with answers, but with questions; not a spectacle to be gazed upon but a window to be gazed through; we are you and you are us; tell us, they asked, where do we go from here?

In January 1994, the Zapatistas made known their intention to continue the rebellion until they took the capital. Over the next few days it became clear that this wouldn't happen anytime soon. But seven years later, in an ultimate gesture of poetic justice, their promise was fulfilled. On March 11, 2001, in the seventh year of the war—seven, the magic number in Zapatista numerology, recalling the Seven Messages that began our tale—the Comandancia entered Mexico City. They were accompanied by thousands of Mexican and international supporters, and welcomed by half a million people in Mexico's Zocalo, *la plaza de la constitucion*. It was the first time that a rebel army had entered the capital since 1914, when Zapata and Pancho Villa's liberating armies briefly occupied the presidential palace, as the famous photo attests. Over the previous seven years, the Zocalo had seen many demonstrations in support of the Zapatista struggle, and had given birth to the contagious sentiment, "Todos somos Marcos." But for Marcos himself to appear there along with twenty-four masked indigenous *comandantes* was something that, only a few months previous—and in all the years since the January uprising—would have been unimaginable. In the first months of the twenty-first century, the Zapatistas were again making history. Indeed, if things went their way, they would be making mythology.

This was the March for Indigenous Dignity, otherwise known as the March the Color of the Earth, otherwise known as the Zapatour. It was early 2001, and a new president had just been elected in Mexico—ousting a sixty-year-old ruling party—requiring the Zapatistas to descend on Mexico City to ensure their place at the center stage of national politics. For almost two years, the EZLN had been silent (though the Zapatista communities themselves continued communicating with the world beyond, for those willing to listen), with occasional brief missives from Marcos punctuating the silence to point out that "silence, too, is a weapon"). The caravan marked such a watershed in civil rights for Mexico's *indigenas* that it was likened to the 1963 March on Washington where Dr. Martin Luther King Jr. gave his "I have a dream" speech. Others called it a ridiculous bid for relevancy at a time when the popular movement in Chiapas was effectively over due to the universal success of neoliberalism (not to mention the success of neoliberalism's structural effects in Chiapas, such as hunger, disease, poverty, and fatigue).

The March for Dignity was another breaking out of the fence for the EZLN. More than that, it showed their ability to make the shift from being a small guerilla army to being a national political force, welcomed into the public debate, and to do it with characteristic dignity, on their own terms. The march, and the speeches and public acts that comprised it, was an attempt to bring the Zapatista voice out of the jungle, to those who couldn't, or wouldn't, seek out the voice on the newsstands during the seven years when no Zapatista insurgent would dare appear masked in a public plaza (though many insurgent youth would). The march to the capital, under the protection of national and international civil society, as well as federal police, took headlines day after day, and proved that their strategy of prolonged resistance could bring victories that armed insurgency never would. Like the freedom rides in the American South in the 1960s and Mahatma Gandhi's Satyagraha that lifted India from British colonial rule, the Zapatista March for Indigenous Dignity marked a moment in history when relations between the ruling minority and the impoverished majority were inexorably changed. One of the slogans that carried the march was "*Nunca mas un México sin nosotros*"—Never again a Mexico without us. The "us," of course, was the indigenous people, the people the color of the earth. And this demand for inclusion, this firm yet deeply nonviolent demand that Mexico's racism against its original inhabitants be confronted and abolished, is precisely the transformational element in the march, and the thing that bears comparison to Dr. King's "I have a dream." For what Dr. King said—"I still have a dream that is deeply rooted in the American dream," with its biblical tone and its quotation of the Declaration of Independence—"We hold these truths to be self-evident, that all men are created equal"—was the pronouncement of a vision where black Americans were part of the larger society, not embittered and marginalized opponents of it. Here were the Zapatistas, *los de abajo*, those without faces, who had picked up weapons in order to be heard and who had covered their faces in order to be seen, removing their masks, laying aside their arms, and asking, simply, to be included. *Nunca mas un México sin nosotros.*

And yet, the primary goal of the march, its concrete footing—to demand that Congress approve the Law of Indigenous Rights and Culture, a fortified version of the San Andrés Accords forged in negotiations between 1995 and 1997, signed and then abandoned by then-President Salinas de Gortari—was not met. The law was offered up in a multitude of watered-down versions that had increasingly less to do with the intentions of its creators; ultimately, Congress members on the left and the right united to reject the sweeping reforms demanded by the San Andrés Accords in favor of a version that failed to offer any substantive changes at all.[62] Mexico, the Congress told the Zapatistas, would continue for a while yet without them. The country, it seemed—or at least the bad government—was not prepared to give the indigenous their due.[63]

In a speech given in January 2003, almost two years later, Comandante Tacho recalled, "The three main political parties of Mexico, the PAN (Partido de Acción Nacional, or National Action Party), the PRI, and the PRD, made a mockery of the demands of all indigenous peoples of Mexico, all the people who supported them…The executive, legislative, and judicial branches rejected a peaceful, political solution to the demands of the Indian people of Mexico." Having exhausted every option—again—the Zapatistas returned home, defeated but resolute.

VI
One No and Many Yeses

> Autonomy is the capacity to decide to create new worlds.
>
> —Jorge Santiago Santiago

Through Our Silence Resounds Our Word

The rejection of the Law of Indigenous Rights and Culture forced the Zapatistas to reckon with what, for the most part, they had known all along—the political process was a dead-end. In the first years of the twenty-first century, after centuries of hunger and resistance, after most of a decade of low-intensity war, after the dialogues and the negotiations, after the massacres and the political cul-de-sacs, after celebrity attention and mass media neglect, the Zapatista communities turned inward, giving their attention to what had been their most profound goal from the beginning: the construction of autonomy.

In a communiqué of March, 2003, Durito addressed the problem:

> Durito says that all the multiple options being offered by the Powers conceal a trap.
>
> "Where there are many paths, and we're presented with the chance to choose, something fundamental is forgotten: all those paths lead to the same place. And so, liberty consists not in choosing the destination, the place, the speed and the company, but in merely choosing the path. The liberty which the Powerful are offering is, in fact, merely the liberty to choose who will walk representing us," Durito says.
>
> And Durito says that, in reality, Power offers no liberty other than choosing among multiple options of death. You can choose

> the nostalgic model, that of forgetting. That is the one being offered, for example, to the Mexican indigenous as the most suitable for their idiosyncrasies.
>
> Or you can choose the modernizing model, that of frenetic exploitation. This is the one being offered, for example, to the Latin American middle classes as the most suitable for their patterns of consumption.
>
> Or, if not, you can choose the futuristic model, that of twenty-first century weapons. This is the one, for example, being offered by the guided missiles in Iraq and which, so there may be no doubt as to their democratic spirit, kill Iraqis as well as North Americans, Saudi Arabians, Iranians, Kurds, Brits and Kuwaitis (the nationalities which have accrued in just one week).
>
> There are many other models, one for almost every taste and preference. Because if there is anything neoliberalism is able to pride itself on, it is on offering an almost infinite variety of deaths. And no other political system in the history of humanity can say that.[1]

In 2001, the Zapatistas teetered on the edge of Durito's perceived trap: they had survived in their villages, had garnered a degree of popular attention, had broken through the barriers isolating them from the rest of Mexico and the world, had visited the seat of power, and had been rejected. The Mexican media both encouraged the rejection and failed to accurately represent it, as ever unable and unwilling to articulate "what the Indians want"; the nation, as a whole, seemed to believe that, by having their day in court, by bringing their demands to the highest authority in the land, the Zapatistas had been given a fair shake, and had either gotten what they wanted, or had at least been heard. What more did they want?

The answer lay, again, in one of their riddles. For years the Zapatistas had said that their movement consisted of "one no and many yeses." The no, in this case, was a rejection of any reliance on the state, whether in the form of constitutional protections, electoral representation, or handouts. The yeses were the many ways forward that are thrown open once dependence on the state is left behind.

And so, entering a new phase of struggle and a new chapter in their narrative, the Zapatistas packed up their demands for legislative change, abandoned their quest for public attention, returned to their villages and their jungle encampments, and retreated into silence for the better part of two years.

There had of course been silences before. For the first half of 1998, a period of frequent military incursions following the Acteal massacre, the EZLN released few communiqués, and in 2000, leading up to the elections, and for periods of several months at a time throughout. The Fifth Declaration of the Lacandon, which broke the silence of 1998, declared:

> Silence, dignity and resistance were our strength and our best weapons. With them we fought and defeated an enemy that was very powerful but lacked reason and justice in its cause... Despite the fact that in the time that our silence lasted, we did not participate directly in the main national problems by giving our position and proposals; despite that our silence permitted the powerful to spread rumors and lies about divisions and internal ruptures among the Zapatistas and make us out to be intolerant, intransigent, weak and obsolete; despite that some became discouraged by our lack of word and others took advantage of our absence to pretend to be our spokespersons; despite the pain and also because of it, we took some giant steps forward.[2]

Antonio Paoli, engaging one of his Tzeltal informants, speaks of the significance of literal silence for the Tzeltales: "Santiago Gómez Miranda comments that silence, whether it goes by the name *lamal* or *Ch'abel*, is the respect that we give to all of the important things in life: *Te ch'abel j ate yich'el muk' te bitni tulan sk'oblal yu'un te kexlejal, yu'un te teetik, te jaetik, sok te sk'op jMejTatik.* (Silence is a way to encompass everything of true value, that which is most important for life, for the trees, for the waters, and for the words of our Mother-Fathers.)"[3]

Silence for the Tzeltales, Paoli notes, is "a practice that brings with it respect; it is a generator of good relations."[4] Reviewing the EZLN's strategic silences, Marcos commented, "When we are silent they don't know what we're doing. When an army that has used the word as a major weapon goes quiet, it makes the government worry."[5] No doubt, from a certain standpoint, the government's worry indicates its respect for the power of silence.

During the silence of 2001, for quite some time, the EZLN's communiqués dried up, and many commentators speculated the worst—they are preparing an offensive, or they have given up in defeat, or Marcos has gone off to Europe, or, any number of absurd notions; the uncertainty was tantamount to a riddle.

But, as Paco Vazquez of *Promedios* points out:

> in these same years, the communities came into their own, and they themselves took up the word. Everybody forgets that, while there weren't communiqués from Marcos, there were any number of communiqués from the communities—*denuncias* of attacks, lists of the names of the dead and missing, human rights reports. There may have been more communication, by more communities, at that time than at any time before. Just that it came from the autonomous municipalities, and not from Marcos. So nobody listened.[6]

The same has been true during all of the silences—and not only then, but constantly. For a movement regularly blanketed with descriptors like "shadowy," and "mysterious," the outpouring of verbiage from the villages of Chiapas and the human rights NGOs that accompany them is, for those who care to listen, anything but mysterious.

To the contrary, the messages come early and often, and are in general startlingly clear. Most of the communiqués issued directly by the base communities take the form of *denuncias*—strict denouncements of specific acts of human rights abuse, lists of grievances, public records of government and paramilitary offenses. The *denuncias* and communiqués issued directly from the Zapatista base communities tend to be received and posted by the web of human rights organizations and solidarity groups that maintain constant links with the movement, many with offices in San Cristóbal de las Casas; generally, though, they are not made available in print nor widely translated on the Internet; they travel on the pathways of communication opened up by Marcos's more poetic tales and are crucial to the day-to-day human rights struggle, but for the most part they maintain a strictly official tone and purpose. Some, though, have their own mordant humor, such as the oft-repeated denouncement issued and signed by thirty-eight Autonomous Municipalities in the spring of 1998: "*Señor Zedillo, es usted in asesino.*" Mister Zedillo, you are a murderer.

One of the crucial tools of autonomy, and of the breaking of silence, is the radio.[7] Even during the periods of so-called silence, the Zapatista communities have steadily broadcast on local radio frequencies—and increasingly on Internet—in order to communicate across the deep canyons and rugged mountain terrain of Chiapas. Their use of radio has included efforts to convert government supporters to their cause and to denounce government and paramilitary abuse of human rights, as well as broadcasting speeches by the Comandancia, educational programming, and—*como no?*—music. The most consistent broadcasts have been under the auspices of Radio Insurgente, the official radio station of the Zapatista communities, which advertises itself as "the voice of the voiceless." Transmitting from various locations, the primary audience of Radio Insurgente is the Zapatista bases, the insurgents, the commanders and local people in general. Programs are broadcast in Spanish, Tzotzil, Tzeltal, Chol and Tojolabal, making it the first radio broadcast that can actually be understood by the majority of the native people of Chiapas, where a third of the men and half of the women cannot read and most women do not speak or understand Spanish. Local, national, and international news are broadcast alongside music, educational and political messages, short stories and radio-plays. In an effort to reach beyond the local, Radio Insurgente broadcasts a weekly shortwave program (in Spanish) offering news on the construction of autonomy, the history of the EZLN, the rights of indigenous women, and reporting on events in Chiapas. All of which is to say that, even as the world beyond Chiapas perceives a silence, the hills of the Mexican southeast have been consistently alive with the sound of insurgent radio.

It was during these same years, while the Autonomous Municipalities of Chiapas focused on constructing their autonomy, that, elsewhere—in fact, everywhere—a great movement of movements arose, connected by the information highway and the ease of jet travel and an evolving global unity of local reactions to the homogeneous abuses of savage capitalism. Following the Battle of Seattle in 1999, where the World Trade Organization was routed by the combined actions of street protest and ministerial dissent, and bolstered by the first World Social Forum in Porto Alegre, Brazil in 2001, attended by no less than 10,000 social movement activists and intellectuals, a series of mass protests arose wherever Big Capital gathered: Davos, Washington, Prague, Genoa, Chiang Mai, Toronto, Cancún. At each gathering, alternative spaces were constructed; the World Water Forum in Kyoto in 2003 saw the coalescence of the popular struggle for the human right to water and the commons; protests against the WTO in Cancún the same year galvanized Vía Campesina, the world's largest unified movement of land-based peoples; a block of developing nations rose up within the World Trade Organization to reject the terms of trade, leading, eventually, to the collapse of the negotiations. (After the ritual suicide of South Korean farmer Kun Hai Lee—the dead of forever, dying, again, in order to live—the cry of "*Todos somos Lee!*" rose from the barricades.)

Neither were the protests limited to the circuit of big global gatherings; worldwide, peoples' movements were surging into action to a degree never before witnessed. The Americas, especially the indigenous Americas, were rising up: in Ecuador, indigenous people mobilized to bring down two presidents in one term; in Bolivia in 2000 a coalition of ad hoc social organizations overturned government plans to sell off the water system in Cochabamba, the nation's second-largest city; in Chile, the Mapuche people successfully blocked unwanted megaprojects; in Colombia, regional federations of indigenous people formed national coordinating bodies and took their message to the nation's capital. None of these movements acted in direct concert with the Zapatistas, for they were generally autonomous, largely spontaneous, and based in local histories and local capacities—but the motivating forces were the same everywhere. And, without doubt, the Zapatistas provided a certain momentum. The Nasa people of Colombia—that nation's largest and most vocal indigenous population, and the principal force behind the nationwide mobilization known as the Minga Indigena—were watching: "the Zapatista march of 2001 had a huge impact on us," Vilma Almendra and Manuel Rozental, of the Minga's communications team told me. "It was after that that we began to really study closely what the Zapatistas were doing."

As *piqueteros* took the streets in Argentina and Ijaw women occupied oil platforms in Nigeria, landless people occupied ranches in Brazil and rural water stewards mobilized with urban rate-payers in Bolivia; the Narmada Bachao Andolan stood in swollen rivers to oppose dam construction on India's sacred Narmada and the Soweto Electricity Crisis Committee lit up townships in South Africa. These events, in turn, inspired a new poetry, a litany of slogans: Another World Is Possible, Our World Is Not for Sale, This Is What Democracy Looks Like, Water for Life—Not for Profit, and the galvanizing call and response chanted like an angry mantra by the ad hoc resistance Reclaim the Streets, born in London and bred in San Francisco and everywhere else: "Whose streets? Our streets!"

Undoubtedly tracking this global explosion of movements from their jungle redoubts, like Brer Rabbit having set the tar-baby trap for Brer Fox, the EZLN lay low.

But out of this "silence" grew the structures of autonomy that the Zapatistas had been building, very slowly, all along. In all areas of community life—health, education, economy, women's rights, agricultural production, delivery of water and sanitation services, autonomous media, and so forth—the Zapatista *bases de apoyo,* or bases of community support, were steadily at work building local capacity and developing local infrastructure.

What Democracy Looks Like

> The Zapatistas take the concept of democracy, but they interpret it through an understanding of ancient indigenous forms of governance. This is their modernity.
>
> —Walter Mignolo[8]

In the 1990s, the practice of radical democracy, or the radical practice of democracy, emerged from several global fronts at once, the Zapatistas among them, at least in part as a response to the tightening noose of global market forces. There was (and is) a sense among the poor and dispossessed, but also among college-educated, relatively privileged "first world" youth, that power had been systematically stripped from individuals, cultures, and communities, and replaced by the generalized humiliation of submission to brute economic force (the so-called "law of the jungle.") One form of resistance to this was (and is) a rebirth of the direct democratic tradition.

Despite the fact that the state has been conventionally held to be the seat of democracy since its primordial development in fourth-century-BC Athens, this democratic tendency did not emerge from the state. To be sure, both the United States and Mexico have suffered unprecedented crises of democracy, best illustrated at the top by the 2000 and 2004 Bush debacles and the Mexican elections of 1988 (when Carlos Salinas de Gortari of the PRI notoriously stole the presidency from front-runner and opposition candidate Cuauhtemoc Cardenas) and 2006 (when current President Felipe Calderón stole the presidency from populist PRD candidate Andres Manuel López Obrador, leading to massive civil unrest).[9]

But the failure of democracy goes far beyond stolen elections, because democracy, its essence, has little to do with elections. When decisions taken by the governors fail utterly to address the concerns of the governed, even the pretense of democracy is undermined. When, in the years leading up to 1994, President Salinas de Gortari, backed by a congress dominated by the PRI, undertook the wholesale reform of the Mexican Constitution, it served to undermine democracy in a way that exemplified changes happening throughout the world, albeit in forms sometimes more brutal, sometimes less. Modifications to Article 3 of the Constitution freed the state of its prior responsibility to guarantee universal access to higher education, leading to the famous strike at the National Autonomous University of Mexico and other student uprisings; modifications to Article 27 wiped out communal property, enclosing the commons with the stroke of a pen, and precipitating the Zapatistas' furious response. Lopez y Rivas comments:

> This conjoining of constitutional reforms, brought about in the shadow of the emerging economic model, neoliberalism, en-

> visioned a notion of the state very different from the heritage handed down from the Revolution. The sovereign nation-state was supplanted by a state beholden entirely to the market and foreign corporate interests, disavowed of any social responsibility and economic control. From being a state apparently given to reconciling diverse class interests, it became a management state for national and international financial oligarchies.[10]

The wind from above, in this case, was trumpeted by the so-called "Washington Consensus"—the bastion of arch-conservative, beltway think tanks such as the Heritage Institute—which reached its intellectual apex when conservative intellectual Francis Fukuyama declared that we had arrived at "the end of history." Fukuyama's thesis, famous at the time in conservative and progressive circles alike, is best summed up in this quote from his book, *The End of History and the Last Man*:

> What we may be witnessing is not just the end of the Cold War, or the passing of a particular period of post-war history, but the end of history as such: that is, the end point of mankind's ideological evolution and the universalization of Western liberal democracy as the final form of human government.[11]

Fukuyama, a former State Department official speaking from the leading edge of the neoconservative movement, was crowing nothing less than the ultimate ascendancy of U.S. and E.U.-style liberal democracy and the totalizing dogma of free trade. A very few years after the fall of Soviet Communism, he seemed to be saying, the greatest ideological battle, not only of the past century, but also of the past ten centuries, was over. Those who had not yet taken part in this victory, the argument implied, should be made to do so for their own good—by force, if need be. But where Fukuyama used the coveted words "Western liberal democracy" we might in fact read something more akin to "savage capitalism unleashed."

It was precisely here at "the end of history" that the nation-state, corroded to the core, began to reveal its disintegration. So-called "failed states" litter the global geography, from Afghanistan to Zimbabwe; even in the nation with the loudest and proudest democratic tradition, the United States, presidential selection has called into question the foundations of representative democracy. As Walter Mignolo points out, "If the 'end of history' has any sense whatsoever, it would be in terms of the end of the history of universal abstractions, Christian, liberal, Marxist,"[12] and I would add here, national, democratic, etcetera.

The meanings and forms of "democracy" are perpetually contested. Mexico's constitutional democracy is largely modeled on that of the United States, which, in itself, is only very distantly related to anything that might be considered "direct democracy." Charles Beard's classic *Economic Interpretation of the Constitution of the United States* (1913) points out that the founding fathers, landowners and aristocrats all, believed that governing was the role of the elite. In their elaboration of the U.S. Constitution, they developed a sort of double discourse in which "We, the people,"—ostensibly the multitude, or *demos*—would in fact be represented by a governing class, essentially eliminating the question of popular power from the halls of government. Political theorist Ellen Meiksins Wood points out that the Constitution defined "the people" not as an active body of engaged citizens, but as "a disarticulated collection of private individuals represented by a distant central State."[13] The result was to empty the concept of democracy of any substantive social content and to institute a concept of "the people" virtually absent of power. Thus, Wood argues, "constitutional capitalism made possible a form of democracy in which the formal equality of political rights has minimal impact on relations of domination and exploitation in other spheres."[14] In other words, the "political" power of voting does not ensure the ability to exercise more subtle and complex forms of social, economic and cultural power. Certainly the mere right to vote does not guarantee that the vote will be counted or, if counted, that it will count.

A similar development occurred in Mexico, where the indigenous majorities were systematically denied access to democracy, as Gilberto López y Rivas points out:

> Despite the interminable conflicts that have arisen from the neglect of the ethnic composition of Latin American societies, the blindness, the incapacity and conservatism of the descendents of

> the colonists to recognize the different ethnic groups as autonomous political-administrative entities, has impeded the nation's progress toward the consolidation of an inclusive democracy.[15]

By the turn of the twenty-first century, the falsehoods underlying representative government "of, by and for the people," complicated by globalization's outer assault on state sovereignty, resulted in a global crisis of democracy; out of this crisis a diverse, decentralized movement emerged simultaneously from the Mexican southeast, from the landless peoples movements of South Africa, Brazil, and India, from the indigenous movements across the Americas, and from the consensus-based direct action movements of North America and Europe. The common thread binding these diverse movements was, and is, a nominal interest in direct democracy, the radical empowerment of the social majorities to take control over the decisions that affect their lives.

Looked at broadly, this kind of popular empowerment is certainly resonant with common understandings of the word "democracy," despite the ownership that the state has historically maintained over the concept. As anthropologist David Graeber says, looking at the historical roots of the phenomenon:

> If democracy is simply a matter of communities managing their own affairs through an open and relatively egalitarian process of public discussion, there is no reason why egalitarian forms of decision-making in rural communities in Africa or Brazil should not be at least as worthy of the name as the constitutional systems that govern most nation-states today—and, in many cases, probably a good deal more worthy.[16]

One such distinctly non-Western, non-statist democratic tradition is found in traditional Mayan forms of authority, including the community assembly, the system of cargos,[17] and the institution of *mandar obediciendo*, all present in the Zapatistas' emergent systems of governance. Indeed, the early Zapatista communiqués were regularly signed off "Libertad! Justicia! Democracia!" (Liberty! Justice! Democracy!); the almost incongruous appearance of this word "democracy" in the pronouncements of an armed and masked guerilla faction served as a kind of shibboleth to appeal to the global community of radical democratists, *altermundistas, globalphobicos*, anti-capitalists, autonomens, as well as, perhaps, to liberal democrats and democratic liberals.

One reason that the Mexican state (like many other states) cannot or will not explicitly recognize indigenous rights and cultural traditions is not only because of its constant pursuit of the material resources to be found within native territory, but, more broadly, because this recognition undermines the profoundly limited modern notion of "democracy." The Zapatista experiment in democracy—attempts, however faltering they may sometimes be, to foster egalitarian, non-coercive decision-making—exists in explicit contrast to the authoritarian state.

Since the Enlightenment, when the modern state emerged from centuries of monarchic rule, the nation-state became associated, by definition, with popular sovereignty (as opposed to the divine right of kings)—which is to say, with democracy. The rhetoric of the Zapatista communiqués and the establishment of autonomous decision-making processes on the ground act to undermine the state's hold on such concepts, producing a metanarrative that cuts against the state's own rhetoric of "liberty, justice, democracy." In essence, if a key aspect of "modernity," as such, is the sovereignty of the nation-state, the Zapatistas propose a new, insurgent form of modernity.

Graeber is onto something crucial when he speculates as to the continuity of decision-making practice among the Maya from the pre-Colombian era to the current moment:

> Sometime in the late first millennium, Classic Maya civilization collapsed. Archeologists argue about the reasons; presumably they always will; but most theories assume popular rebellions played at least some role. By the time the Spaniards arrived six hundred years later, Mayan societies were thoroughly decentralized, with an endless variety of tiny city-states, some apparently with elected leaders. Conquest took much longer than it did in Peru and Mexico, and Maya communities have proved so consistently rebellious that, over the last five hundred years, there has been virtually no point during which at least some have not been in a state of armed

> insurrection. Most ironic of all, the current wave of the global justice movement was largely kicked off by the EZLN, a group of largely Maya-speaking rebels in Chiapas.... The Zapatistas developed an elaborate system in which communal assemblies, operating on consensus, supplemented by women and youth caucuses to counterbalance the traditional dominance of adult males, are knitted together by councils with recallable delegates. They claim it to be rooted in, but a radicalization of, the way that Maya-speaking communities have governed themselves for thousands of years. We do know that most highland Maya communities have been governed by some kind of consensus system since we have records: that is, for at least five hundred years. While it's possible that nothing of the sort existed in rural communities during the Classic Maya heyday a little over a thousand years ago, it seems rather unlikely.[18]

Graeber goes on to cite historian and theorist Walter Mignolo, who notes that:

> The Zapatistas have used the word democracy, although it has a different meaning for them than it has for the Mexican government. Democracy for the Zapatistas is not conceptualized in terms of European political philosophy but in terms of Maya social organization based on reciprocity, communal (instead of individual) values, the value of wisdom rather than epistemology, and so forth... The Zapatistas have no choice but to use the word that political hegemony imposed, though using that word does not mean bending to its mono-logic interpretation.

On this point Graeber differs: "of course they have a choice... The Zapatista dccision to embrace the term, it seems to me, was more than anything else a decision to reject anything that smacked of a politics of identity, and to appeal for allies, in Mexico and elsewhere, among those interested in a broader conversation about forms of self-organization."[19]

In other words, Graeber believes, the Zapatistas' use of the word "democracy," like their decision to uphold the Mexican flag, was less a reaching back into history than a reaching out to a larger constituency; as such, it was pure propaganda. I would argue that this is, at best, only partially true. Like their embrace of the symbols of nationalism—the flag, the myth of Zapata, the singing of the Mexican national anthem at *encuentros* and gatherings, an adherence to the well-worn theme "*patria o muerte*," fatherland or death, the demand, "Never again a Mexico without us!"—the use of the word "democracy" may serve to ingratiate the indigenous Zapatistas to Mexico's nationalist multitudes, and may at least serve as a bridge to the political class. Certainly, it has the function of reaching out to broaden the movement, to "open a space for democracy." But, doubtless, for communities that are heir to a thousand years of direct democratic tradition, the word also has a deeper resonance.

While they maintain an extraordinary level of political awareness and a well-honed ability to articulate a critique of power, the Zapatistas are not unique among Mesoamerican *campesinos* in their belief in direct democracy and their capture of the word itself. In *Una Tierra para Sembrar Sueños,* the third volume of his comprehensive history of the Lacandon region, Jan de Vos tells the story of a group of Guatemalan refugees—236 families—who had fled across the border during the war in their country. Upon returning home after the signing of peace accords in Guatemala in 1996, they held a ceremony at the Mayan archaeological site of Tikal, in the Petén just south of the frontier with Mexico. There they gave a strikingly clear articulation of their demands in reclaiming their historic territory:

> Our return should be the dawning of a new era, a time when equality reigns in our lands. Democracy is an empty word in the mouths of politicians who make themselves wealthy with their power and contribute to maintaining an unjust order in which the very few decide in the name of the many. True democracy is based in permanent *consultas*, in the participation of everyone, in respecting the word of everyone. Democracy is our practice and our demand. Together, with everyone's participation, we will build a new democracy, the new power of the people.[20]

Similarly, Luis Macas, former president of the Confederación de Nacionalidades Indígenas del Ecuador (CONAIE), asks:

> What does democracy mean for us, as indigenous nations and peoples? What has been the conception of democracy as it's been constructed in América?[21] The construction of nation states, what does it respond to? When we speak of the democracy from the epoch of Aristotle, passing through the French Revolution and arriving in our territories, what does this mean for us, and is it valid for the well-being of our peoples?[22]

These questions are virtually the same ones asked by the Zapatistas. How the notion of radical democracy promulgated by the Zapatistas evolves remains to be seen (especially given the patriarchal and authoritarian legacies present in Mexican society, the pressures of resource scarcity and militarization, and the personality cult that clings to Marcos like a nylon stocking); but it cannot be doubted that the principle of democracy as expounded by the Zapatistas has been central to both their appeal and their influence. Regardless of its long-term success, perhaps the most crucial project of the Zapatistas in the twenty-first century, accompanying the construction of autonomy that followed the March for Indigenous Dignity, has been the construction of new forms of direct democratic leadership. Among the Zapatista communities, as reflected in the communiqués, there is a profound awareness that democracy is, at best, a practice. As Gustavo Esteva and Madhu Suri Prakash have written:

> Radical democracy is not a historically existing institution, but a historical project which can only exist as a never-ending horizon. It is not about "a government" but about governance. It is not about any of the existing "democracies" or "democratic institutions," but about the thing itself, the root of democracy, the essential form taken in the exercise of people's power.[23]

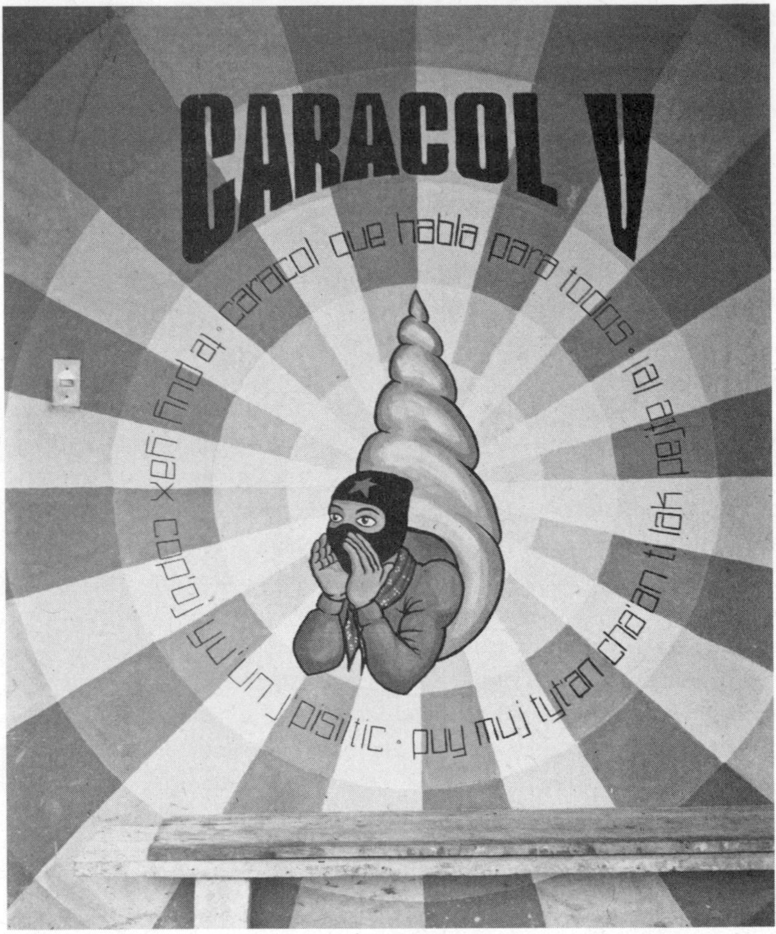

The Caracoles and the Good Government Councils: Traveling Outward to Journey Inward

From the beginning, the Zapatista struggle was about autonomy, that elusive concept that Lopez y Rivas defines as, "in essence, the recognition of communal, municipal, or regional self-governments within the framework of the national state."[24] But it was with the construction of new local governance bodies in 2003 that autonomy began to gain a real foothold. As far back as December 8, 1994, the Zapatistas announced the end of their truce with the government and launched their campaign, "Paz con Justicia y Dignidad para los Pueblos Indios" (Peace with Justice and Dignity for the Indian Peoples),[25] the entry point for the construction of thirty autonomous municipalities within Zapatista territory. From this point on, one of the most crucial projects was redrawing the map of Chiapas, building material autonomy within the communities, and developing autonomous local government councils.

The Municipios Autónomos Rebeldes Zapatistas (Autonomous Rebel Zapatista Municipalities) functioned distinctly from the municipalities of the Mexican state; their functioning, in one reading of history, can be traced back through earlier forms of governance:

> Each community of communities has been traditionally known in the Tseltal world as a "regional municipality," in contrast to the "constitutional municipality," and it is from this tradition that the new perspective emerges: the "autonomous municipality." But it is worth stressing that the defining of the autonomous municipalities derives from a long historical experience of "regional municipalities," and forms part of the cultural equipment deeply rooted in the Tseltal-Tsotsil consciousness and that of the other cultures of the region.[26]

The communiqué that announced the construction of the autonomous municipalities declared that "the civilian populations of these municipalities would name new authorities," who, in their role of leading by obeying, would carry out the following laws: "The political Constitution of the United States of Mexico, 1917; the revolutionary Zapatista laws of 1993; the local laws of the municipal committees as determined by the popular will of the civilian population."[27]

At the very beginning of the uprising, the Zapatistas had announced a set of "revolutionary laws" that were to be applied to all of the communities within their territory. The most famous was the "Ley Revolucionaria de las Mujeres," or "Revolutionary Women's Law," which aimed to turn around centuries of gender oppression by giving women the right to decide how many children they would bear, to decline to be married, and to serve in the EZLN, among other rights. Certainly the need for such a law reveals that "democracy" in the indigenous communities of Chiapas had never been ideal (that is, had never extended to women), and the women's law became emblematic of the profound changes the Zapatistas were instituting; such a law was shockingly progressive in the Mexican context. But there were other laws which, under the guidance of the municipal councils, governed questions of justice, agricultural production, health, education, and so forth.

For the Zapatista communities, neoliberalism is represented as much by the megaprojects that would threaten to displace their villages and despoil their territory as by the more micro "development projects" that would arrive to the villages in government trucks, with government financing: community stores, or agricultural support, or health clinics, or scholarships from the National Indigenist Institute (INI, in its Spanish acronym), all calculated, in principle, to buy votes and suppress rebellion and generate dependency. These projects, and government aid in general, have a double aspect, of which the Zapatista communities are acutely aware: on the one hand, they offer basic shelter and sustenance—the government as kindly, fostering father figure taking care of hapless children; on the other hand, government aid is often seen as part and parcel of a historical program that also brings starvation, violence, denial of language and land and culture and values—the government as cruel *patrón* bringing arbitrary punishment and fierce neglect. On the one hand, the "generous" construction of health centers, schools, and water systems; on the other, no one to staff those schools, no medicines for those health centers, no pumps or cisterns to move and store water—essentially, a rather ungenerous sense of dependency on the state.

With the uprising, the villagers responded (not for the first time, certainly) by expelling government teachers and rejecting social welfare programs and starting fresh. Resistance, constructed on a daily basis from the heart of these communities, was, and is, a direct response to the double discourse of government patronage. As one Zapatista said, "The state has never come through; it doesn't want us alive, except as slaves, as cheap labor. That is why we decided to organize with our own resources and our own ideas, to resolve our problems ourselves, to liberate ourselves."[28]

The redrawing of the map and the construction of autonomy during the first years was slow, and under constant threat; under the Zedillo administration, and especially during the years between 1997 and 2000, autonomous municipalities were occupied—and some "dismantled" –almost as quickly as they could be established, often through military incursions using overwhelming force.[29] It was not until the period of silence following the March for Indigenous Dignity, a time in which President Vicente Fox chose to avoid "the problem of Chiapas," rather than to approach it head-on (even announcing to the World Economic Forum in Davos, Switzerland that the problem had "gone away"), that the Zapatista communities were able to truly consolidate their gains and establish revolutionary new structures of local authority. Having seen the Law of Indigenous Rights and Culture (the Ley Cocopa, which grew out of the hard-won San Andrés Accords)[30] mocked by the press, shredded by the Congress, and profoundly miscomprehended by every political institution in the land, the Zapatistas decided to apply the law themselves in their own territory.

In a series of ceremonies held between August 8–10, 2003 (August 8 being, significantly, the birthday of Zapata and the date on which the first Aguascalientes was inaugurated), the Aguascalientes were declared dead. In a long series of communiqués called "The Thirteenth Stella," Marcos details the history of the Aguascalientes and the many difficulties the Zapatista communities had suffered in working with the international community. As centers of receiving "autonomous" aid from solidarity organizations (as opposed to government aid from the *mal gobierno)* the Aguascalientes were bound, from the start, to be fraught with challenges. The five regional centers had served as often as not, Marcos suggests, as centers for receiving pity and charity rather than true solidarity for their struggle for autonomy. He writes:

> For all these reasons, and for other things that will be seen later, on this August 8, 2003, the anniversary of the first "Aguascalientes," the well-died death of the "Aguascalientes" will be decreed. The *fiesta* (because there are deaths which must be celebrated) will be in Oventik, and all of you are invited who, over these ten years, have supported the rebel communities, whether with projects, or with peace camps, or with caravans, or with an attentive ear, or

with the *compañera* word, whatever it may be, as long as it is not with pity and charity.[31]

Following their death, in true Mayan fashion, the regional centers are reborn, and renamed. Now they are to be known as *Caracoles*, conch shells, or spirals, to reflect their new function. From "The Thirteenth Stella, Second Part: A Death":

> They say around here that the oldest ones say that others even older than them said that the first ones in these lands had a high esteem for the figure of the conch shell. They say that they say that they said that the conch shell represents entering into the heart, which is what the very first people said when they talked about knowledge. And they say that they say that they said that the conch shell also represents leaving the heart to walk in the world, which is what the very first people said when they talked about life.[32]

The conch shell, traditionally used in Mesoamerica to call communities to meeting, became, as well, a symbol of the doorway through which the outside world would enter the Zapatista zone, and through which the Zapatistas would know the outside. Rather than serving only as centers of resistance and *encuentro*, these five villages—La Realidad, Morelia, La Garrucha, Roberto Barrios, and Oventic—would now function as regional entry points where visitors would be received and their solidarity efforts evaluated before being directed to the areas of greatest need. The Caracoles would continue to act as centers of resistance, but would serve other functions as well; importantly, aid received there would be shared more widely and with greater vigilance than before.

Names, as always, mattered; the new Caracoles would be named, "The Mother of *Caracoles*—Sea of Dreams" (La Realidad), "The Whirlwind of Our Words" (Morelia), "Resistance Until the New Dawn" (La Garrucha/Francisco Gómez), "The Caracol That Speaks for All" (Roberto Barrios), and "Resistance for Humanity" (Oventik). Together, the Caracoles covered twenty-nine autonomous municipalities comprising, according to the EZLN, 2,222 villages—a total population of perhaps 100,000 people.[33]

Decisions would be taken by newly established Juntas de Buen Gobierno, or Good Government Councils (in stark contrast to the oft-cited *mal gobierno* or bad government), made up of community members elected on a rotating basis. The Councils were, and continue to be, an astonishingly bold attempt to create direct democracy. Each of the Councils functions a bit differently, but a report on the Councils published in *La Jornada* gives a snapshot view of one:

> [Good Government Council] members rotate every eight days, in such a way that they return to repeat their term various times. Each member travels from her or his municipality to the Caracol, where they remain day and night for a week until returning to their houses to continue working the fields and taking care of family and domestic chores. They receive no salary. It is a responsibility, not a privilege. The practice of rotation, revocability, and rendering of accounts in the Good Government Councils, and the fact that over time every community member has the expe-

> rience of governing and being governed, has as a consequence nothing short of *the elimination of the governing class*.[34]

The form of governance represented by the Juntas is clearly modeled on traditional systems of cargo, where village leaders occupy posts voluntarily, in service to the village. The words of Roel, a member of the Junta de Buen Gobierno of La Realidad, serve to illustrate the Zapatista vision of authority, the *mandar obediciendo*: "The authority should serve but not serve itself, propose, not impose."[35] Astonishingly, Roel's choice of words echoes Tzvetan Todorov's formula for distinguishing between the influence of internal colonialism and the kind of authority constituted by community self-reliance:

> To establish an ethical criterion to judge the form of influences… the essential thing…is to know whether they are *imposed* or *proposed*…. No one asked the Indians if they wanted the wheel, or looms, or forges; they were obliged to accept them. Here is where the violence resides, and it does not depend upon the possible utility of these objects.[36]

Within the Zapatista communities, the establishment of the Councils was essential to the growth of autonomy; for those on the outside, it served as both a demonstration and a test of Zapatista ethics and values. More than simply territories liberated, to an extent, from the logic of capital, the Caracoles and the Good Government Councils are a model of new social relations in embryonic form, encouraging the development of new forms and practices of education, of medicine, of assimilating and recuperating technologies both ancient and modern, along with new ways of understanding and practicing governance, of managing natural resources, and of organizing communities. Islands of autonomy in the global archipelago of resistance, the Juntas de Buen Gobierno and the communities they represent demonstrate a unique form of horizontal community-based governance. The Juntas are unique; at the same time, they are one among many experiments in governance in what might be seen as a new phase of global decolonization.

As the Juntas sought to subvert the communities' relationship of dependency on the state, they also changed the way the communities would interact with solidarity activists and nongovernmental organizations (NGOs). Previous to 2003, the best-known and easiest-to-access communities (generally, the Aguascalientes), would receive the most aid; certain villages, families, and even individuals would receive more of the benefits of solidarity than others. As Marcos pointed out in "The Thirteenth Stella," this was commonplace in human relations, but "it could produce disequilibrium in the life of the community if there were no counter-balance."[37] In a word, solidarity aid poorly distributed could disturb the *lekil kuxlejal*.

Jorge Santiago of DESMI, a development NGO present in Chiapas since 1970, says, "This manner of working turns the question of 'participation' on its head: where standard NGO behavior is to engage community groups in self-improvement projects and to measure success by the level of participation, in the case of the Zapatista communities, people participate to the degree they want to, and then demand that the NGOs offer up their services upon request. The NGOs are no longer central."

With an ideology based in community life, Santiago explains, the Juntas insist on only small projects, small loans, small bits of help along the way, because they believe that less support means more empowerment. "They follow the law of '*poco a poco*' (little by little)."

> The good government councils ensure that the benefits brought by the NGOs are not for individuals, or even for individual communities, but for everyone. This forces the NGOs to stop responding to their own criteria, and to respond to the criteria of the communities, by way of the Councils. It's a different demand; now the goal is no longer development, or progress, or technical production, but consciousness.[38]

Even without the explicit goal of "progress," the turning inward of the Zapatista communities, the clear need to attend to the development of autonomous infrastructure, led to some stunning advances: according to Gloria Muñoz, the first ten years of the uprising had seen the construction of 800 community health centers, 300 schools, eighteen clinics, and two hospitals within rebel territory, as well as the training of 1,000 "education promoters"—teachers of teachers—and 500 health promoters,[39] all trained according to criteria developed by the Zapatistas themselves, which is to say, from the perspective that both health and education are built on a foundation of dignity.[40] In one year alone, fifty schools were built and equipped without a single peso from the government. This, indeed, was what they called "resistance."

These advances mark both a real victory and a propaganda victory for the Zapatista communities who, after more than a decade in resistance, must show the real bread-and-butter improvements to their quality of life in order to maintain both territorial and psychological advantage. A further advantage of the Good Government Councils, both in terms of building capacity within the communities and in terms of the way the Zapatistas represent their values, is in their participatory structure. Cecilia Santiago Vera, a Chiapanecan psychologist and human rights advocate with close ties to the movement, points out that:

> The people who make up the Good Government Councils are not insurgents, not full-time activists—they are mothers and fathers, people making a living, family people. By taking the lead in guiding community decision-making and the political process, they remind us that the struggle is for day-to-day life. Autonomy is about the land; for *campesinos*, the land is a matter of everyday life. This is why the Good Government Councils are so important; it's also why, in the cities, the struggle is so easily fragmented.[41]

Entering the Caracol of Oventik you encounter a sign that says "Welcome to Oventik. Here the people lead and the government obeys." The sign underscores the sense that the Juntas de Buen Gobierno embody an understanding of politics, and of power, fundamentally different, and even diametrically opposed, to conventional notions. Where conventional politics is practiced "from above" by professional politicians who are expected or assumed to be "experts," who are practiced at public speaking and image management and exercising authority, who are recognized as individuals of rare and exceptional ability, and who are, without question, paid for their service, the Juntas, both in theory and in practice, undermine all of this. Chosen by their communities to serve unpaid, expected to learn on the job regardless of their ability to read or write or even to speak Spanish, expected to share decision-making power and to step down when asked, and held to an ethical standard in which their decisions must reflect the greater good of the community with no sectarian advantage or will for personal gain, members of the Juntas are precisely the opposite of what convention says the politician must be.

The Juntas also put into practice concepts of human rights and justice far-removed from conventional approaches. Says Victor Hugo López of the Fray Bartolomé de Las Casas Center for Human Rights:

> The Juntas' approach to justice is holistic: when a person has committed a crime, he isn't simply treated as a bad person deserving of punishment. Instead, the authorities look at the structural causes of the crime, in poverty, unemployment, and other social factors. The response is not simply to punish the individual, but to work towards addressing the root causes. The Juntas' approach is not focused on individual justice, but on social justice."[42]

Not surprisingly, the Juntas de Buen Gobierno, as an expression of indigenous autonomy, received recrimination and abuse from the state institutions they served to replace. By promoting collective human rights and community-based restorative justice, they threaten individual human rights and judicial process; by settling disputes locally they threaten federal and state jurisdiction; above all, by implementing autonomous governance, they suggest the very disintegration of the state.

In a communiqué issued in August 2004, called "Four Fallacies about the Good Government Juntas,"[43] Marcos addressed these concerns directly. The Juntas, he writes, do not deny the Mexicanidad of their struggle:

> With the creation of the Caracoles and the Good Government Juntas, the Zapatistas decided to put the San Andrés Accords into practice and to demonstrate, in action, that we wanted to be part of Mexico (of which we were not a part without ceasing to be what we are).

Nor, Marcos writes, do the Juntas exclude anyone: "The JBGs were created in order to attend to everyone, to Zapatistas, to non-Zapatistas and even to anti-Zapatistas."

Further, Marcos writes, the Juntas, propose a system of justice that is both fair and adequate:

> Now non-Zapatista and anti-Zapatista persons and organizations know that they can go to the JBGs in order to deal with any kind of problem, that they will not be detained (the JBGs are bodies of dialogue, not of punishment), that their case will be assessed and that justice will be done. If someone wants punishment for something, they go to an official municipality or to an autonomía, but if someone wants resolution through dialogue and accord, they go to the Good Government Junta.

As an incipient form of rights-based governance, Marcos declares, the Juntas challenge conventional notions of human rights:

> Collective rights (like the decision as to the use and enjoyment of natural resources) are not only *not* in contradiction with individual rights, but they allow them to be extended to everyone, not just to a few.

And, ultimately, Marcos suggests, the movement toward autonomy represented by the Juntas is the best way forward for a nation in crisis: "The disintegration of the Mexican nation is not evolving on Zapatista lands. On the contrary, what is being created here is a chance for its reconstruction."

That a system of authority so clearly anti-authoritarian should come under criticism on many fronts, governmental as well as nongovernmental, well-intentioned as well as ill-intentioned, comes as no surprise; and there is no doubt that the establishment of the Juntas has caused confusion within the territory where this anti-authoritarian authority has taken up its position. Perhaps most challenging to conventional state and local officials—and even to conventional notions of human rights and government accountability—is the fact that these anti-authorities now serve not only Zapatistas, but "non-Zapatistas and even anti-Zapatistas." By extending autonomy even to those who have not sought it, have not understood it, and much less struggled and sacrificed for it, the Zapatistas made another strikingly bold move—resisting internal colonialism directly by decolonizing territory and allowing the decolonization of the territory, and the establishment of non-conventional anti-authoritarian authority, to act upon all who find themselves within that territory.

The fact that this "new" form of governance is modeled, to an extent, on forms of governance that precede the conquest and colonization, is precisely to the point. The establishment, in the twenty-first century, of a "pre-modern" practice of direct democracy goes to the heart of the Zapatistas' program—to construct a new sense of modernity that is insurgent in its disobedience toward—its *rejection of*—the most common notions handed down from the Enlightenment—justice, democracy, liberalism, and the authority of the nation-state.

Having developed a new way to interact with the outside world, the autonomous communities revolutionize the way in which they are seen and represented—a new public relations strategy; putting into practice radical forms of everyday governance, they offer up a new identity, both political and cultural—a profound rebranding; without ski masks and without weapons, they declare their autonomy from the state and reconstruct social relations, *poco a poco*, in ways that turn 500 years of colonialism on its head—a new modernity.

If There Is a Tomorrow, It Will Be Made by the Women

And what of turning many thousands of years of patriarchy on its head? Back in that early long communiqué called "The Long Journey from Despair to Hope," Marcos had included a short section titled, "The Women: Double Dream, Double Nightmare, Double Awakening," in which he wrote:

> For women from below and from the basement, everything is duplicated (except respect): among women, levels of illiteracy, of miserable living conditions, of low salaries, of marginalization, grow into a nightmare that the system prefers to ignore or to cover with the makeup of general indicators that fail to recognize the gender exploitation that makes possible exploitation in general.
>
> But something begins to cause discomfort in this double submission; the double nightmare doubles the awakening.
>
> Women from below and from further below awake fighting against the present, and against a past that threatens them with a certain future.
>
> The conscience of humanity passes through the conscience of the feminine; knowing that one is human implies knowing that one is woman and must struggle. They no longer need anyone to speak for them, their word follows the double path of rebellion under its own power.[44]

The double nightmare of being marginalized and excluded from the ranks of the marginalized—voiceless among the voiceless; the double burden of earning a living day after day while conducting the minute-to-minute work of child-rearing, hauling water, and producing and preparing food; among radical cadres and revolutionary mass movements, the triple burden of earning the daily bread, keeping the house, and transforming society.

From the beginning, the Zapatista struggle gave priority to women's leadership, to women's voices, to the feminine; it voiced a challenge to traditional Mexican patriarchal relations, and, further, to the patterns of patriarchy and domination that existed, and continue to exist, in the indigenous communities. For many, it was this challenge that signaled the radical break that Zapatismo was making with previous Latin American guerilla struggles. The double awakening was written into Zapatista legal code through the Zapatista Revolutionary Women's Law, laid out in ten points:

> First—Women, regardless of their race, creed, color or political affiliation, have the right to participate in the revolutionary struggle in a way determined by their desire and capacity.
>
> Second—Women have the right to work and receive a just salary.
>
> Third—Women have the right to decide the number of children they have and care for.
>
> Fourth—Women have the right to participate in community affairs and to hold office if they are freely and democratically elected.
>
> Fifth—Women and their children have the right to primary consideration in their health and nutrition.
>
> Sixth—Women have the right to education.
>
> Seventh—Women have the right to select their partner and not be forced to marry.
>
> Eighth—No woman shall be beaten or physically mistreated by her family members or strangers. The crimes of rape and attempted rape will be severely punished.
>
> Ninth—Women can occupy leadership positions and hold military ranks in the revolutionary armed forces.
>
> Tenth—Women will have all the rights and obligations stated in the Revolutionary Laws and Regulations.

Other aspects of the Zapatista uprising revealed a new approach to popular rebellion, but simply putting down in words that women "have the right to participate in the revolutionary struggle in a way determined by their desire and capacity"—acknowledging, to begin with, that women have desire, and have capacity—was like the proverbial "revolution within the revolution." The women's law was, without doubt, a shock to their adversaries and an inspiration to their potential allies; aside from whatever its impact within the ranks of the indigenous women of Chiapas, it gave

Zapatismo a strong and urgent appeal to women on the outside. Thousands of women from around the world made the journey to Chiapas to witness and to work and to take part in this "double awakening."

The women's law was underwritten by the appearance of several women within the ranks of the CCRI-CG. Major Ana Maria, one of the first military leaders of the EZLN, was in charge of the takeover of San Cristóbal during the initial uprising; Comandanta Ramona, another early Zapatista leader, was part of the EZLN's team of negotiators in the peace talks with the Mexican government and became, in an instant, an icon of feminine and feminist rebellion. Her role in history was further solidified when, in 1996, she became the first Zapatista to break out of the Mexican military's encirclement of Zapatista territory, traveling to Mexico City to help found the National Indigenous Congress.

A year before they declared war on the Mexican government, the Zapatistas, led by the women, implemented another law, prohibiting alcohol in their communities. The prohibition had to do with a need for security and for vigilance, certainly, as well as with breaking historical patterns of addiction that came with colonialism and domination; just as certainly, the renunciation of alcohol had the immediate effect of decreasing domestic violence and increasing indices of family nutrition and welfare. It was the men who drank, and when the men stopped drinking, the women's lot improved considerably; many anecdotal accounts of the history tell that the prohibition was a demand of organized women in the base communities. The law had an additional tactical side effect: the EZLN could hardly be accused of narco-trafficking—a typical vocation of the Latin American guerilla—if they were teetotalers.

The Zapatistas make clear that, just as oppression may be gendered, so is resistance. As Marcos writes, "Knowing that one is human implies knowing that one is woman and must struggle." Any struggle against internal and internalized colonialism, and for dignity, the Zapatistas seemed to propose, must be a struggle also against patriarchy and gender-oppression. "If the transformation we seek does not include the radical transformation of gender relations between men and women," wrote Marcos, "the generational relations between the old and the young, relations between homosexuals and to-each-his-own, the cultural relations between indigenous and non-indigenous people, the relations of life between humans and nature, then this transformation will be nothing more than one more caricature among those that abound in the great book of history."[45]

Conversely, just as resistance is gendered, so is oppression. Many Zapatista women would be forced to pay a terrible price for their resistance. As is always the case with counter-revolutionary violence, acts of violence against the Zapatistas have a symbolic aspect, to "send a message"; in many cases, the message, encoded in a gendered language, is directed at women. In the grisly massacre at Acteal on December 22, 1997, of the 47 people killed (including the unborn), 32 were women and girls. Their killings were unspeakably brutal: "Testimonies of survivors tell of the paramilitaries macheteing the bodies of the dead women, cutting off their breasts and hacking the fetuses out of their bellies. Other testimonies tell of the paramilitaries tossing the fetuses from machete to machete, laughing and saying 'Let's do away with the seed.'"[46]

Anthropologist Shannon Speed points out that "the paramilitary violence waged against women in Acteal was not incidental—its motivation was the silencing of political opposition, and its logic and symbology was gendered in such a way that rendered women most vulnerable to attack."[47] From the first, women were on the front lines in every way, as witnessed by the atrocity in Acteal and as best represented, perhaps, by the famous photograph from 1998 of the small, unarmed women of Polho physically repelling a platoon of heavily armed soldiers.

The rebellion of the Zapatista women is, as Marcos suggested, a double rebellion—a rebellion against the historical implications that women are inferior, and are thus to remain subservient and submissive, and a rebellion against the infantilization of all indigenous people by the colonist. It is also a rebellion against patriarchy *within* the indigenous communities. And if anything endangers the social order more than native men bearing automatic rifles, it is native women bearing automatic rifles. Revolt against the patriarchy presents a real threat. Perhaps it is for this reason that images of women make up an important part of the Zapatista imaginary. From the graffiti to the T-shirts to the classic photographs of popular resistance as women's resistance, you can see that this is a rebellion made by women.

At the same time, women's leadership, and the image of women in command, has been continually jeopardized by the often macho posturing of Marcos, his big nose always too much in the spotlight. Again, Marcos acknowledges the contradictions he embodies, and is no more shy about women's leadership than he is, in his often flirtatious writings, about their courtship.

Most years, on or around International Women's Day, the EZLN holds a ceremony and releases a communiqué. In 1996 it was to celebrate the insurgent women who led the initial uprising.

Twelve Women in the Twelfth Year: The Moment of War[48]

During the twelfth year of the Zapatistas, many kilometers and at a great distance from Beijing, twelve women meet March 8 with their faces erased…

I. Yesterday…

Although her face is wreathed in black, still one can see a few strands of hair upon her forehead, and the eyes with the spark of one who searches. Before her she holds an M-I carbine in the "assault" position. She has a pistol strapped to her waist. Over the left side of the chest, that place where hopes and convictions reside, she carries the rank of infantry major of an insurgent army that has called itself, this cold dawn of January 1, 1994, the Zapatista National Liberation Army.

> Under her command, a rebel column takes the former capital of the southeastern Mexican state of Chiapas, San Cristóbal de Las Casas. The central square of San Cristóbal is deserted. Only the indigenous men and women under her command are witnesses to the moment in which the major, a rebel indigenous Tzotzil woman, takes the national flag and gives it to the commanders of the rebellion, those called "The Indigenous Clandestine Revolutionary Committee." At 02:00 southeastern time, January 1 of 1994, over the radio, the major says, "We have recovered the flag. 10-23 over."
>
> For the rest of the world, it is 01:00 hours of the New Year, but for her, those words mark a decade-long wait. In December 1984, not yet twenty years old, she arrives in the mountains of the Lacandon Jungle, carrying the marks of the whole history of indigenous humiliation on her body. In December 1984 this brown woman says, "Enough is enough!" so softly that only she hears herself. In January 1994 this woman and several thousand indigenous people do not just say, but yell, "Enough is enough!" so loudly that all the world hears them...
>
> Outside San Cristóbal another column of indigenous rebels, who attack the city under the command of the only man with light skin and a large nose, has just taken the police headquarters. It frees from these clandestine jails the indigenous who were spending the New Year locked up, guilty of the most terrible crime in the Chiapanecan southeast: being poor.

Marcos describes some of the events of the uprising, and then introduces Comandanta Ramona:

> Among the indigenous commanders there is a tiny woman, even tinier than those around her. Her face is wreathed in black; still, one can see a few strands of hair upon her forehead, and the gaze with the spark of one who searches. A twelve-gauge sawed-off shotgun hangs from her back. Wearing the traditional dress of the women from San Andrés, Ramona, together with hundreds of women, walks down from the mountains toward the city of San

> Cristóbal on that last night of 1993. Together with Susana and other indigenous people, she is part of that indigenous war command which, in 1994, gives birth to the CCRI-CG, the Clandestine Indigenous Revolutionary Committee of the General Command of the Zapatista National Liberation Army, the EZLN.
>
> Comandante Ramona's size and brilliance will surprise the international press when she appears in the Cathedral—where the first Dialogues for Peace are held—and pulls from her backpack the national flag, seized by the Major in January. Ramona does not know then, nor do we, that she carries an illness that takes huge bites of her body, eats away at her life and dims her voice and her gaze. Ramona and the Major, the only women in the Zapatista delegation who show themselves to the world for the first time, declare, "For all intents and purposes, we were already dead. We meant absolutely nothing." With these words they can almost convey the humiliation and abandonment. The major translates to Ramona the questions of the reporters. Ramona nods and understands, as though the answers she is asked for had always been there, in her tiny figure that laughs at the Spanish language and at the ways of the city women. Ramona laughs when she does not know she is dying. And when she knows, she still laughs. Before she did not exist for anyone; now she exists, as a woman, as an indigenous woman, as a rebel woman. Now Ramona lives, a woman belonging to that race that must die in order to live...
>
> The major watches as the light takes possession the streets of San Cristóbal. Her soldiers secure the defense of the old city of Jovel and the protection of the men and women who are now sleeping, indigenous and mestizos, all equally surprised. The major, this indigenous rebel woman, has taken their city. Hundreds of armed indigenous people surround the old city. An armed woman commands them...

Marcos goes on to narrate the role of twelve women in the January 1 uprising: Capitán Irma, who leads the attack on the Municipal Palace in Ocosingo and, after victory, "undoes her braid and lets her hair falls to her waist as though to say, 'Here I am, free and new;'" Capitán Laura, a

Tzotzil woman, "fierce in battle and fiercely committed to learning and teaching," and captain of a unit composed only of men; Capitán Elisa, who still carries mortar fragments in her body as a war trophy; Capitán Silvia who, "after ten days trapped in the rathole that Ocosingo became after January 2," escapes dressed as a civilian, the soldiers at the checkpoint saying, "It isn't possible that such a young and fragile woman could be a rebel"; Capitán Maribel, who took the radio station in Las Margaritas and then, days later, served as guard for a prisoner of war, General Absalón Castellanos Domínguez; Capitán Isidora, who refuses to let the mortar fragments in her arms and legs prevent her from rescuing fallen comrades; and other insurgents for whom January 1 represents an unimaginable leap in their struggle for empowerment as women. The narrative then returns to the present tense and the melee of that New Year:

> In San Cristóbal, that morning of January 1, 1994, she communicates with the great white nose: "Someone just came here asking questions, but I don't understand the language, I think it's English. I don't know if he's a photographer, but he has a camera."
>
> "I'll be there soon," answers the nose as he rearranges the ski mask. Putting the weapons that have been taken from the police station into a vehicle, he travels to the center of the city. They take the weapons out and distribute them among the indigenous who are guarding the Municipal Palace. The foreigner is a tourist who asks if he may leave the city. "No," answers the ski mask with the oversize nose. "It's better that you return to your hotel. We don't know what will happen." The tourist leaves after asking permission to film with his video camera. Meanwhile the morning advances, and with the curious arrive the journalists and questions. The nose responds and explains to the locals, tourists, and journalists. The major is behind him. The ski mask talks and makes jokes. A woman who is armed watches his back.
>
> A journalist, from behind a television camera, asks, "And who are you?"
>
> "Who am I?" repeats the ski mask hesitantly, fighting off sleep after a long night.
>
> "Yes," insists the journalist. "Are you 'Commander Tiger' or

'Commander Lion'?"

"No," responds the ski mask, rubbing his eyes, which are now filled with boredom.

"So, what's your name?" asks the journalist as he thrusts his camera and microphone forward. The big-nosed ski mask answers, "Marcos. Subcomandante Marcos."

Overhead, Pilatus planes begin to circle.

From that moment on, the impeccable military action of the taking of San Cristóbal is blurred, and with it, the fact that it was a woman—a rebel indigenous woman—who commanded the entire operation, is erased. The participation of other rebel women in the actions of January 1, and during the ten-year-long road since the birth of the Zapatistas, become secondary. The faces covered with ski masks become even more anonymous when the lights focus on Marcos. The major says nothing, and she continues to watch the back of that enormous nose, which now has a name for the rest of the world. No one asks her name.

At dawn on January 2, 1994, that same woman directs the retreat from San Cristóbal and the return to the mountains. Fifty days later, she comes back to San Cristóbal as part of the escort that safeguards the delegates of the CCRI-CG of the Zapatista National Liberation Army to the Dialogues for Peace at the Cathedral. Some women journalists interview her and ask her name. "Ana María, Mayor Insurgente Ana María," she answers with her dark gaze. She leaves the cathedral and disappears for the rest of the year, 1994. Like her other *compañeras*, she must wait, she must be silent…

In December 1994, ten years after becoming a soldier, Ana María receives the order to prepare to break out of the military blockade established by government forces around the Lacandon jungle. At dawn on December 19, the Zapatistas take positions in thirty-eight municipalities. Ana María leads the action in the municipalities of the Altos of Chiapas. Twelve women officers are with her: Monica, Isabela, Yuri, Patricia, Juana, Ofelia, Celina, María, Gabriela, Alicia, Zenaida, and María Luisa. Ana María herself takes the municipality of Bochil.

After the Zapatista deployment, the high command of the federal army surrounds their ruptured blockade with silence, and, represented by the mass media, declares it is pure propaganda on the part of the EZLN. The *federales'* pride is deeply wounded: the Zapatistas have broken the blockade and, adding insult to injury, various municipalities have been taken by a unit headed by a woman. Much money is spent to keep this unacceptable event from the people. Due to the involuntary actions of her armed *compañeros*, and the deliberate actions of the government, Ana María and the Zapatista women at her side are ignored and kept invisible.

II. Today...

I have almost finished writing this when someone arrives...

Doña Juanita. After Old Don Antonio dies, Doña Juanita allows her life to slow down to the gentle pace she uses when preparing coffee. Physically strong, Doña Juanita has announced she will die. "Don't be silly, grandmother," I say, refusing to meet her eyes. "Look, you," she answers. "If we must die in order to live, nothing will keep me from dying, much less a young brat like yourself," scolds Doña Juanita, Old Don Antonio's woman, a rebel woman all her life, and apparently, a rebel even in response to her death.

Meanwhile, on the other side of the blockade, she appears.

The narrative describes a woman who, "much like the Zapatistas, has no face or name," and the high cost of her joining the rebels: "She has already fought against everyone—against her husband, her lover, her boyfriend, her children, her friend, her brother, her father, her grandfather. 'You are insane,' they say. She leaves a great deal behind."

She meets March 8 with her face erased, and her name hidden. With her come thousands of women. More and more arrive. Dozens, hundreds, thousands, millions of women who remember all over the world that there is much to be done and remember that there is still much to fight for. It appears that dignity is contagious, and it is the women who are more likely to become infected with this uncomfortable ill...

This March 8 is a good time to remember and to give their rightful place to the insurgent Zapatistas, to the women who are armed and unarmed.

To remember the rebels and those uncomfortable Mexican women now bent over knitting that history which, without them, is nothing more than a badly made fable.

III. Tomorrow...

If there is to be one, it will be made with the women, and above all, by them...

In "Twelve Women in the Twelfth Year," Marcos retells the story of January 1, 1994 with a focus on the lead roles played by women. Though the story has been told so often as to become legend, it is very rare to hear in such detail about the participation of women in these world-changing events; even the legend itself, such as it is, negates this part of the story. And yet, if Marcos's narrative is historically accurate—and there is no reason to suppose otherwise—most of the key protagonists were women. But, as Marcos notes, "Due to the involuntary actions of her armed *compañeros*, and the deliberate actions of the government, Ana María and the Zapatista women at her side are ignored and kept invisible."

This communiqué is clearly crucial in narrating the essential, and essentially invisible, role of women in the uprising. But of equal interest is the way it reveals the means by which the role of women has been systematically marginalized, not only by "the deliberate actions of the government" and the corporate media, but also by "the involuntary actions of her armed *compañeros*," including the "involuntary" sexism implicit in Marcos's role as chief protagonist and in the very manner in which he constructs the narrative.

Marcos acknowledges that, rewarded with the role of speaking on behalf of the EZLN, he is also speaking for—or in lieu of—the women. That there is acknowledgment of the injustice of the women's further marginalization is significant. But our speaker, Marcos, characterizing himself (comically?) by the overtly phallic representation "of that enormous nose," does not retreat from the lights or suggest that there might be something he could do to ensure that the women are heard. Too often we speak of "the voiceless," when we mean "the disregarded"—those whose voices, when raised, go unheard. Even among those who cover their faces in order to be seen, some are seen and not heard.

Major Ana María, for example, despite having led the occupation of San Cristóbal—one of the most outrageous and revolutionary acts imaginable—is seen and not heard, and fades immediately into the background. Fifty days later she returns unarmed, and is interviewed by the media; but still all we know of her is her name. Notable that her interviewers are identified by Marcos as "some women journalists;" presumably, the "men journalists" were granted interviews with Marcos himself, and the other leaders, that is, the "men insurgents."

In the litany of heroic achievements credited to the women—Irma, Laura, Elisa, Sylvia, Maribel, Isadora, Amalia, and Elena—they are celebrated for their bravery, their valiance, their bold leadership, their determination—in short, for their display of conventionally *masculine* characteristics. These women, called out as exceptional, are war heroes; essentially, we might say, they are "as good as men." The only woman celebrated in a conventionally feminine, i.e. domestic, role is the elderly Doña Juanita. She is "physically strong" but clearly too old to fight.

In the brief portrait we have of her, amid the fast-paced action and heroics of battle, she is reduced to moving at "the gentle pace she uses when preparing coffee." One feels that she has always prepared coffee, and always at this gentle pace. Doña Juanita—"old Don Antonio's woman"—is essentially passive, even servile. Scanning the earlier Old Antonio stories, we find that her role is, in fact, largely confined to making coffee. While Marcos deferentially characterizes her as "a rebel," what we see of her is not, in fact, rebelliousness, but *scolding*, which, like preparing coffee, is a conventionally and pejoratively feminine act. And, while Marcos, for fear or shame, cannot meet her eyes, in a reversal of the traditional penetrating male-gaze, it is Doña Juanita who is engaged in the ultimate gesture of feminine passivity, that is, dying.

Despite Marcos's attempts at chivalry, and despite even his attempts to create an equalizing narrative, a feminist reading of this and many other communiqués—that is, a reading informed by "the double awakening" from the dream of male privilege, an eye tendered toward Marcos's representation of women, and of himself in the light of women—reveals unresolved contradictions. In essence, he challenges many conventional Mexican values, but, perhaps despite all intentions, leaves one—machismo—very much intact.

Twelve years later, from December 28, 2007 to January 1, 2008, the Zapatistas celebrated the First Encuentro of Zapatista Women with the Women of the World. Of the many large gatherings the Zapatistas had organized in their territory since 1994, this was the first devoted solely to women. "Why a women's encounter?" the masked women who organized the event asked rhetorically. "Because it is time."

Reports from the event indicate a mix of inspiring, transformative discussion and a bittersweet impression that, in the realm of women's rights, much remains to be done. Hilary Klein, one of many women from around the world who attended the *encuentro*, reported back: "Women recognized that increasing their political participation is not something that can happen overnight." Klein gives us several women's perspectives, in their own words:

> Rebecca, a member of the autonomous council, said: "At first we didn't participate much as women. Little by little we began to participate more."
>
> Laura, a member of the Agrarian Commission, explained: "Before, they didn't take us into consideration as women. Later they realized that we needed to have women authorities too, to strengthen our autonomy. Now, as women, we are conscious and we're moving forward. We don't know much, but as authorities we learn as we go, by doing the work."
>
> And Daisy, a local authority: "A lot of times we're still nervous and shy. There are still a lot of men who think that we can't do the work."[49]

"As they talked about the obstacles they have faced and how they have organized as women," Klein points out, "they were also telling the story of the Zapatista movement."

The women's *encuentro* provided a public space to examine and evaluate the progress of the feminist cause as it played out through *Za-*

patismo, and the examination showed that there had been, perhaps, less progress than one might hope. Of course, progress is slow, and patterns that have persisted for centuries cannot be expected to change overnight. At the same time, at the level of representation, one might speculate to what degree the macho figure of Marcos had distracted, over the years, from the feminist cause.

On the positive side, there had been a conscious opening of spaces of political participation specifically for women; permitted to engage in political decision-making, women engender social transformation and change the cultural perception of what is possible. By revealing the shared oppression of women, and by acting to transform their conditions, a sense of collective resistance emerges from what, previously, was merely the difficult lot—the triple burden—of each individual. Yet, some have argued, the EZLN structure is fundamentally patriarchal, and there is a distinction between a movement that engages women in positions of leadership, and a movement that is truly feminist, challenging altogether conventional patriarchal structures of authority and domination.

A close reading of "Twelve Women in the Twelfth Year" reveals that the classic, sexist representation of woman as either virgin or whore is unfortunately reproduced in the dichotomy of woman as either domestic servant or as warrior. While there is great effort on the part of Marcos's narrative, and on the part of the Zapatistas' organizing efforts, to invert capitalist and patriarchal gender relations, this representation serves, to a certain extent, to reinforce them. The resolution of opposing expressions of gendered humanness—woman as war hero and woman as family provider—is perhaps, the ultimate objective of the Zapatistas' Revolutionary Women's Law, out of which a "new woman," like Che Guevara's insistence on a "new man," might come about. That these contradictions have yet to be resolved there is little doubt; numerous anecdotal tales from the *encuentros* and the real life of Zapatista women reveal that there is a long way to go before the image and the reality cohere.

The Sixth Declaration and the Other Campaign

In June, 2005, the Zapatistas issued a red alert in Chiapas, asking foreigners to leave the villages for an indefinite period of time, and called their communities together to consult on a question whose outcome, as

Marcos put it, "would risk the little that we have gained." What the question was remains something of a mystery, and how the *consulta* happened is a matter of heated discussion among people close to the movement. Whatever the case, the outcome, appearing mere days after the red alert was called, was the "Sixth Declaration of the Lacandon Jungle," which promises a "new political direction" for the movement. It begins with a lengthy history of the twelve years of struggle, an analysis of global capitalism, a description of the Zapatistas' goals, a promise of material solidarity (meager as that might turn out to be) for allied movements and peoples, and then, toward the end, offers the diligent reader the longed-for new direction:

> We are inviting all indigenous, workers, *campesinos*, teachers, students, housewives, neighbors, small businesspersons, small shop owners, micro-businesspersons, pensioners, handicapped persons, religious men and women, scientists, artists, intellectuals, young persons, women, old persons, homosexuals and lesbians, boys and girls, to participate, whether individually or collectively, directly with the Zapatistas in this NATIONAL CAMPAIGN for building another way of doing politics, for a program of national struggle of the left, and for a new Constitution.[50]

To understand the Sixth Declaration, it helps to have a sense of the previous five. The First Declaration, recall, had been read at dawn on January 1, 1994, a declaration of war and a first clarion-call for resistance. Of the rest, John Ross offers a summary:

> The Second Declaration, issued in the summer of 1994, was an invitation for the outside to come in, summoning the civil society to the National Democratic Convention to figure out how to deal with coming presidential elections. The Third, promulgated in February 1995 just before Zedillo's invasion, called for the building of a Movement of National Liberation, a cross-class coalition to save the nation as the economy plunged into freefall. The Fourth, in December 1995, as negotiations between the EZLN and the *mal gobierno* got real, affirmed the primacy of the Word over the Fire, advertised that the rebels really did not want

state power, and called for the 1996 Intergaláctica and the formation of the FZLN [the Frente Zapatista de Liberación Nacional, a short-lived political front group for the EZLN]. The *Sexta* contained a similar thrusting outside. For four years, the *compas* had been building autonomy, getting off the grid under the trees, seemingly having turned their backs on the rest of Mexico. Now they were turning back.[51]

The Sixth Declaration, or Sexta, as it quickly became known, proposed platforms both global and national. On the national level the EZLN outlined four primary goals:

1. To "continue fighting for the Indian peoples of Mexico," including "the brothers and sisters who have had to go to the United States in order to survive."
2. To build "a national program of struggle...which will be clearly of the left, anti-capitalist, or anti-neoliberal, and for justice, democracy and liberty for the Mexican people."
3. "To build, or rebuild, another way of doing politics...which has the spirit of serving others, without material interests, with sacrifice, with dedication, with honesty..."
4. "To go about raising a struggle in order to demand...a new Constitution...which defends the weak in the face of the powerful."

While the Sexta was a declaration of the Zapatistas' new direction, it was also a call to Mexican civil society to organize, and to build a common front, or many fronts, "from down below and to the left."

Six months after its release, the Sixth Declaration was put into practice by way of la Otra Campaña, the Other Campaign. It was a *campaign* because, as a national organizing effort, it ran directly counter to the concurrent electoral campaign in which archconservative Felipé Calderon faced off against the populist social democrat Andrés Manuel López Obrador. (One of *la Otra's* key mottoes was "Vote or don't vote: organize.") And it was *otra* because it was not about winning state power, raising massive amounts of funds, making promises of reform, or offering concrete improvements to peoples' lives from above. Rather, it was, and is, other, in the sense that it is about building power from "down below and to the left," about linking popular struggles across the nation, about developing the capacity of *los otros, los de abajo*, to restore dignity and justice to their own struggles and their own lives. The campaign that was not a campaign began as an alternative to the 2006 electoral bid, but more than that, as an alternative to bankrupt party politics in general.

Journalist John Gibler, who accompanied the first phase of the Other Campaign from beginning to end, writes:

> The tour visited rural communities, inner-city slums, and downtown plazas. Marcos often spoke in public to encourage people to join and participate in the Other Campaign, but the backbone of the tour consisted in the hours-long meetings where Marcos—and the ragtag crew of organizational representatives and independent media correspondents who followed him—sat listening to tales of repression and exclusion, of resistance and autonomous governance projects. The listening sessions were long and arduous, stretching for hours, several times a day, seven days a week. Most meetings were held either in boxlike concrete rooms in union offices and public halls or outdoors, sometimes with and sometimes without thatched roofs or tarps to block the force of Mexico's sun and rain. When the agenda was tight, meeting organizers set a time limit for each participant, but most often there was no limit. And while no one ever screened for content, two topics were explicitly unwelcome: speaking in favor of either capitalism or political parties.[52]

The Otra Campaña was an effort to scale up the gains of the Zapatistas' first ten years of above-ground organizing into a national platform of struggle. Rather than a movement limited to one sector of society, *la Otra* made a bid to build a movement among multiple social actors—women, students, working classes, landless people, etc.—and on many fronts of struggle—gender oppression, land reform, urban decay, access to basic services, labor rights, and on down the line. It was a veritable movement of movements, reaching out to the most marginalized in an antisystemic campaign that hoped to grow organically and permanently, based on principles of diversity, plurality, and *el mandar obediciendo*.

In organizing the Other Campaign, participants were asked to formally adhere to the tenets of the Sixth Declaration as a general statement of principals. Adhering to these principals had the very important effect of building a massive block of social movement activists who clearly and consciously recognized that their struggle is *anti-systemic* and *anti-capitalist*. By identifying capitalism itself as the source of many ills—patriarchy, racism, violence, environmental degradation, human rights abuse, and so forth—the Otra Campaña provided a common framework for many movements that have historically found themselves diverging into distinct issue areas. This would be the first time since the advent of the information age that a popular, explicitly anti-capitalist struggle was launched at the national level, with hopes of unifying people across all sectors of society.

With the goal of traversing Mexican territory in two phases—first Marcos himself, and then a corps of other *comandantes* and Zapatistas—*la Otra* sought, in some sense, to expand the Zapatistas' theoretical territory from the remote southeast to the entire nation. In a symbolic acknowledgment of the Other Campaign's bid to start from nothing, Marcos dubbed himself "Delegate Zero," and on January 1, 2006 began coursing across deep Mexico on a black motorcycle, appearing for all the world as a simulacrum of Don Durito on his faithful steed Pegasus. Delegate Zero rode solo, drawing shades of the young Che Guevara on his Latin American odyssey; but unlike the young Che, Marcos was accompanied the entire way by a flock of fans and independent media correspondents. Marcos called the tour "Plan La Realidad–Tijuana" in response to the Plan Puebla–Panama, the government's massive infrastructure project that planned to construct highways, rails, ports, dams, and other essentials of modernity from south-central Mexico to the bottom of the Central American isthmus.

In building a national platform of struggle with goals and strategies that would be defined as it went, the Other Campaign was less *Campaign* and more *Other:* in contrast to politics as usual, it sought to build *other* social relations by giving *other* interlocutors the opportunity to engage *other* actors and social classes toward *other* objectives, using *other* methods; in the language of critical theory it was about raising alterity, or otherness, from its marginal position in the dominant society to a central role. It was about defining an *other* politics in order to build an *other* social system.

Writer Carlos Antonio Aguirre makes the important and easily overlooked point that *la Otra* also employed *una otra temporalidad*—an other sense of time:[53]

> Given that the Zapatistas grasp the essential lesson that "we have learned that we should never subject ourselves to the schedule of power but that we have always had to follow our own calendar, and impose our time frame on that which comes down from above," it is clear that the time frame of the Other Campaign has nothing to do with the timing of the official electoral campaign, and affirms itself, on the contrary, from within a very different temporal register and in a very different evolutionary rhythm.[54]

While it was initially called for as a direct response to the election campaigns then in progress, the Other Campaign would not build toward an electoral climax or a moment of grand political spectacle, but would develop according to its own internal rhythm, taking the time needed to do whatever needed to be done. In this sense, *la Otra* is very much still in progress. Aguirre's description of this *otra temporalidad* mirrors Jorge Santiago's assessment of the Caracoles as consciously practicing the philosophy of *poco a poco*:

> The time of the Other Campaign exists before, during, and after, transcending the time of the presidential campaign, leading the Zapatistas to affirm that this is a process that might take ten years—a calculation derived from the Zapatistas' own experience developing between 1984 and 1994, that is to say, during the ten years in which the EZLN went from being an organization with six members to comprising tens and hundreds of thousands of rebellious indigenous Chiapanecos, transforming into one of the most important social movements in Mexico and Latin America and, indeed, the world.[55]

This extension of time beyond the immediate and strategic present, of course, can be seen to reflect the generational vision of indigenous social movements. Beyond the immediate, daily struggle for survival, for rights, and for territory, is the millennial struggle against centuries of an oppression which, no one doubts, could easily take centuries to lift. As Trinidad Perez Cruz of Roberto Barrios had told me, "Our grandchildren want justice."

Unlike a conventional electoral campaign, whose primary protagonists are the most powerful sectors of society—the politicians, the bosses, the business elite—and which is only marginally directed toward the multitudes in order to win their confidence and their votes, the Other Campaign engaged the most marginal sectors of the population as social subjects and agents of change. With no concrete campaign strategy and no explicit goal, the Other Campaign, more than anything, was about raising the voices of resistance; one might say that the Other Campaign was, and continues to be, about telling the stories of a people in resistance—or, more importantly perhaps, about listening to them.

As Gibler writes, "the listening is strenuous, at times exhausting: the length of the meetings, the relentless seven-days a week, two-to-three meetings a day pace, the heat…Truly listening, as the Other Campaign proposes, is a mental marathon unlike anything I have known."[56]

As Marcos toured the country and convened meetings in countless cities and *pueblos*, fishermen in Campeche told of their resistance to increasing rates for electricity; students in Yucatán told of resisting the closure of their schools; cancer patients in Jalisco told of their resistance to industrial effluent clogging the Santiago River; Yaqui elders in Sonora told of their resistance to the dams that blocked their river and the agrochemicals that poisoned their blood and that threatened, altogether, to extinguish their people; retirees decried the years that had passed without a social security check; coastal villagers condemned the government engineering projects that had flooded their homes. After each testimony, Marcos would take the stage and call for a rejection of politics as usual, demanding that the people present weave stories into a vast social movement that would transform the nation village by village and state by state.

In February, 2006, commenting on what he had witnessed and heard on the first leg of the Other Campaign, Marcos said,

> What we have heard in these nine states we have traversed is a boiling from down below...The people have had enough and they don't believe in any political party, none, nor do they believe in the electoral path; they are rising up down below, preparing an enormous explosion, enormous, like we didn't see even in the Mexican Revolution or in the War for Independence; what we are doing is joining all of these rebellions, all of these rebels, into something good, so that in the end it won't be that everyone decides that some leader is the big bad dude and everything stays the same, so that in the end there won't be some group, some little clique that grabs power and everything stays the same.[57]

Somehow, by allowing a lot of little stories to come forth, the big story would change.

Of course, stories of resistance, as much as they strengthen that resistance, also attract repression. Violence against *los de abajo* continued, and in many ways grew worse during the Other Campaign. In May 2006, while Marcos and *la Otra* were bivouacked in nearby Mexico City, the town of Atenco, already infamous for its residents' resistance in 2002 to the construction of a new airport, witnessed the worst brutality that Mexico had seen since the student massacres of 1968. After state police blocked sixty flower vendors from setting up their carts in nearby Texcoco, the merchants called on the people of Atenco for solidarity. When Atenco residents blocked the highway to demand justice, the police response was unprecedented. Hundreds of federal and state police arrived to lift the blockade and were fought back by citizens wielding machetes, clubs, Molotov cocktails, and homemade missiles. In the ensuing days, the police launched an all-out war, shutting down the streets with barricades and teargas, killing several youths, and openly raping both men and women. Throughout Mexico, the name Atenco has become synonymous with state terror.[58]

Looking back, Gloria Muñoz and Herman Bellinghausen wrote:

> Brutal and hateful government attacks took place against the Front of the Peoples in Defense of Land in the town of San Salvador Atenco, in the state of Mexico, and against the extraordi-

> nary people's movement of Oaxaca. These aggressions sparked a large number of mobilizations of solidarity in Mexico and abroad. They were hard times, during which the Other Campaign tested its ability to organize nationally, its international legitimacy, and its capacity to convene international solidarity (for Atenco alone there were 209 mobilizations in 77 cities of 30 countries). The Zapatista communities expressed their unconditional support for Atenco and Oaxaca not only with words, but, for the first time, tens of thousands of Zapatistas mobilized against the repression of another movement, in accordance with the Other Campaign's principle "if they strike one of us, they strike us all."[59]

Marcos spoke out, and the Zapatistas marched, but for the usual reasons, they were hard-pressed to respond with more then gestures: what was there to gain but more bloodshed? Faced with open war, the EZLN held its fire. They called a red alert, the Other Campaign put on the brakes, and Delegate Zero returned to Chiapas for a time, to regroup.

Unsurprisingly, *la Otra* became a target of criticism from all sides. The organizing effort centered, for better or worse, on the subcomandante himself. Gibler, reporting for *Z Magazine*, pointed out that "nearly everyone on the outside of the campaign reduces the entire effort to a failed display of Marcos's enormous ego."[60] Some academics revealed their latent racism, decrying *la Otra* as "primitive,"[61] while others abandoned their sympathy for the EZLN in favor of the safer and more pragmatic option of siding with the progressive candidate for president. At a moment when Mexico had, in Andres Manuel López Obrador (or AMLO as he is fondly called), its first real possibility of a progressive victory in the national elections, the Zapatistas chose to spurn his candidacy. Stumping from his pulpit, Marcos did everything in his power to stain Lopez Obrador's reputation, devoting endless hours of speechifying to denouncing the popular, center-left candidate. Years later under the *mano dura* of right-wing President Felipé Calderon, much of the Mexican left has refused to forgive *el Sup* for relentlessly attacking AMLO with his own hard fist.

The sting of the Zapatista's scorn for López Obrador shows the depth of their disdain for the political process and for the Party of the Democratic Revolution (PRD), under whose banner AMLO speaks. Indeed, since the victory of Vicente Fox in 2000, the PRD has become a refuge for defectors from the PRI; Adolfo Gilly noted at the time that former officials of the Salinas administration have become "the pillars of the presidential campaign of the PRD and its candidate, Andres Manuel López Obrador."[62] The Other Campaign, pronouncing these truths at a moment when left-wing governments were on the rise across the continent, produced a discomforting sense of disillusion.

Commenting in 2006, John Gibler wrote, "The challenge of the first phase of the Other Campaign is not whether it can fill plazas, parks, and auditoriums ... but whether it can pull people into a new, national social movement that overcomes the deep and historic divisions amongst the left."[63] Looking backwards from 2010, the Other Campaign has not only failed to overcome these divisions—it has turned them into apparently unbreachable chasms.[64]

John Ross, highly critical of the Otra Campaña, wrote in 2006, "As Marcos has moved farther and farther away from the Zapatista communities in Chiapas, his connection to the *compas* who confer upon him both authority and authenticity has frayed." Even more concerning, he wrote about the Otra, "What was missing? The *Sexta* had tried to answer that question: the rest of Mexico. Now out here in the rest of Mexico, what was missing was the heart of the Zapatista rebellion; the Indians."[65]

"The Zapatistas are marginalized," Ross told me at the Festival de la Digna Rabia in Mexico City at the end of 2008. "The movement's stuck.... again. Even *La Jornada* is marginalizing them," he said. Gustavo Castro, a sociologist who has worked closely with the Zapatistas both on the ground and in the heady realm of analysis, echoes the sentiment: "As soon as Marcos left the communities, he isolated himself. He created a vacuum."[66]

Many others, however, do not agree, and, diffuse as it is, *la Otra* continues in various forms as an organizing platform throughout Mexico. If it indeed follows an *other* temporality, not in any rush to overturn the truths of yesterday, then no conclusions may yet be drawn; if it indeed is about building an *other* power, one based not in individuals, or even in individual social movements, but in the vast collectivity that is the entire *Mexico de abajo*, then no immediate results may be forthcoming. While some commentators say that the EZLN has "disappeared," and Marcos has become an object of no little scorn even (and especially) among his former admirers, down below, in the Mayan communities of Chiapas, the construction of autonomy continues, *poco a poco*.

Diversity, Pluriethnicity, and Insurgent Modernity: A World in which Many Worlds Fit

> In the case of Mexico, we have to reconstruct the concept of the nation, and to reconstruct does not mean to return to the past, it's not to return to [the time of Benito] Juarez, or to liberalism in the face of the new conservatism. This is not the history that we need to rescue. We need to reconstruct the nation on a different base, and this has to be a recognition of difference.
>
> —Subcomandante Marcos[67]

In Mexico, the historical yoke of Spanish rule was thrown off with the Independence of 1810, but the persistent traits of colonialism—subjugation of the peasantry, enclosure of the commons, plunder of natural and cultural resources, religious persecution and deracination of the indigenous cultures, suppression of the insurgent imagination—remained, enforced now by the republic rather than by the distant crown. Colonial patterns of domination came to characterize the emergent Mexican republic through the nineteenth century. The Revolution of 1910 gave a solid blow to the colonial legacy, but ultimately the narrative of empire, and what Edward Said calls "the mental attitude of the colonist," was galvanized by the further consolidation of the nation-state following the revolution, reinforcing an ongoing pattern of internal colonialism. The narrative of the nation—*la patria*—as the seat of identity and belonging of the many peoples that make up Mexico endured through the twentieth century.

Canadian scholar Michael Ignatieff offers a summary of the emergence of national consciousness in Europe precisely in the years coinciding with both the Mexican Revolution and the Russian:

> Right up to the First World War, the very idea of being a citizen, of belonging to a society or a nation, would have seemed a distant abstraction to the peasants who made up the majority of the European population. Such belonging as a peasant felt was bounded by the distances his legs could walk and his cart could roll. Until 1914, most European peasants spoke in regional dialects; national languages were apparatuses of the state rather than the living speech of those they administered. It was only as the school, the medical officer and the census taker—the institutions of the national state—began to permeate the village world that the nation became a living entity and national belonging became a felt need of millions. With the mass mobilization of the European peasantry in August 1914, modern nationalism found its voice and the need for belonging finally spoke in the cries for war which resounded around Europe. In those cries, the other possible belonging—the *internationale* of working men (*sic*) of all nations—was swept aside like a pile of leaflets in the wind.[68]

With the galvanizing of national consciousness the imperial expansion of the European states persisted throughout the twentieth century; colonialism unraveled throughout the global South in the decades following World War II, but even the axis of power that emerged in the Cold War was clearly built on the midden of European imperialism, with the globe now divided into first, second, and third worlds for the sake of strategic alliances (a world in which not all worlds fit equally).[69] Even under the new Cold War axis, the nation-state—now stronger than ever—was the ultimate source of community identity and collective power. Even through the anti-colonial, national independence movements of the period following World War II, indigenous peoples everywhere remained subject to internal colonialism, perpetrated now not by a distant monarch but by the centralized power of the state.

In Mexico, as elsewhere, indigenous cultures were a stumbling block in the project of "nation-building," the construction of a unified national identity. When it wasn't possible to eliminate them altogether, the state tried to integrate the indigenous cultures into the national culture, thereby silencing their distinctive voices and doing away with their particular histories.[70]

Gilberto Lopez y Rivas tells of Manuel Gamio, the *padre fundador*, founding father, of Mexican anthropology, for whom Mexico in the early years of the twentieth century would never consolidate into a modern nation as long as it persisted to be made up of some "seventy small nations," each with its own language and culture. For Gamio, and the school of scientific and social thought that accompanied the growth of the modern nation, the way to integrate the "backwards Indians" into the project of civilization was for the state to assimilate them into the dominant culture, and to submit their languages and cultures to the homogenizing influence of progress and development.

In a strange backward echo, Gamio defined anthropology as "the science of good government." At the VIII Panamerican Education Conference in Lima, Peru in 1938, the indigenous were declared to "have a special right to the protection of public authorities to make up for their deficient physical and mental development"; further, governments should "develop policies that would bring about their complete integration." Soon after, at the first Interamerican Indigenist Congress in Patzcuaro, Michoacan in 1940, the policy of total assimilation was taken up as state policy not only in Mexico, but throughout Latin America. So it was that "plurinationality"—the consideration that a nation might reasonably include many ethnicities, linguistic groupings, and cultural beliefs, and that these beliefs were, in fact, the source of the nation's cultural wealth—was swept aside in favor of a monocultural nation. But, like the maize that is born again each spring from buried seed, the pluriethnic composition of the nation would be back. As Lopez y Rivas points out, "The argument of national unity is unsustainable, among other reasons because the nation is the result of a hegemony imposed by a minority sector, at the price of the exclusion of the majority."[71]

The kinder, gentler face of this hegemony came to be known as indigenism, and was characterized by "a particular rhetoric with respect to indigenous languages and customs, accompanied by the practice of destroying the ethnic make-up."[72] In Mexico the doctrine came to be represented by the Instituto Nacional Indigenista (the INI, or National

Indigenist Institute), created in 1948 to represent the interests of the indigenous peoples as defined by the state. The very purpose of the Instituto Nacional Indigenista was to assimilate Mexico's disparate cultures under one banner, albeit through paternalism rather than coercion; hence the Zapatistas' resistance to both paternalism and outright occupation as two faces of the same bad coin, and hence their assault on the INI offices in San Cristóbal on that fabled January dawn. Until 1994, the policy of indigenism was largely unquestioned in the national debate. But by 2003 the INI, under heavy criticism, was closed down and replaced by the Comisión Nacional para el Desarrollo de los Pueblos Indígenas (National Commission for the Development of Indigenous Peoples)—shifting the emphasis from assimilation to "sustainable development and the full enjoyment of rights."[73]

"The creators of indigenist policies," Lopez y Rivas writes, "would never have imagined that the 'indigenous question' would return as a national problem at the end of the century, due to an armed rebellion of the indigenous peoples of Chiapas. Since the thirties, the pluriethnic character of the nation and the rights of indigenous peoples had not caused much concern among intellectuals and politicians. In the best of cases, the indigenous appeared recurrently as subject-victims, objects of exploitation and paternalist politics. Even within the framework of Marxist analysis, the indigenous and the *campesinos* were not seen as subjects of their own liberation."[74]

As a movement born in resistance to a particular history, *Zapatismo* is, in its roots, deeply Mexican—indeed, deeply local. A long history of *latifundias* and debt peonage, *caciquismo* and local corruption, a struggle between Ladino cattle ranchers and indigenous subsistence farmers, and local and national resistance to these forms of domination, are the conditions that allowed the movement to be born when and where it was. In principle, the movement is about *tierra y libertad*, land and liberty, about agrarian reform—all part of the menu of rebellion within the national culture.

But if it were not also something more, *Zapatismo* would not have emerged overnight as the face of a global resistance movement. The Zapatistas' project of autonomy and resistance, and Marcos's hybrid insurgent narrative, aims to change the common interpretation of history, and to reveal undetected patterns of internal colonialism, in order to once and for all undermine the imperial and arbitrary basis of state authority.

However, as distinct from the anti-colonial movements of the post-World War II moment, the basis of authority now resides not merely in the nation state, but in the neo-imperial domination of transnational capital. By the 1990s, several decades after the first stirrings of decolonization, the sovereignty of the nation-state had come under assault, though not, as left theorists would have hoped, from the side of internationalist popular movements. Instead it was the emergence of neoliberal economics and the breaking down of national borders due to the deregulation of trade that ushered in a new phase of resource colonization and a global undermining of progressive social policies. In Mexico, as throughout Latin America, the most recent embodiments of Empire are seen in NAFTA, FTAA, the WTO, the Plan Puebla Panama, etcetera: the massive infrastructure projects, bureaucratic restructurings, and international trade agreements that yearn to replace the nation-state with something akin to a World Market. If the nation-state required the homogenization of diverse cultures in order to form national identity, the World Market—the full-spectrum dominance of transnational capital—demands it even more.

The Zapatistas, as we've seen, are vocal about their desire not to separate from the Mexican nation, but rather to participate in it, albeit with autonomy. From the first, and most clearly with the San Andrés Accords and the March for Indigenous Dignity, *Zapatismo* asserted its primary demand to be the social and political recognition of indigenous cultures within the Mexican nation. Yet, at the same time a violent nationalism—whose own roots are in the national resistance to historical forces that have sought to relieve Mexico of its unity and its sovereignty—underlies Mexican opposition to *Zapatismo*. In the context of the "Balkanization" of nations in the twenty-first century, many Mexicans fear that the indigenous movements threaten national unity.

In fact, despite the Zapatistas saluting the Mexican flag, these movements *do* threaten national unity, and they do so on a profound level. One of the chief aims of *Zapatismo* is embodied in their slogan "a world in which many worlds fit." More than a simple plea for diversity, what is at stake is the will toward making of Mexico a *pluricultural*, *pluriethnic* state—and by so doing to reinvent the nation-state altogether.

Generally speaking, the modern state, as a system of governance, is organized with the primary objective of uniting a dominant class in order to regulate and legislate the ongoing exploitation of human and natural resources. The process of "nation-building," then, tends to disintegrate human communities and the ecosystems of which human communities are a part; where local forms of resource management and governance once existed—often guided by ethics along the lines of *el lekil kuxlejal*—bureaucracies and laws, including those that define the so-called democratic tradition, are created to manage the fragments; flags and anthems are created to weave and sing together the broken pieces; national mythologies are developed to give a sense of belonging to disparate cultures united under the illusory banner of the nation-state.

In contrast, many leaders of indigenous movements will tell you that their project is to rebuild human systems and to reestablish a relationship in balance with the natural world. In confronting five hundred years of state capitalism, one of the ways indigenous movements throughout the Americas are attempting to reconstruct social relationships is by proposing a new model of a "pluriethnic state"—one that fundamentally challenges the cyclopic, monocultural hegemony of the state as it came to be in the twentieth century.

Historian Walter Mignolo suggests that *Zapatismo*, by virtue of its hybridity, advances a form of modernity that is entirely distinct from what preceded it. Modernity, he suggests, can be viewed as a mentality of salvation—the "Western," "modern" nations venturing to save the rest through an evolving set of paternalistic concepts: first the arrival of Christianity with the colonizers brought the saving of souls: *salvation through conversion*; in the eighteenth century, the Enlightenment burst out of France and England, bringing what Mignolo calls "epistemic salvation," or *salvation through civilization*; with the massive change wrought in the twentieth century, and specifically the Second World War, technology becomes the savior and we have *salvation through development* (and the birth of the "developing world," a term coined by Harry Truman in order to establish the clear need of the "less developed" nations of the third world to be managed by the "more developed" nations of the first); finally, when Milton Friedman, Ronald Reagan and Margaret Thatcher usher in the great wave of neoliberalism, where free markets become synonymous with democracy, and democracy with civilization, we arrive in the age of *salvation through democracy*, where the Washington Consensus promises salvation through the market and the "end of history" is declared.[75]

Only, the Zapatistas tell us, History with a capital H is but one among many stories, and if it has ended, it is for other narratives to emerge from its detritus. When we reach the ends of time, it is said, we arrive at the roots of eternity, where all stories are conceived. Rather than one Power (capital P), one History (capital H) and one State (capital S), *Zapatismo*—in time with other emerging movements—declares that there are many powers, many histories, and many states, the most notable being the state of constant flux.

"Modernity," says Mignolo, "is a political project based in the control of economies, gender, sexuality, knowledge, etcetera, and the marginalization of everything that does not fit within these categories. The geopolitics of knowledge allows us to create arguments in terms of a hierarchy of knowledge. For example, philosophy necessarily responds only to the Western tradition—Aristotle and so forth. If it does not do this, it is not philosophy, and therefore it is not serious thinking. Therefore, anything outside of the Western frame of mind is not to be taken seriously."[76]

By the same token, any social construction that takes place outside of the sphere of the nation-state lacks modernity, and therefore, is also not to be taken seriously.

Zapatismo challenges all of that. In *The Uncomfortable Dead*, the 2005 pulp noir novel he co-wrote with Paco Ignacio Taibo II, Marcos visits the question of modernity somewhat more gruffly. A character known only as "the Russian," who, in an extreme example of pluricultural hybridity, is also a Purepecha Indian who runs a tortilla stand "over by the cathedral" in Guadalajara, says:

> "They can't come to me with that crock of shit that globalization is modernity." The Russian wasn't angry, that was just the way he talked. And without stopping his talking, he went on making tor-

> tillas. "What the hell modernity are they talking about? Go ahead, you tell me. That's old as the hills. They been trying to globalize us for bout 500 years. First the fuckin Spanish, then the fuckin gringos, then the fuckin French. And now they're all getting together to gang up on us... even the fuckin Japanese."[77]

The upshot is that, while the nation-state—from the "fuckin Spanish" to the "fuckin Japanese"—has been, up to now, the site of modernity, the very basis of social relations and the imagined communities that serve as templates for our private lives since the Enlightenment, it is time for this particular form of modernity to give up the ghost. What the Zapatistas bring, at the crest of a wave of indigenous and peasant uprisings throughout the world, is a rejection of each and all of the forms of salvationism that Mignolo posits as the fundaments of modernity, in favor of a new, insurgent form of modernity built on territorial autonomy, on cultural diversity, on human dignity, on radical democracy, and on local initiative and community stewardship.

As Peruvian scholar Roberto Espinoza of the Coordinadora Andina de Organizaciones Indígenas stated the problem at the Americas Social Forum on Guatemala City in October 2008, "Why do countries with dozens or hundreds of indigenous nations need to be governed by one single type of ideology that descends from the French Revolution through Simon Bolivar and that continues to rule to this day? Why can't this dominant form of governance be replaced by local, community self-government?"[78] In some sense this is the riddle posed throughout the communiqués and throughout the Zapatista resistance to that stifling modernity that has, by the beginnings of the twenty-first century, led to an impasse. And though he died those many years ago, Old Antonio, who died below in order to live up above, who has disappeared in order to be seen, made a surprise appearance on the outskirts of San Cristóbal de las Casas as lately as January 2009, to help clear the impasse, with a story...

> A frigid dawn, icy and silent, finds us awake just like fifteen years past. And like twenty-five years ago, Old Antonio draws a little light among the shadows we are as he lights his handmade cigarette. We keep our mouths shut. Nobody says anything. Wait.

Then, Old Antonio looses the warmth of his words, words that give relief, that console, that give hope.

"The oldest of our old people, our most ancient wise people, said that the first gods, those that gave birth to the world, that it looked like they had done it without the slightest rhyme or reason. That they just went making pieces of the world and throwing them wherever. That the world they created wasn't one, but that they were many, and each one very different. That's to say, as you say, there were many geographies. And our wise people say that then the times got together, the past, the present and the future, and they went to protest to the gods.

"You can't do it like that, because if you do, we can't do our work with this big mess of different worlds you've made. There needs to be just one world, so that time can walk in an orderly way, along just one road."

That's what the times said.

Then the gods listened to what the past, the present and the future said, and they answered: "Alright then, let's see." So the first gods, those that gave birth to the world, got together, and who knows what they talked about, but they took awhile to talk, that much is certain.

After a while the first gods called out to the times, and they said, "We thought about what you guys said, and we want to tell you we don't like how you think." The times began to moan, what the hey, what the flock is this about, just because we're not gods or whatever, blah blah blah. The gods told them to wait, that they hadn't quite finished talking. "That's okay," said the times and they stood by and waited for what came next. Then the first gods explained to them that a time would come when the Big Boss would show up and would want to dominate the whole world and enslave everybody and everything that the world had in it, and that He was going to kill and destroy. That the Big Boss's strength was for reals and that there was no force equal to it in the whole world. That the only way to resist and to struggle against the Big Boss was to be many and different, so that that way the Big Boss couldn't just grab one and trash everyone.

The gods understood that it was a pain in the ass for the times to make themselves many and different in order to do their work and to make different roads in every one of the worlds that the world had in it, but whatever, that's the way it had to be. And they said, so then there wasn't going to be one time that would fit all the worlds that there were in the world, but that there would be many times. Which is to say, as you say, there would be many calendars. And the first gods said to the times: there's gonna be in each one of these worlds that form the world some who are gonna know how to read the map and the calendars. And there's going to come a time when the past, the present, and the future are gonna get together and then all the times are going to overthrow the Big Boss. That's what the first gods said. And the times, just to be stubborn because they already knew the answer, asked if, when they had overthrown the Big Boss, if then all the worlds would join together in one world. And the first gods told them, that's for the men and women of that time to see for themselves, that they would see if being different made them weak or if it made them strong so they could beat all the Big Bosses that were going to keep showing up.'

Old Antonio left. It continued being cold, but a little light remained, as if to give the shadows some company.

The end.[79]

The Zapatista project is perceived as a threat to the nation-state; what it proposes in fact, is not the end of the nation as a geopolitical entity, but its reformulation to formally recognize the existence within its boundaries of diverse ethnic, cultural, linguistic, and religious groups—that is, pluriethnicity. And from the concept of pluriethnicity—a world in which many worlds fit—we arrive at the concept of plurinationality—a nation in which fit many nations.

Luis Macas of Ecuador's CONAIE writes:

> Interculturality begins with the recognition of the diversity of our societies, which for many years has been ignored by the nation states in which we live. In this sense the indigenous movement in

> Latin America has forced the state to stop in its tracks; interculturality is first the recognition of the diversity of peoples, cultures, and historical processes with distinct identities; beyond that it implies that the original peoples must return to and be conscious of our origins.[80]

Ecuadorian philosopher/historian Bolívar Echeverría points out the same when he says, "For the indigenous to continue surviving, for them to maintain their mode of existence, the Latin American states must change… The only possible way for these human beings who are the indigenous to continue existing as they are and as they want to be, is through the *radical self-transformation* of political modernity as such.[81]

Interculturality, as Macas proposes it, differs in many ways from mere multiculturalism, as recognized in the U.S. While it signals inclusion of multicultural narratives, education and social programs oriented toward diverse ethnic populations, and so forth, for Latin American indigenous people it also signals something more fundamental and more palpable: respect for collective claims to territory and for collective rights.

Prior to a resurgence of indigenous organizing that can be roughly traced to 1992—the five-hundredth anniversary of Columbus's "discovery"—indigenous people in the Americas were deeply marginalized and their movements largely defensive; in a Latin America that has taken a distinct leftward turn at the government level, thanks in large part to this surge of popular consciousness from below, these movements have assumed center stage. A 2002 report from the U.S. National Intelligence Council, a branch of the CIA, announced that indigenous movements had emerged as a serious threat: "Such movements will increase, assisted by transnational networks of indigenous rights activists, supported by well-intentioned international human rights groups and environmentalists."[82]

Though these movements are broadly critical of the state, in general, for all the reasons we have witnessed, the changes they propose have filtered upward rapidly. The Ecuadorian constitution, ratified in 2008, and the Bolivian constitution, ratified in 2009, are the first in the world to recognize plurinationality, and are the fruit of popular indigenous struggles based as much in the demand for resource rights—access to safe water, food sovereignty, and territory—as in the reclaiming of historico-cultural identity, self-determination, and, again, dignity. The movements that have tossed out unpopular presidents, expelled transnational corporations, forced the exit of the International Monetary Fund and other agents of capital, and led to what is universally seen as a new era of democratization throughout Latin America, are based, clearly and unequivocally, in the resurgence of the indigenous struggle. And, even while the Zapatistas themselves maintain a distance from these struggles, as many critics have noted, their influence has been decisive. In a Latin America without borders, a struggle that arises in the *cañadas* of Chiapas in 1994 easily resurfaces in the uprisings in the streets of Cochabamba in 2000, in the popular assaults on Quito's presidential palace in 2007, in the blocking of highways in the Peruvian Amazon in 2009.

These uprisings—this uprising—is nothing less than a new and more profound phase of the decolonialization of the Americas.[83] While earlier phases of decolonization threw out the forces of imperial Europe and then built constitutional republics on European enlightenment values, the current phase, is, at bottom, about the restoration of collective rights and collective subjectivity. NAFTA's erasure of collective property rights in Mexico in 1993—the beginning of a wave of free trade agreements—pushed popular outrage at the legalization of private property over the tipping point, leading to the blowback we are seeing now. The meeting of two winds that Marcos prophesied almost twenty years ago may be read, in the current moment, as a struggle between the isolating modernity of state and corporate capitalism, and an entirely *other* modernity manifesting as a collective engagement fundamental to indigenous worldviews.[84]

An Extremely Brief and Irascible Aside on Old Antonio and the Problem of "Development"

Zapatismo challenges not only the notion of the monolithic state, but also the equally imperial and imperious notion of "development." Recalling Todorov's notion that the *indigena*, the native, was (is?) assigned value by the conqueror only in terms of "absence" or the things she lacks—clothes, firearms, religion, science—let's take advantage of the recent appearance of Old Antonio to visit with him one last time.

Old Antonio is a fiction, but he is a fiction invented to represent a particular set of values that, we can presume, describe the aspirations of *Zapatismo*; yet, from the standpoint of "modernity" or "development" or "progress," Old Antonio is hardly an enviable figure. He has no car, no office, no suburban tract home, no refrigerator, no air conditioning; he owns neither a laptop nor a mobile phone nor a washer-dryer. Poor, disconnected, Old Antonio doesn't even have an email account. We do not see his house, as he is always walking in the hills or crouching on his haunches by a fire outside in the night. He smokes borrowed tobacco rolled in newspaper, and when his old leather *huaraches* wear out, we don't know—nor does he—where he will find another pair of shoes. Certainly he has no retirement fund, pension, bank account, or AARP membership. Which notion, in fact, may signal his most important and substantive lack: Old Antonio does not have a job.

Jobless (not to say unemployed), tending his *milpa* and collecting vines to mend his shoes, his belt, and his house, Old Antonio yet lives what the indigenous-led movements of the Americas today are calling "*el buen vivir,*" what the Tzeltal call *el lekil kuxlejal*. The good life. So, while he is by no means free of worry, pain, fear, suffering, etcetera (who is?), the character of Old Antonio represents, in his daily actions, a way of being beyond the bounds of economic development, whether by the nation-state, the private sector, or the NGO-led development industry.

What we may observe by this is that, while supposedly universal notions of human rights and dignity include economic opportunity, they also include the capacity to eschew economic opportunity in order to cultivate the earth, to raise one's family, to practice one's craft.

Where development offers employment, Old Antonio wants territory. Where development offers money, Old Antonio wants dignity. Where development—falsely indeed–offers social security, Old Antonio wants social sovereignty, resilience. In a word, autonomy.

Of course, it would be equally absurd to suggest that Old Antonio represents the desires of all indigenous people, or all *campesinos,* as it would to say that he represents all old people, or all Mexicans, or all men named Antonio. Old Antonio is a fiction. But by inventing the character of Old Antonio and shining a spotlight on him in so many tales, Marcos is offering a commentary on, among other things, the question of "development." He is not suggesting, necessarily, that you or I should renounce our luxuries, relative as they may be, and choose to live like Antonio. He is merely showing us the possibility that we might be doing Old Antonio a favor by allowing him to live that way himself if he wants.

P.S.: A Postscript which Masquerades as an Aside but Is in Fact an Important Point

If the stories of Don Durito, by making a mockery of the Western canon, act to undermine grand narratives of History (like that, with a capital H), Old Antonio, perhaps, does the opposite. If the effort to dismantle grand narratives allows space for living history to emerge, as I've suggested, Antonio comes to represent precisely that living history. But where official History tells one story, Antonio, the village storyteller, tells many. What he represents may be, in some sense, its own sort of grand narrative—the inclusion of myth in history, a sense of time that spirals like a *caracol*, a world of old gods and old ways that offers a solid ethical compass—but it is a narrative made up of many narratives—and this is precisely the point. Where Don Durito is an anti-hero, breaking down grand narratives and fragmenting and fracturing and decomposing them (a job certainly fit for a beetle), Old Antonio is a mythic hero in the conventional sense, offering gestures of hope, and the certitude that as long as we walk by asking questions, we will at least be walking, and that as long as we employ our inverted periscopes we will see that "down below is not only the world, but the possibility of a better world."[85] Tan-tan.

Launching the Carnival against Capital

The cultural and political influence of *Zapatismo*, within Mexico and around the world, is indisputable, and it runs deep. Oscar Olivera, the Bolivian shoemaker and union leader whose voice was heard around the world in 2000 as the spokesman for a mass popular movement that evicted transnational corporation Bechtel from his hometown of Cochabamba, recognizes "many points in common" between the movements in Bolivia and in Mexico, such as:

> the concept of power, the concept of new forms of social organization, the understanding that power, the construction of democracy, has to be accompanied by the occupation of territory. Here [in Bolivia] the struggles for water and for gas have been at the same time mobilizations to occupy territory. The concept of territory itself is being recuperated from the historical memory of the indigenous peoples, and this is transmitted through the popular

> movements. In Peru, in Mexico, here in Bolivia, in Guatemala, very important struggles have been established against the multinationals, whether they be mining companies, water, electric, oil, and I believe that these struggles, more than disputes over the control of these companies or these resources, are struggles for the recuperation and reappropriation of territory, understanding territory not only as a geographic space, but as a social space that has been violated by neoliberalism, and "development" as such, which wants to do away with community values.
>
> Without saying that we are Zapatistas, I believe that this is an echo of January 1, 1994. This "*Ya Basta!*" has been repeated in many countries, in many forms, with differing characteristics, but with several things in common, such as new forms of organization based in horizontalism, collective leadership, and the recovery of historical memory. The language, the vocabulary, the way these movements act—they have common roots, a sort of unity in the struggle for life itself, and not only for our common goods, but, from a globalized perspective, for a new form of well-being altogether.[86]

So, the struggle, in Bolivia as in Chiapas, is for territory, but also for "the social space that has been violated by neoliberalism," a collective mind-set based in "the recovery of historical memory." In *Culture and Imperialism*, Edward Said quotes D. K. Fieldhouse, conservative historian of empire, on the mutually reinforcing psychology of imperialism: "The basis of imperial authority was the mental attitude of the colonist. His acceptance of subordination—whether through a positive sense of common interest with the parent state, or through inability to conceive of any alternative—made empire durable." Said elaborates: "the durability of empire was sustained on both sides, that of the rulers and that of the distant ruled, and in turn each had a set of interpretations of their common history with its own perspective, historical sense, emotions, and traditions."[87] The current global movements, by reclaiming historical memory and redefining human relationships through an ever-evolving lexicon of resistance, attempt to emerge, once and for all, from under the centuries-long shadow of imperialism.

Mexico, the site of the first revolution of the twentieth century as the feudal isolation of the peasantry gave way to the age of the railroad and the telegraph, brought another revolution at the close of the century when *campesinos* and indigenous people, previously relegated to being objects of exotic inquiry in the frame of modernity, became the subjects of modernity; indeed when they began to change the notion of what modernity is. Despite—or because of—its local roots, the faceless mask of *Zapatismo* has seen its image mirrored in Seattle and Davos, Prague and Toronto, Nice and Porto Alegre. As a struggle for the survival of local cultures, *Zapatismo* is emblematic of global resistance to homogenization and the selling off of culture at any price. January 1, 1994 is a critical date in the global movement of resistance against corporate globalization, and *Zapatismo*, now a cultural force that is more or less taken for granted on the left, offered the ideological base from which myriad opposition movements have sprung. The World Trade Organization, established in 1995, suffered major routs in 1999 (Seattle) and 2003 (Cancún); by 2007 the Doha Round of talks had collapsed entirely, preceding by only a year the largest crisis of capital the world has seen since 1929. Before January 1, 1994—though the bankruptcy and ultimate collapse of capital have been envisioned by many since Marx's predictions a century ago—none of this was immediately foreseeable.

One of the ways in which the Zapatistas have built their base has been through a series of open-ended, inclusive gatherings, generally known as *encuentros* or *convocatorias*, which, along with the marches and the endless public pronouncements, have created a social space for dialogue and discussion, and for what has come to be a sort of ritual participation in the spectacle of *Zapatismo*. This aspect of the poetics began with the National Democratic Convention in the summer of 1994; the Consulta of August 27, 1995, when the Mexican people as a whole were asked to help determine the Zapatistas' strategy through a popular vote; the Encuentro Intercontinental por la Humanidad y contra el Neoliberalismo held at all of the Aguascalientes in July and August of 1996, attended by over 3,000 people from over 40 countries; the March of 1,111 Zapatistas to Mexico City in September 1996; the founding conference of the National Indigenous Congress and the appearance of Comandanta Ramona in the Zocalo in Mexico City on October 12, 1996; a second

Consulta in March 1999, organized by over 120,000 people, including 5,000 Zapatistas who visited municipalities across Mexico, resulting in a popular vote by 2.8 million Mexicans and some 58,000 voters in 29 foreign countries;[88] the March for Indigenous Dignity, also known as the March the Color of the Earth, in February and March, 2001; and so on.

At the closing of the first Encuentro the EZLN issued the Second Declaration of La Realidad for Humanity and against Neoliberalism, which called for the creation of "a collective network of resistance against neoliberalism, an intercontinental network of resistance for humanity."[89] This network would have "no central head or decision maker," "no central command or hierarchies," but would provide communication and support for struggles against neoliberalism around the world.[90] The EZLN also called, in the Second Declaration, for a second *encuentro* to be held on another continent.

That *encuentro*, the Second Intercontinental Encuentro for Humanity and Against Neoliberalism, was held in Spain the following year, in July 1997, attended by 4,000 activists from 50 countries. At the European *encuentro,* plans were laid to form a group called People's Global Action (PGA), which would answer the Zapatistas' call. Olivier de Marcellus, one of the founders of PGA, explains:

> PGA is an offshoot of the international Zapatista movement, founded in a meeting that prolonged the Second *Encuentro* in southern Spain, and drawing a lot of its European support from people who also support the Zapatistas. There is also a certain ideological and organizational resemblance, both being rather unorthodox, eclectic networks attempting to stimulate radical opposition worldwide.[91]

PGA (whose slogan is "May the resistance be as transnational as capital!") became an important organizing forum for the series of global protests that followed, coordinating Days of Action against the WTO, the G8, and the World Bank, and convening numerous gatherings around the world. PGA was also instrumental in the formation and evolution of the World Social Forum—a sort of Zapatista *encuentro* writ large.

At the World Economic Forum, held every January in Davos, Switzerland, the leaders of the capitalist class, from presidents to multilateral investment banks to the Bill Gates' and Jeffrey Sachs' of the world, come together to discuss global economic policy, and to forge alliances. The World Social Forum established itself as a grassroots alternative; at the first Forum, held by the Workers' Party in Porto Alegre, Brazil in 2001, more than 10,000 social movement activists attended from all over the world, and gave rise to the simple but fundamental chant, "Another World is Possible!" Within a few years, the numbers had grown to over 100,000, with the forum moving between its home in Porto Alegre and sites on other continents, and giving birth to regional and national fora such as the Social Forum of the Americas, the U.S. Social Forum, the European Social Forum, and any number of smaller, local gatherings.

People's Global Action and the Social Forum process are indicative of the emergent rhizomatic organizing structures prefigured by *Zapatismo*, and recognized early on by the Rand Corporation; anti-capitalist and anti-authoritarian in spirit, they are based on decentralized power, collective decision-making, and continual evolution of both form and function.

It is not only the cause of *Zapatismo* and its methodologies that have been taken up by the global resistance movement; the poetics of *Zapatismo* have given birth to renewed forms of protest, a new vocabulary of street action and struggle. The cry of "*Zapata vive, la lucha sigue*" is heard across Europe and the Americas. The demand *everything for everyone, nothing for ourselves* has become something of a theoretical framework for a global counterculture that refuses to tolerate the inequalities that further divide North from South, uptown from downtown, richer from poorer. The movement is marked by public spectacles, giant puppets, street theater, direct action, music, masks, uniforms; in short, a global poetics of resistance where the struggle is housed in costumes that stir the heart as well as the intellect. The spirit of Don Durito de la Lacandona was alive in the sea turtles that marched for ecological justice in Seattle in November 1999. The sense of the Zapatistas' black ski masks has been taken up by the Italian direct action collective Ya Basta, who wear white overalls to distinguish themselves as peaceful warriors and perform group actions under the name Tutti Bianchi, all in white, a.k.a. Monos Blancos, or White Monkeys.

Ever the contrarian, Subcomandante Marcos takes a measured approach to such a genealogy of resistance:

> We conceived of our movement, and this is what we declared in 1994, as a symptom of something that was happening and was about to happen. We used the image of the iceberg: we are, we said, the tip of the iceberg that is sticking up and soon other tips will emerge in other places, and something larger will surge up to the surface.
>
> In this sense, Chiapas doesn't precede Seattle as much as it announces Seattle. Seattle is the continuation. Seattle is another manifestation of this world rebellion that is gestating outside of political parties, outside of traditional channels of politics. And it's that way with every one of the demonstrations, and I don't mean only those that have followed the WTO around and have become its worst nightmare, but other kinds of more lasting demonstrations or mobilizations or movements against the globalization of death and destruction.
>
> We are more modest as to our place. We are a symptom and we think that our duty is to maintain ourselves as much as possible as a handle, a point of reference. But not as a model to follow. That's why we never argued, nor will we say, that Chiapas and the Continental and Intercontinental Meetings were the beginning. The rebellion in Chiapas is called Zapatista; but in Seattle it's called something else; in the European Union something else; in Asia something else; in Australia something else. Even in Mexico, in other places the rebellion has other names."[92]

Other names, yes, and other uniforms—or better, pluriforms. When white monkeys march in Milan, sea turtles dance in the streets of Seattle, and a little beetle lectures on neoliberalism from the jungle of southeastern Mexico, these are perhaps signs of a reinvigorated resistant ecopoetic consciousness; an ancient new voice making itself heard across the globe.

In "The Twilight of Vanguardism," David Graeber reminds us that Karl Marx, a century and a half ago, emerged from a tradition of revolutionary vanguardist intellectuals to introduce "the notion that the proletariat were the true revolutionary class…because they were the most oppressed or, as he put it, 'negated' by capitalism, and therefore had the least to lose by its abolition." Graeber then points out that it is no surprise that indigenous uprising(s) should figure largely in the emergence of the so-called "anti-globalization" movement: indigenous people "tend to be simultaneously the very least alienated and most oppressed people on earth and, once it is technologically possible to include them in revolutionary coalitions, it is almost inevitable that they should take a leading role."[93]

These coalitions—Vía Campesina defining food sovereignty as a right of all peoples and then struggling to defend it, *la Red VIDA* fighting for the human right to water in Latin America, the People's Health Movement with huge contingents in South Asia and considerable numbers elsewhere demanding the human right to health with dignity, the Jubilee South Network repudiating illegitimate national debt, the innumerable alliances of indigenous peoples that have emerged throughout the Americas such as the Confederation of Indigenous Nations of Ecuador (CONAIE) and the Civic Council of Popular and Indigenous Organizations of Honduras (COPINH) to name just two, People's Global Action "following the WTO around and becoming its worst nightmare"—tend to construct themselves on principals such as self-organization, voluntary association, mutual aid, a questioning of state power, and other ideological tools that, again, echo the Zapatista cry of "everything for everyone, nothing for us."

This conjunction of forces that has become known as the global justice movement, not unlike the Zapatistas within Mexico, has received criticism (when it has received any substantive media attention at all), for being merely *anti*, and lacking a programmatic vision.

On the one hand, this movement of movements is *anti* because, apart from being against exclusion and exploitation generally, it is against the dominant narratives of history. That is the "One no" in the Zapatista slogan "One no and many yeses." In this sense we are witness to a literal, physical manifestation of the obscure theoretical tenets of postmodernism—countless local struggles against the imposition of both a dominant narrative (History with a capital H) and a dominating physical superstructure (the alienating built environment, and the impoverishment that accompanies it).

On the other hand, neither the Zapatistas nor the larger global movement(s) are limited to the "no"; like *Zapatismo*, the global movement is in favor of diverse, plural, culturally embedded community and is engaged in increasingly concrete efforts to build social and political structures that support food sovereignty, water justice, democracy in trade, and a revival of economic frameworks like the commons that propose alternatives to both government control and free market free-for-all—real, grounded, strategies, many of them based in notions of autonomy, liberty, justice, and dignity. Beyond that, as Graeber, among many others, has pointed out, "these new forms of organization, which presume and are ways of articulating diverse perspectives, *are* [the global justice movement's] ideology."[94] It is precisely this diverse, horizontal, open-ended network style of organizing that embodies the prophecy and the hope of a world in which many worlds fit. This is the "many yeses."

Unfortunately, as noted, "a revolutionary strategy of permanent, open-ended global uprising (from Chiapas to Seattle, Genoa, and Argentina) has been so successful that it is now being answered with a doctrine of permanent, open-ended global war."[95]

The New Horizon: From Resistance to Re-existence

> Utopia is on the horizon. You walk two steps, and it retreats two steps. You walk ten steps and it retreats ten steps.
>
> So, then what is utopia for? For that—to make you keep walking.
>
> —Eduardo Galeano

Fifteen years into the uprising, the challenges to *Zapatismo* have not diminished; neither has the Zapatistas' novelty as masters of the grassroots spectacle. At the turn of the year 2008–2009, the First International Festival of Dignified Rage (*la digna rabia*), part *encuentro*, part seminar, and part cultural bash, drew many thousands of participants to the Lienzo Charro, an occupied rodeo ground in Ixtapalapa at the edge of Mexico City, and to the Centro Indígena de Capacitación Integral (CIDECI), a radical, social-movement-based popular education center also known as the Universidad de la Tierra, in Chiapas. For the better part of ten days,

Mexican luminaries like Pablo González Casanova, Adolfo Gilly, and Gustavo Esteva shared the microphone with foreign journalists like Raul Zibechi, social movement leaders like Mónica Baltodano of Nicaragua's neo-Sandinista movement and Oscar Olivera, and the EZLN Comandancia, paying homage to the Zapatistas' "fifteen and twenty-five" years of struggle and theorizing the ways forward, making the road by walking. The scene at the Universidad de la Tierra, small by World Cup standards, was enough to give a sense that the Zapatistas still draw a crowd.

Still, due to the splits caused by the Otra Campaña and to an apparently successful Mexican media campaign to marginalize them, even many people on the Mexican left have assigned the Zapatistas to oblivion. *La Jornada's* coverage has shrunk, with new communiqués no longer published in their entirety in its pages, though they can still be found on line. With the spectacular failure of the global economy grabbing headlines, and with the rapid growth of narco-trafficking across the Mexican countryside—as one taxi driver said to me, "too many decapitated heads too many days of the week"—the EZLN as a political force is no longer at the center of national debate. Between Felipé Calderon's election in 2006 and midterm elections in 2009 estimates of deaths in Mexico's drug war ran as high as 10,000;[96] bullet for bullet, the EZLN, pacifist teetotalers that they are, simply cannot compete for the attention. In the United States, press coverage of the movement—never profound—has diminished to the likes of a mocking travel piece in the *New York Times* and a box in "The Lonely Planet Guide to La Ruta Maya" updated every few years. But the poetics of resistance that imbued *Zapatismo* with its initial resonance has entered the political vocabulary; the EZLN itself may be largely out of the picture, but *Zapatismo* as a theoretical approach and "a way of doing politics," is everywhere.

At the same time, "the fire" in "the fire and the word," is kindling dangerously. The administration of Felipe Calderón has taken a hard line, reestablishing military bases throughout Chiapas; paramilitary threats—incursions, confrontations, beatings, killings—are on the rise like at no time since the mid-1990s; in the second half of 2009 and the first months of 2010, *denuncias* of Zapatistas and their allies killed, generally one-by-one in disperse, remote communities, appear almost weekly. Impunity, it appears, is at an all-time high. In August, 2009, 12 years after the massacre at Acteal, the killers previously convicted of carrying out the massacre were ordered released from prison because of "procedural errors in their prosecutions."[97] Commenting on the prevalence of such "procedural errors," Mexican human rights attorney Barbara Zamora, lawyer for the prisoners of Atenco and other high profile government targets, said, "The Mexican judicial system is rotten to the core. From now on, whether they are guilty or not, anyone who can afford a powerful lawyer and has been sentenced for homicide, narco, kidnapping, or organized crime will be able to claim judicial impropriety and appeal to the Supreme Court to be set free. This could empty out the jails."[98]

With impunity reigning, the drug war raging, the *peso* plummeting, and the price of basic commodities such as corn, beans, and rice on a steady upward trajectory, the Zapatista communities, according to many first-hand accounts, are shrinking. The challenge of maintaining resistance in the face of hunger and misery is no doubt taking its toll, and the Zapatista communities are far from immune to the pressures that empty out towns and villages throughout the nation in a steady stream of migration northward in search of a world that is not necessarily better, but that at least offers a paycheck.

Still, in the face of it, Zapata lives, and the struggle, as always, continues.

Regardless of how Marcos or the Zapatistas are perceived at the present juncture, and despite continued repression, there can be no doubt that the changes they have brought to Mexico are profound. While Marcos's ceaseless disparaging of Andrés Manuel Lopez Obrador caused fractures in the national left and, according to some, gave the election to Felipé Calderón (earning Marcos the very unfortunate moniker "the Ralph Nader of Mexico"), it is just as certain that, had it not been for the emergence of *Zapatismo* on the dawn of Mexico's emergence into the First World that dark January of 1994, López Obrador's candidacy, and the popular movement he continues to spearhead, would likely never have come to pass.

Beyond ephemeral questions of the shape of electoral politics at the surface of Mexican life, more far-reaching changes have been wrought in the fabric of race relations. In late 2008, Wixarika lawyer Santos de La Cruz Carillo told me:

> Within the process of struggle there was always a threat, a racism against us. But in 1994, the EZLN entered into a state of war, they made many demands; these demands were for all indigenous peoples. They brought to light our demands, as indigenous peoples, and many of us in Mexico realized that we had to fight for our constitutional rights. Many things have changed since 1994. Before that, many people in Mexico didn't know what we, the indigenous, what we wanted.[99]

Paco Vazquez of ProMedios makes a similar point: "In my family, in my *pueblo*, we're Momoxca, from near Mexico City. Does racism continue in Mexico? Of course it does. But after 1994, my family began to reclaim its heritage by reclaiming our language. Since 1994, at home, our language is spoken again."[100]

During the Festival de la Digna Rabia, a woman stood up, waving a machete in the air, symbol of struggle for the people of Atenco, and she said, "This is what we learned from the EZLN—love for our roots, and love for our dignity. Our *pueblo*, Atenco, has been bathed in blood. Unfortunately, this is not only true of us. But what we have in common with the EZLN is not merely that we have suffered bloodshed. What we have in common is that we have recovered our dignity."

These testimonies bear witness to what such a poet as Marcos might call "*el efecto mariposa*:" that the flap of a butterfly's wings in La Realidad might set off a tornado in Mexico City, or in Washington D.C., or everywhere.

Walter Mignolo has pointed out that "*Zapatismo* is not an anti-capitalist movement, but a decolonial movement. Why decolonial? Because movements that are "anti" are merely about resistance, while decolonial movements are about 're-existence.'"[101] With the decline of Marxist national liberation movements, the multiple crises of nation-states, and the rise of corporate globalization, *Zapatismo* is one face of the indigenous movements emerging throughout the world in search of new forms of popular power based in territorial autonomy, cultural rights, and political self-determination; in short, an entirely new—and at the same time, resurgently old—set of principles.

As a movement toward re-existence, a final analogy might be drawn to an earlier peasant revolution faraway in time and across the globe.

John Berger, discussing the "strange dynamic" of the Russian peasantry during the revolutionary moment of 1917 says, "their backwardness had become the very condition of their seizing a future, far in advance of the rest of Europe. Instead of a present, they had a past and a future. Instead of compromises, they had extremes. Instead of limited possibilities, they had open prophecies."[102]

Our insurgent narrative began with "A Storm and a Prophecy," and, in spiral fashion like a *caracol*, this is where it leaves off. If all of Latin America in the first decade of the twenty-first century is a laboratory of resistance, then Chiapas in the 1990s was the crucible for this resistance, the fundament for a series of alchemical reactions that have brought social movements across the continent to a boil.

The storm is the greatest crisis of global capital since 1929. And the prophecy?

The popular notion of prophecy is a telling of fortunes, the mystical divination of future events, and certainly we can see in the communiqués, the masks, the dolls and the guns (both imitation and real), and in the actions of the Zapatistas, a prefiguring of what has since come to pass—a global struggle of *los de abajo* for justice with dignity. But the older meaning of prophecy is less sideshow attraction and more integrated into the meaning of events; it is the interjection into ordinary life of a divine clarity, a sense of the fullness of time and the greater world. Anthropologist Armin Geertz, considering Hopi culture, wrote, "Prophecy is not prediction, even though it purports to be so. Prophecy is a thread in the total fabric of meaning, in the total worldview. In this way it can be seen as a way of life and of being."[103] Mythologist Michael Meade says, in a similar vein, "Prophecy doesn't mean to tell what's going to happen in the future, it means to visit the ancient past and the future, to gather language and words, to bring them back and drop them into the present."[104] Prophecy in the old sense indicates those flashes of consciousness when the stream of time, both time past and time future, become momently visible in time present. If the storm is the problem—a clash of cultural values and systems of power, or, as it was named by the indigenous-led movements at the 2009 World Social Forum, *a crisis of civilization*—then the prophecy is the solution, the way forward reckoned against the real costs of history, the turning of the world toward greater harmony.

Without doubt we live in prophetic times.

It is commonly noted by Mexicans and Mexicologists these days that there is an interesting numerological coincidence at hand. As John Ross puts it, "Mexico's political metabolism seems to break out in insurgencies every 100 years on the 10th year of the century. In 1810, the country priest Miguel Hidalgo launched the struggle for independence from the Crown. In 1910, Francisco Madero ignited the fuse of the epic Mexican revolution."[105] Could 2010 bring another outbreak of sustained social upheaval?

As anthropologist Guillermo Bonfil Batalla noted, in the construction of an imaginary nation that is Mexico, "Power and Western civilization coincide on one pole, and subjugation and Mesoamerican civilization on the other."[106] The Zapatista project is to shift the balance of power not, as is so common, by moving to the side of Western civilization, but by changing the social meanings of what power is.

If what we are living is a war against the imagination, part of what the Zapatistas have wrought is the notion that imagination is a foundational act, an act of will that is not merely individual, as many of us in the North (or West, or wherever it is we locate ourselves in the shifting compass of psychogeography) tend to believe, but collective, and that by engaging in collective acts of imagination, we transform the world.

And, they remind us, these transformations happen everywhere, all the time.

In answer to criticisms that *Zapatismo* is merely anti-, or that it does not go far enough, or has little to offer, or is riddled with flaws, Subcomandante Marcos has said, "The specialty of the Zapatistas is to create problems and then see who can fix them."[107] The problem they have created for the western mind-set, for the corporate state, for the development industry, and for everyone to one degree or another, is that of collectively imagining a way to fix what Galeano called "five centuries of the pillage of a continent." And while, as we have seen, *Zapatismo* is not a model on which all social movements can be based, for over fifteen years and counting they have, at their great peril, continued to offer us a language, at once pragmatic, beautiful, and absurd, in which we can collectively discuss the problem.

Acknowledgments

This book began its long journey in 1994, when the communiqués first appeared on the Internet, and I, like many others, began translating them, studying them, interpreting them, and apprehending them, quite literally, as a riddle to be teased out. In 1995 I found my way to Chiapas and got involved in the work there—installing potable drinking water systems, helping with agricultural production, and "observing the human rights situation," which meant, *mas que nada,* taking testimonies from members of Zapatista communities about military and paramilitary abuses they had witnessed and lived through. After most of three years living in Chiapas, in 1998, like a good number of other human rights workers, I was, rather suddenly, arrested and expelled from the country, and it was some years before I was able to return.

Following my expulsion, I began work on this book, first as an academic thesis, and, later, with hopes of seeing it published. A brief stay in Mexico during and after the Zapatista caravan in early 2001 allowed me to reestablish contact with many people, and to meet a new generation of activists who had arrived in Chiapas after the events of Seattle in 1999. Additional visits in 2004 and 2008 allowed me to glean new insights and to update the material here. As well, the web of activists and scholars for whom Chiapas is the crossroads of the global justice movement continued to grow, many of them crossing my doorstep along the way, keeping me apprised of events in the Mexican Southeast. At the same time, nearly a decade working on a popular education manual about grassroots environmental health efforts in the developing world, followed by further work organizing around the human right to water, gave me the opportunity to widen my understanding of social movements globally, as I visited and spent time with community activists in numerous countries. The similarity among struggles against oppression across the globe is astonishing; astonishing, as well, is the diversity of means employed to construct resistance.

Having first arrived in Chiapas in 1995, I've been fortunate to have access to an ongoing dialogue among many people who've been close to the Zapatista movement for over a decade; some of them live daily in Zapatista communities helping to cultivate programs of education, health, solidarity economy, agricultural production; others report on the movement for media both marginal and mainstream, or lead delegations and fact-finding missions, or build digital networks or publish and distribute communiqués. A few of those who've kept me informed and made me feel a part of the movement, to an extent that has allowed me to write this book in good faith, and to whom I offer my most profound gratitude and respect, are Mariana Mora, Eva Schulte, Lisa Sanderson-Fox, Gustavo Castro Soto, Jorge Santiago Santiago, Rosa Luz Perez, Jutta Meier-Weidenbach, Paco Vasquez, and Cecilia Santiago Vera. The Chiapas Support Committee of Oakland and the Comité Emiliano Zapata, the Mexico Solidarity Network, the National Commission for Democracy in Mexico, Global Exchange, and the Centro de Derechos Humanos Fray Bartolomé de Las Casas were, and are, essential in providing information and support. Others who've helped shape these ideas and allowed room for them to grow, whether through simple encouragement and accompaniment or through editing and feedback, include Todd Jailer, Wendy Call, Jennifer Whitney, David Solnit, Charlotte Saenz, Christy Rogers, Beverly Bell, Steve Solnit, John Gibler, Ramor Ryan, Manolo Callahan, Gopal Dayaneni, and Innosanto Nagara. Hilary Klein deserves an extra shout-out for having read the manuscript with great care and for sending extraordinarily detailed and attentive feedback.

Among the poets who've mentored me, five in particular, all of the perpetual San Francisco renaissance, merit a tip of the hat: Lyn Hejinian's New College course "Language and Paradise" tendered great mental ferment, and her fearlessness in all matters of academic and postcolonial freedom encouraged my pursuit of the material early on; Gloria Frym supported my first efforts at translation by giving them academic credence; David Meltzer was an early, enthusiastic reader of the manuscript and cheerleader for its publication; former San Francisco poet laureate Jack Hirschman suggested a list of readings which opened many paths into the dark landscapes of colonial occupation and resistance. The omnipresent John Ross provided a high stylistic objective for which to strive, both in writing the annals of rebellion and, be it said, in living them.

For putting a roof over my head during a few lost weekends in Mexico (not to mention a summer in *la Mision*) I thank Nancy Charraga, Jeff Juris, and Hena Moreno Corzo-Cruz (who most gracefully wore a clown nose as the EZLN occupied the Zocalo in her beloved Tenochtitlán). Annick Garcia gave me a month of shelter and kind company in East L.A. where I began the book lo those many years ago; the Mesa Writers' Refuge offered me two weeks of uninterrupted writing time in the marshlands at Point Reyes, where I finished it. Thanks to Claudia Campero of Chilangolandia and Maria Gonzalez of Guadalajara for offering their perspectives on la Otra Campaña and *las demas luchas que siguen por alli*. A visit to Potam pueblo in Yaqui territory hosted by Andrea Carmen and the International Indian Treaty Council deepened my perception of deep Mexico, and the occasional phone call from Angél Valencia, a native of that territory, made me feel welcome to return, which I someday will. Pedro Gonzalez of Otros Mundos, aside from providing shelter in San Cristóbal one cold but bright New Year, brought to my attention the Tzeltal concept of *lekil kuxlejal*, a crucial contribution. Thanks to the kind intervention of my Bolivian *colega en lucha* Marcela Olivera I was able to meet and spend precious time with members of Colombia's Minga Indigena, Vilma Almendra and Manuel Rozental, who generously shared with me their perspectives, their history, and their profoundly brilliant organizing and communications strategy. *Mil gracias,* Marcela, for keeping me on track, and *mil gracias, tambien,* to your esteemed brother Oscar.

Brian Awehali's publication of an adapted portion of the manuscript in the marvelous and sadly defunct *LiP Magazine* revived my interest in the material at a time when my attention had long been turned elsewhere; his generous efforts to promote it led, eventually, to AK Press's request to have a look. Thanks to Chuck Morse whose kind and attentive editing helped clarify some of the principal concepts and called my attention to some rather serious inconsistencies in an earlier draft, and to Charles Weigl and the AK Press Collective for their commitment to bringing the book into the world. For permission to use their gorgeous photos, I thank Mariana Mora, Gustavo Gilabert, Tim Russo, John Gibler, Andy Lin, and Jutta Meier-Weidenbach.

Finally, eternal thanks to my companion and *compañera* Kristen, whose steadfast support has allowed these scribblings to coalesce into a book; whose forbearance, understanding, and self-sacrifice gave me time to write even when there was no time; and whose love has nurtured my creative spirit; and to Sacha Rain Conant, born kicking on the fourteenth New Year's Eve of the Zapatista uprising. Sacha Rain, you are the illumination of the better world I strive for everyday.

Photo credits:

John Gibler: 39, 104, 290, 293;

Gustavo Gilabert: 22, 48, 152, 176, 325;

Andy Lin: 276, 280, 285;

Jutta Meier-Weidenbach: 148, 185, 245, 260;

Mariana Mora: 10, 118;

Tim Russo: 128, 162, 191, 210

Notes

Introduction

1 From an audio recording of Marcos, transcribed in Muñoz, Gloria, *The Fire and the Word* (San Francisco: City Lights Books, 2008), 283.

2 Jan De Vos, *Una Tierra para Sembrar Sueños* (México, D.F.: Fondo de Cultura Económica, Centro de Investigaciones y Estudios Superiores en Antropología Social, 2002), 326.

Chapter I

1 See Roger Burbach, "Roots of the Postmodern Rebellion in Chiapas," *New Left Review*, Vol. 205 (May-June, 1994), 113-124.

2 Communiqué of 17 November, 1994, in de Leon, and Monsivais, eds. *EZLN: Documentos y Comunicados*, Vol. 2, *15 de agosto - 29 de septiembre, 1995* (México, D.F.: Ediciones Era, 1996), 139.

3 These are the predominant ethnic groups in Chiapas whose historic unification in struggle was brought about by the Zapatista uprising.

4 The hilariously apt "Make-sicko City," is, I think, Carlos Fuentes's coinage.

5 Televisa and TV Azteca, both family-owned conglomerates, dominate the Mexican airwaves with more than 95 percent of the viewing audience. Televisa operates 225 television channels while TV Azteca operates 42. Seven out of ten viewers in Mexico watch channels belonging to Televisa, while two out of ten watch TV Azteca channels.

6 In a 1990 debate with Mexican poet Octavio Paz, the Peruvian novelist Mario Vargas Llosa described Mexico's political system as "the perfect dictatorship," in reference to the way the PRI (Partido Revolucionario Institucional), Mexico's monolithic political party, had controlled nearly every aspect of the country's life for over sixty years.

7 "Mysterious" because, printed in an edition of 1,000 copies and sold for 900 pesos, or almost $70 US (the profits support the communities in resistance), it is hard to get one's hands on the book; mysterious also because Marcos's turn toward erotic poetry has mystified many followers of the Zapatista movement. Some charge that the recent literary work has dubious political value at best; at worst, that it compromises the hard-won Zapatista name.

8 From an interview with Gabriel García Marquéz and Roberto Pombo, in Tom Mertes, *A Movement of Movements: Is Another World Really Possible?* (London, New York: Verso, 2004), 4.

9 John Berger, *Art and Revolution: Ernst Neizvestny and the Role of the Artists in the U.S.S.R.* (New York: Pantheon Books, 1969), 22.

10 From a communiqué of July 15, 1998, signed "Speedy Gonzalez."

11 From a communiqué, "To 500 Years of Resistance," February 1, 1994.

12 From a definition of postmodernism at http://www.georgetown.edu/faculty/irvinem/technoculture/pomo.html.

13 William Carlos Williams, from *Asphodel, That Greeny Flower* in *Journey to Love*, 1955.
14 Personal communication, December 2008.
15 Communiqué of 12 June, 1994, in de Leon, and Monsivais, eds. *EZLN: Documentos y Comunicados,* Vol.1, 269.
16 A *huipil* (from the Nahuatl *uipilli*, meaning "blouse" or "dress") is a form tunic or blouse worn by indigenous Mayan, Zapotec, and other women in central to southern Mexico, and the northern parts of Central America. The elaborate patterns of a traditional woman's huipil convey the wearer's village, marital status, and personal beliefs.
17 John Ross, *Zapatistas!* (New York: Nation Books, 2006), 331.
18 From her speech at the Festival de la Digna Rabia, México, D.F., December, 2008.
19 Quoted in Alex Khashnabish, *Zapatismo Beyond Borders* (Toronto: University of Toronto Press, 2008), 266.
20 Naomi Klein, *No Logo* (New York: Picador, 2000), 73.
21 Gloria Muñoz Ramirez, *The Fire and The Word: A History of the Zapatista Movement*. (San Francisco: City Lights Books, 2008), 20.
22 Klein, *No Logo*, 2000, xix–xxii.
23 Ibid., 3.
24 Ibid., 5.
25 Guy Debord, *Society of the Spectacle,* (Detroit: Black and Red, 1983), 32.
26 Ibid., 1.
27 Figures from *Para Entender Chiapas*, (*La Coordinacion de Organismos No Gobernementales por la Paz de Chiapas* San Cristobal de las Casas, 1997), 31.
28 From the magazine *El Cuarto Poder,* Comision Nacional para la Proteccion y Defensa de los Usuarios de los Sistemas Financieros (CONDUSEF).
29 Figures from Ana Carrigan, "Chiapas, The First Postmodern Revolution," in Juana Ponce de Leon, ed., *Our Word is Our Weapon: Selected Writings of Subcomandante Insurgente Marcos (*New York: Seven Stories Press, 2001).
30 Resist! Collective, eds., *Zapatista! Documents from the New Mexican Revolution* (New York: Semiotext(e), 1995), 114.
31 Personal communication, October 2008.
32 Personal communication, interview, December 2008.

Chapter II

1 Klein, *No Logo*, xix.
2 "The Table of San Andrés: Between the Oblivion Above and the Memory Below," in *La Jornada*, February 28, 1998.
3 *EZLN Documentos y Comunicados*, Vol. 1, 1994, Declaration of the Lacandon Jungle, 33–35. See also *Our Word is Our Weapon,* 13.
4 Originally reported in the *Guardian*, January 5, 1994, quoted in Tello Diaz, *La rebelion de las Cañadas*, 1995–2000, 19.
5 As quoted in Mihalis Mentinis, *Zapatistas: The Chiapas Revolt and What it*

Means for Radical Politics (London: Pluto Press, 2006), 9.

6 Gilberto López y Rivas, *Autonomías: Democracia o Contrainsurgencia* (México, D.F., Ediciones ERA, 2004), 75.

7 As quoted in Mentinis, *Zapatistas*, 12.

8 Yvon LeBot, *Subcomandante Marcos, El Sueño Zapatista* (Barcelona: Plaza & Janes Editores, 1997), 115.

9 Ronald Wright, *Stolen Continents: The New World through Indian Eyes* (Boston: Houghton Mifflin, 1992), 5.

10 Victoria Bricker, *El Cristo Indigena, El Rey Nativo: El Sustrato historico de la mitologia del ritual de los mayas,* (México, D.F.: Fondo de Cultura Economica, 1989), 22.

11 Dennis Tedlock, trans., *Popul Vuh* (New York: Simon & Schuster, 1985), 63–64.

12 Vine Deloria, "Myth and the Origin of Religion," in *Spirit and Reason* (Golden Colorado:Fulcrum Publishing,1999), 340.

13 Ibid., 344.

14 Tzvetan Todorov, *The Conquest of America: The Question of the Other* (New York: Harper Perennial, 1992), 54.

15 Ward Churchill, *Fantasies of the Master Race* (San Francisco: City Lights, 1998), 15.

16 Neal Salisbury, "American Indians and American History," in Deloria and Salisbury, eds., *A Companion to American Indian History* (Malden, Maine: Blackwell Publishing, 2004), 46.

17 Edward Said, *Culture and Imperialism* (London, Chatto and Windus, Ltd.,1991), xiii.

18 cf. Adolfo Gilly,"*Chiapas and the Rebellion of the Enchanted World,*" in Nugent, Daniel, ed., *Rural Revolt in Mexico: U.S. Intervention and the Domain of Subaltern Politics* (Durham: Duke University Press, 1998).

19 Garcia de Leon, ed., *EZLN Documentos y Comunicados*, Vol. 2 (México, D.F.: Ediciones Era), 1995, "The Long Journey from Despair to Hope," 68, translation by the author.

20 Serge Gruzinski, *The Conquest of Mexico* (Cambridge, England: Polity Press, 1993), 52.

21 *EZLN Documentos y Comunicados*, Vol. 1 (México, D.F.: Ediciones Era), 1994, from "Chiapas: The Southeast in Two Winds, a Storm and a Prophecy," 50, translation by the author. Full translations of the text can be found in *Zapatista! Documents from the New Mexican Revolution*, (Resist! Collective, eds., New York, Semiotext(e), 1995, 25, and in Juana Ponce de León, ed., *Our Word is Our Weapon* (New York: Seven Stories Press, 2001), 22.

22 The Age of Discovery quickly bled into "the age of empire," of which Edward Said has this to say: "Most historians of empire speak of the 'age of empire' as formally beginning around 1878, with 'the scramble for Africa.' A closer look at the cultural actuality reveals a much earlier, more deeply and stubbornly held view about overseas European hegemony; we can locate a

coherent, fully mobilized system of ideas near the end of the eighteenth century, and there follows the set of integral developments such as the first great systematic conquests by Napoleon, the rise of nationalism and the European nation-state, the advent of large-scale industrialization, and the consolidation of power in the bourgeoisie. This is also the period in which the novel form and the new historical narrative become pre-eminent, and in which the importance of subjectivity to historical time takes firm hold." (Said, *Cultural Imperialism*, 68–69).

23 *EZLN Documentos y Comunicados*, Vol. 1, 1994, from "Chiapas: The Southeast in Two Winds, a Storm and a Prophecy," 50, translation by the author.

24 Ibid., 51.

25 Pemex is Petroleo Mexicano, Mexico's state oil company.

26 Ibid., 51.

27 Ibid., 52.

28 Ibid., 58.

29 See Ward Churchill, *A Little Matter of Genocide* (San Francisco: City Lights, 1998), and Ronald Wright, *Stolen Continents*, as well as Dee Brown's classic *Bury My Heart at Wounded Knee*, for the gory details.

30 Said, *Culture and Imperialism*, 13.

31 Personal communication, June 2000.

32 See Tom Barry, *Zapata's Revenge: Free Trade and the Farm Crisis in Mexico*, (Boston: South End Press, 1995), and Noam Chomsky, *Year 501: The Conquest Continues* (Boston: South End Press, 1993).

33 *EZLN Documentos y Comunicados*, Vol. 1, 61–62.

34 This oft-cited quote is, in fact, inaccurate. In *The 18th Brumaire of Louis Bonaparte*, Chapter 1, Marx wrote: "Hegel remarks somewhere that all great world-historic facts and personages appear, so to speak, twice. He forgot to add: the first time as tragedy, the second time as farce."

35 Gross, Matt, "*Frugal Mexico*," *New York Times* Travel Section, November 16, 2008.

36 Armando Bartra, Introduction to *Relatos de El Viejo Antonio* (San Cristóbal de Las Casas, México: Centro de Informacion y Analisis de Chiapas, A.C., 1999), 14, translation mine.

37 *EZLN Documentos y Comunicados*, Vol. 1, 65.

38 The *milpa* is the traditional family plot where corn, beans, squash and other crops are grown.

39 Carlos Montemayor, *Chiapas: La Rebelion indigena de Mexico* (México, D.F.: Joaquin Mortiz, 1997), 142.

40 Le Bot, *El Sueño Zapatista,* 153.

41 Jan De Vos, *Una Tierra para Sembrar Sueños* (México, D.F.: Fondo de Cultura Económica, Centro de Investigaciones y Estudios Superiores en Antropología Social, 2002), 369, translation mine.

42 John Bierhorst, John, *The Mythology of Mexico and Central America* (New York, HarperCollins, 1990), 37.

43 Ibid., 38.
44 EZLN Documentos y Comunicados, Vol. 1, *Los Arroyos Cuando Bajan,* 240–241.
45 Antonio Garcia de Leon as quoted in César Romero, *Marcos: ¿un profesional de la esperanza? (*México D.F.: Planeta, 1994).
46 The Lacandon are the only ethnic group in Chiapas not to join or support the EZLN. Much has been written about them; suffice it to say here that longstanding conflicts over territory, perpetuated by the government, are a chief cause of their distance from the Zapatista movement.
47 Antonio Paoli, *Educación, autonomía, y lekil kuxlejal: Aproximaciones sociolinguisticas a la sabiduria de los tseltales* (México, D.F.: Universidad Autonoma Metropalitana, Unidad Xochimilco, 2003), 53.
48 *EZLN Documentos y Comunicados,* Vol. 2, 43, translation mine.
49 *EZLN Documentos y Comunicados,* Vol. 1, 159-164, translation mine.
50 From "The Story of the Skimasks," *EZLN Documentos y Comunicados,* Vol. 2, in "The Long Journey from Despair to Hope," 74-78, translation mine.
51 José Rabasa, "Of *Zapatismo*: Reflections on the Folkloric and the Impossible in a Subaltern Insurrection," in L. Lowe and D. Lloyd, *The Politics of Culture in the Shadow of Capital,* (Durham, London: Duke University Press, 1997), 400.
52 Bierhorst, *Mythology of Mexico and Central America,* 162.
53 Bricker, *El Cristo Indigena, El Rey Nativo: El Sustrato historico de la mitologia del ritual de los mayas,* 278, translation mine.
54 A *Katún* is a twenty-year segment in the Mayan long-count calendar. According to the cyclical calendar each day has a name, a number, and a specific character. A particular day, on which the same name and number combine, comes around every twenty years. Specific events are prophesied to occur on specific days, and can be foreseen according to the character of the day.
55 For more on the Tojol abal, the true word, see Chapter 4.
56 Antonio García de Leon, "*La Vuelta de Katun,*" in *Los Hombres Sin Rostro,* Vol. 2, (México, D.F., Centro de Estudios Ecumenicos, 1995), 289, translation mine.
57 Adolfo Gilly, "*Chiapas and the Rebellion of the Enchanted World,*" in Daniel Nugent, ed., *Rural Revolt in Mexico: U.S. Intervention and the Domain of Subaltern Politics* (Durham: Duke University,1998), 322.
58 Le Bot, *El Sueño Zapatista.*
59 Lucio Cabañas Barrientos was a Mexican schoolteacher who became a revolutionary in the mold of Emiliano Zapata. Cabañas led a guerilla group, the Army of the Poor and Peasant's Brigade against Injustice, in the mountains of Guerrero in the 1970s. He financed the group through kidnappings and bank robberies. In December 1974 Cabañas kidnapped Rubén Figueroa, senator and future governor of Guerrero. When government troops tried to rescue the senator, Cabañas committed suicide before being captured.
60 See Bertrand de la Grange and Maite Rico, *Marcos, La Genial Impostura,*

for a biased but detailed historical account. The book was distributed by the Mexican government after Acteal to discredit the Zapatistas. De la Grange later lost his position at the French newspaper *Le Monde* for his strongly reactionary view of the indigenous struggle.

61 Dennis Tedlock, trans., *Popul Vuh*, 1985, 153.

62 For mythology of the region, among many other books, see the *Popul Vuh* and Robert Laughlin, *Of Cabbages and Kings: Tales from Zinacantán*, Smithsonian Contributions to Anthropology 23. (Washington DC: Smithsonian Institution,1977).

63 Communiqué of November 1, 1999, in *Our Word is Our Weapon (*Ponce de Leon, Juana, ed. New York: Seven Stories Press, 2001), 359–363.

64 Mircea Eliade, *The Myth of the Eternal Return* (Princeton: Bollingen, 1971), 28

65 Gilly, "*Chiapas and the Rebellion of the Enchanted World,*" in Nugent, ed., *Rural Revolt in Mexico: U.S. Intervention and the Domain of Subaltern Politics*, 324–325.

66 Ibid., 325–326.

67 For a discussion of this topic, see José Rabasa, *Of Zapatismo: Reflections on the Folkloric and the Impossible in a Subaltern Insurrection.*

68 EZLN *Documentos y Comunicados*, Vol. I, 307, translation mine.

69 Eliade, *The Myth of the Eternal Return,* 27–28.

70 John Berger, *Pig Earth* (London: Writers and Readers Publishing Cooperative, 1979), 210.

71 Enrique S. Rajchenberg and Catherine Héau-Lamber, "Historia y simbolismo en el movimiento zapatista," *CHIAPAS* #2, 44.

72 For history and analysis see: John Womack, Jr., *Zapata and The Mexican Revolution*, 1968; John Ross, *Rebellion from the Roots: The Zapatista Uprising in Chiapas*, 1995; John Ross, *The Annexation of Mexico: From the Aztecs to the I.M.F.*, 1998; John Mason Hart, *Revolutionary Mexico: The Coming and Process of the Mexican Revolution*, 1987; George Collier, *Basta! Land and the Zapatista Rebellion in Chiapas*, 1994; and Tom Barry *Zapata's Revenge: Free Trade and the Farm Crisis in Mexico*, 1995.

73 George A. Collier, "*Zapatismo Resurgent: Land and Autonomy in Chiapas,*" *NACLA*, March/April 2000.

74 Rajchenberg, and Héau-Lamber, "Historia y simbolismo en el movimiento zapatista," *CHIAPAS* #2, 45.

75 Montemayor, *Chiapas: La Rebelion indigena de Mexico*, 115.

76 Gilly, "*Chiapas and the Rebellion of the Enchanted World,*" in Nugent, ed., *Rural Revolt in Mexico: U.S. Intervention and the Domain of Subaltern Politics*, 315.

77 Rajchenberg and Héau-Lamber, "Historia y simbolismo en el movimiento zapatista," *CHIAPAS* #2, 41.

78 Montemayor, *Chiapas: La Rebelion indigena de Mexico*, 151.

79 See my personal account, "Death of a Zapatista," in *We Are Everywhere*

(London: Verso, 2003), 80–86.

80 From Subcomandante Marcos, *La Treceava Estela, Segunda Parte: Una Muerte*; translation mine.

81 In his classic 1967 study, *Democracy in Mexico*, Mexican sociologist Pablo González Casanova, recognizes "internal colonialism as a defining characteristic of Mexican political culture.

82 From *El Periscopio Invertido*, printed in *La Jornada*, February 24, 1998, translated and reprinted in *Memory from Below, EZLN Communiqués* (Oakland: Agit Press, 1998), 17–18.

83 Gilly, "*Chiapas and the Rebellion of the Enchanted World*," in Nugent, ed., *Rural Revolt in Mexico: U.S. Intervention and the Domain of Subaltern Politics*, 319.

84 The term "deep Mexico" refers to the classic book, *México Profundo*, by Guillermo Bonfil, which makes the case that the urban poor, rural mestizos, and indigenous peoples of the México have been dominated by an "imaginary México" imposed by the West, that denies the cultural reality lived daily by most Mexicans.

85 Serge Gruzinski, *Painting the Conquest: The Mexican Indians and the European Renaissance* (Paris: Flamarion,1992), 135.

86 Montemayor, *Chiapas: La Rebelion indigena de Mexico*, 106–107.

87 John Ross, "The EZLN, A History: Miracles, *Coyunturas*, Communiqués," in *Shadows of Tender Fury* (New York: Monthly Review Press, 1995), 8–9.

88 See de la Grange and Rico, *Marcos, La Genial Impostura*, 1998; Le Bot, *El Sueño Zapatista*, 1997; and Montemayor, *Chiapas: La Rebelion indigena de México*, 1997.

89 Mentinis, *Zapatistas*, 4.

90 See Beas, Ballesteros, and Maldonado, *Magonismo y Movimiento Indígena en Mexico*, (México, D.F.: Ce-Acatl, A.C., 1997).

91 Ross, *Shadows of Tender Fury*, 7; and Antonio García de Leon, *Resistencia y utopia*, 1994.

92 Ross., 7, and see also Antonio García de Leon, *Resistencia y utopia*, 1994.

93 J. M. G. Le Clézio, *The Mexican Dream* (Chicago: University of Chicago Press, 1993), 164.

94 From *Les Tarahumaras, Tome 9, Oevres compléts d'Antonin Artaud*, as quoted in J.M.G. Le Clézio, *The Mexican Dream*, 1993, 164.

95 Ibid.,168.

96 Ibid.

Chapter III

1 Michael Taussig, *Shamanism, Colonialism and the Wild Man: A Study in Terror and Healing (Chicago: University of Chicago Press,* 1987), 8.

2 The nineteenth-century Cuban poet and revolutionary Jose Martí termed the continent "Nuestra America," Our America, in a bid to build a sense of hemispheric unity.

3 Taussig, *Shamanism, Colonialism and the Wild Man*, 5.
4 *EZLN Documentos y Comunicados*, Vol. 2, "*Carta a Adolfo Gilly*," 109.
5 *EZLN Documentos y Comunicados*, Vol. 2, from "The Long Journey from Despair to Hope," 74–78.
6 Rushdie, Salman, *The Jaguar Smiles* (New York: Henry Holt and Company, 1987), 26.
7 Personal communication, January, 2010, all thanks and praises to Steve Solnit for facilitating the collection of this information.
8 See Juan Anzaldo Meneses, "*Máscaras y Sombras: Del concepto ritual a la práctica cuotidiana del anonimato*" ("Masks and Shadows: From the Ritual Concept to the Quotidian Practice of Anonymity"), *Ce-Acatal* # 81, June 1996.
9 A dance practiced in Puebla, Mexico, in which the dancers wear headdresses representing the extravagant colors of the sacred quetzal bird.
10 A ritual dance in Veracruz, Mexico performed by the Totonac and Olmec people. There is an initial dance in which five men, representing the five elements of the indigenous world, climb a pole. One stays on the pole playing a flute and dancing while the remaining four descend with a rope tied by one of their feet. The rope unwraps itself thirteen times for each of the four flyers, symbolizing the fifty-two weeks of the year.
11 Ibid., 6.
12 Ibid., 7.
13 John Ross, *The War Against Oblivion* (Monroe, Maine: Common Courage, 2000), 83.
14 *EZLN Documentos y Comunicados*, Vol. 1, 1994, 98.
15 A satirical reference to a traditional communist guerilla.
16 A character from an Argentine comic strip. He is a fictional Vietnam veteran, soldier, and bounty hunter, and is used to parody racism, violence, nationalism, and sexism, through his exaggerated character traits.
17 Octavio Paz, *The Labyrinth of Solitude* (New York: Grove Press, 1961), 89.
18 Ibid., 29.
19 The electoral fraud perpetrated in 1988 by PRI candidate—then president—Carlos Salinas de Gortari is universally acknowledged. The election results, contested to the point of mass riots in Mexico, were immediately recognized (even before a recount of the votes) by then U.S. president Ronald Reagan. Salinas de Gortari went on to work closely with the U.S. and international multilateral institutions in the architecture of NAFTA. He pursued a schizophrenic policy regarding the Zapatistas, and after his brother was implicated in the murder of PRI secretary-general José Francisco Ruiz Massieu, fled on a round-the-world tour, eventually settling in Ireland where he found diplomatic immunity. There are a myriad of popular jokes about this giant electoral fraud, as well as about the fact that Mexican presidents who speak of "patriotic values" and vilify the Zapatistas as a movement controlled by foreigners, are to a large extent in the service of U.S. and multinational interests.

20 Article 27 is the portion of the Mexican Constitution dealing with agrarian reform. It is based directly on the Plan de Ayala, the land reform plan proposed by Emiliano Zapata as a condition for his laying down arms during the Mexican Revolution. Agrarian reform has been undertaken at various times throughout the recent history of Mexico, especially during and after the Mexican Revolution, but plans for reform have consistently been weakened, and were effectively dismantled by Carlos Salinas de Gortari's redefinition of Article 27.

21 Paz, *The Labyrinth of Solitude,* 43.

22 From Subcomandante Marcos, *La Treceava Estela, Primera Parte: Un Caracol*; translation mine.

23 Carlos Monsivais, "Chronicle of a Convention (That Really Wasn't) and of a Very Significant Event," in *EZLN Documentos y Comunicados,* Vol. 1, 1994, 323, translation mine.

24 *EZLN Documentos y Comunicados,* Vol. 2, 88-90, translation mine.

25 I was subject to such treatment myself following the invasion of Taniperla in April, 1998. For an account, see my article, "Against Oblivion," in *Left Curve,* 1999.

26 See Frederick Engels, *The Origin of the Family, Private Property and the State,* (New York: International Publishers, 1972).

27 Colin M. MacLachlan, *Anarchism and the Mexican Revolution* (Berkeley, Los Angeles: University of California Press, 1991), 70.

28 Beas, Ballesteros, and Maldonado, *Magonismo y Movimiento Indígena en Mexico,* 41. Translation mine.

29 Ibid., 41-42.

30 Ibid., 45.

31 Roberta Markman and Peter Markman, *The Flayed God: The Mythology of MesoAmerica, Sacred texts and Images from PreColombian Mexico and Central America* (San Francsico: Harper San Francisco,1992), 37–38.

32 Ibid., 41.

33 Ibid., 40.

34 Taussig, *Shamanism, Colonialism, and the Wild Man,* 7.

35 See Gary Gossen, *Telling Maya Tales,* 1999.

36 Paula Gunn Allen, "Thus Spake Pocahontas" in *Off the Reservation: Reflections of Boundary-Busting, Border-Crossing, Loose Canons* (Boston: Beacon Press, 1998).

37 Personal communication: interview, May 25, 2009, Bogota, Colombia.

38 Gustavo Esteva and Madhu Suri Prakash, in their book *Grassroots Postmodernism,* employ the term "social majorities" as a positive way to frame those who, until recently, were called simply "minorities."

39 J. Ginés de Sepúlveda, "*Democrates secundo: De las justas causas de la guerra contra los indios*" (Madrid: Instituto F. de Vitoria, 1951), cited in Tzvetan Todorov, *The Conquest of America: The Question of the Other* (New York: Harper Perennial, 1992), 156.

40 From Guillermo Gomez-Peña, "The Subcomandante of Performance," in Elaine Katzenberger, ed., *First World, Ha Ha Ha!* (San Francisco: City Lights, 1995), 90.

41 Former U.S. Attorney General and tireless defender of human rights Ramsey Clark has pointed out that this is triple the number of U.N. peacekeeping troops that were stationed in Serbo-Croatia at the height of the conflict there in 1998.

42 Le Bot, *El Sueño Zapatista*, 99.

43 Subcomandante Marcos writes on July 1, 1997: "*No matter how far away, tomorrow is still closer than yesterday…May we never lose the shadow or memory. Even though it does not seem like it, both define hope.*" Communiqué, in *Tierra & Libertad*, Newsletter of the Comité Emiliano Zapata, Oakland, 1997.

44 Interview with Xunka' López Díaz by Teresa Ortiz, from *Never Again a World Without Us: Voices of Mayan Women in Chiapas, Mexico* (Washington, D.C.: EPICA, 2001), 79.

45 Todorov, *The Conquest of America*, 115.

46 Quote from Armand Mattelart, *Networking the World* (Minneapolis: University of Minnesota Press, 2000), 105.

47 Le Bot, *El Sueño Zapatista*, 114.

48 For elucidation of this framework for developing campaign strategies, see Patrick Reinsborough, "Decolonizing the Revolutionary Imagination," in David Solnit ed., *Globalize Liberation* (San Francisco: City Lights, 2005), 161–211.

49 Ibid., 185.

50 Communiqué printed in *La Jornada*, August 31, 1996.

51 As quoted in Robert J. C. Young, *Postcolonialism: A Very Short Introduction* (Oxford: Oxford University Press, 2003), 129.

52 In Noam Chomsky, *Turning the Tide: U.S. Intervention in Central America and the Struggle for Peace* (Boston: South End Press, 1985), 6.

53 Interview with Gabriel García Marquéz and Roberto Pombo in Tom Mertes, ed., *A Movement of Movements: Is Another World Really Possible?* (London: Verso, 2004), 4.

54 Ibid., 4.

55 From an interview with Gustavo Esteva, *In Motion Magazine*, http://www.inmotionmagazine.com/global/gest_int_1.html#Anchor-Because-44867.

56 Ibid.

57 Personal communication, October 2008.

58 Lopez y Rivas, among others, use this metaphor in *Autonomías* (México, D.F.: Ediciones ERA, 2004), 88.

59 Widely sung anywhere that Zapatistas gather, the words and music of the Zapatista Hymn can be found in Subcomandante Marcos, *The Speed of Dreams* (San Francisco: City Lights Books, 2007), 32.

60 Lopez y Rivas, *Autonomías*, 63.

61 George Orwell, "Reflections on Ghandi," in *All Art is Propaganda* (New

York: Harcourt, 2008).

62 Communiqué of October 27, 1995, translation mine. See also *Our Word Is Our Weapon,* 310.

63 Communiqué of August 7, 1995, translation mine. See also *Our Word Is Our Weapon,* 308.

64 For a lucid and extensive treatment of the trickster figure in myth, history, and literature, see Lewis Hyde's *Trickster Makes This World.* Hyde examines the trickster nature of figures from Coyote and Brer Rabbit to Charlie Chaplin and Allen Ginsberg and cites the essential social role that enacted by their often anti-social antics; Marcos and the Zapatistas do not appear in the book, but they clearly fit the profile.

65 Lanzarote is home to the Nobel Prize–winning Portuguese novelist and Zapatista sympathizer José Saramago.

66 Translated by Irlandesa.

67 Translated by Irlandesa.

68 *Pozol* is a drink of fermented cornmeal in water; a staple of the indigenous people of Chiapas, and a survival food. In times when there is no other food, there is *pozol.*

69 Translated by Irlandesa.

Chapter IV

1 See Ken Silverstein and Alexander Cockburn, "The Killers and the Killing," *Nation,* V. 260, No. 9 (1995):306.

2 *Relatos de El Viejo Antonio*, San Cristóbal de Las Casas, México: Centro de Informacion y Analisis de Chiapas, A.C., 1999), 62–67.

3 Gary Gossen, *Telling Maya Tales*, 84.

4 Of the several indigenous languages in Chiapas, Tzeltal (spoken largely throughout the *cañadas*), Tzotzil (spoken primarily in the highlands), and Tojolabal (spoken in the southern portion of the conflict zone, toward Guatemala) are the most widely spoken.

5 Ibid, 23.

6 Antonio Paoli, in *Educación, autonomía, y lekil kuxlejal*: *Aproximaciones sociolinguisticas a la sabiduria de los tseltales* (México, D.F.: *Universidad Autonoma Metropalitana, Unidad Xochimilco,* 2003), a participatory study of Tzteltal socio-linguistics, finds similar structures in Tzeltal and other Mayan tongues.

7 Carl Lenkersdorf, *Los Hombres Verdaderos: Voces y Testimonios Tojolobales* (México, D.F.: Siglo XXI Editores, 1996), 29.

8 Ibid., 29.

9 Ibid., 35.

10 Ibid., 31.

11 Ibid.

12 See John Ross, *Shadows of Tender Fury,* and Antonio García de Leon, *Resistencia y utopia.*

13 Paoli, *Educación, autonomía, y lekil kuxlejal*, 71, translation mine.

14 Ibid., 85.
15 Montemayor, *Chiapas: La Rebelion indigena de Mexico*, 56.
16 *EZLN Documentos y Comunicados*, Vol. 1, 89–90, translation mine. See also *Our Word Is Our Weapon*, 68.
17 *EZLN Documentos y Comunicados*, Vol. 1, 268.
18 José Rabasa, "*Of Zapatismo: Reflections on the Folkloric and the Impossible in a Subaltern Insurrection*," in *The Politics of Culture in the Shadow of Capital*, eds. Lisa Lowe and David Lloyd (Durham: Duke University Press, 1997), 425.
19 Todorov, *The Conquest of America*, 147.
20 Ibid., 148.
21 Rabasa, "*Of Zapatismo*," 403.
22 "*The Zapatista "Social Netwar" in Mexico (*Rand Corporation, 1998), 86.
23 De la Grange, and Rico, *Marcos, La Genial Impostura*, 390.
24 When seeking out *La Jornada* on several occasions in a Mexican city other than San Cristóbal or Mexico City between 1995 and 1998, I was accused of "being a Zapatista" and threatened with being run out of town. During the height of the conflict, the San Cristóbal newsstand that carried *La Jornada* by subscription was regularly watched by federal police and immigration agents. John Ross recounts at least one incidence of disappearing periodicals: "When *La Jornada* reported [Chiapas governor] Roberto Albores Guillén's pecadillos, his communication director Manuel de la Torre sent agents out into the streets to buy up every issue of *La Jornada* in Chiapas when the Mexico City gazette was flown into Tuxtla at noon each day." (*Against Oblivion*, 321.)
25 Harry Cleaver, *The Zapatistas and the New Electronic Fabric of Struggle*, public domain, 1995.
26 Rand Corporation, *Zapatista 'Social Netwar' in Mexico*, 1998, 78.
27 Ibid., 79.
28 In a perverse example of history's eternal returns, there is a parallel to be found here: just as bombardment from the air was first used against Pancho Villa's army before becoming the decisive tactic in two World Wars—an example of a new technology developed by the United States being tested on a Mexican revolutionary army before being employed against the real enemy—the imperative to respond to the social netwar launched by the EZLN created fertile ground in U.S. policy circles to build the conceptual and strategic armature of the so-called "War on Terror."
29 Rand Corporation, *Zapatista "Social Netwar" in Mexico*, 82.
30 Miguel Pickard, *Las Redes y la Guerra en Redes: Apuntes sobre las Hormigas y la Aplanadora*, CIEPAC, 2002.
31 Ibid.
32 Ibid.
33 Subcomandante Marcos, *Don Durito de La Lacandona* (San Cristóbal de las Casas: Centro de Información y Análisis de Chiapas, A.C.1999), 136, translation mine.
34 Frantz Fanon, *A Dying Colonialism* (New York: Grove Press, 1967), 84.

35 Ibid., 89.
36 From a talk given at CIDESE, San Cristóbal de Las Casas, Chiapas, October 12, 2008.
37 Cleaver, *The Zapatistas and the New Electronic Fabric of Struggle*.
38 Mattelart, *Networking the World,* 100.
39 From Surui's presentation at the Twentieth Annual Bioneers Conference, San Rafael, California, October 18, 2009.
40 Las Fuerzas Armadas Revolucionarias de Colombia, or Revolutionary Armed Forces of Colombia.
41 Personal communication, interview May 25, 2009, Bogotá, Colombia.
42 See Wright, *Stolen Continents*.
43 Montemayor, *Chiapas: La Rebelion indigena de Mexico*, 38.
44 Gruzinski, *The Conquest of Mexico*, 46.
45 Ibid., 53.
46 Ibid., 54.
47 Ibid., 70–71.
48 Ibid., 72–73.
49 Ibid., 80.
50 See Beas, Ballesteros, and Maldonado, *Magonismo y Movimiento Indígena en México*.

Chapter V

1 Miguel de Cervantes, *Don Quixote de la Mancha*, trans. Charles Jarvis (Oxford: Oxford University Press, 1992), 28.
2 *Conversations with Durito*, "Durito III: The Story of Neoliberalism and the Labor Movement," 72.
3 See http://www.acropolis.org.
4 Matthew Gutmann, *The Romance of Democracy: Compliant Defiance in Modern Mexico* (Berkeley: University of California Press, 2002), 105.
5 Khashnabish, *Zapatismo Beyond Borders*, 30.
6 *EZLN Documentos y Comunicados,* Vol. 1, 217–219, translation mine.
7 EZLN Documentos y Comunicados, Vol. 2, 413–419, translation mine.
8 Cervantes, 70–71.
9 Milan Kundera, "The Depreciated Legacy of Cervantes," in *The Art of the Novel* (New York: Perennial Classics, 1986), 6.
10 Michael Ignatieff, *The Needs of Strangers* (New York: Picador), 139.
11 Raymond Williams, *The Country and the City* (London: Chatto and Windus, 1973), 31.
12 John Holloway, "The Concept of Power and the Zapatistas," in *Take the Power to Change the World*, 131.
13 Holloway, 'Zapatismo and the Social Sciences," *Capital and Class* 78: 153–60, 2002.
14 Interview by Al Giordano of Narconews, posted at http://narcosphere.narconews.com/notebook/al-giordano/2006/01/marcos-zapatistas-will-not-

attend-evos-inauguration-bolivia.

15 Ibid.

16 Published in 2002 at ezln.org; this translation lifted, with slight adaptations, from *Conversations with Durito*, 309-310.

17 Frank McLynn, *Villa and Zapata: A History of the Mexican Revolution* (New York: Carroll & Graf, 2000).

18 Gilly, "Chiapas and the Rebellion of the Enchanted World".

19 From Gilly as quoted in, *Zapatismo Beyond Borders*, 99.

20 Lopez y Rivas, *Autonomías: Democracia o Contrainsurgencia*, 37.

21 Anthropologist Mariana Mora, in *Decolonizing Politics*, conducts numerous interviews with Zapatista community members concerning state patronage versus autonomy. Regarding the words of two Zapatistas she refers to as Macario and Don Leopold, she writes: "They denounced that the Mexican government only offered 'projects' in order to buy votes, to maintain loyalty toward the (then) state party, the *Partido Revolucionario Institucional* (PRI), and to 'discourage the people' from participating in *campesino* organizations or in the guerillas that were rumored to exist.

"Many criticized the government for a series of contradictory actions, for acting simultaneously like 'father government' and like an *ajvalil*, a governing boss that maintained a relationship of tutelage toward the local population and offered only crumbs, as if they were children incapable of taking their own social and political action. At the same time, they criticized the government's failure to carry out its mandate of ensuring health services, education programs, and other projects to improve the standard of living of the indigenous *campesino* population…With anger they pointed out that it wasn't that the state was passively withdrawing from its responsibilities, but that it was systematically excluding them through its failure to offer social programs. This reflected an expression of the same state violence that intensified into repression, military vigilance, and frequent patrols by the armed forces." (M. Mora, *Decolonizing Politics*, 17–18.)

22 Personal communication, December, 2008.

23 Holloway, "The Concept of Power and the Zapatistas," in *Take the Power to Change the World*, 131.

24 Personal communication: a not uncommon notion, it came up in conversation with Flavio Santi, Quichua/Shuar activist from Amazanga, Ecuador, and member of Organizacion de Pueblos Indigenas de Pastaza (OPIP).

25 Eliade, *Cosmos and History*, 28.

26 *EZLN Documentos y Comunicados*, Vol. 1, 120.

27 Paoli, *Educación, autonomía, y lekil kuxlejal.*

28 *EZLN Documentos y Comunicados*, Vol. 1, 175.

29 From Michel Foucault, "The Order of Discourse," 1981.

30 Communiqué of May 28, 1994, widely translated and published.

31 In John Womack, Jr., *Rebellion in Chiapas* (New York: New Press, 1999), 326.

32 Le Bot, *El Sueño Zapatista*, 161.
33 See de Vos, *Una Tierra Para Sembrar Sueños*, 332.
34 Medea Benjamin, "Interview with Subcomandante Marcos," in Katzenberger, *First World, Ha Ha Ha!* (San Francisco: City Lights Books, 1995), 70.
35 From *EZLN Documentos y Comunicados*, Vol. 5, 194: "*Marcos no existe. No es. Es una sombra. Es el marco de la ventana. Si ustedes estan viendo que detras de mi estan mis compañeros, comandantes y jefes, deben ponerse del otro lado, del lado de las comunidades, y darse cuenta de que cuando los vemos a ellos es precisamente al reves, ellos estan primero de nosotros.*"
36 From *EZLN Documentos y Comunicados*, Vol. 5, 194: "*Pero es sobre todo una ventana. Nosotros decimos el marco de una ventana que nosotros queríamos que sirviera para que ustedes se asomaran a lo que somos nosotros, lo que está detrás de mí y detrás de nuestros comandantes: los pueblos indígenas. Y toda la situación que había de injusticia y de pobreza y de miseria, y sobre todo de tristeza, que había en las comunidades indígenas.*"
37 From Subcomandante Marcos, *La Treceava Estela, Primera Parte: Un Caracol*; translation mine.
38 Cantinflas, often referred to as the Charlie Chaplin of Mexico, was (and is) an extremely popular stage and film persona usually portraying an impoverished *campesino*. Pedro Infante was the most famous entertainer in Mexico from the thirties until his death in 1957.
39 *Newseek*, March 7, 1994.
40 Kristine Vanden Berghe, *Narrativa de la rebellión Zapatista: Los relatos del Subcomandante Marcos* (Vervuert, Belgium: Iberoamericana, 2005), 96, translation mine.
41 Ramor Ryan, personal communication, January, 2009. Albeit slightly sarcastic.
42 Nick Henck, *Subcomandante Marcos: The Man and the Mask* (Durham: Duke University Press, 2007), 228–229.
43 Ibid., 229.
44 Personal communication, interview, Bogota, Colombia, May 25, 2009.
45 *EZLN Documentos y Comunicados*, Vol. 5, 339, translation mine.
46 Juan Charrasqueado is a character from Mexican romantic cinema.
47 Laura Castellanos, *Corte de Caja: Entrevista al Subcomandante Marcos* (Naucalpan, Mexico: Grupo Editorial Endira México, 2008), 92.
48 Octavio Paz, "The Media Spectacle Comes to Mexico," *New Perspectives Quarterly*11 (Spring 1994): 59–60.
49 From an interview with Adolfo Gilly; the source is unfortunately unknown at the time of publication.
50 John Ross, *Rebellion from the Roots* (Monroe, Maine: Common Courage, 1995), 288.
51 Le Bot, *El Sueño Zapatista*, 203.
52 Henck, *Subcomandante Marcos: The Man and the Mask*.
53 In the original, "*Donner un sens plus pur aux mots du tribu*," from "*Le Tombeau*

d'Edgar Poe," Mallarmé, *Oevres Complétes*, 189.

54 Paz, *The Labyrinth of Solitude,* 190.

55 Vanden Berghe (*Narativa de la rebellion Zapatista*, 2005, 51) tells us that Marcos has been nominated for the Premio Chiapas de Literatura (by noted Chiapanecan poets Emilio Pacheco, Juan Bañuelos and Oscar Oliva), and for the Premio Chiapas en Arte, with support from esteemed literary figures such as Eduardo Galeano, Elena Poniatowska, and Jose Emilio Pacheco, among others, and cites Corona and Jorgenson, *The Contemporary Mexican Chronicle: Theoretical Perspectives on the Liminal Genre*, 2005, 13, in refernce to Marcos's challenge to universal theories of aesthetics.

56 Carlos Monsivais, *Mexican Postcards,* 1997.

57 *EZLN Documentos y Comunicados,* Vol. 2, 153, *Carta de Marcos a Remitentes que Aun No Obtienen Respuesta,*

58 LeBot, *El Sueño Zapatista,* 356.

59 *EZLN Documentos y Comunicados* Vol. 3, 72.

60 Subcomandante Marcos, *Cuentos Para Una Soledad Desvelada* (México, D.F.: Ediciones del Frente Zapatista, 1997), 41, translation mine.

61 Manuel Vázquez Montalbán, "*Marcos, el mestizaje que viene,*" in *El País*, February 22, 1999.

62 Gilberto Lopez y Rivas, in *Autonomias: Democracia o Contrainsurgencia (2004)*, offers a clear but detailed look at the changes wrought to the "*ley Cocopa,*" the proposed constitutional reform that emerged from the long process of the San Andrés Accords. Among other points, he notes that "the constitutional reforms in the area of indigenous rights realized in April of 2001 contain judicial impediments which imply that for every right granted or conceded, a precautionary note is added that narrows, limits, and impedes its effective implementation."

One of the more striking revisions is the replacement of the notion that indigenous peoples are "entities with public rights" ("*entidades de derecho público*") with the notion that they are "entities of public interest" ("*interés público*"). With the sweep of the pen entire cultures are transformed from active agents of their own development to, in the words of Lopez y Rivas, "objects of public policy, or museum pieces, as they say."

63 Gilberto Lopez y Rivas underlines the importance of such a rejection: "With the decision to approve a law contrary to the San Andrés Accords, the Congress of the Union and the federal government lost the historic opportunity to consider that the indigenous peoples could form part of the Mexican state as dignified political subjects." *Autonomias: Democracia o Contrainsurgencia*, 56.

Chapter VI

1 Originally issued in March 2003, this translation of *Durito and One about False Options* is from *Ya Basta! Ten Years of the Zapatista Uprising*, ed. Ziga Vodovnik (Oakland: AK Press, 2004).

2 From the Fifth Declaration of the Lacandon.
3 Paoli, *Educación, autonomía, y lekil kuxlejal,* 29.
4 Ibid., 29.
5 From an audio recording made in September, 2003, transcribed in Muñoz, *The Fire and the Word*, 292.
6 Personal communication, October, 2008.
7 The importance of radio to popular revolt is described nowhere better than by Che Guevara in *Guerilla Warfare*: "The radio is a factor of extraordinary importance. At moments when war fever is more or less palpitating in every region or throughout a country, the inspiring, burning word increases this fever and communicates it to every one of the future combatants. It explains, teaches, fires, and fixes the future positions of both friends and enemies. However, the radio should be ruled by the fundamental principle of popular propaganda, which is truth; it is preferable to tell the truth, small in its dimension, than a large lie artfully embellished." (*Guerilla Warfare*, 1961)
8 From a talk given at the Universidad de la Tierra, San Cristóbal de las Casas, October 13, 2008.
9 See Ross, *Zapatistas!,* 361–374, for a concise history of the latter.
10 Lopez y Rivas, *Autonomias,* 173.
11 Francis Fukuyama, *The End of History and the Last Man* (New York: Avon Books, 1992), 4.
12 Walter Mignolo, *La Revolucion Teorica del Zapatismo* (San Cristóbal de Las Casas, Chiapas: Universidad de la Tierra, 2008), 42.
13 Ellen Meiksins Wood, *Democracy Against Capitalism* (London: Cambridge University Press, 1995), 219.
14 Ibid., 224.
15 López y Rivas, *Autonomías,* 37.
16 David Graeber, "There Never Was a West, or, Democracy Emerges from the Spaces in Between," in *Possibilities* (Oakland: AK Press, 2007), 331.
17 The Spanish term *cargo* means burden or task; and basic to all variations of the cargo system is the expenditure of wealth in the sponsorship of religious fiestas in order to accumulate prestige within one's community. The cargo system has been compared to the potlatch of the Northwest Coast and the Big Man redistribution system of the Pacific Islands. Like these other redistribution festivals, the cargo system reduced the wealth of all in exchange for status in the community.
18 Graeber, *Possibilities*, 362. The author continues, at this point, to narrate a personal account of a Chol-speaking Zapatista, pointing to the ruins of Palenque and saying, "we managed to get rid of those guys." Although I regrettably cannot recall her name, I had a similar conversation with a Mayan woman from Guatemala who said (to paraphrase), "They say Maya civilization collapsed. It didn't collapse—we just got tired of being told what to do, and we walked away."
19 Ibid., 364.

20 From "*La Declaración de Tikal*," as read by Dominga Matías, a young Kanjobal Mayan woman, in de Vos, *Una Tierra Para Sembrar Sueños,* 320, translation mine.

21 It should go without saying that "América" here refers to the entire hemisphere, not the United States of.

22 From Luis Macas, *Diversidąd y plurinacionalidad*, in *La Otra América en Debate* (Quito, Consejo Hemisferico, 2006), 263, translation mine.

23 Esteva and Prakash, *Grassroots Postmodernism* (London: Zed Books, 1998), 159–160.

24 Lopez y Rivas, *Autonomias,* 37.

25 *EZLN Documentos y Comunicados*, Vol. 1, 170–182.

26 Paoli, *Educación, autonomía, y lekil kuxlejal*, 26.

27 *EZLN Documentos y Comunicados*, Vol. 1, 181–182.

28 Macario and don Leopoldo as quoted in M. Mora, *Decolonizing Politics*, 17.

29 I had the good fortune to be present, on April 10, 1998, for the establishment of the autonomous munipality Ricardo Flores Magón, as well as for its violent dismantling by a thousand government troops and federal authorities the following day.

30 All of the major books on the Zapatistas deal directly or indirectly with the San Andrés Accords, so I refrain from delving into the precise history here.

31 From Subcomandante Marcos, *Chiapas, La Treceava Estela, Segunda Parte: Una Muerte* (*Ediciones del Frente Zapatista de Liberación Nacional,* August, 2003), translation mine.

32 *La treceava estela.quinta parte.*

33 See Ross, *Zapatistas!,* 194.

34 Fernanda Navarro, "*Reseña de una visita a Chiapas,*" *La Jornada*, Michoacan, March 14 and 15, 2005, as quoted in Raul Zibechi, *Autonomías y Emancipaciones* (México, D.F.: Bajo Tierra), 148.

35 From John Gibler, *Mexico Unconquered* (San Francisco: City Lights Books: 2008), 210.

36 Todorov, *The Conquest of America,* 179.

37 *La treceava estela. Una historia, quinta parte.*

38 Personal communication, October, 2008.

39 From Muñoz, *The Fire and the Word*, figures collected throughout.

40 Educational materials are developed within the communities in such a way that they "emerge from the thinking of the people," such that "the children go to consult with the old people from the villages and together with them they develop their own educational curriculum." (Muñoz, 2004/2008)

41 Personal communication, January, 2009, translation mine.

42 Victor Hugo Lopez speaking at La Peña Cultural Center, Oakland, February, 2010, translation mine.

43 Communiqué issued in August 2004. Translation by Irlandesa.

44 *EZLN Documentos y Comunicados Vol. 2,* 58–59.

45 Subcomandante Insurgente Marcos, "*Carta a ONG, Colectivos, Grupos, etc…*"

August 30, 2005, published in the magazine *Rebeldía*, no. 34, 72, translation mine.

46 Shannon Speed, "Actions Speak Louder than Words: Indigenous Women and Gendered Resistance in the Wake of Acteal," in Christine Eber and Christine Kovic eds., *Women of Chiapas: Making History in Times of Trouble and Hope* (New York: Routledge, 2003).

47 Speed, "Actions Speak Louder than Words," in Eber and Kovic, *Women of Chiapas*.

48 Communiqué of March 11, 1996, in *Our Word is Our Weapon*, 5-12.

49 Hillary Klein, "'We Learn as We Go': Zapatista Women Share Their Experiences," unpublished, 2008.

50 Translated by Irlandesa.

51 Ross, *Zapatistas!*, 302.

52 Gibler, *Mexico Unconquered*, 209–210.

53 Carlos Antonio Aguirre, *Chiapas, Planeta Tierra* (Bogotá, Colombia: *Ediciones Desde Abajo,* 2007), 148.

54 Ibid.

55 Ibid., 149.

56 John Gibler, "The Politics of Listening," ZNet, February 5, 2006.

57 Marcos talk in the "*Reunion con el Magisterio y otros sectores de Tlaxcala,*" February 20, 2006, as quoted in Aguirre, *Chiapas, Planeta Tierra,* 150.

58 Gibler, "Police Brutality in Mexico," ZNet, May 6, 2006.

59 From "The Next Step: The Sixth Declaration of the Lacandon Jungle," by Hermann Bellinghausen and Gloria Muñoz Ramirez, in *The Fire and the Word*, 321.

60 Gibler, "The Politics of Listening," ZNet, February 5, 2006.

61 Gibler, "The Orphans of July Third," ZNet, June 24, 2006.

62 As quoted in Gibler, "The Orphans of July Third," ZNet, June 24, 2006.

63 Gibler, "Time and Urgency: Reflections on the Politics of Listening in the Other Campaign, A Defense and a Critique," ZNet, July 20, 2006.

64 While this might seem to be a matter of opinion, this assessment is based on informal interviews with a half-dozen largely unassociated Mexican activists, some of whom were associated with *la Otra*, others not.

65 Ross, *Zapatistas!*, 337 and 343.

66 Personal communication, October, 2008.

67 From *EZLN Documentos y Comunicados*, Vol. 5, Interview with Marcos by Julio Scherer García, broadcast by Televisa from Milpa Alta on March 10, 2001, upon the Zapatistas' arrival in Mexico City with the March for Indigenous Dignity.

68 Michael Ignatieff, *The Needs of Strangers,* 138.

69 The terms were coined by French economist Alfred Sauvy in 1952, with "third world" referring to the countries of Latin America, Africa, Oceania, and Asia which were not aligned with the U.S. bloc (the "first world") or the Soviet Union (the "second world") during the Cold War. "Third world" was

a reference to the French Third Estate (*Tiers Etat*) from the French Revolution. (The First Estate was the clergy, the Second Estate was the nobility, and the Third Estate was the common people.) "Like the Third Estate," wrote Sauvy, "the Third World has nothing, and it wants to be something." The term therefore implies that the Third World is exploited, much as Third Estate commoners were exploited, and that, like the Third Estate, its destiny is a revolutionary one. A more recent commentator, Indian writer and scientist Vandana Shiva, says: "The third world is that part of the world which became the colonies in the last colonization. It wasn't impoverished then; in fact the reason it was colonized is because it had the wealth. Today [these countries] are the poorer parts of the world because the wealth has been drained out."

70 One of the great books on the topic is Enrique Florescano, *Memoria Indigena* (México, D.F.: Taurus, 1999).

71 Ibid., 41.

72 López y Rivas, *Autonomias,* 17.

73 http://www.cdi.gob.mx/.

74 López y Rivas, *Autonomias,* 24–25.

75 From a talk by Mignolo before an audience of Zapatistas and their supporters at CIDECI (Centro Indígena de Capacitación Integral, a.k.a. Universidad de la Tierra), San Cristóbal de Las Casas, October, 12, 2008.

76 Ibid.

77 Subcomandante Marcos and Paco Ignacio Taibo II, *The Uncomfortable Dead* (New York: Akashic Books, 2005), 125.

78 Roberto Espinoza, from a talk given at the Americas Social Forum, Guatemala City, October, 2008.

79 This story, titled simply "*Old Antonio tells a story...*" was read by Subcomandante Marcos during the First International Festival of Dignifed Rage, Universidad de la Tierra, Chiapas, January 5, 2009. Translation mine.

80 Luis Macas, "*Diversidad y plurinacionalidad,*" in *La Otra America en debate,* 2006, translation mine.

81 Bolívar Echeverría, *Vuelta de siglo* (México: Era, 2006), as quoted in Gibler, *Mexico Unconquered*, 283.

82 See Juan Houghton and Beverly Bell, *Indigenous Movements in Latin America* (Albuquerque: Center for Economic Justice, 2004), 4. In this report, Bell and Houghton cite this report as well as an article concerning it in *La Jornada* December 19, 2002.

83 Mignolo, *Universidad de la Tierra*, San Cristóbal de Las Casas, Chiapas, October 12, 2008.

84 See Lopez y Rivas, *Autonomias,* 43.

85 From *El Periscopio Invertido*, printed in *La Jornada*, February 24, 1998, translated and reprinted in *Memory From Below, EZLN Communiqués* (Oakland: Agit Press, 1998), 17–18.

86 Personal communication, Cochabamba, Bolivia, September, 2008, translation mine.

87 Said, *Culture and Imperialism*, 11.

88 This data is drawn from *Conversations with Durito*, 23; in the interests of public relations, it's worth mentioning that among the foreigners who voted in the *Consulta* were such high-profile and high-fashion figures as Antonio Banderas, Susan Sarandon, Melanie Griffith, Oliver Stone, and Quentin Tarantino.

89 Khashnabish, *Zapatismo Beyond Borders*, 236.

90 Ibid.

91 Ibid.

92 From an audio recording of Marcos in September 2003, as transcribed in Muñoz, *The Fire and the Word*, 305.

93 From "The Twilight of Vanguardism," in Graeber, *Possibilities,* 310.

94 Graeber, *Possibilities,* 386.

95 Ibid.

96 Figure taken from John Ross, "Politics as Drugs/Drugs as Politics," *Blindman's Buff* #243, June 2, 2009.

97 See Ross, "Supreme Impunity: Mexico's High Court Frees Convicted Killers of 49 Indians in Chiapas," *Blindman's Buff* #254, August 28, 2009.

98 Ibid.

99 Personal communication, December, 2008.

100 Personal communication, October, 2008.

101 Mignolo, *Universidad de la Tierra*, San Cristóbal de Las Casas, Chiapas, October 12, 2008.

102 John Berger, *Art and Revolution: Ernst Neizvestny and the Role of the Artists in the U.S.S.R.* (New York: Pantheon, 1969), 30.

103 Armin Geertz, *The Invention of Prophecy* (Berkeley: University of California Press, 1994).

104 From Michael Meade, "Dreaming of War Again," on *Poetics of Peace*, sound recording (Seattle: Mosaic, 2007).

105 Ross, "Millionaire Mummies Mourn in Davos/South Sambas in Brazil," *Blindman's Buff* #237, February, 2009.

106 Guillermo Bonfil Batalla, *Mexico Profundo* (Austin: University of Texas Press, 1996), xvi.

107 From Subcomandante Marcos, *La Treceava Estela, Primera Parte: Un Caracol.*

Bibliography

Agit Press Collective, eds. *Memory From Below, EZLN Communiqués*. Oakland: Agit Press, 1998.

Aguirre, Carlos Antonio. *Chiapas, Planeta Tierra*. Bogotá, Colombia: Ediciones Desde Abajo, 2007.

Allen, Paula Gunn. *Off the Reservation: Reflections of Boundary-Busting, Border-Crossing, Loose Canons*. Boston: Beacon Press, 1998.

Asturias, Miguel Angel. *Men of Maize*. Trans. Gerald Martin. Pittsburgh: University of Pittsburgh Press, 1993.

Barrera Vasquez, Alfredo, and Silvia Redon. *El Libro de Los Libros de Chilam Balam*. México, D.F.: Fondo de Cultura Economica, 1948.

Barry, Tom. *Zapata's Revenge: Free Trade and the Farm Crisis in Mexico*. Boston: South End Press, 1995.

Batalla, Guillermo Bonfil. *México Profundo: Reclaming a Civilization*. Trans. Philip A. Dennis, Austin: University of Texas Press, 1996.

Beas, Juan Carlos, Manuel Ballesteros, and Benjamin Maldonado. *Magonismo y Movimiento Indígena en México*. México, D.F.: Ce-Acatl, A.C., 1997.

Bell, Beverly, and Juan Houghton. *Indigenous Movements in Latin America*, Albuquerque: Center for Economic Justice, 2004.

Berger, John. *Art and Revolution: Ernst Neizvestny and the Role of the Artists in the U.S.S.R.* New York: Pantheon Books, 1969.

Berger, John. *Pig Earth*. London: Writers and Readers Publishing Cooperative, 1979.

Berghe, Kristine Vanden. *Narrativa de la rebellión Zapatista: Los relatos del Subcomandante Marcos*. Vervuert, Belgium: Iberoamericana, 2005.

Bierhorst, John. *The Mythology of Mexico and Central America*. New York: Harper Collins, 1990.

Bricker, Victoria. *El Cristo Indigena, El Rey Nativo: El Sustrato historico de la mitologia del ritual de los mayas*, México, D.F.: Fondo de Cultura Economica, 1989.

Bricker, Victoria. *The Indian Christ, the Indian King*, Austin: University of Texas Press, 1981.

Brown, Dee. *Bury My Heart at Wounded Knee*, New York: Henry Holt and Company, 1970.

Burbach, Roger. *Globalization and Postmodern Politics: From Zapatistas to High-Tech Robber Barons*. Sterling, VA: Pluto Press, 2001.

Burbach, Roger. "Roots of the Postmodern Rebellion in Chiapas," *New Left Review*, Vol. 205 (May–June, 1994): 113–124.

Camejo, Pedro, and Fred Murphy. *The Nicaraguan Revolution*. New York:

Pathfinder Press, 1979.
Canby, Peter. *The Heart of the Sky: Travels Among the Maya.* Tokyo: Kodansha International, 1992.
Castellanos, Laura. *Corte de Caja: Entrevista al Subcomandante Marcos.* Naucalpan, Mexico: Grupo Editorial Endira México, 2008.
Centro de Estudios Ecumenicos, ed. *Los Hombres Sin Rostro*, vol. 2, México, D.F.: Centro de Estudios Ecumenicos,1995 .
Cervantes, Miguel de. *Don Quixote de la Mancha.* Trans. Charles Jarvis. Oxford: Oxford University Press, 1992.
Chomsky, Noam. *Turning the Tide: U.S. Intervention in Central America and the Struggle for Peace.* Boston: South End Press, 1985.
Chomsky, Noam. *Year 501: The Conquest Continues.* Boston: South End Press, 1993.
Churchill, Ward. *Fantasies of the Master Race: Literature, Cinema and the Colonization of American Indians.* San Francisco: City Lights Books, 1998.
Churchill, Ward. *A Little Matter of Genocide: Genocide and Denial in the Americas, 1492 to the Present.* San Francisco: City Lights Books, 1998.
Clarke, Ben, and Clifton Ross, eds. *Voice of Fire: Communiqués and Interviews from the Zapatista National Liberation Army.* Berkeley: New Earth Publications, 1994.
Collier, George. *Basta!: Land and the Zapatista Rebellion in Chiapas.* Oakland: Food First Books, 1994.
De la Grange, Bertrand, and Maite Rico. *Marcos, La Genial Impostura.* México, D.F.: Nuevo Siglo, 1998.
De Landa, Friar Diego. Trans. William Gates. *Yucatan Before and After the Conquest.* New York: Dover Press, 1978.
De Leon, Antonio García. "*La Vuelta de Katun.*" In *Los Hombres Sin Rostros*, México, D.F., Centro de Estudios Ecumenicos, 1995.
De Leon, Antonio García. *Resistencia y Utopia.* México, D.F.: Ediciones Era, 1994.
De Leon, Antonio García, and Carlos Monsivais. *EZLN: Documentos y Comunicados, Vol. 1, 1 de enero - 8 de agosto, 1994.* México, D.F.: Ediciones Era, 1994.
De Leon, Antonio García, and Carlos Monsivais. *EZLN: Documentos y Comunicados, Vol.2, 15 de agosto - 29 de septiembre, 1995.* México, D.F.: Ediciones Era, 1996.
De Leon, Antonio García, and Carlos Monsivais. *EZLN: Documentos y Comunicados, Vol.5, La Marcha el Color de la Tierra.* México, D.F.: Ediciones Era, 2003.
Debord, Guy. *The Society of the Spectacle.* Detroit: Black and Red, 1983.
Deloria, Phillip, and Neal Salisbury, eds. *A Companion to American Indian History.* Malden, Maine: Blackwell Publishing, 2004.
Deloria, Vine. *Spirit and Reason: The Vine Deloria, Jr. Reader.* Golden, Colo-

rado: Fulcrum Publishing, 1999.

Díaz-Polanca, Héctor. *Elogio de la Diversidad: Globalización, multiculturalismo y etnofagia*. México, D.F.: Siglo XXI, 2006.

Eber, Christine, and Christine Kovic, eds. *Women of Chiapas*. New York: Routledge, 2003.

Eliade, Mircea. *Cosmos and History: The Myth of the Eternal Return, or Cosmos and History*. Princeton: Bollingen, 1971.

Engels, Frederick. *The Origin of the Family, Private Property and the State*, New York: International Publishers, 1972.

Esteva, Gustavo, and Madhu Suri Prakash. *Grassroots Postmodernism: Remaking the Soil of Cultures*, London and New York: Zed Books, 1998.

Fanon, Frantz. *A Dying Colonialism*. New York: Grove Press, 1967.

Florescano, Enrique. *Memoria Indigena*. México, D.F.: Taurus, 1999.

Foucault, Michel. "The Order of Discourse," trans. Ian McLeod, in *Untying the Text*, ed. Robert Young, 48-78. Boston: Routledge, 1981.

Fuentes, Carlos. *A New Time for Mexico*. Berkeley and Los Angeles: UC Press, 1997.

Fukuyama, Francis. *The End of History and The Last Man*, New York: Avon Books, 1992.

Galeano, Eduardo. *Memory of Fire*. New York: Pantheon Books, 1987.

Galeano, Eduardo. *The Open Veins of Latin America: Five Centuries of the Pillage of a Continent*. New York: Monthly Review Press, 1973.

Geertz, Armin. *The Invention of Prophecy*. Berkeley: University of California Press, 1994.

Gibler, John. *Mexico Unconquered*. San Francisco: City Lights Books, 2008.

Gillette, Douglas. *The Shaman's Secret: The Lost Resurrection Teachings of the Ancient Maya*. New York: Bantam Books, 1997.

Gilly, Adolfo. "*Chiapas and the Rebellion of the Enchanted World*," in *Rural Revolt in Mexico: U.S. Intervention and the Domain of Subaltern Politics*, Nugent, Daniel, ed. 261–233. Durham and London: Duke University Press, 1998.

Goetz, Delia, trans. *Popul Vuh: The Sacred Book of the Ancient Quiche Maya*. Norman, OK: University of Oklahoma Press, 1950.

Gossen, George. "*From Olmecs to Zapatistas: A Once and Future History of Souls*," *American Anthropologist*, vol. 96 no. 3 (1994): 553–570.

Gossen, Gary. *Telling Maya Tales: Tzotzil Identities in Modern Mexico*. New York and London: Routledge Press, 1999.

Gott, Richard. *Guerilla Movements in Latin America*. Garden City, NY: Doubleday & Co., 1972.

Graeber, David. *Possibilities: Essays on Hierarchy, Rebellion, and Desire*. Oakland: AK Press, 2007.

Gross, Matt. "*Frugal Mexico*," *New York Times* Travel Section, November 16, 2008.

Gruzinski, Serge. *La Colonisation de lo Imaginario.* México, D.F.: Fondacion de Cultura Economica, 1988.
Gruzinski, Serge. *Conquering the Mind of the Native,* Cambridge, MA.: Polity Press, 1992.
Gruzinski, Serge. *The Conquest of Mexico*, Cambridge, England: Polity Press, 1993.
Gruzinski, Serge. *Painting the Conquest: The Mexican Indians and the European Renaissance.* Paris: Flamarion, 1992.
Guevara, Che. *Guerilla Warfare*, New York: Monthly Review Press, 1961.
Gutmann, Matthew C. *The Romance of Democracy: Compliant Defiance in Modern Mexico.* Berkeley: University of California Press, 2002.
Harss, Luis, and Dohmann, Barbara. "*Miguel Angel Asturias, or The Land Where the Flowers Bloom,*" in Miguel Angel Asturias, *Men of Maize*, trans. Gerald Martin. Pittsburgh and London: University of Pittsburgh Press, 1993.
Hart, John Mason. *Revolutionary Mexico: The Coming and Process of the Mexican Revolution.* Berkeley: UC Press, 1987.
Hearse, Phil, ed. *Take the Power to Change the World: Globalization ad the Debate on Power.* London: Socialist Resistance, 2007.
Henck, Nick. *Broadening the Struggle and Winning the Media War.* Self-published pamphlet, 2002.
Henck, Nick. *Subcomandante Marcos: The Man and the Mask*, Durham: Duke University Press, 2007.
Holloway, John, and Bensaid, Daniel. *Take the Power to Change the World: Globalisation and the Debate on Power.* London: IMG Publications, 2007.
Holloway, John. "Zapatismo and the Social Sciences," *Capital and Class* 78 (2002): 153–60.
Hyde, Lewis. *Trickster Makes This World: Mischief, Myth, and Art.* New York: North Point Press, 1998.
Ignatieff, Michael. *The Needs of Strangers.* New York: Picador, 1984.
Juris, Jeffrey S. *Networking Futures: The Movements Against Corporate Globalization.* Durham: Duke University Press, 2008.
Katzenburger, Elaine, ed. *First World, Ha Ha Ha!.* San Francisco: City Lights Books, 1995.
Kehoe, Alice Beck. *The Ghost Dance: Ethnohistory and Revitalization.* Chicago: Holt, Rhinehart and Winston, 1989.
Khashnabish, Alex. *Zapatismo Beyond Borders: New Imaginations of Political Possibility.* Toronto: University of Toronto Press, 2008.
Klein, Naomi. *No Logo.* New York: Picador, 2000.
Kundera, Milan. *The Art of the Novel.* New York: Perennial Classics, 1986.
Laughlin, Robert. *Of Cabbages and Kings: Tales from Zinacantan.* Smithsonian Contributions to Anthropology 23. Washington D.C.: Smithsonian Institution, 1977.

Le Clézio, J. M. G. *The Mexican Dream, or The Interrupted Thought of Amerindian Civilizations*. Chicago and London: University of Chicago Press, 1993.

LeBot, Yvon. Subcomandante Marcos, *El Sueño Zapatista*. Barcelona: Plaza & Janes Editores, 1997.

Lenkersdorf, Carlos. *Los Hombres Verdaderos: Voces y Testimonios Tojolobales*. México, D.F.: Siglo XXI Editores, 1996.

Leon, Irene, ed. *La Otra América en Debate: Aportes del I Foro Social Américas*. Quito, Ecuador: Consejo Hemisférico, 2006.

Leon-Portilla, Miguel. *Pre-Columbian Literatures of Mexico*. Norman, OK.: University of Oklahoma Press, 1969.

López Y Rivas, Gilberto. *Autonomías: Democracia o Contrainsurgencia*. México, D.F., Ediciones ERA, 2004.

Lowe, L., and Lloyd, D., eds. *The Politics of Culture in the Shadow of Capital*. Durham and London: Duke University Press, 1997.

Magón, Ricardo Flores. *Land and Liberty*. Montreal: Black Rose Books, 1977.

MacLachlin, Colin M., *Anarchism and the Mexican Revolution: The Political Trials of Ricardo Flores Magon*. Berkeley: University of California Press, 1991.

Marcos, Subcomandante Insurgente, *Chiapas, La Treceava Estela, Segunda Parte: Una Muerte, Ediciones del Frente Zapatista de Liberación Nacional,* August, 2003.

Marcos, Subcomandante Insurgente. *Conversations With Durito: Stories of the Zapatistas and Neoliberalism*. Edited and introduced by Acción Zapatista Editorial Collective. New York: Autonomedia, 2005.

Marcos, Subcomandante Insurgente. *Cuentos para una soledad desvelada*. México, D.F.: Ediciones del Frente Zapatista, 1997.

Marcos, Subcomandante Insurgente. *Desde las montanas del Sureste Mexicano*. México, D.F.: Plaza and Janes Editores, 1999.

Marcos, Subcomandante Insurgente. *Don Durito de la Lacandona*. San Cristóbal de Las Casas, México: Centro de Informacion y Analisis de Chiapas, A.C., 1999.

Marcos, Subcomandante Insurgente. *Our Word is Our Weapon: Selected Writings of Subcomandante Insurgente Marcos*. Ponce de Leon, Juana, ed. New York: Seven Stories Press, 2001.

Marcos, Subcomandante Insurgente. *Questions and Swords: Folktales of the Zapatista Revolution*. El Paso, Cinco Puntos Press, 2001.

Marcos, Subcomandante Insurgente. *Relatos de El Viejo Antonio*. San Cristóbal de Las Casas, México: Centro de Informacion y Analisis de Chiapas, A.C., 1999.

Marcos, Subcomandante Insurgente. *The Speed of Dreams: Selected Writings 2001-2007*. San Francisco: City Lights Books, 2007.

Marcos, Subcomandante Insurgente, and Paco Ignacio Taibo II. *The Uncomfortable Dead*. New York: Akashic Books, 2005.
Markman, Roberta, and Peter Markman. *The Flayed God: The Mythology of Mesoamerica, Sacred Texts and Images from Pre-Columbian Mexico and Central America*. San Francisco: Harper San Francisco, 1992.
Martin, Calvin, ed. *The American Indian and the Problem of History*. Oxford: Oxford University Press, 1987.
Mattelart, Armand. *Networking the World, 1794-2000*. Minneapolis: University of Minnesota Press, 2000.
Meade, Michael. *Poetics of Peace*. Seattle: Mosaic, 2007.
McLynn, Frank. *Villa and Zapata: A History of the Mexican Revolution*, New York: Carroll & Graf, 2000.
Mentinis, Mihalis. *Zapatistas: The Chiapas Revolt and What it Means for Radical Politics*. London: Pluto Press, 2006.
Mertes, Tom, ed. *A Movement of Movements: Is Another World Really Possible?*. London, New York: Verso, 2004.
Midnight Notes Collective, ed. *Auroras of the Zapatistas: Local and Global Struggles of the Fourth World War. New York:* Autonomedia, 2001.
Mignolo, Walter. *La revolución teórica del Zapatismo y pensamiento decolonial*. San Cristóbàl de Las Casas, Chiapas: Universidad de la tierra, 2008.
Mignolo, Walter. "*When Speaking Was Not Good Enough: Illiterates, Barbarians, Savages and Cannibals.*" In *Amerindian Images and the Legacy of Columbus*. Minneapolis: University of Minnesota Press, 1992.
Monsivais, Carlos. *Mexican Postcards*, trans. J. Kraniauskas. London: Verso, 1997.
Montemayor, Carlos. *Chiapas: La Rebelion indigena de México*. México, D.F.: Joaquin Mortiz, 1997.
Mora, Mariana. *Decolonizing Politics: Zapatista Indigenous Autonomy in an Era of Neoliberal Governance and Low Intensity Warfare*. Unpublishcd, presented as a dissertation for doctorate in philosophy, University of Texas, Austin, 2008.
Muñoz Ramirez, Gloria. *The Fire and The Word, A History of the Zapatista Movement*. San Francisco: City Lights Books, 2008.
Notes from Nowhere Collective, eds. *We Are Everywhere*. London: Verso, 2003.
Ortiz, Teresa. *Never Again A World Without Us: Voices of Mayan Women in Chiapas, Mexico*. Washington, DC.: EPICA, 2001.
Orwell, George. *All Art is Propaganda*. New York: Harcourt, 2008.
Paoli, Antonio. *Educación, autonomía, y Lekil kuxlejal: Aproximaciones sociolinguisticas a la sabiduria de los tseltales*. México, D.F.: *Universidad Autonoma Metropalitana, Unidad Xochimilco*, 2003.
Paz, Octavio. *The Labyrinth of Solitude: Life and Thought in Mexico*. New York: Grove Press, 1961.

Paz, Octavio. *The Other Mexico: Critique of the Pyramid*. New York: Grove Press, 1972.

Rabasa, José. "*Of Zapatismo: Reflections on the Folkloric and the Impossible in a Subaltern Insurrection*," in *The Politics of Culture in the Shadow of Capital*, eds. Lowe, Lisa and Lloyd, David. Durham and London: Duke University Press, 1997.

Rajchenberg, Enrique S., and Héau-Lamber, Catherine. "Historia y simbolismo en el movimiento Zapatista." In *CHIAPAS* #2, México D.F., 1996.

Resist! Collective, eds. *Zapatista! Documents from the New Mexican Revolution*. New York: Semiotext(e), 1995.

Retamar, Roberto Fernandéz. *Caliban and Other Essays*. Minneapolis: University of Minnesota Press, 1989.

Ross, John. *The Annexation of Mexico: From the Aztecs to the I.M.F.* Monroe, Maine: Common Courage Press, 1998.

Ross, John. "The EZLN, A History: Miracles, *Coyunturas*, Communiqués," in *Shadows of Tender Fury: The Letters and Communiques of Subcomandante Marcos and the Zapatista Army of National Liberation*. New York: Monthly Review Press, 1995.

Ross, John. *Rebellion from the Roots: the Zapatista Uprising in Chiapas*. Monroe, Maine: Common Courage Press, 1995.

Ross, John. *The War Against Oblivion*. Monroe, Maine: Common Courage Press, 2000.

Ross, John. *Zapatistas!: Making Another World Possible, Chronicles of Resistance 2000–2006*. New York: Nation Books, 2006.

Rovira, Guiomar. *Mujeres de Maiz*. México D.F.: Ediciones Era, 1997.

Rushdie, Salman. *The Jaguar Smiles*, New York: Henry Holt and Company, 1987

Ryan, Ramor. *Clandestines: The Pirate Journals of an Irish Exile*. Oakland: AK Press, 2006.

Said, Edward W. *Culture and Imperialism*. London: Chatto and Windus, Ltd., 1993.

Selbin, Eric. *Modern Latin American Revolutions*. Boulder, CO: Westview Press, 1993.

Silverstein, Ken, and Cockburn, Alexander. "The Killers and the Killing," *Nation*, v. 260, no. 9 (1995): 306.

Solnit, David, ed. *Globalize Liberation: How to Uproot the System and Build a Better World*. San Francisco: City Lights Books, 2004.

Solnit, Rebecca. *Hope in the Dark: Untold Histories, Wild Possibilities*. New York: Nation Books, 2006.

Sullivan, Paul. *Unfinished Conversations: Maya and Foreigners Between Two Wars*. Berkeley: University of California Press, 1989.

Taussig, Michael. *Mimesis and Alterity: A Particular History of the Senses*. New York: Routledge, 1993.

Taussig, Michael. *Shamanism, Colonialism and the Wild Man: A Study in Terror and Healing*. Chicago: University of Chicago Press, 1987.

Tedlock, Barbara. *Time and the Highland Maya*. Albuquerque: University of New Mexico Press, 1982.

Tedlock, Dennis. *Breath on the Mirror: Living Myth of the Highland Maya*. New York: Harper Perennial, 1994.

Tedlock, Dennis, trans. *Popul Vuh*. New York: Simon & Schuster, 1985.

Tello Díaz, Carlos. *La Rebelion de las Cañadas*. México, D.F.: Cal y Arena, 1995-2000.

Thompson, J. Eric S. *Maya History and Religion*. Norman: University of Oklahoma Press, 1970.

Todorov, Tzvetan. *The Conquest of America: The Question of the Other*. New York: Harper Perennial, 1992.

Tomlinson, John. *Cultural Imperialism*. Baltimore, MD: Johns Hopkins University Press, 1991.

Vos, Jan de. *Una Tierra Para Sembrar Sueños: Historia Reciente de la Selva Lacandona, 1950-2000*. México, D.F.: Fondo de Cultura Económica, Centro de Investigaciones y Estudios Superiores en Antropología Social, 2002.

Wallerstein, Immanuel. *Historical Capitalism*. London: Verso, 1996.

Weinberg, Bill. *Homage to Chiapas: The New Indigenous Struggles in Mexico*. London: Verso, 2000.

Wheaton, Philip E. *Unmasking the Powers in Mexico: The Zapatista Prophetic Alternative to the New World Order*. Washington D.C.: EPICA, 1998.

Williams, Raymond. *The Country and the City*. London: Chatto and Windus, 1973.

Womack, John. *Rebellion in Chiapas: An Historical Reader*. New York: The New Press, 1999.

Womack, John, Jr. *Zapata and the Mexican Revolution*. New York: Alfred A. Knopf, 1968.

Wood, Ellen Meiksins. *Democracy against Capitalism: Renewing Historical Materialism*. London: Cambridge University Press, 1995.

Wright, Ronald. *Stolen Continents, The "New World" through Indian Eyes*. Boston: Houghton Mifflin, 1992.

Young, Robert J. C. *Postcolonialism: A Very Short Introduction*. Oxford: Oxford University Press, 2003.

Zibechi, Raúl. *Autonomías y Emancipaciones: América Latina en Movimiento*. México, D.F.: Bajo Tierra, 2008.

Ziga, Vodovnik, ed. "*Ya Basta! Ten Years of the Zapatista Uprising*," Oakland: AK Press, 2004.

Index